Pilgrimage

Pilgrimage was a vital element in the religious life of England from the death of Thomas Becket to the suppression of the shrines by Henry VIII. By reaching beyond the Reformation to explore the transformation of the idea of the pilgrim in Protestant spirituality, this book confronts the religious experience of the English laity over half a millennium.

The attractions for pilgrims of journeys to Jerusalem and to Canterbury and other English religious shrines are considered in the light of theories of the 'liminality' of pilgrimages, and in relation to the therapeutic qualities of 'miracle cures' and penitential undertakings to visit and venerate holy relics. The political aspects of pilgrimage in the aspirations of the Angevin kings and in the reactions to the Henrician Reformation are discussed in relation to the architectural, documentary and pictorial evidence for the expression of lay piety in late medieval England. The cult of St Thomas of Canterbury, England's premier saint, is studied in its iconography as well as in its manifestation as civic ritual, while the role of drama as propaganda in the suppression and in the revival of the cult is explored in the context of the iconoclasm of the sixteenth century.

COLIN MORRIS is Emeritus Professor of Medieval History, University of Southampton, and Emeritus Fellow of Pembroke College, Oxford.

PETER ROBERTS is Senior Lecturer in History, University of Kent at Canterbury.

Pilgrimage

The English Experience from Becket to Bunyan

Edited by

Colin Morris and Peter Roberts

CAMBRIDGE
UNIVERSITY PRESS

PUBLISHED BY THE PRESS SYNDICATE OF THE UNIVERSITY OF CAMBRIDGE
The Pitt Building, Trumpington Street, Cambridge, United Kingdom

CAMBRIDGE UNIVERSITY PRESS
The Edinburgh Building, Cambridge CB2 2RU, UK
40 West 20th Street, New York, NY 10011-4211, USA
477 Williamstown Road, Port Melbourne, VIC 3207, Australia
Ruiz de Alarcón 13, 28014 Madrid, Spain
Dock House, The Waterfront, Cape Town 8001, South Africa

http://www.cambridge.org

First published 2002

Printed in the United Kingdom at the University Press, Cambridge

Typeface Plantin 10/12 pt.   *System* LaTeX 2$_\varepsilon$ [TB]

A catalogue record for this book is available from the British Library

Library of Congress Cataloging in Publication data

Pilgrimage: the English experience from Becket to Bunyan / edited by
Colin Morris and Peter Roberts.
    p.   cm.
Includes bibliographical references and index.
ISBN 0 521 80811 1
1. England – Religious life and customs.   2. Christian pilgrims
and pilgrimages – England – History   I. Morris, Colin,
1928–   II. Roberts, Peter.
BR747 .P57 2002
263′.04242–dc21   2001043673

ISBN 0 521 80811 1 hardback

Contents

List of illustrations	*page* vii
Notes on contributors	x
Preface	xii
Acknowledgements	xiii
List of abbreviations	xv
PETER ROBERTS	

Introduction   1
COLIN MORRIS

1   The pilgrimages of the Angevin kings of England, 1154–1272   12
NICHOLAS VINCENT

2   The early imagery of Thomas Becket   46
RICHARD GAMESON

3   Canterbury and the architecture of pilgrimage shrines in England   90
TIM TATTON-BROWN

4   Curing bodies and healing souls: pilgrimage and the sick in medieval East Anglia   108
CAROLE RAWCLIFFE

5   Pilgrimage to Jerusalem in the late Middle Ages   141
COLIN MORRIS

6   The dynamics of pilgrimage in late medieval England   164
EAMON DUFFY

7   The Pilgrimage of Grace and the pilgrim tradition of holy war   178
MICHAEL BUSH

8   Politics, drama and the cult of Thomas Becket in
    the sixteenth century   199
    PETER ROBERTS

9   'To be a pilgrim': constructing the Protestant life in
    early modern England   238
    N. H. KEEBLE

    Index   257

Illustrations

PLATES

1   Tarrasa, S. Maria, south transept, apse. Photo:
    Gameson   *page* 54
2   New York, Metropolitan Museum of Art, Purchase,
    Rogers Fund and Schimmel Foundation, Inc. and
    others, 1988. Ivory comb. Photo: Metropolitan
    Museum of Art   56
3   Twill silk mitre. Photo: Bayerisches Nationalmuseum,
    Munich   57
4   Twill silk mitre. Photo: Bayerisches Nationalmuseum,
    Munich   58
5   New York, Metropolitan Museum of Art, Gift of
    J. Pierpont Morgan, 1917. Silver reliquary casket.
    Photo: Metropolitan Museum of Art   60
6   New York, Metropolitan Museum of Art, Gift of
    J. Pierpont Morgan, 1917. Silver reliquary casket.
    Photo: Metropolitan Museum of Art   61
7   London, Victoria and Albert Museum. Gilt copper
    and champlevé enamel reliquary châsse. Photo:
    © Victoria and Albert Museum, by permission of
    the Trustees   62
8   Amiens, Bibliothèque municipale, MS 19, fol. 8r
    (prefatory miniature to the 'Saint-Fuscien'
    Psalter-hymnal). Photo: after Leroquais   65
9   MS Cotton Claudius B. ii. fol. 214v Photo: © British
    Library, by permission of the Trustees   66
10 Lyngsjö, Sweden. Font. Photo: Gameson   68
11 Chartres, Cathédrale de Notre-Dame. South-east
    apsidal chapel, westernmost window (*Corpus
    vitrearum*, baie 18, detail). Photo: Gameson   69

12 Chartres, Cathédrale de Notre-Dame. South-east
    apsidal chapel, westernmost window (detail). Photo:
    Gameson   70
13 Sens, Cathédrale de Saint-Etienne. North ambulatory
    (*Corpus vitrearum*, baies 23 and 21). Photo: Gameson   73
14 Sens, Cathédrale de Saint-Etienne. North ambulatory,
    westernmost window (*Corpus vitrearum*, baie 23).
    Photo: Gameson   74
15 Canterbury Cathedral. Trinity Chapel ambulatory
    (*Corpus vitrearum* n. III, detail). Photo: Gameson   76
16 Canterbury Cathedral. Trinity Chapel ambulatory
    (*Corpus vitrearum* n. IV, detail). Photo: Gameson   77
17 New York, Pierpont Morgan Library. M 43, fol., 24v.
    Photo: Morgan Library   79
18 Canterbury Cathedral. Trinity Chapel ambulatory
    (*Corpus vitrearum* n. IV, III and II). Photo: Gameson   82
19 Canterbury Cathedral. Trinity Chapel ambulatory
    (*Corpus vitrearum* n. II, detail). Photo: Gameson   86
20 Canterbury Cathedral. Trinity Chapel ambulatory
    (*Corpus vitrearum* n. II, detail). Photo: Gameson   88
21 Horning, Norfolk. Pilgrim Hospital of St James.
    Photo: © Tim Pestell   115
22 The shrine of St Edmund at the Abbey of Bury
    St Edmunds, from Harley MS 2278, fol. 106. Photo:
    © The British Library, by permission of the Trustees   118
23 The healing of a female leper at the shrine of St William
    of York, in the St William window, n. VII 22c. Photo:
    © The Dean and Chapter, York Minster   122
24 The Lady/Pilgrim Chapel, Holy Trinity Church, Long
    Melford, Suffolk. Photo: © Carole Rawcliffe   124
25 A sick pilgrim being transported in a wheelbarrow,
    from Add MS 42130, fol. 186v. Photo: © The British
    Library, by permission of the Trustees   130
26 Copper alloy badge from Cologne showing the *Sancta
    roba*. Photo: © Norfolk Museum Service   137
27 Bruges, Belgium. The Jerusalem Church, *c*. 1480.
    From Sanderus, *Flandria illustrata*, Keulen, 1641.
    Photo: © The Bodleian Library, Oxford   152
28 Lincoln Cathedral. The Easter Sepulchre, *c*. 1300.
    Photo: Country Frames, Dunholm, Lincolnshire   157
29 Heckington, Lincolnshire. The Easter Sepulchre,
    c. 1345. Photo: the Rev. David Boutle, Heckington   158

30 Corpus Christi College, Cambridge. MS 298, fol. 2r
    (from the English verse translation of the Becket *vita*
    by Laurence Wade, 1497). Photo: © Corpus Christi
    College, Cambridge, by permission of the Master and
    Fellows   204

FIGURES

1   Plan of Canterbury Cathedral showing tombs and
    shrines in the Middle Ages. Drawing by John Atherton   92
2   Major healing shrines of medieval East Anglia   109

Notes on contributors

MICHAEL BUSH is Research Professor of History at Manchester Metropolitan University. He has written several books and articles on the Pilgrimage of Grace, and on the English nobilities and peasantries. His other publications include *The Governmental Policy of Protector Somerset* (1975), *What is Love? Richard Carlisle's Philosophy of Sex*, and *Servitude in Modern Times* (2000).

EAMON DUFFY is Reader in Church History, University of Cambridge, and Fellow and President of Magdalene College. He is Chairman of the editorial committee of the Calendar of Papal Letters relating to Great Britain and Ireland, and a member of the Pontifical Historical Commission. His publications include *The Stripping of the Altars: Traditional Religion in England 1400–1570* (1992); *Saints and Sinners: A History of the Popes* (1997), and *The Voices of Morebath: Reformation and Rebellion in an English Village* (2001).

RICHARD GAMESON is Reader in Medieval History at the University of Kent, Canterbury. He has published numerous studies of early manuscripts and cultural history; his most recent books are *The Manuscripts of Early Norman England, c. 1066–1130* (1999), and *The Codex Aureus* (2001).

N. H. KEEBLE is Professor of English Studies and Deputy Principal at the University of Stirling, Scotland. His research interests lie in the field of English literary and religious history of the early modern period, and his publications include: *Richard Baxter: Puritan Man of Letters* (1982) and *The Literary Culture of Nonconformity in Later Seventeenth-Century England* (1987).

COLIN MORRIS has taught at Pembroke College, Oxford, and Southampton University, where he was Professor of Medieval History. He was recently President of Ecclesiastical History Society. He is the author of *The Papal Monarchy: The Western Church from 1050 to 1250*

(1989), and has long had an interest in pilgrimage and the history of the crusades.

CAROLE RAWCLIFFE, Reader in the History of Medicine at the University of East Anglia, is the author of a number of books and articles on late medieval medical and social history. Her most recent work explores the connection between healing and religion in a regional context: *The Hospitals of Medieval Norwich* (1995), and *Medicine for the Soul: The Life, Death and Resurrection of an English Medieval Hospital: St Giles's, Norwich, c. 1249–1550* (1999).

PETER ROBERTS is Senior Lecturer in History at the University of Kent and editor of *The Transactions of the Honourable Society of Cymmrodorion*. He has researched and published on Tudor Canterbury, Anglo-Welsh relations and the concept of Britain in the sixteenth century, and cultural and theatre history in the early modern period. He is co-editor of *Religion, Culture and Society in Early Modern Britain* (1994), *Christopher Marlowe and English Renaissance Culture* (1996), and *British Consciousness and Identity* (1998).

TIM TATTON-BROWN, formerly Director of the Canterbury Archaeological Trust (1975 85), is now a freelance archaeologist and architectural historian. He is consultant archaeologist to Salisbury and Rochester Cathedrals and the Royal Peculiars of Westminster Abbey and St George's Chapel, Windsor. He has written extensively on the history and buildings of Canterbury Cathedral; his latest publication is *Lambeth Palace: A History of the Archbishops of Canterbury and their Houses* (2000).

NICHOLAS VINCENT, Professor of Medieval History at Christ Church University College, Canterbury, is Director of the British Academy Angevin Acta project and author of *Peter des Roches: An Alien in English Politics, 1205–1238* (1996), and *The Holy Blood: King Henry III and the Blood Relics of Westminster* (2001).

Preface

This book makes a distinctive contribution to the growing body of historical literature on the concept and experience of pilgrimage. In straddling the Reformation to consider Protestant as well as Catholic piety this collection of specialist studies, which is more than the sum of its parts, seeks to open new perspectives on English spiritual, cultural and political life over five centuries. All the chapters originated in papers presented to a colloquium on English Pilgrimage held at the University of Kent as part of Canterbury's celebration of the turn of the Millennium. The papers have been rewritten for this volume in the light of the discussions on that occasion and further research.

The colloquium was sponsored by the Roger Anstey Memorial Trust administered by the University of Kent School of History. The Editors would like to record their thanks to the Trustees and to the participants in the colloquium, as well as to the following for valuable help in its preparation: John Butler, Hugh Cunningham, Richard Eales, Sheila Hingley, Christopher Holdsworth, Nigel Ramsay, Michael Stansfield, and Jackie Waller.

Corpus Christi 2001   PETER ROBERTS

Acknowledgements

The editors, authors and publisher make grateful acknowledgement to the following institutions and authorities for photographs and for kind permission to reproduce them.

The Bayerisches Nationalmuseum, Munich:
Photograph of mitre (3–4).

The Delegates, The Bodleian Library, Oxford (28–29):
Sanderus, *Flandria Illustrata*, Keulen, 1641.

The Rev. David Boutle, Heckington (29):
Photograph of Easter Sepulchre, Heckington, Lincs, *c*. 1345.

The Trustees, The British Library, London:
Harleian MS 2278, fol. 106 (22);
Additional MS 42130, fol. 186v (25);
Cotton MS, Claudius B. ii, fol. 214v (9).

The Master and Fellows, Corpus Christi College, Cambridge:
Photograph of CCC MS 298, fol. 2r (31).

County Frames, Dunholm, Lincoln (29):
Photograph of Easter Sepulchre, Lincoln Cathedral.

The Metropolitan Museum of Art, New York:
Photographs of Ivory comb (Purchase, Rogers Fund and Schimmel Foundation, Mr and Mrs Maxime L. Mermanos, Lila Acheson Wallace, Nathaniel Spear Jr., Mrs Katherine S. Rorimer, William Kelly Simpson, Alastair B. Martin and anon. Gifts. 1988) (2); and Silver Reliquary Casket (gift of J. Pierpont Morgan) (5–6).

Norfolk Museum Service, Norwich:
Photograph of a copper alloy pilgrim badge from Cologne (26).

The Pierpont Morgan Library, New York:
Photograph of MS 43, fol. 24v (17);

The Dean and Chapter of York Minster:
Photograph of 'the healing of a female leper at the shrine' in the
St William window of York Minster (Green Collection Plate
BB89/2802) (23);

The Trustees, The Victoria and Albert Museum, London:
Photograph of reliquary châsse (7).

Abbreviations

AS	*Acta Sanctorum*, ed. J. Bollandus and others (Antwerp, Tongerloo and Paris, 1643–)
ANS	*Anglo-Norman Studies: Proceedings of the Battle Conference* (Ipswich: Boydell, 1978–)
Ant. Jnl	*Antiquaries Journal*
Arch.	Archaeological
Arch. Cant.	*Archaeologia Cantiana: The Journal of the Kent Archaeological Society*
BL	British Library
CCA	Canterbury Cathedral Archives
CVMA	*Corpus Vitrearum Medii Aevi*
DNB	*Dictionary of National Biography*
EETS	Early English Text Society
EHR	*English Historical Review*
Hist. Canterbury Cath.	*The History of Canterbury Cathedral*, ed. Patrick Collinson, Nigel Ramsay and Margaret Sparks (Oxford, 1995)
HJ	*Historical Journal*
HMC	Historical Manuscripts Commission
JBAA	*Journal of the British Archaeological Association*
JEH	*Journal of Ecclesiastical History*
Jnl	Journal
Jour. Soc. Archit. Historian	*Journal of the Society of Architectural Historians*
LP	*Letters and Papers, Foreign and Domestic, of the Reign of Henry VIII, 1509–47*, ed. J. Brewer *et al.*, 21 vols. in 33 parts (London, 1862–1910)

Materials	*Materials for the History of Thomas Becket, Archbishop of Canterbury,* ed. J. C. Robertson and J. B. Sheppard, 7 vols., Rolls Series (London, 1875–85)
MGH SS	*Monumenta Germaniae Historica, Scriptores*
MW	*The Miscellaneous Works of John Bunyan,* 13 vols. (Oxford, 1976–94)
NCC	Norfolk County Council
NLW	National Library of Wales
OMT	Oxford Medieval Texts
PCC	Prerogative Court of Canterbury
PL	*Patrologiae cursus completus series Latina,* ed. J.-P. Migne (Paris, 1841–64)
PP	*The Pilgrim's Progress,* ed. J. B. Wharey, rev. R. Sharrock, 2nd edn (Oxford, 1960)
PRO	Public Record Office
RCHM	Royal Commission on Historic Monuments
RHGF	*Recueil des Historiens des Gaules et de la France,* ed. M. Bouquet *et al.* (Paris: Libraires Associés, 1983–)
RS	Rolls Series
SCH	Studies in Church History
SJ	Society of Jesus
Soc.	Society
SP, Henry VIII	*State Papers, Henry VIII,* 11 vols. (London, 1830–52)
Trans. St Paul's Eccles. Soc.	*Transactions of the St Paul's Ecclesialogical Society*
TRHS	*Transactions of the Royal Historical Society*
V&A	Victoria and Albert Museum
VCH	*Victoria County History*

Introduction

Colin Morris

It is notoriously difficult to define a pilgrim. The original Latin word *peregrinus* was an unspecific term, meaning a traveller, stranger, alien or immigrant. Such people were not necessarily involved in a religious journey, and did not even have to be travelling at all. When Cicero contrasted the *civis* (citizen) with the *peregrinus*, he was apparently thinking of the 'pilgrim' as a resident alien.

By the period with which this volume is concerned, the term had become more specific and had hardened to an institution. The pilgrim was a man or woman who travelled in order to reach a shrine. For Chaucer, April was the time when people long to go on pilgrimage, to seek out foreign places and distant shrines. Pilgrims had their own ceremonial, and a conventional insignia consisting of staff and wallet or bag. They hoped to bring back 'blessings', memorials or relics from the shrine that they had visited. Most shrines, even quite local ones, had their own badge. From at least the thirteenth century, canon law provided for the pilgrims special guarantees and a particular status. Social and architectural provisions were made for them. They had hostels and hospitals, and, as Tim Tatton-Brown indicates in his chapter, many of the great churches had east ends accommodated to dealing with the traffic problems posed by the large numbers of visitors. In a real sense 'pilgrim architecture' goes back to the great churches built by Constantine in the fourth century, but the twelfth and subsequent centuries saw their own special versions, adapted to the commemoration of particular saints. In architectural terms, the greatest pilgrimage church of our period was the Church of the Holy Sepulchre at Jerusalem, as it was reconstructed in the twelfth century. It can be seen either as an imitation in the East of pilgrimage styles already in development in the West, or as an inspiration for their spread in the West. It may, indeed, have been both.

Most of the pilgrims who appear in this volume were shrine-seekers, but wider meanings of the word persisted. Crusaders almost invariably saw themselves as pilgrims. Words cognate with 'crusade', such as *croiserie* or *crucesignati*, can be found from the end of the twelfth century, but they scarcely became standard usage. In English, surprisingly, 'crusade' and 'crusader' only established themselves in the nineteenth century: earlier instances were obvious foreign borrowings, such as *crusado* or *croisader*. 'Pilgrim' continued to be the word that came most readily to medieval minds. Some of the contemporary historians of the First Crusade, such as Albert of Aachen, structured their whole account round the idea of pilgrimage. True, many crusaders were indeed seekers after a shrine, that of the Holy Sepulchre at Jerusalem, but, throughout the centuries, the crusading vow led others to unexpected places and distant complications.

Even more generally, pilgrimage could act as a symbol of the whole Christian life. This interpretation was authorised by Hebrews xi.13, which presented the holy people of the Old Testament as 'pilgrims and strangers', *peregrini et hospites* as the Vulgate version had it. The idea was incorporated into Patristic thought. As Gregory the Great trenchantly observed, 'pilgrimage is our present life'.[1] In the eleventh and twelfth centuries, the fashion grew, in liturgy and hymns, of presenting the life of faith as a journey towards the heavenly Jerusalem, an idea designed especially, but not exclusively, for monks. Peter Abelard's hymn for Saturday vespers,

> O what the joy and the glory must be,

still appears in most standard hymn-books. It is true that such writers did not directly use contemporary pilgrim terminology for this spiritual journey. They followed the Epistle to the Hebrews in seeing the journey of Abraham, the forty years spent by the Israelites in the wilderness, or the return from exile in Babylon as representations of the journey to the Jerusalem above. The use of pilgrimage as a metaphor for the journey of the Christian soul was developed by the three long *Pèlerinage* poems of Guillaume de Deguileville in the middle years of the fourteenth century, and appeared also in Walter Hilton and in a speech by the parson in Chaucer's *Canterbury Tales*. For those who accept this long-enduring theological tradition, 'pilgrims and pilgrimages do not belong simply to the external forms of Christian piety, but are signs of an important characteristic of the Church, signs of the messianic people of God, who draw near to their Lord'.[2]

---

[1] For this and other references, see G. B. Ladner, '*Homo viator*: Medieval Ideas on Alienation and Order', *Speculum*, 42 (1967), 233–59.

[2] N. Egender, 'Jerusalem – Ziel der Pilger damals und heute', in L. Kriss-Rettenbeck and G. Möhler (eds.), *Wallfahrt kennt keine Grenzen* (Munich/Zürich: Schnell and Steiner, 1984), p. 308; and J. M. Keenan, 'The Cistercian Pilgrimage to Jerusalem in Guillaume de Deguileville's *Pèlerinage de la vie humaine*', in J. R. Sommerfeldt (ed.), *Studies in Medieval Cistercian History*, vol. II (Kalamazoo: Cistercian Publications, 1976), pp. 166–85.

Most of this volume, however, is concerned with pilgrims in the more usual medieval sense of shrine-seekers. Their travels were enormously important in the culture of medieval England, and have generated a long tradition of studies in this country. It is time, however, to ask some new questions, and this is the purpose of the present collection, which took its origin in a symposium under the auspices of the Anstey Foundation at the University of Kent in September 1999. The volume of recent continental studies of pilgrimage is enormous.[3] This is not to say that British historians have been snorting in the Seven Sleepers' den, but there are substantial reasons why our continental colleagues have been in the lead. For all the cultural significance of pilgrimage within England, the country was on the margin of the European circuit. Only the shrine of Archbishop Thomas at Canterbury was of truly international status, although there certainly were others that were held in honour nationally. English travellers to shrines abroad appear to have been much more numerous than foreign visitors to England, and some of the great continental centres generated documentary and narrative records that it is hard to match in this country. My own chapter in this collection is an attempt to see the English participation in the Jerusalem pilgrimage within the context of the whole Western European experience. Other chapters, in particular those of Carole Rawcliffe and Eamon Duffy, examine the nature of local pilgrimage within England.

A further discouragement to the study of late medieval pilgrimage has been its sudden disappearance in the late 1530s. Effectively, there are no shrines left, although some cathedral chapters have made serious efforts to reconstruct them as far as possible.[4] Very nearly the whole of medieval English art has been destroyed. The losses have been put at 97 per cent. That is hardly a serious statistical calculation, but it gives an indication

---

[3] Important recent examples are Kriss-Rettenbeck and Möhler (as above); B. N. Sargent-Bauer (ed.), *Journeys towards God: Pilgrimage and Crusade* (Kalamazoo: Western Michigan University, 1992); *Pèlerinages et croisades: Actes du 118e Congrès National des Sociétés Historiques et Scientifiques* (Paris: CTHS, 1995); B. Abou-el-Haj, *The Medieval Cult of Saints: Formations and Transformations* (Cambridge University Press, 1995); *Voyages et voyageurs au Moyen Age: XXVIe Congrès de la Société des Historiens Médiévistes de l'Enseignement Supérieur Public* (Paris: Sorbonne, 1996); I. Erfen and K.-H. Speiss (eds.), *Fremdheit und Reisen im Mittelalter* (Stuttgart: Steiner, 1997); R. Oursel, *Sanctuaires et chemins de pèlerinage* (Paris: Le Cerf, 1997); G. Vitolo (ed.), *Pellegrinaggi e itinerari dei santi nel Mezzogiorno medievale* (Naples: Liguori, 1999); and D. Webb, 'St James in Tuscany: The Opera di San Jacopo of Pistoia and Pilgrimage to Compostella', *JEH*, 50 (1999), 207–34; as well as a long series of studies by E. R. Labande and by P. A. Sigal. There is an interesting collection of recent studies edited by J. Stopford, *Pilgrimage Explored* (York Medieval Press, 1999) covering a wide range of periods; three of these fall within the subject of the present collection, late medieval English pilgrimage.

[4] For a recent survey, see B. Nilson, *Cathedral Shrines of Medieval England* (Woodbridge: Boydell, 1998).

of the scale of the destruction. Most difficult for the historian has been the failure of continuity. In many continental societies, we are able to observe the way in which pilgrimage was to evolve in the sixteenth century: *sacri monti*, the Calvary, the Way of the Cross, entombment chapels, pilgrim brotherhoods and indulgences can all be observed in the process of evolution. We know, so to speak, where late medieval pilgrimage was going. An outstanding recent study by Marie-Christine Gomez-Géraud has provided a new basis for an understanding of the Jerusalem pilgrimage and other devotions in the early modern period, but the nature of the material necessarily means that its coverage of England is less than that of other countries.[5]

These lectures were prepared before the publication of this important volume. It is, however, largely true that the history of Reformation and post-Reformation pilgrimage has not been much explored in England. This is hardly surprising, since the discontinuities are more obvious than on the continent.[6] One of the originalities of this present collection, I believe, is its concern with Reformation and post-Reformation pilgrimage in England. Michael Bush considers the status of the Pilgrimage of Grace as the last, perhaps anomalous, expression of Catholic pilgrimage. The greatest of the medieval cults, that of Thomas Becket, provides some particularly interesting material on conflicting theologies and politics, which are explored by Peter Roberts. One element of continuity, which co-existed with the fierce criticism of shrines, indulgences and traditional pilgrimage, was provided by the strand of Protestant spirituality that adopted the pilgrim as the figure of the Christian. This was an ancient idea, one indeed with Biblical foundations, and its post-Reformation development is traced by Neil Keeble. My own chapter considers the interaction between the end of the Jerusalem pilgrimage and the English publications about Oceanic exploration.

The general study of cult and liturgy has also opened new ways of looking at pilgrimage. The shrine of a great church constituted its 'memory': it defined its character, its worship, its power and its symbolism. This was true to such an extent that early in the sixteenth century Angelo Fiorenzuola could observe in his *Ragionamenti d'amore* that at Venice

[5] M.-C. Gomez-Géraud, *Le crépuscule du Grand Voyage: les récits des pèlerins à Jérusalem (1458–1612)* (Paris: Honoré Champion, 1999).

[6] The exceptions to this statement include the magisterial works of E. Duffy, *The Stripping of the Altars: Traditional Religion in England c.1400–c.1580* (New Haven, CT: Yale University Press, 1992), and M. Aston, *England's Iconoclasts*, vol. I: *Laws against Images* (Oxford University Press, 1988). See also recent articles by G. W. Bernard, 'Vitality and Vulnerability in the Late Medieval Church: Pilgrimage on the Eve of the Break with Rome', in J. L. Watts (ed.), *The End of the Middle Ages? England in the Fifteenth and Sixteenth Centuries* (Stroud: Sutton, 1998), pp. 199–233; and P. Marshall, 'Papist as Heretic: The Burning of John Forest, 1538', *Historical Jnl*, 41 (1998), 351–74.

St Mark was honoured more highly than God himself. (Certainly Mark had as much impact as the deity on the Venetian calendar, and more on its panoply of state.) Given that, as Jacques le Goff has put it, 'Christianity is memory', the character of the relics as *memoria* is crucial to the understanding of the medieval perception of religion and pilgrimage.[7] To see the relics, if possible to touch them, at least to draw near to them, to spend the night in their presence, was fundamental to access to their power. The enormous importance of the visual imagination in worship and devotion has been a central theme in the scholarship of the past ten years.[8] In this collection, shrine imagery is closely examined in the studies by Richard Gameson and Carole Rawcliffe; and Tim Tatton-Brown sets the shrines within the context of the communities that supported them, and benefited from them.

The experiences of the shrine-seekers were inevitably of varied kinds. Historians and sociologists have attempted to define a normative version of pilgrimage, most notably among them Victor and Edith Turner, *Image and Pilgrimage in Christian Culture: Anthropological Perspectives.*[9] These two authors drew on a wide range of evidence, including medieval

[7] The theme has been examined in a diverse range of works, including M. Halbwachs, *The Collective Memory* (New York: Harper and Row, 1980); K. Schmid and J. Wollasch, *Memoria: der geschichtliche Zeugniswert des liturgischen Gedenkens im Mittelalter* (Munich 1984); J. Le Goff, *History and Memory* (New York, 1992); S. Schama, *Landscape and Memory* (London: Fontana, 1995); and E. Palazzo, 'Le livre dans les trésors du Moyen Age: contribution à l'histoire de la *Memoria* universelle', *Annales – Histoire, Sciences Sociales*, 52 (1997), 93–118.

[8] The scale of interest, and the variety of approaches, are both enormous. The following list is confined to the past ten years, and primarily, but not wholly, to England: S. Beckwith, *Christ's Body: Identity, Culture and Society in Late Medieval Writings* (London: Routledge, 1993); B. Cassidy (ed.), *Iconography at the Crossroads* (Princeton University Press, 1993); S. Kay and M. Rubin (eds.), *Framing Medieval Bodies* (Manchester University Press, 1994); J.-C. Schmitt, 'Au Moyen Age: l'église, l'argent et les images', in M. Aubrun *et al.* (eds.), *Entre idéal et réalité* (Clermont-Ferrand: Institut d'études du Massif Central, 1994), pp. 407–15; H. van Os *et al.* (eds.), *The Art of Devotion in the Late Middle Ages in Europe 1300–1500* (Princeton University Press, 1994); D. Aers, 'Altars of Power: Reflections on Eamon Duffy's *The Stripping of the Altars*', *Literature and History*, 3 (1994), 90–105; N. Watson, 'Censorship and Cultural Change in Late Medieval England: Vernacular Theology, the Oxford Translation Debate and Arundel's *Constitutions*', *Speculum* 70 (1995), 822–65; J.-C. Schmitt, 'La culture de l'image' and J. Baschet, 'Inventivité et sérialité des images médiévales', in *Annales – Histoire, Sciences Sociales*, 51 (1996), 3–36 and 93–133; D. Aers and L. Staley (eds.), *The Powers of the Holy: Religion, Politics and Gender in Late Medieval English Culture* (Pennsylvania University Press, 1996); E. M. Ross, *The Grief of God: Images of the Suffering Jesus in Late Medieval England* (Oxford University Press, 1997); B. C. Raw, *Anglo-Saxon Crucifixion Iconography* (Cambridge University Press, 1990); J. F. Hamburger, *Nuns as Artists: The Visual Culture of a Medieval Convent* (Berkeley University Press, 1997); J. B. Friedman and J. M. Wegmann, *Medieval Iconography: A Research Guide* (New York: Garland, 1998); M. B. Merback, *The Thief, the Cross and the Wheel* (London: Reaktion, 1999); and G. Finaldi (ed.), *The Image of Christ* (London: National Gallery, 2000).

[9] Oxford: Blackwell, 1978.

Europe, modern Mexico and Marian shrines in the post-industrial world. Nonetheless there are difficulties in accepting their interpretation of pilgrimage as characteristically a rite of passage, or a crossing of the threshold from ordinary life (a 'liminal phenomenon', as they call it).[10] Many of the journeys by English pilgrims studied in this group of essays did not take the traveller far from his normal context. Most of them involved a few days' travel at most. Over half the pilgrim badges that have been recovered from a deposit at King's Lynn were from nearby Walsingham, and similar badges found at Salisbury were mostly from southern England. Scarcely any in these two groups came from shrines across the sea. It seems fair to describe these journeys as 'rather like visits which become a part of family piety'. Local pilgrimage of this sort belongs to a world in which we know that people trusted in the protection of the saints of their own region.[11] Eamon Duffy's chapter stresses the essentially local character of a great deal of medieval devotion: 'going on pilgrimage is a liminal phenomenon only if, and to much the same extent that, going to market was a liminal phenomenon'. It is often supposed that the belief and practice of medieval Catholicism were universal, in contrast with the diversity introduced by the new religion, and of course there is truth in that. There is also an opposite truth. The attack on shrines and pilgrimages was one of the many ways in which the Reformation set itself against local variants, popular cults and diverse uses. A standard translation of the Bible was, by royal decree, to be available in each church for the faithful to read, and a uniform liturgy replaced the variety that characterised medieval churches. The Preface to the 1549 Prayer Book proclaimed triumphantly: 'Now, from henceforth, all the whole realm shall have but one use'; although few aspirations can have been so disappointed in their fulfilment.

At the opposite extreme from local outings was the great pilgrimage to Jerusalem. Then the participants did travel outside their familiar world, and the language of renewal and rebirth was used by travellers of their experience in the Church of the Holy Sepulchre, and still more obviously by those who went on to bathe in the River Jordan. Only a small number of English pilgrims shared this experience, although its features made it specially normative in medieval thinking. In spite of the unfamiliarity of its setting, the Jerusalem pilgrimage of the late Middle Ages was a tightly organised experience, directed to shaping the participants' vision according to the norms of accepted Latin piety. The package tours from Venice,

---

[10] Apart from the comments in the present volume, see the remarks by Jennifer Stopford in her introduction to *Pilgrimage Explored* (see above, note 3), esp. p. xii.

[11] The evidence is summarised by D. Bruna, 'La diffusion des enseignes de pèlerinage', in *Pèlerinages et croisades* (above), pp. 201–14.

the easiest way of travelling to Palestine in the later Middle Ages, were designed to confirm, not to question, the prejudices that pilgrims had brought with them from home. Throughout history, whenever the authorities of Church and State were in a position to do so, they had shown a desire to regulate and standardise the pilgrim experience. David Hunt has noticed this tendency even in the fifth century: 'The imposition of [a] Christian character on the pilgrim's journey was a conscious development which came with the consolidation of Christian empire and the increasing vogue for pilgrimage itself'.[12] The strictly regulated pilgrim traffic of the fifteenth century reflected in an exaggerated way this concern to shape pilgrim piety according to norms that were much more narrowly Latin, and isolated from the societies through which the pilgrims travelled.

A further reason for avoiding an explanation of English pilgrimage as a rite of passage or a 'liminal' experience is the extent to which it was incorporated within the normal structures of social aspiration. It is true that the Christian pilgrim was never awarded the precise standing of the pilgrim to Mecca, the *haji*, within the world of Islam, but pilgrimage was contained within the normal social expectations of the time. Kings and nobles were patrons of major shrines, such as Westminster and Saint-Denis, and many families had a strong tradition of pilgrimage, including the great journeys to Rome, Jerusalem and Compostela. The binding character of these commitments is illustrated by the fact that five successive kings of France went on crusade, and five successive kings of England vowed to do so. The irregularities of this essentially voluntary system are also shown by the fact that only one of the French kings and none of the English ones reached Jerusalem; indeed (alas, perfidious Albion) only one of the English kings even set out during his reign, and that was Richard I, the least 'English' of all. Nevertheless pilgrimage and crusade were structural parts of the politics of the medieval world, and of its land-owning, too. By and large, the most influential churches were the ones with the best relics and the greatest saints, and therefore the major claim on patronage and pilgrimage. Pilgrims could rewrite the history of a countryside, as the rise to prominence of Walsingham did in East Anglia, or even reshape the government of a great church, as the pilgrims to Compostela did in Spain. Pilgrimage could indeed add directly to a man's social status. To become a knight of the Holy Sepulchre, a title that could only be bestowed at the place itself, was to acquire a proud and valued rank.

Given the relative strength of English government throughout the Middle Ages and early modern period, the political implications of pilgrimage were bound to be important. It is a nice question, on which

---

[12] E. D. Hunt, *Holy Land Pilgrimage in the Later Roman Empire 312–460* (Oxford: Clarendon, 1982), p. 62.

Richard Gameson provides material, how far the imagery of the Becket cult was anti-royal. Certainly the devotion to Thomas was in the end suppressed because it seemed traitorous in the sight of Tudor absolutists. On the other hand, visits to shrines could also be a normal part of the functioning of royal authority. Nicholas Vincent's analysis of Angevin devotion provides an original perception of their aims in the cultivation of such major centres. Here again, as with Jerusalem, we have travel on a supranational scale, but it can hardly be perceived as a 'liminal' experience, because all Angevin government involved international travel at its very heart. Indeed, one might say that the special genius of the Angevin kings was their unusual capacity to govern *in absentia*.

As these observations have shown, there were many different pilgrimages, and many reasons for going. Innumerable people went to obtain a favour, which would often be healing for themselves or a member of the family. The close link between the saints and healing has long been recognised, but Carole Rawcliffe's chapter analyses the connection with particular precision, and considers the way in which it was expressed in imagery. Successful healings, or other blessings, would be advertised by the custodians of the shrines through inclusion in the legends of their saints (occasionally with a report of the failure of other shrines to solve the problem) and also by the display of offerings made by gratified pilgrims. Except in the very general sense that the unfortunate could hope for mercies that they needed, the whole pilgrimage system strikes one as curiously devoid of moral content; although none of our English saints seems quite to have rivalled St Ranieri of Pisa, who master-minded a jailbreak by some prisoners accused of necromancy, and received a gift of silver thread to his shrine in gratitude.[13]

That many people travelled out of social expectation, combined with an interest in seeing nearby places, there is no doubt. Some of Chaucer's Canterbury pilgrims are presented as genuinely pious, but the whole expedition can hardly be said to be filled with devotion. We may find some literary artifice and satire here, but even in the much more demanding context of a journey through the Mediterranean, some devout travellers took a keen interest in what they were seeing, quite aside from their visits to holy places. Others went in search of holy people. This had been a marked feature of pilgrimage long before, in the fifth century, but we continue to meet it throughout pilgrim history. Richard I ignored the relics of Rome on his way to the Third Crusade, but he found time for an interview with Abbot Joachim of Fiore. Visitors to Jerusalem who undertook the very demanding extra journey to St Catherine's at Sinai

---

[13] C. Morris, 'San Ranieri of Pisa: The Power and Limitations of Sanctity in Twelfth-century Italy', *JEH*, 45 (1994), 596.

sometimes noted with interest the piety of the Egyptian monks they met. Much of Margery Kempe's travelling was directed to the consultation of spiritual advisers.

What is probably true is that the devotion at popular shrines was much more designed to speak to the laity than was the liturgy of home churches. We know little about worship in parish churches. It is exasperating that we do not even know what proportion of the population of a parish attended Sunday worship regularly, while we do know that on the whole access by lay worshippers to cathedrals and abbeys (aside from pilgrims) was subject to considerable limitations. Evidence from pilgrimage is therefore an important part of our knowledge of lay devotion. It is true that the shrines were controlled by clergy, and that their forms of worship and legends were probably composed by the clerks, but they were often directed to a lay constituency. From collections of miracles we hear, albeit briefly, the concerns of lay visitors. Stories of the lives of the saints are addressed to lay audiences. Lay visitors are assisted by images: in the ambitious presentation of the miracles of Thomas of Canterbury in the windows surrounding his shrine, elsewhere through a simple depiction or relic. All of this gave a visible focus to devotion, which might be a tomb, a well, or an altar, which gave a physical expression to what was seen as spiritual reality. The power of a saint could be made present through his body, and the graces of the Holy Land through a fragment of the cross or oil from the lamps at the Holy Sepulchre. Walsingham brought the saving power of Palestine to Norfolk by creating there a representation of the Virgin's house.

That is not to say that clergy were uninterested in devotions which spoke readily to the laity: the gap between 'learned' and 'popular' religion is much narrower than was at one time thought. Among the vast mass of narratives of the Jerusalem journey in the last two medieval centuries, we can readily perceive the directing hand of the Franciscans who acted as guides to the holy places, but it must also be said that a great many of the accounts were composed by lay people, often writing in their vernacular language. The fact that the pilgrimage ethos and ceremonies were more addressed to the laity than was the normal liturgy of the Church helps to explain the popularity of pilgrimage in a world in which lay demands and desires were becoming increasingly influential in the life of the church.[14]

I noted earlier that medieval writers were familiar with the idea of pilgrimage as a representation of the human condition. From the point of view of the present collection of essays, this concept has a special

---

[14] P. Boglioni, 'Pèlerinage et religion populaire au Moyen Age', in Kriss-Rettenbeck and Möhler (eds.), *Wallfahrt kennt keine Grenzen* (above), pp. 66–75, extending the ideas of the Turners into a different area.

importance. Protestant reformers rejected the sanctity of shrines, ridiculed their relics, and denied the value of visiting them. In spite of the ferocity of this criticism, it was still possible for 'pilgrimage' to survive as an important cultural phenomenon.

The pilgrim ideal had some interesting successors. The word came to be secularised, to mean a journey, usually a journey of importance and dignity. About 1600, there was *The Pilgrimage to Parnassus*, a journey of scholars. In 1625, *Purchas his Pilgrims* was published as a successor to Hakluyt, but now without any reference to the Jerusalem journeys created by the devotion of past ages. A 'pilgrim' in this collection of works was an explorer of the world.[15] It also spilled out into the Grand Tour. A visit to Italy might combine Catholic devotion with art patronage, with the one hiding behind the other. In their great art tour of 1613–14 the earl and countess of Arundel, themselves Roman Catholics, were accompanied by a party that included not only Inigo Jones, but some outstanding Recusants, including Tobie Matthew, who was priested at Rome. The journey to Italy of Nicholas Lanier in 1625, to buy pictures for Charles I, was disguised as a pilgrimage for the Holy Year, so as not to 'enhance the prices'.[16]

Even more striking is the way in which the image of pilgrimage as a symbol of the Christian life was able to pass from Catholic to Protestant spirituality. Catholics had usually read 'the pilgrimage of life' as a deeper and fuller expression of shrine pilgrimage, as we can see in the sermons of James of Vitry, early in the thirteenth century.[17] Protestants separated the two sharply. In 1552, Bishop Latimer told his hearers that 'I Have to tell you at this present time of a certain Pilgrimage, which may be called the Christian man's pilgrimage: but ye shall not think that I will speake of the Popish pilgrimage, which we were wont to use in times past, in running hither and thither'. The fact that Latimer's conceit is rather forced, in seeing the Beatitudes as the eight steps of the true pilgrimage to heaven, impresses one all the more with his concern to divide the two sorts of pilgrimage.[18] A more polished and famous expression of this idea, Bunyan's *Pilgrim's Progress*, published in 1678, was essentially original in its structure, but as Neil Keeble demonstrates here, it drew on a considerable Protestant tradition of thought about the pilgrimage of

---

[15] *Hakluytus Posthumus, or Purchas his Pilgrims: contayning a History of the World in Sea Voyages and Lande Travells by Englishmen and Others: Printed in Pauls Churchyard 1625.*

[16] See the interesting discussion in E. Chaney, *The Evolution of the Grand Tour* (London: Cass, 1998), ch. 8.

[17] D. J. Birch, 'Jacques de Vitry and the Ideology of Pilgrimage', in Stopford (ed.), *Pilgrimage Explored* (see above, note 3), pp. 95–122.

[18] Gomez-Géraud, *Le crépuscule du Grand Voyage* (see above, note 5), pp. 118–19.

the human soul. Perhaps the poem, *The Passionate Man's Pilgrimage*, may serve as a 'missing link' to illustrate the process of change.

Its authorship is disputed. Seventeenth-century report was that it was written by Sir Walter Ralegh as he was awaiting execution late in 1603 – which, in the event, was to be very long delayed. The original attribution is not secure. One would not expect Catholic language from Ralegh, and this *is* traditional Catholicism, seeing shrine pilgrimage as the outer symbol for the pilgrimage of life. As a result, several scholars have flatly denied his authorship. On the other hand, the poem certainly reads like a meditation on death, written by an unsuccessful courtier confronted by the prospect of execution; and, as to the language, Ralegh was a man whose imagination encompassed oceans. Whoever wrote it, the poem was a place where the tradition of medieval pilgrimage became the vehicle for an understanding of the human condition:

> Give me my scallop-shell of quiet,
> My staff of faith to walk upon,
> My scrip of joy, immortal diet,
> My bottle of salvation,
> My gown of glory, hope's true gage,
> And thus I'll take my pilgrimage.[19]

[19] G. Hammond (ed.), *Sir Walter Ralegh: Selected Writings* (Manchester, 1984), pp. 53–5, 284–5.

1   The pilgrimages of the Angevin kings of England 1154–1272*

Nicholas Vincent

The present investigation is to be read as but one small part of a much larger study of the religion of England's medieval kings: a study that richly deserves to be written, but that as yet has failed to attract an author. Here I intend to confine myself to a single aspect of the king's religion: the royal pilgrimage. In doing so, I hope to challenge what little secondary writing there exists on the subject, and in particular to suggest that the pilgrimages made by the Angevin kings of England represent a far more complex and significant phenomenon than just ordinary pilgrimage writ large.[1] A consideration of royal pilgrims may also lead us to raise yet a further challenge to the anthropological model of pilgrimage, imported into historical studies in the 1970s, and at the same time may dissuade us from drawing too rigid a distinction between pilgrimage and the king's more general religious devotions. As I hope to prove, it may also force us to reconsider an issue with which English historians have shown themselves somewhat reluctant to engage: the king's sacrality. My field of study will be limited to the period from the accession of Henry II in 1154, to the death of his grandson, Henry III, in 1272, spanning the reigns of the first four Plantagenet kings. There is no real justification for these limits, save that they coincide conveniently with my own area of expertise, and that they incorporate what might be described as the 'Golden Age' of English pilgrimage. I might also, in defence, plead that after 1272, and as a result of the work of Michael Prestwich and others, we have a slightly better understanding of the dynamics of kingly piety than we do for the preceding two centuries.[2]

---

* I am grateful to Henry Mayr-Harting, Bernard Hamilton and to various of the speakers at the Canterbury Colloquium for their assistance in the writing of this chapter.

[1] See here the remarks of Ben Nilson, 'The Medieval Experience at the Shrine', in J. Stopford (ed.), *Pilgrimage Explored* (Woodbridge, 1999), p. 122: 'The substance of these beliefs did not change with social status, only the scale and style with which they were acted out. Thus the actions of a king...were directed with the same hopes and expectations as [those of] the average supplicant.' I must apologise to Dr Nilson for making merry with what is otherwise an extremely compelling piece of work.

[2] See M. Prestwich, 'The Piety of Edward I', in W. M. Ormrod (ed.), *England in the Thirteenth Century: Proceedings of the 1984 Harlaxton Symposium* (Harlaxton, 1985),

Pilgrimage ran in the blood of Henry II, the first of the Angevin kings, as a tradition inherited from all sides of his family, from his Angevin, Norman and Anglo-Saxon ancestors. From his native Anjou, Henry's paternal great-great-great-grandfather, Count Fulk Nerra, had made at least three and possibly four penitential pilgrimages to Jerusalem, establishing a tradition whereby, a century later, Henry's grandfather, another Count Fulk, came not only to visit but to rule in the Holy Land.[3] From the east, the counts returned with relics, of the true Cross and of St Nicholas, that in due course were to provide the focus for pilgrimage to various of the city churches of Angers and Tours, in addition to the relics, most notably of St Martin, that those churches already possessed.[4] Jerusalem had also been the object of the penitential pilgrimage undertaken in the 1030s by Henry II's maternal great-grandfather, Duke Robert of Normandy, and thereafter had attracted large numbers of Robert's subjects and descendants to serve in the first and all subsequent crusades.[5] Although, after their Conquest of England in 1066, there had been been some resistance by the Normans to the cult of the Anglo-Saxon saints, by the 1090s Anglo-Saxon relics were being translated with enthusiasm to shrines newly constructed by England's Norman bishops and kings.[6] William the Conqueror himself passed the night before Hastings with phylacteries around his neck containing relics of the saints. Others, which he had acquired from the treasury of the Anglo-Saxon kings, he bequeathed to his monastery at Battle, where they are said to have

---

pp. 120–8; A. J. Taylor, 'Edward I and the Shrine of St Thomas at Canterbury', *JBAA*, 132 (1979), 22–8; A. Taylor, 'Royal Alms and Oblations in the Later 13th Century', in F. Emmison and R. Stephens (eds.), *Tribute to an Antiquary: Essays presented to Marc Fitch* (London, 1976), pp. 93–125; D. W. Burton, 'Requests for Prayers and Royal Propaganda under Edward I', in P. R. Coss and S. D. Lloyd (eds.), *Thirteenth Century England*, vol. III (Woodbridge, 1991), pp. 25–35.

[3] B. S. Bachrach, 'The Pilgrimages of Fulk Nerra Count of the Angevins, 987–1040', in T. F. X. Noble and J. J. Contreni (eds.), *Religion, Culture and Society in the Early Middle Ages: Studies in Honor of Richard E. Sullivan* (Kalamazoo, 1987), pp. 205–17.

[4] Y. Mailfert, 'Fondation du monastére Bénédictin de Saint-Nicolas d'Angers', *Bibliothèque de l'Ecole des Chartes*, 92 (1931), 43–61, esp. 55–6; J. Riley-Smith, 'King Fulk of Jerusalem and "the Sultan of Babylon"', in B. Z. Kedar et al. (eds.), *Montjoie: Studies in Crusade History in Honour of Hans Eberhard Mayer* (London, 1997), pp. 55–8, including the special arrangements made at St Laud at Angers in the 1130s for the reception of the count of Anjou whenever he should return to Angers from pilgrimage.

[5] E. C. M. Van Houts (ed.), *The Gesta Normannorum Ducum of William of Jumièges, Orderic Vitalis and Robert of Torigni*, 2 vols., OMT (Oxford, 1992–5), vol. II, pp. 78–85; R. H. C. Davis and M. Chibnall (eds.),*The Gesta Guillelmi of William of Poitiers*, OMT (Oxford, 1998), pp. 78–9, with some extremely interesting but speculative remarks by Bachrach, 'Pilgrimages of Fulk Nerra', pp. 208–10.

[6] Amongst many other studies, see S. J. Ridyard, '"Condigna Veneratio": Post-Conquest Attitudes to the Saints of the Anglo-Saxons', *ANS*; vol. IX, (1986), pp. 179–206.

been employed in a not entirely successful attempt to attract pilgrims.[7] No Anglo-Saxon king of England had visited Jerusalem, but several had made pilgrimages to the almost equally distinguished shrines of Rome. It was during a pilgrimage to Rome, in 1027, that king Cnut sought special privileges for English pilgrims travelling to the Holy City, whilst the very earliest surviving correspondence between an English and a continental king, that between Offa and Charlemagne, concerns the rights of English pilgrims to free passage through Carolingian France.[8] Henry II's lands, from Durham to Limoges, were criss-crossed by pilgrim routes, scattered with shrines and piled high with holy relics, often of considerable antiquity. It is therefore hardly surprising that Henry, like most of his ancestors and successors, should have proved both an enthusiastic and a frequent pilgrim.

Here, however, at the very start of our enquiry, we come up against a major problem. If we seek to apply the anthropological model of pilgrimage, championed most notably by Victor and Edith Turner, we find that England's pilgrim kings differed in several important respects from what the Turners would regard as the pilgrim norm. For the Turners, pilgrimage can be defined as a ritual practice, carrying the pilgrim beyond the frontiers of daily experience, and characterised by such concepts as 'liminality', 'transience' and 'communitas'. Turnerian pilgrimage stands outside the normal structures of authority, requiring its participants to enter a nomadic state in which the individual pilgrim may transcend the more conventional distinctions of class and social status.[9] Putting aside, for the moment, any scepticism we might feel towards an analysis that, in its search for meaning, seeks to reinvent the English language, it is clear that such concepts as 'transience' and 'communitas' cannot easily be applied to the pilgrimage experience of England's medieval kings. To begin with, and unlike, say, a peasant who might pass the larger part of his life in one place and in one set of social relations, the Plantagenet kings

---

[7] Davis and Chibnall (eds.), *William of Poitiers*, pp. 124–5; E. Searle (ed.), *The Chronicle of Battle Abbey*, OMT (Oxford, 1980), pp. 90–1, 102–5. For another reliquary, given by William to the monks of Rochester, and for relics of SS Denis, Nicaise, Eustace and Rumbald reputedly given by the king to Westminster Abbey, see J. Thorpe, *Registrum Roffense* (London, 1769), p. 120; John Flete, *The History of Westminster Abbey*, ed. J. A. Robinson (Cambridge, 1909), p. 71.

[8] V. Ortenberg, *The English Church and the Continent in the Tenth and Eleventh Centuries* (Oxford, 1992), p. 59, and for the burial of Kings Offa and Ceadwalla at Rome, see p. 135. For the letters of Charlemagne to Offa, AD795, see *PL*, 98, col. 907.

[9] These ideas are most fully expressed in V. and E. Turner, *Image and Pilgrimage in Christian Culture* (Oxford, 1978), with a particularly illuminating attempt to define terms at pp. 249–51. For a recent critique, see Stopford in *Pilgrimage Explored*, p. xii, citing various of the more recent anthropological studies edited by J. Eade and M. J. Sallnow, *Contesting the Sacred: The Anthropology of Christian Pilgrimage* (London, 1991).

were of their essence itinerant, travelling ceaselessly from one region of their dominion to another. Even Henry III, the first post-Conquest king to begin to establish a permanent administrative capital for himself, spent far more time touring his realm than he ever did in residence at his palace in Westminster. It was the royal itinerary, and the near ceaseless round of campaigning, hunting expeditions, crown-wearings, solemn entries and local visitations, that characterised all western European monarchies from the fall of Rome until at least the fourteenth century. Even earlier, it has been argued that the very idea of Christian pilgrimage may have developed in emulation of the journey to Jerusalem conducted by Helena, mother of the fourth-century Roman emperor Constantine. Helena's journey can be regarded as merely the latest in a long tradition of visitations, the *itinera principum*, orchestrated by the imperial court since the time of Augustus, and in this particular instance intended to forge an alliance between Constantine's troubled family and the Christian God. It may thus have been the Roman imperial itinerary that first brought pilgrimage into vogue, rather than any pre-existing idea of pilgrimage which first encouraged Helena to journey to Jerusalem.[10] With the fall of Rome, and in the absence of any more stable form of government, it was the royal itinerary that more than anything else served to impose order, justice and authority upon the otherwise disunited regions of barbarian and early medieval Europe.[11] The Plantagenets, and their itinerant court, so graphically described by Walter Map or Peter of Blois, were heirs to this long tradition.[12] To this extent, there was often no more 'transience' in the decision made by a Plantagenet king to set out for a pilgrim shrine than there was in the daily run of his nomadic existence.

Likewise, if we take another of the Turners' ideas, 'communitas', we shall find that, both in import and magnificence, the king's pilgrimage remained very much a royal phenomenon, set apart from the experience of less exalted pilgrims. The significance attached to royal pilgrimage and

---

[10] See here the stimulating essay by K. G. Holum, 'Hadrian and St Helena: Imperial Travel and the Origins of Christian Holy Land Pilgrimage', in R. Ousterhout (ed.), *The Blessings of Pilgrimage*, Illinois Byzantine Studies 1 (Urbana and Chicago, 1990), pp. 66–81.

[11] See in general J. W. Bernhardt, *Itinerant Kingship and Royal Monasteries in Early Medieval Germany, c. 936–1075* (Cambridge, 1993), esp. p. 45ff.

[12] The Plantagenet itinerary is best approached through the work of J. E. A. Jolliffe, *Angevin Kingship* (London, 1955), esp. ch. 7, and R. Bartlett, *England Under the Norman and Angevin Kings 1075–1225* (Oxford, 2000), pp. 133–43. See also the image of the diabolic hunt, developed as an image of Henry II's court by Walter Map, *De Nugis Curialium: Courtiers' Trifles*, ed. M. R. James, C. N. L. Brooke and R. A. B. Mynors, OMT (Oxford, 1983), pp. 26–31, 370–3, with commentary by L. Harf-Lancner, 'L'Enfer de la cour: la cour d'Henri II Plantagenet et la Mesnie Hellequin', in P. Contamine (ed.), *L'Etat et les aristocraties (France, Angleterre, Ecosse) XIIe–XVIIe siècle* (Paris, 1989), pp. 38–9, as drawn to my attention by Martin Aurell.

the status bestowed upon a church or relic by its ability to attract royal visitors, inevitably set a pilgrim king apart from any more humble visitor to a shrine. The king's degree and status were preserved, even in the act of pilgrimage. Long before the advent of written record, there is evidence to suggest that the social elites of prehistoric Britain may have been guaranteed a different reception at their holy sites from the average run of visitors.[13] With the Plantagenets, we might care to remember the experience of Henry II, during his penitential visit to the shrine of Thomas Becket in 1174. In theory, Henry came in all humility, dismounting at his first sight of Becket's cathedral, and processing thereafter through the streets of Canterbury from St Dunstans to the shrine, barefoot and wearing nothing more than a hair shirt and a smock.[14] In practice, so accustomed were the monks of Canterbury to laying on a special display for their royal visitors, that Henry had sternly to forbid them from greeting him in procession at the city's outskirts, or from escorting him in majesty to their church.[15] To become a pilgrim, it would seem, Henry had first to command his subjects to respect his pilgrim status. A king who has to command the observation of his own humility cannot be said to be truly humbled.

Moreover, for all that Henry might spend the night in tears by Becket's shrine, and on the morrow instruct the monks and clergy to discipline him with more than two hundred strokes of the rod, no ordinary pilgrim could then have made the rich offerings that Henry bestowed upon the monks, of four marks of pure gold, a silk pall and an annual rent of £40 from the royal manor of Milton.[16] Here again we might recall the chronicler Salimbene's description of King Louis IX of France, on his departure for crusade in 1248. To Salimbene it was the very fact that Louis arrived at Sens dressed as a humble pilgrim, on foot and with scrip and staff, that appeared so remarkable. What Salimbene observed is in fact a common phenomenon: the royal display of humility that remains royal precisely because it is so ostentatiously humble. Having arrived dressed as a pilgrim, Louis did not depart from Sens until his court had been served with a sumptuous banquet that included cherries, crayfish,

---

[13] R. Bradley, 'Pilgrimage in Prehistoric Britain?', in Stopford (ed.), *Pilgrimage Explored*, pp. 11, 23.

[14] For an account of this pilgrimage, drawn from several sources, see F. Barlow, *Thomas Becket* (London, 1986), pp. 269–70

[15] E. Grim, in *Materials*, vol. II, p. 445: 'Moris quidem fuerat conventum regibus festive procedere, et nonnulla reverentie obsequia solemniter exhibere, sed hec universa sibi prohibebat impendi, qui magis luctu quam letitia pascebatur'.

[16] *Materials*, vol. II, pp. 446–7; Barlow, *Becket*, p. 270, and for the rent, originally of £30, awarded at Easter 1173, raised after Henry's pilgrimage in July 1174 to £40, see Henry's charter, now CCA Chartae Antiquae B337; *Pipe Roll 19 Henry II*, pp. 80–1; *Pipe Roll 21 Henry II*, p. 208.

and eels cooked in the finest sauce.[17] Over and over again, as we shall see, the royal experience of pilgrimage was distinguished by particular traditions and by a particular, privileged approach to the shrine and its relics, that render it unlikely that such pilgrimages were governed by much sense of 'communitas', or freedom from the normal social distinctions that set king and subjects apart. As any reader of Chaucer can appreciate – although it seems to have escaped the notice of anthropologists – there was almost as great an awareness of social distinction amongst the Canterbury pilgrims as there would be today amongst visitors to the royal enclosure at Ascot.

Thus far we have referred to pilgrimage as if it were a neatly definable phenomenon – a journey in pursuit of the Holy that can be distinguished from the more ordinary run of religious devotions. Medieval writers were clearly at pains to establish such a distinction, if only to set the genuine pilgrim apart from his more disreputable counterpart, the vagabond or commercial traveller. In canon law, a pilgrimage was defined as either an obligatory journey imposed in penance for wrongdoing, or as a voluntary act that nonetheless involved a preliminary vow, and that was accomplished thereafter in the proper habit of a pilgrim, carrying the pilgrim insignia of scrip and staff.[18] If we seek to apply such distinctions to the Plantagenet kings, we shall again run into difficulty. Of penitential royal pilgrimage, we have no evidence during our period, since even the remarkable visit paid to Becket's shrine by Henry II in 1174 was made at the king's own insistence, and not in obedience to a sentence imposed by the Church.[19] As to the elements of the pilgrim's vow, scrip and staff, we have precious little proof that these things played much part in the king's devotions. Richard I, it is true, accepted the insignia of staff and scrip on setting out for crusade – depending upon which account one reads, at Tours or at Vézelay, but in either case in a location that itself could boast a rich tradition of pilgrimage, to St Martin or

---

[17] Salimbene de Adam, *Cronica*, ed. F. Bernini, 2 vols. (Bari, 1942), vol. I, pp. 316–21, whence L. Carolus-Barré, *Le Procès de canonisation de Saint Louis (1272–1297): Essai de reconstruction*, Collections de l'Ecole française de Rome 195 (Rome, 1994), pp. 294–5.

[18] H. Gilles, 'Lex Peregrinorum', *Cahiers de Fanjeaux 15: Le Pèlerinage* (1980), 161–89, esp. 163–70.

[19] Edward Grim (in *Materials*, vol. II, p. 445) suggests that in 1174 Henry was inspired by a dream to visit Canterbury. His agreement to take the Cross within nine months of the compromise of Avranches (1172) might to some extent be regarded as an enforced pilgrimage, but in the event he was to evade this stipulation, and only took the Cross, on his own terms, in 1188: H. E. Mayer, 'Henry II of England and the Holy Land', *EHR*, 97 (1982), 721–39, esp. 721–2. For penitential pilgrimage in general, see the classic study by C. Vogel, 'Le Pèlerinage pénitentiel', *Revue des Sciences Religieuses*, 38 (1964), 113–53, reprinted in Vogel, *En Rémission de péchés* (London, 1994), ch. 7.

to St Mary Magdalene. The staff is said to have broken in his hand.[20] Thereafter, and with the exception of their signings with the cross – a ceremony that already stood outside the pilgrim norm – the only other occasions on which the Plantagenets are known to have put on the theatrical props of pilgrimage came in the 1190s, when Richard sought to disguise himself as a pilgrim in returning via Austria, and in 1242, when at the bridge of Taillebourg, faced by a vastly superior French army, Henry III's brother Richard of Cornwall went unarmed into the enemy camp, carrying nothing more than a pilgrim staff as a reminder of the services that he had rendered to the French on crusade.[21] Elsewhere, the most that we can hope for from the chronicle sources is some comment that a particular journey was made by a king *orationis gratia*, or *voto et devotione*, phrases that are applied, for example, to the visits made by King John to the shrines of Bury St Edmunds and St Albans immediately after his coronation.[22]

Medieval Christendom boasted three great pilgrim destinations: Jerusalem, Rome and Compostela. It is a remarkable fact that during our period not one of these shrines was visited by a Plantagenet king. All four of our kings took vows to depart on crusade, and hence to visit the Holy Land. Only one of them, Richard I, actually set sail, and, as is well known, Richard was never to enter the city of Jerusalem. More remarkably still, and despite having travelled from Marseilles to Sicily with frequent stops along the Italian coast, Richard deliberately passed up the opportunity to visit the Holy Places of Rome.[23] For the rest, Henry the Young King, Richard's elder brother, although never a pilgrim to Jerusalem, accomplished a pilgrimage there by proxy, on his deathbed dispatching William Marshal as a pilgrim in his stead.[24] Henry III, whose own son, the future Edward I, was in the Holy Land at the time of his father's death, obtained,

---

[20] Roger of Howden, *Chronica*, ed. W. Stubbs, 4 vols., RS (London, 1868–71), vol. III, pp. 36–7; (Roger of Howden), *Gesta Regis Henrici Secundi Benedicti abbatis*, ed. W. Stubbs, 2 vols., RS (London, 1867), vol. II, p. 111.

[21] For Richard I, see Howden, *Chronica*, vol. III, pp. 185–6, also remarked by the Salzburg annalist, 'Annalium Salisburgensium additamentun', ed. W. Wattenbach, *MGH SS*, vol. XIII p. 240. For Richard of Cornwall, see Matthew Paris, *Chronica Majora*, ed. H. R. Luard, 7 vols., RS (London, 1872–83), vol. IV, p. 211. For other, non-royal examples of the pilgrim habit being used as disguise, see Y. Dossat, 'Types exceptionnels de pèlerins: l'hérétique, le voyageur déguisé, le professionel', *Cahiers de Fanjeaux 15* (1980), 213–19.

[22] Roger of Wendover, in Paris, *Chronica Majora*, vol. II, p. 456; H. E. Butler (ed.), *The Chronicle of Jocelin of Brakelond* (London, 1949), pp. 116–17, and note that before returning to France in June 1199, John also visited Becket's shrine at Canterbury: 'Itinerary of King John', in T. D. Hardy (ed.), *Rotuli Litterarum Patentium* (London, 1835), *sub dat.* 12 June 1199; *Radulphi de Diceto Opera Historica*, ed. W. Stubbs, 2 vols., RS (London, 1876), vol. II, p. 166.

[23] J. Gillingham, *Richard I* (New Haven, CT, 1999), p. 130.

[24] D. Crouch, *William Marshal* (London, 1990), pp. 49, 51–2.

via Edward, a grant of plenary indulgence from the church of Jerusalem, forgiving him all the sins of which he was truly penitent and confessed, and extending a similar indulgence to Henry's long-dead father and mother, King John and Queen Isabella, deemed to be participators in the indulgence available to those who lent aid to the Holy Land. However since this award was made only a few days before Henry died, and more than a thousand miles away, he can never have learned of its provisions.[25] Both Henry II and his son Henry the Young King voiced a desire to visit Compostela. Neither actually accomplished this desire, and in both cases they may have had other considerations in mind than religious devotion. Henry II may have been angling for diplomatic contacts with the kingdom of Leon: the Young King to escape from his overbearing father.[26]

It is worth asking why the Plantagenet kings failed to follow in the footsteps of their ancestors, beyond the confines of the Plantagenet realm. A similar reluctance has been observed in the case of Louis IX of France, a notable crusader, and an avid pilgrim, but a king who failed to follow Capetian tradition by visiting any European shrine outside the boundaries of France.[27] Henry III, it is true, visited Saint-Denis, the passion relics of the Sainte-Chapelle, and a round of French shrines, including those of St Edmund of Canterbury at Pontigny and of the Virgin Mary at Chartres, during the Anglo-French negotiations of 1254, 1259–60, and 1262.[28] However, for the rest, it was the shrines of England and the Plantagenet dominion that received the vast majority of royal visits, perhaps because of the simple logistical difficulty of venturing beyond the realm, but more likely through a perceived, dare one say patriotic, sense that it was the saints of England and the Angevin realm, or at least those saints whose relics reposed within the king's dominion, who were the king's chief spiritual protectors. It was the hand of St James at Reading, not the body of Santiago at Compostela, to which the Plantagenets rendered their devotion.

---

[25] PRO E36/274 fol.250r (211r), apparently unprinted, issued by Brother Bernard the penitentiary of Jerusalem, at Acre on 20 September 1272.

[26] Howden, *Gesta*, vol. I, pp. 114–15, 157; D. W. Lomax, 'The First English Pilgrims to Santiago de Compostela', in H. Mayr-Harting and R. I. Moore (eds.), *Studies in Medieval History Presented to R. H. C. Davis* (London, 1985), pp. 173–4.

[27] E.-R. Labande, 'Saint Louis Pèlerin', *Revue d'Histoire de l'Eglise de France*, 57 (1971), 5–18, esp. 9–10, reprinted in Labande, *Spiritualité et vie littéraire de l'occident, Xe–XIVe siècle* (London, 1974), ch. 16.

[28] Paris, *Chronica Majora*, vol. v, pp. 467, 475–83; *Close Rolls 1259–61*, pp. 267–8; *Close Rolls 1261–4*, p. 145. Note, too, the pilgrimage made by the Lord Edward, son of Henry III, to the shrine of St Ninian, at Whithorn in Galloway in southern Scotland, in July 1256: R. Studd, *An Itinerary of the Lord Edward*, List and Index Society, 284 (2000), p. 30, as drawn to my attention by Robin Studd.

The fact that the kings of England made no pilgrimages to Jerusalem, Rome or Compostela; the fact that they seem rarely to have vowed their pilgrimages; and that they travelled without the insignia of scrip and staff, all suggest that we need to rethink any attempt we might otherwise make to distinguish between 'genuine' royal pilgrimage, and the more general run of royal devotions. When the king visited a monastery or church, it was customary for him to make offerings, of money, gold, silk, or more exceptionally of privileges or lands. Very seldom, though, can these awards be used to define a pilgrimage. To take just one example: Henry II issued numerous surviving charters on behalf of the monks of St Albans, keepers of the shrine not only of the English protomartyr Alban, but of Alban's teacher, the entirely apocryphal St Amphibalus, whose remains were rediscovered in dramatic circumstances, being translated to a new shrine in June 1178, and again, to a more fitting location, in June 1186.[29] There is no evidence, for or against, to suggest whether Henry II attended either of these translations. Of his dozen or so charters to the abbey, at least two were issued at St Albans itself, early in the reign, and of these two, the longer, confirming exemption from interference by the king's officers, was specifically made for the soul of the king, of Eleanor his wife and of his heirs and ancestors, an unusual formula which suggests a particular personal concern.[30] However, we have no proof that these awards were made *ex voto*, as the result of a pilgrimage, and our only indication that Henry took any interest in the abbey's shrine occurs in a brief reference in the St Albans' chronicle to his having supplied a precious cup for the reservation of the sacrament, matching gifts that had been made to the shrine by Abbot Simon.[31] Not until the reign of Henry III do we begin to read of the king making regular visits to pray at St Albans, and of his bestowing offerings there of gold, silk and other precious objects: gifts, it should be noticed, including silk cloths indelibly marked with the king's name, and amulets permanently nailed to the shrine, that were intended for public display, presumably to advertise the king's largesse.[32] Even then,

---

[29] For Amphibalus, see Howden, *Gesta*, vol. I, pp. 175–7; Matthew Paris, 'Gesta Abbatum', in *Chronica Monasterii S. Albani*, ed. H. T. Riley, 7 vols. RS (London, 1863–76), vol. IV part 1, pp. 192–3, 199–206; Paris, *Chronica Majora*, vol. II, pp. 301–8; F. McCulloch, 'Saints Alban and Amphibalus in the Works of Matthew Paris: Dublin, Trinity College MS 177', *Speculum*, 56 (1981), 761–85.

[30] *Calendar of Charter Rolls 1300–26*, pp. 17 no. 5, 19 no. 2.

[31] Paris, 'Gesta Abbatum', pp. 189–90.

[32] *Chronica Majora*, vol. IV, p. 402; vol. V, pp. 233–4, 257–8, 319–20, 489–90, 574, 617, 653–4; vol. VI, pp. 389–92. For a cloth embroidered with the words *Henricus rex*, given in 1182 to the shrine of St Martial at Limoges by Henry the Young King, see Geoffrey of Vigeois, in *RHGF*, vol. XVIII, p. 212. For special cloths given to Le Mans Cathedral by

none of the many accounts of these visits specifically refers to them as a pilgrimage.

Here we may well care to rethink our attempt to define pilgrimage as a specific and distinct category of the king's religious devotions. As an itinerant ruler, the king inevitably visited a whole series of locations that possessed shrines or relics worthy of veneration. It is hard, indeed, to name many places on the royal itinerary where relics and shrines were not to be found. As we shall see, the kings themselves travelled with a chapel that included a substantial collection of relics.[33] Rather than attempt to distinguish between the extraordinary ('pilgrimage'), and the ordinary ('devotion' or 'mere visitation'), it may be better to picture the king as being by his very nature a near-perpetual pilgrim. Seen in this light, the daily round of royal devotions, carried out in many different places across the realm, can be regarded as yet another means, and a significant one, by which the royal itinerary served to impose the king's authority upon realm and subjects alike. Kings might complain that their time was short, just as Henry II is said to have complained, towards the end of his life, that he had few spare moments in which to pray. Even at mass, where he could utter barely two paternosters, he was beset by petitioners, not only laymen, but clerks and monks who, showing no respect for the sacrament, ceaselessly bombarded him with their pleas.[34] Well might King John have sent up a note to Hugh of Lincoln during the Easter service in 1200, not once but three times, imploring the bishop to cut short his sermon and to get on with the mass, so that the king might dine after his Easter fasting.[35] Nonetheless, as even this story, so often quoted as a sign of John's impiety, should make plain, the king was not only sufficiently pious to fast during Holy Week, but better placed than anyone else to listen to the finest sermons and to visit the greatest shrines, virtually wherever his itinerary might take him. In doing so, kings not only brought their

Henry II, see Paris, Bibliothèque Nationale MS Latin 5211B, p. 81: 'Nobis modo dedit xi. pallia, pannumque illum sericum cum auratis imaginibus qui dicitur pannus regius, qui in magnis festiuis super altare beati Iuliani suspenditur.'

[33] See below pp. 34–6.

[34] Peter of Blois, 'Dialogus inter regem Henricum secundum et abbatem Bonevallis', ed. R. B. C. Huygens, *Revue Bénédictine*, 68 (1958), pp. 104–5. Sir Richard Southern, whilst continuing to cite this treatise from its unsatisfactory printing in *PL* 207, gives good reasons for accepting its basic accuracy, identifying the king's interlocutor as Christian abbot of Bonneval, and dating their interview to some time between February and May 1189: Southern, 'Peter of Blois and the Third Crusade', in Mayr-Harting and Moore (eds.), *Studies in Medieval History*, pp. 208–11.

[35] Adam of Eynsham, *Magna Vita Sancti Hugonis*, ed. D. L. Douie and D. H. Farmer, 2 vols., OMT, 2nd edn (Oxford, 1985), vol. II, pp. 142–3.

own problems and the problems of their realm before the saints for intercession, but, through their near ceaseless round of devotions, served to link one shrine to another into a chain of spiritual support, sanctifying their journeys around the realm and underpinning their attempts to impose royal authority upon their diverse dominions. Where previously the West Saxon kings had sought to introduce unity to their realm by translating the relics of the saints from outlying regions to the vicinity of the great royal necropolis at Winchester, the Plantagenets made a virtue out of necessity, employing the shrines of the saints, and the churches and monasteries that housed them, as stopping-off points in an otherwise ceaseless pattern of movement that encompassed even the most far-flung outposts of Plantagenet rule.[36] A glance at the accounts for the household expenses of King John, or later of Edward I, is sufficient to show that frequent oblations at the shrines of the saints take their place alongside hunting and warfare as an essential feature of the king's itinerary.[37]

With this thought in mind, let us proceed to the king's devotions, and to those in particular that involved shrines, penitence or prayer, all of them features common to pilgrimage. Here, and without too rigid an attempt at classification, we can at least suggest some broad categories into which the king's devotions may be divided. We might begin with those many religious acts intended to procure or to offer thanks for recovery from illness, spritual or physical. In 1170, as is well known, Henry II broke camp in Normandy and travelled as far south as Rocamadour in Quercy, to give thanks to the Virgin for his restoration to health.[38] At

---

[36] For the Anglo-Saxon period, see especially D. W. Rollason, 'Lists of Saints' Resting-Places in Anglo-Saxon England', *Anglo-Saxon England*, 7 (1978), 61–93, at 82–6; Rollason, 'The Shrines of Saints in Later Anglo-Saxon England: Distribution and Significance', in L. A. S. Butler and R. K. Morris (eds.), *The Anglo-Saxon Church*, Council for British Archaeology Research Report 60 (1986), pp. 32–43; Rollason, *Saints and Relics in Anglo-Saxon England* (Oxford, 1989), ch. 6, pp. 133–68. For continental parallels, see E. Bozóky, 'La Politique des reliques des premiers comtes de Flandre (fin du IXe–fin du XIe siècle)', in Bozóky and A.-M. Helvétius (eds.), *Les Reliques: objets, cultes, symboles. Actes du colloque international de l'Université du Littoral-Côte d'Opale (Boulogne-sur-Mer) 4–6 septembre 1997* (Turnhout, 1999), pp. 271–92.

[37] The household accounts of King John (1209–10, and 1212–13) are printed in T. D. Hardy (ed.), *Rotuli de Liberate ac de misis et praestitis* (London, 1844), pp. 109–71; H. Cole (ed.), *Documents Illustrative of English History in the Thirteenth and Fourteenth Centuries* (London, 1844), pp. 231–69, with some analysis by C. R. Young, 'King John of England: An Illustration of the Medieval Practice of Charity', *Church History*, 24 (1960), 264–74. For a glimpse of the religious itinerary of Edward I, see Taylor, 'Royal Alms and Oblations' (above n. 2), pp. 112–16.

[38] E. Mason, ' "Rocamadour in Quercy Above All Other Churches": The Healing of Henry II', in W. J. Sheils (ed.), *The Church and Healing*, SCH 19 (Oxford, 1982), 39–54. For the supposed divinely imposed sickness from which the king had suffered, having failed to heed the advice of the blessed Hamo of Savigny to pardon a knight accused of plotting his death, sentenced to blinding and castration, see E. P. Sauvage, 'Vitae B.

Pontigny in 1254, Henry III is said to have recovered from illness at the shrine of St Edmund.[39] Linked to these are the journeys, such as that of Henry II to Canterbury in 1174, intended to acquire remission from spiritual sickness and sin. Kings, more perhaps than the average believer, were burdened with a sense of their own wrongdoing. After Becket's murder, in 1171, Henry II is said to have retired for forty days of penance and fasting, refusing to leave his apartments at Argentan.[40] Richard I, perhaps for sexual misconduct, undertook public penance at least twice, on the first occasion throwing himself naked before the feet of the assembled bishops.[41] Even John is said to have undergone an, albeit temporary, conversion to good living as a result of viewing the images of kings condemned to damnation in the portal of Fontevraud, whilst his son the excessively pious Henry III is said to have confessed that he knew only too well the extent to which he had sinned against God and his saints by promoting his half-brother Aymer to the bishopric of Winchester.[42] Towards the end of his life, Henry III granted significant alms to the nuns of Amesbury, for the souls of Arthur and Eleanor of Brittany, suggesting a particular desire to atone for the sins of his father King John.[43] Uneasy lies the head that wears a crown. As Henry II is said to have remarked, 'I have sinned more than most, for the whole life of the knight is passed in sin, nor have I time for proper repentance unless the Lord have mercy upon me.'[44]

Particular events in a king's life might focus his mind upon the need for divine intercession with especial urgency. The king's accession and coronation were followed, in the case of both Richard I and John, by a brief progress around the greater pilgrim shrines of southern England: Bury, St Albans and Canterbury.[45] Marriage, or the birth of an heir, might inspire offerings to the saints, such as the statue of his wife, Eleanor of Provence, which Henry III commanded be placed upon the shrine of St Edward at Westminster, shortly after his marriage in 1236.[46] Sea-crossings and negotiations with foreign powers might well lead the king to invoke divine aid, all the more so since the Plantagenets were rulers of

Petri Abrincensis et B. Hamonis monachorum coenobii Saviniacensis in Normannia', *Analecta Bollandiana*, 2 (1883), 534–5.

[39] Paris, *Chronica Majora*, vol. v, p. 475.

[40] Herbert of Bosham, in *Materials*, vol. iii, pp. 541–3.

[41] Howden, *Chronica*, vol. iii, pp. 74–5, 288–90, and for commentary on the possibility that Richard's crimes included sodomy, see Gillingham, *Richard I*, pp. 263–5.

[42] Adam of Eynsham, *Vita Sancti Hugonis*, vol. ii, pp. 140–2; Paris, *Chronica Majora*, vol. v, pp. 332–3.

[43] *Calendar of Charter Rolls 1257–1300*, p. 100, as drawn to my attention by David Carpenter.

[44] Peter of Blois, 'Dialogus' (above n. 34), p. 111, lines 422–4.

[45] For John, see above note 22. For Richard, see L. Landon, *The Itinerary of King Richard I*, Pipe Roll Society n. s. 13 (1935), pp. 5, 16–21.

[46] *Calendar of Liberate Rolls 1226–40*, p. 243.

a cross-Channel dominion, many of whose subjects, including courtiers or even close royal kinsmen, had been drowned at sea, from the time of the wreck of the White Ship onwards.[47] In journeying to Ireland in 1171, Henry II passed via the shrine of St David's in Pembroke, and having subdued the Irish, returned to St David's the following year *orandi causa*.[48] According to Howden, he deliberately delayed his departure from Ireland so as not to set sail on Easter day.[49] Henry II on at least one occasion sent to Reading Abbey for the hand of St James, so that he might pray before it and obtain the saint's protection before crossing the Channel.[50] On the eve of taking ship from Barfleur into England, in the 1150s or 60s, he is said to have made a full confession of his sins committed from the cradle onwards, to the bishop of Evreux and a monk of Savigny.[51] In 1259, before embarking for his negotiations with Louis IX, Henry III came to St Albans where he commanded that the shrine of St Alban be placed upon the high altar, beseeching the monks for their prayers in his forthcoming journey.[52] As for journeys or devotions intended to obtain or to give thanks for the succesful completion of international treaties, we might cite the various visits made by Henry II to Mont-Saint-Michel: in 1158, having secured the restoration of Nantes from the Bretons and before setting out to besiege Thouars, and again in 1166, *causa orationis*, following a second victory against the Bretons.[53] It may be that in 1172, during the settlement of the Becket dispute, negotations between Henry and the papal legates were deliberately timed to take place at Avranches around Michaelmas, so that the king might thereafter render devotion to St Michael, in the event ruled out because Henry fell ill.[54]

When negotiations failed, and warfare loomed, kings also sought to invoke the aid of the saints. The timing of Henry II's visit to Reading in March 1163 may have been providential, although it immediately preceded an expedition against the Welsh.[55] In 1183, and with Limoges under siege by Henry II, the rebellious Henry the Young King attended

---

[47] For the death of Plantagenet courtiers by drowning, see, for example, Howden, *Chronica*, vol. II, pp. 3–4; vol. III, pp. 105–6.

[48] J. Williams ab Ithel (ed.), *Annales Cambriae*, RS (London, 1860), pp. 53–4.

[49] Howden, *Gesta*, vol. I, p. 30.

[50] B. Kemp, 'The Miracles of the Hand of St James', *Berkshire Archaeological Jnl*, 65 (1970), 18 no. 26.

[51] Sauvage, 'Vita B. Hamonis' (above n. 38), 531–2.

[52] H. R. Luard (ed.), *Flores Historiarum*, 3 vols., RS (London, 1890), vol. II, pp. 431–2.

[53] Robert of Torigny, 'Chronica', in R. Howlett (ed.), *Chronicles of the Reigns of Stephen, Henry II and Richard I*, 4 vols., RS (London, 1885–9), vol. IV, pp. 197, 228.

[54] Torigny, 'Chronica', p. 254, and for pilgrimage, especially penitential pilgrimage to Mont-St-Michel, see E.-R. Labande, 'Les pèlerinages au Mont Saint-Michel pendant le Moyen Age', in M. Baudet (ed.), *Millénaire Monastique du Mont Saint-Michel III: Culte de Saint Michel et pèlerinage au Mont* (Paris, 1971), pp. 237–50, esp. pp. 241, 243, reprinted in Labande, *Spiritualité et vie littéraire*, ch. 15.

[55] R. W. Eyton, *Court, Household and Itinerary of King Henry II* (London, 1878), pp. 61–2.

a procession of the relics of St Martial, no doubt in the hope of obtaining the saint's assistance against his father.[56] A century later, in 1264, Henry III travelled to Oxford, to the shrine of St Frideswide, *orationis gratia*, before joining battle with the barons at Northampton.[57] Although there is less evidence from Plantagenet England than from early medieval Europe for the deliberate timing of battles to coincide with the feasts of the saints, having made landfall at Cyprus around the feast of the translation of St Edmund (29 April) 1191, and having defeated the local tyrant a week later, it is perhaps no coincidence that Richard I sent back a newly captured golden banner to the shrine of St Edmund at Bury.[58] Henry II may have attached a particular significance to the feast day of St James (25 July), whose arm the king considered to be amongst the most precious of relics.[59] In 1166 or 1167, he originally planned to do battle with the Breton rebels on the feast day of SS Peter and Paul, 29 June, but was dissuaded by the blessed Hamo of Savigny, who prophesied that if the king chose a less holy day, he would be rewarded with victory.[60] Likewise, I would suggest that it was more than mere coincidence that led the monks of Westminster, acting in close co-operation with Henry II, to select Sunday 13 October 1163 as the date for the translation of the relics of the newly canonised St Edward the Confessor. We should bear in mind here that the Battle of Hastings had been fought on Saturday 14 October 1066, and that the canonisation of St Edward was widely linked to prophecies of Henry II as the heir to St Edward who would unite the stock of Normandy and England.[61] William the Conqueror, after all, had made land at Pevensey in 1066 on the feast day of St Michael, the greatest of the warrior angels.[62] Henry III spent the feast of the translation of St Edward at Westminster in all save fifteen of his fifty-six years as

[56] Geoffrey of Vigeois, in *RHGF*, vol. xviii, p. 215

[57] William Rishanger, *Chronica et Annales*, ed. H. T. Riley, RS (London, 1865), p. 20. Rishanger's claim that no previous king had dared enter Oxford, for fear of the saint and her curse, is clearly a later fabrication. For other examples, see the useful article by W. T. Mitchell, 'The Shrines of English Saints in War-Time before the Reformation', *Pax: The Quarterly Review of the Benedictines of Prinknash*, 30 (1940), 71–80, whose date of publication is worth noting.

[58] Howden, *Chronica*, vol. iii, pp. 107–8, and for earlier, continental evidence of the deliberate timing of battles, see H. M. Schaller, 'Der heilige Tag als Termin in mittelalterlicher Staatsakte', *Deutsches Archiv für Erforschung des Mittelalters*, 30 (1974), 1–24. The pilgrims who chose St James's day 1190 to launch an attack upon Saladin, were surely not acting by random coincidence: Howden, *Chronica*, vol. iii, p. 70.

[59] Kemp, 'Miracles of the Hand of St James', 17 no. 25.

[60] Sauvage, 'Vita B. Hamonis' (above n. 38), 523–4, dated 1167 but more likely to refer to the Breton campaign of 1166.

[61] See Ailred of Rievaulx's letter to Henry II and his life of St Edward, itself delivered to Westminster in the king's presence at the time of the translation of 1163: *PL*, 195, cols. 711–38 at 717, and 737–40, 773–4, tracing the descent of the Anglo-Saxon kings back through Woden to Noah and thence to Adam.

[62] As noted by Labande, 'Les pèlerinages au Mont St-Michel', p. 239.

king, and from 1238, although not before, he also made it his practice to be at Westminster for the feast of Edward's deposition (5 January).[63] By comparison, in only seven years did he arrange to spend any of the three feast days of St Thomas Becket at Canterbury.[64] As David Carpenter has recently suggested, the timing of Henry's re-translation of the relics of St Edward, in October 1269, was almost certainly determined by the fact that the Easter calendar of 1269 coincided precisely with the calendar of 1163, the year in which the saint's body had first been translated.[65]

So far, we have considered royal acts of devotion, pilgrimages in the broadest sense, that were intended to invoke the aid, or offer thanks to the saints for very particular benefits. More subtle were those journeys or devotions that appear to mark changes of the king's mind or policy. We find something of this intention in Henry II's visit to Canterbury in 1174. Where previously Henry's hostility to St Thomas and his attempt to prohibit the veneration of Becket's shrine were believed to have called down civil war upon his realm, his tearful reconciliation with the martyr's remains was widely regarded as having altered the course of the war between Henry and his sons, being followed almost immediately by news of the cancellation of the threatened Flemish invasion and of the capture of the King of Scots at Alnwick.[66] Emma Mason has suggested that Henry's earlier visit to Rocamadour in 1170 was intended not merely to give thanks for his bodily healing, but to effect a reconciliation with his southern subjects in Aquitaine.[67] In much the same way, on a visit to the Limousin in 1182, Henry is said to have taken a particular interest in the

---

[63] The typescript 'Itinerary' of Henry III at the PRO suggests that Henry was at Westminster on 13 October in every year of his reign save 1223, 1228–32, 1236–7, 1242, 1245, 1253–4, 1262–3 and 1266, these absences for the most being explained by his preoccupations in campaigning and overseas. He was at Westminster on 5 January in 1220, 1225, and thereafter from 1238, save for the years 1243, 1252, 1254, 1257, 1260, 1264 and 1266.

[64] Henry was at Canterbury for the feast of Becket's return from exile (2 December) in 1220, 1237 and 1263; for the feast of Becket's translation (7 July) in 1220, 1222, 1228 and 1262, and for the feast of Becket's martyrdom (29 December) in 1240, 1254, 1262 and 1263.

[65] As argued in a paper by David Carpenter, to appear in M. Prestwich (ed.), *Thirteenth Century England*, vol. VIII (Woodbridge, forthcoming).

[66] The coincidence between Henry's pilgrimage and the capture of William of Scots was noted by virtually every contemporary chronicler, on occasion with exaggerated detail. See, for example, Howden, *Gesta*, vol. I, p. 72; *Materials*, vol. III, p. 547; Geoffrey of Vigeois, in *RHGF*, vol. XII, p. 443; and the chronicle of Saint-Aubin at Angers, P. Marchegay and E. Mabille (eds.), *Chroniques des églises d'Anjou* (Paris, 1869), pp. 42–3. For Henry's earlier attempts to discourage pilgrims to Canterbury, see *Materials*, vol. IV, pp. 160–1.

[67] Mason, 'Rocamadour in Quercy', p. 51. See also the interesting mixture of motives that may have drawn Louis IX to Rocamadour in 1244, as examined by J. Juillet, 'Saint Louis à Rocamadour', *Bulletin de la Société des Etudes littéraires, scientifiques et artistiques du Lot*, 92 (1971), 19–30.

cult of St Yrieix, sending for a life of the saint, and, even more remarkably, reading it, before leaving offerings at the shrine. In doing so, he may have hoped to stamp royal approval upon a cult, previously dominated by the independently minded viscounts of Limoges.[68]

By the summer of 1232, King Henry III was anxious to escape from the tutelage of his justiciar Hubert de Burgh, yet apprehensive of the consequences. He used the ritual of a journey to the Holy Rood of Bromholm in Norfolk as an opportunity to effect major changes in his counsel. This change had been signalled a few weeks earlier, when at Worcester, in May 1232, Henry had presided over the removal of the body of his father King John to a new tomb in the cathedral, thereby signalling the final passing of the old order whilst at the same time honouring his father's memory by generous gifts to the Worcester monks. In the same way, in 1234, following a disastrous flirtation with the regime presided over by Peter des Roches, Henry signalled his intention to break with des Roches by retracing his steps to the same shrine at Bromholm that had witnessed his political conversion two years earlier. In 1234 he placed a silver likeness of himself on the shrine, almost certainly a votive offering to commemorate a recovery, not from physical but from what the king conceived to have been his political and intellectual infirmity.[69] Twenty years later, in 1254, having conducted a fruitless campaign in Gascony, and by now surely aware of the futility of any further attempt to reconquer the lost Plantagenet lands in France, Henry travelled to Fontevraud and there with his own hands helped to translate the body of his mother, Isabella of Angoulême, from her original resting place in the chapter-house to a more fitting tomb close to those of the Plantagenet rulers Henry II, Richard and Eleanor of Aquitaine.[70] If we care to read it as such, this translation can be regarded as Henry's fond farewell to the old Plantegenet order. It was followed within a few days by the King's visit to Paris and the opening of negotiations with Louis IX that were to culminate, five years later, in Henry's official renunciation of his claims to Normandy and much of his long-lost French dominion. In 1232 with his father, John, and in 1254 with his mother, Isabella, Henry III came to his parents' remains, not merely to honour them but to bury them, both in the body and the spirit. As Henry Mayr-Harting has pointed out, 'Ritual may sometimes allow a reversal of an action or an attitude of an individual or a society where the

---

[68] Geoffrey of Vigeois, in *RHGF*, vol. XII, p. 448; vol. XVIII, pp. 212, 219, and for the saint, see *AS August*, 5: 171–8, esp. 174–5; Abbé Arbellot, *Vie de Saint-Yrieix, ses miracles et son culte* (Paris/Limoges, 1900).

[69] N. Vincent, *Peter des Roches* (Cambridge, 1996), pp. 291–303, 431–2.

[70] N. Vincent, 'Isabella of Angoulême: John's Jezebel', in S. D. Church (ed.), *King John: New Interpretations* (Woodbridge, 1999), pp. 214, 219; Paris, *Chronica Majora*, vol. V, p. 475.

loss of face would be too great without it'.[71] Here perhaps we approach something of that 'liminality' that social anthropologists have sought to present as the defining feature of pilgrimage.

Throughout, we must beware of drawing too rigid a distinction between the king's 'political' and 'spiritual' motives. Just as the Plantagenets themselves might have found it hard to appreciate any distinction between pilgrimage and their daily, itinerant devotions, so there was always a political element to their spirituality, and a spirtual element to their politics. Nor should we suppose that pilgrimage became a significant feature of court life only in the aftermath of the Becket dispute, or following the perceived success of Henry II's Canterbury pilgrimage of 1174 in bringing divine justice to bear upon his enemies. Certainly, after 1174, Henry made a number of further pilgrimages – to Canterbury, Bury and Ely in 1177, for example all of these being described specifically as *peregrinationes*.[72] However, there are as many examples of such journeys being made by the king before as after 1174. We have already cited the king's journey to Rocamadour in 1170, and his visits to Mont-Saint-Michel in 1158 and 1166, closely connected to his campaigns in Brittany. In July 1166 he is said to have attended the translation of the relics of St Brieuc at Angers – in many ways a political act, carried out in the aftermath of the Breton rebellion, to commemorate the removal several centuries before of the relics of a leading Breton saint to the Angevin capital.[73] Three years earlier he had been present for the translation of St Edward at Westminster, whose canonisation had been obtained with Henry's active support in 1161.[74] In March 1162 he had been present at Fécamp for the ceremonial reburial of the bodies of Dukes Richard I and Richard II of Normandy.[75] The gifts he made before 1172 to the abbeys of Cerisy, Lisieux and St Augustine's Bristol to mark their dedications

---

[71] H. Mayr-Harting, 'Functions of a Twelfth-Century Shrine: The Miracles of St Frideswide', in Mayr-Harting and Moore (eds.), *Studies in Medieval History*, p. 206.

[72] Howden, *Gesta*, vol. I, pp. 158–9; W. Stubbs (ed.), *Gervase of Canterbury, Historical Works*, 2 vols., RS (London, 1879–80), vol. I, pp. 261–2.

[73] L. Delisle and E. Berger (eds.), *Recueil des Actes de Henri II roi d'Angleterre et duc de Normandie concernant les provinces françaises et les affaires de France*, 3 vols. (Paris, 1916–27), vol. I, no. 258; Marchegay and Mabille (eds.), *Chroniques des églises d'Anjou*, pp. 149–50, and for the saint, part of whose remains were eventually restored to the church of St-Brieuc, following the Plantagenet loss of Normandy and Anjou, see F. Plaine (ed.), *Vie inédite de Saint Brieuc évêque et confesseur (420–515)* (Saint-Brieuc, 1883), esp. pp. xv–xvii, 29–30; *AS May*, 1: 91–4.

[74] B. W. Scholz, 'The Canonization of Edward the Confessor', *Speculum*, 36 (1961), 38–60, esp. pp. 49–60.

[75] Delisle and Berger (eds.), *Recueil des Actes de Henri II*, vol. I, nos. 222–3; Torigny, 'Chronica', pp. 212–13, and for a possible gift made on this occasion, see S. E. Jones, 'The Twelfth-Century Reliefs from Fécamp: New Evidence for their Dating and Original Purpose', *JBAA*, 138 (1985), 79–88.

suggest strongly that he had attended these ceremonies in person, whilst there is no doubt that he was present for the dedication of Reading Abbey by Archbishop Becket in April 1164, followed by three days of junketings paid for by the king.[76] It was Reading that housed the most precious and in some ways the most personal of the dynasty's relics, the hand of St James, and it was at Reading that several members of Henry's family, including his eldest son William, were buried *ad limina*.[77] Depending upon how we interpret them, all of these ceremonies and journeys before 1174 have a greater or lesser degree of political or spiritual significance. Taken *en masse*, they suggest that there was nothing new or extraordinary about the king's enthusiasm for pilgrimages and religious ceremonial in the aftermath of Becket's death.

Beyond his own participation in pilgrimages and religious devotions, the king also had a role to play in fostering the pilgrimages of others. Here we should think not just of the contributions made by various kings towards the cost of the crusades, or of their support for the military orders in the East, established to protect the pilgrim route to Jerusalem. Shortly after his accession to the throne, Henry II awarded land at Havering for the foundation of a priory attached to the hospital of Montjoux in the Grand Saint-Bernard Pass, intended to assist pilgrims crossing the Alps to Rome.[78] King John likewise granted the Essex church of Writtle as the endowment for a small English congregation attached to the hospital of the Holy Ghost in S. Maria in Sassia, a foundation that had provided shelter to English pilgrims in Rome since long before the Norman

---

[76] Delisle and Berger (eds.), *Recueil des Actes de Henri II*, vol. I, nos. 188, 407; 2, supplement no. 31; D. Walker (ed.), *The Cartulary of St Augustine's Abbey, Bristol*, Gloucestershire Record Series 10 (1998), p. 5 no. 7; Torigny, 'Chronica', p. 221, and for the precise date of the dedication of Reading, see C. W. Previté-Orton, 'Annales Radingenses Posteriores, 1135–1264', *EHR*, 37 (1922), 400.

[77] For the relic, see Kemp, 'Miracles of the Hand of St James'; K. Leyser, 'Frederick Barbarossa, Henry II and the Hand of St James', *EHR*, 90 (1975), 481–506. For the burial at Reading of the king's eldest son William (d.1156), and cousin Earl Reginald (d.1175), and for gifts made with specific reference to the hand of St James by the future King John, see Torigny, 'Chronica' pp. 189, 268; B. R. Kemp (ed.), *Reading Abbey Cartularies*, 2 vols., Camden Society 4th series 31 and 33 (1986–7), vol. I, pp. 68–9, nos. 42–3. For the possibly special significance that may have attached to the saint's hand as an object appropriate to a cult of kings, see W. A. Chaney, *The Cult of Kingship in Anglo-Saxon England: The Transition from Paganism to Christianity* (Manchester, 1970), p. 116, citing the example of the hand of St Oswald, for which see also D. Rollason, 'St Oswald in Post-Conquest England', and V. Tudor, 'Reginald's Life of Oswald', in C. Stancliffe and E. Cambridge (eds.), *Oswald: Northumbrian King to European Saint* (Stamford, 1995), pp. 168–9, 190–3.

[78] Delisle and Berger (eds.), *Recueil des Actes de Henri II*, vol. I, nos. 93, 235, 379; vol. II, nos. 722, 755; *VCH Essex*, vol. II, pp. 195–6; H. F. Westlake, *Hornchurch Priory* (London, 1923), and for the priory's mother house, see A. Donnet, *Saint Bernard et les origines de l'hospice du Mont-Joux (Grand-St-Bernard)* (Saint-Maurice, 1942), esp. p. 108ff.

Conquest.[79] Although he himself made no pilgrimage to St James, in the 1170s, as count of Poitiers, the future Richard I had rained warfare upon various southern lords accused of robbing pilgrims to Compostela. Richard thereby greatly extended the Plantagenet dominion over Gascony, albeit on the pretext of offering shelter and protection to the region's pilgrims.[80] Likewise, shortly before embarking for crusade, he issued privileges for the Abbey of Saint-Sever and abolished tolls for those crossing the Garonne by the bridge at Agen, both of them not only prominent landmarks on the pilgrim route to St James, but crucial to Plantagenet control of the south.[81] In the Plantagenet, as in most royal law courts, special privileges were accorded to those unable to answer pleas because of their absence on pilgrimage, most notably to the Holy Land, but also to Compostela and Rome.[82] Just as the king's pilgrim itinerary served to impose authority upon his realm, so that authority was strengthened by the practical measures, by sword and by statute, that the king undertook for the protection of lesser pilgrims.

This is turn must carry us on to consider one final, but much broader theme. The average pilgrim to a shrine brought with him gifts of wax or silver. Kings brought gold, silk, and sometimes significant grants of land. Their gifts, it should be noted, were publicly offered and displayed, specially recorded in the places to which they were given, and often governed by peculiar custom, such as the offering of the 'King's great penny' – a particular coin that was carried from shrine to shrine, offered by the king and then redeemed by his officials for cash – or the Capetian custom of offering four bezants each year to Saint-Denis by first placing them on the king's head and then bowing so that the shrine might receive them as a token of royal homage: a practice already echoed in the eleventh century at Saint-Hilaire in Poitiers, where Henry II and his sons were later to rule as lay abbots.[83] But not only did the king bring material gifts. By visiting

[79] *VCH Essex*, vol. II, pp. 200–1; C. R. Cheney, *Pope Innocent III and England* (Stuttgart, 1976), pp. 237–8; Ortenberg, *English Church and the Continent*, pp. 132–6.

[80] Howden, *Chronica*, vol. II, pp. 117–18.

[81] E. Martène and U. Durand, *Thesaurus novus anecdotorum* (Paris, 1717), vol. I, pp. 636–7; A. Magen and G. Tholin (eds.), *Archives Municipales d'Agen: Chartes première série (1189–1328)* (Villeneuve-sur-Lot, 1876), pp. 1–2, no. 1, and see Howden, *Chronica*, vol. I, p. 35; Gillingham, *Richard I*, pp. 55–6, 124.

[82] G. D. G. Hall and M. T. Clanchy (eds.), *The Treatise on the Laws and Customs of the Realm of England Commonly Called Glanvill*, OMT (Oxford, 1993), pp. 16–17, 150–1, and for specific cases, see the many examples cited in the printed *Curia Regis Rolls*, subject index *sub* pilgrimage.

[83] For the king's great penny, see Nilson, 'The Medieval Experience at the Shrine' (above n. 1), pp. 120–2. For the ceremonies at Saint-Denis and Poitiers, see Labande, 'St Louis pèlerin' p. 16, citing *RHGF*, vol. XX, pp. 51–2; *Catalogus codicum hagiographicorum latinorum . . . in Bibliotheca Nationali Parisiensi*, 3 vols. (Brussels, 1889–93), vol. II, pp. 106–7. For a suggestion that similar pennies were reserved for the use of the Anglo-Saxon kings of England, see Chaney, *Cult of kingship*, pp. 70–1.

the saints and their shrines he conferred upon them something equally, or even more precious: his own royal person and presence. To adapt some recent remarks of Alphonse Dupront: the royal pilgrim, by virtue of his own royal presence, conferred upon his chosen place of pilgrimage a particular mark, especially when king succeeded king in making pilgrimage to any one location.[84] Here too we may need to rethink the accepted view of the role played by pilgrimage in the lives of the Plantagenet kings. Not only were Henry II and his successors itinerant, engaged in a near permanent process of journeying from one church or shrine to another, but they themselves could inspire practices and obeisance from their subjects that might be viewed as a species of secular pilgrimage.

In the Angevin realm, saints needed kings almost as much as kings needed saints. After the Norman conquest, Paul Hayward has shown how hagiographers deliberately, and often fraudulently, introduced the Anglo-Saxon kings into the lives of the saints, in the hope that this royal connection might increase the saints' appeal to their new Norman patrons.[85] The hagiography of Plantagenet England is littered with examples of saints whose dealings with the king were recorded in the minutest of detail, sometimes, as in the case of St Hugh of Lincoln or St Thomas of Canterbury, almost to the exclusion of their dealings with lesser mortals; in other cases, as with St Gilbert of Sempringham, or St Robert of Knaresborough, as an incidental but nonetheless significant fact.[86] Not many of these dealings, of course, showed the king in a favourable light. Consider, for example, the prophecy attributed by Gerald of Wales to St Bernard of Clairvaux, who when asked to predict the future of the young Henry II, is said to have announced that 'From the Devil he came, and to the Devil he will surely go'.[87] Nonetheless, either for good or for ill, the king's presence is an essential feature of most English saints' lives: a feature that distinguishes the Plantagenet saints from their counterparts in less strongly governed regions, such as northern Italy or Germany, and

---

[84] A. Dupront, *Du Sacré: Croisades et pèlerinages, images et langages* (Paris, 1987), pp. 317–18, also cited by J. Le Goff, *Saint Louis* (Paris, 1996), p. 539.

[85] P. A. Hayward, 'Translation-Narratives in Post-Conquest Hagiography and English Resistance to the Norman Conquest', in *ANS*, vol. XXI (1999), pp. 67–93. For the nonetheless significant role of the Anglo-Saxon kings in promoting the cult of the saints, see Rollason, *Saints and Relics*, pp. 114–20.

[86] For St Robert and St Gilbert, see B. Golding, 'The Hermit and the Hunter', in J. Blair and B. Golding (eds.), *The Cloister and the World: Essays in Medieval History in Honour of Barbara Harvey* (Oxford, 1996), pp. 95–117; R. Foreville and G. Keir (eds.), *The Book of St Gilbert*, OMT (Oxford, 1987), pp. 72–5, 82–5, 92–3, 104–7. The case of St Thomas hardly requires further reference here. For St Hugh, see the extraordinarily perceptive essay by K. Leyser, 'The Angevin Kings and the Holy Man', in H. Mayr-Harting (ed.), *St Hugh of Lincoln* (Oxford, 1987), pp. 49–73.

[87] Gerald of Wales, 'De principis instructione', in Gerald, *Opera*, ed. J. S. Brewer and J. F. Dimock, 8 vols., RS (London, 1861–91), vol. VIII, p. 309.

that clearly exposes the extent to which the Plantagenets towered over the politics of their realm.[88]

Just as kings might invoke the aid of the saints before approaching their enemies or the sea, so lesser men would approach the saints before setting out to visit the king. In the twelfth century, both Godric of Finchale and Christina of Markyate are to be found offering advice to men who had come to them for solace and intercession prior to attending the royal court.[89] If prophecy was a gift of the saints, then it is remarkable how many saintly prophecies concerned the person of the king. An ability to read the king's mind, his intentions or his fate, was seen as an attribute of the saints hardly less remarkable than their ability to interpret the mind of God.[90] Both St Godric and St Gilbert of Sempringham, for example, made statements to their followers, later interpreted as prophecies concerning King Henry II: St Godric, by predicting that the king would have his eldest son crowned in his own lifetime, St Gilbert by predicting the king's death.[91] Wulfric of Haselbury, having made several prophecies of kings Henry I and Stephen, is said to have gone on to inform the future King Henry II that he would succeed to the throne of England.[92] Such

---

[88] A point that is not made in the otherwise extremely useful survey by R. Bartlett, 'The Hagiography of Angevin England', in *Thirteenth Century England*, vol. v (Woodbridge, 1995), pp. 37–52. For a classic account of the differences between English and Italian sanctity in the thirteenth century, see R. Brentano, *Two Churches; England and Italy in the Thirteenth Century*, revised edn (Berkeley, 1988), ch. 3. It is worth noting the absence of the king from the hagiography of Plantagenet Aquitaine, a further indication of the weakness of Plantagenet government in the south. See for example, the entire absence of either the ducal or royal family from M. Aubrun (ed.), *Vie de Saint Etienne d'Obazine* (Clermont-Ferrand, 1970), and for a more general analysis of Plantagenet power in the south, N. Vincent, 'King Henry II and the Poitevins', in M. Aurell (ed.), *Le Cour Plantagênet (1154–1204)* (Poitiers, 2000), pp. 103–35.

[89] Reginald of Durham, *Libellus de vita et miraculis S. Godrici, heremite de Finchale*, ed. J. Stevenson, Surtees Society 20 (1847), p. 302; Matthew Paris, 'Gesta Abbatum' (above n. 29), pp. 104–5.

[90] For the earlier role of saintly prophecy in the lives of the Anglo-Saxon kings, see Rollason, *Saints and Relics*, pp. 99–100.

[91] Foreville and Keir (eds.), *Book of St Gilbert*, pp. 104–7; Reginald of Durham, *Vita S. Godrici*, pp. 302–4, although note that the author of St Godric's life misdates the gift of land at Sadberge by Henry II, that cannot in fact have been made until some years after Godric's death: J. Raine (ed.), *The Charters of Endowment . . . of the Priory of Finchale*, Surtees Society 6 (1837), p. 192. For futher examples, amongst many, see the prophecies attributed to St Thomas, in Paris, 'Gesta Abbatum', pp. 186–7, and, perhaps above all, to St Edward: *PL*, 195, cols. 738–9, 771–4; F. Barlow (ed.), *The Life of King Edward Who Rests at Westminster*, OMT, 2nd edn (Oxford, 1992), pp. 131–2. For the much more ancient tradition in which these prophecies can be set, see Chaney, *Cult of Kingship*, pp. 152–5. Chaney's book has been much criticised in recent scholarship, as, for example, by S. J. Ridyard, *The Royal Saints of Anglo-Saxon England* (Cambridge, 1988). However, for all its tendency to overstatement, it deserves respect for the way that it assembles evidence of the popular/emotional, as opposed to the literary/intellectual reception of royal sacrality.

[92] M. Bell (ed.), *Wulfric of Haselbury by John Abbot of Ford*, Somerset Record Society 47 (1933), pp. lix–lxiii; Stubbs (ed.), *Gervase of Canterbury*, vol. I, pp. 130–1.

stories were recorded, of course, to demonstrate that the saints possessed a foresight superior to that of mere mortal kings. The figure of the king was nonetheless essential for this point to be made.

Kings had an important role to play, not only in the translation and veneration, but in the canonisation of saints. Most notably in the case of St Edward the Confessor, but also in support of the processes for St Gilbert of Sempringham, St Richard of Chichester, and later for Robert Grosseteste, the Plantagenets wrote letters to the pope, in several cases specifically referred to in the official papal letters of canonisation.[93] At the time of the canonisation of St Hugh of Lincoln, the King, Henry III, was a mere boy. Even so, the fact that King John had attended the funeral of St Hugh was judged sufficiently significant to be mentioned in the canonisation report – a reminder, incidentally, that John had not as yet been cast in the role of outright bogey-man to which he was later to be condemned.[94]

The royal court, with its processions, ceremonies and particular traditions, mirrors many of the features of pilgrimage to the saints. From his ritual almsgiving at Easter, to his special Christmas festivities, the king was an active participant in the Christian calendar.[95] To judge from the surviving almoners' accounts, his court teemed with many hundreds of paupers and religious, in receipt of near daily dispensations of food, drink and charity. Even when the king himself chose to ignore various of the fasts and feasts of the Church, as seems to have been the case under King John, he would make up for such lapses by increased almsgiving. Having hunted for cranes on Holy Innocents' day 1212, for example, John fed fifty paupers for each of the seven birds that he had taken.[96]

---

[93] Scholz, 'Canonization of Edward the Confessor', p. 49; Foreville and Keir (eds.), *Book of St Gilbert*, pp. 170–1; D. Jones (ed.), *Saint Richard of Chichester; The Sources for his Life*, Sussex Record Society 79 (1995), pp. 225–6, 231; R. E. G. Cole, 'Proceedings Relative to the Canonization of Robert Grosseteste Bishop of Lincoln', *Associated Architectural Societies' Reports and Papers*, 33, part 1 (1915), pp. 27–8. Besides the various translation ceremonies described above, see the role that Henry II may have played in the translation of St Frideswide at Oxford in 1180: *AS October*, 8: 568–9. For the extraordinary record of Louis IX in attending such ceremonies, see L. Carolus-Barré, 'Saint Louis et la translation des corps saints', in *Etudes d'histoire du droit canonique dédiées à Gabriel le Bras*, 2 vols. (Paris, 1965), vol. II, pp. 1087–112.

[94] D. H. Farmer, 'The Canonization of St Hugh of Lincoln', *Lincolnshire Architectural and Archaeological Society Reports and Papers*, 6, part 2 (1956), pp. 93, 95–6, and cf. Adam of Eynsham, *Vita Sancti Hugonis*, vol. II, pp. 188, 225.

[95] See, for example, the ceremony of the royal Maundy, which clearly predates its first recorded appearance in 1210: A. Kellett, 'King John in Knaresborough: The First Known Royal Maundy', *Yorkshire Archaeological Jnl*, 62 (1990), 69–90, esp. 84–7. The court etiquette of the Plantagenets is a subject that has been inadequately studied: potential Ph.D. students please take note. For a much later period, see N. Saul, *Richard II* (London, 1996), p. 339ff.

[96] H. Johnstone, 'Poor-Relief in the Royal Households of Thirteenth-Century England', *Speculum*, 4 (1929), 149–67, esp. 153, citing the account in Cole (ed.), *Documents* (above n. 37), p. 250. For an analysis of later almsgiving, see Taylor, 'Royal Alms and Oblations' (above n. 2), pp. 98–109.

The court was also a place of worship in its own right, since the king travelled with his own private chapel, furnished with relics in abundance. These may well have included the finger bone of St Bernard, acquired by Henry II in 1178, following his gift of lead to roof the new church at Clairvaux.[97] In rescuing the relics of St Petroc from a thief who had carried them from Cornwall into Brittany, Henry ensured not only that he was allowed to handle and venerate the relics, but that he himself retained three finger bones and a rib.[98] One reason why not all churches welcomed kings or noblemen at the translation of their saints was that such men were too accustomed to pocketing relics as souvenirs.[99] From his Canterbury pilgrimage of 1174, Henry II is said to have left with a flask of the water of St Thomas, that most fashionable and sought-after of secondary relics.[100] When a miraculous flow of blood was reported from a statue of the Virgin Mary at Déols, in the late 1180s, it was the future King John who stepped in to claim both statue and blood.[101] Relics from the sack of Constantinople, including part of the head of St Philip, passed via King John to Reading Abbey.[102] Henry III acquired portions not only of the Crown of Thorns and of the blood of Christ, but of the head of St Maurice – a good example of the way in which relics could serve as diplomatic gifts, in this case almost certainly dispatched from the treasury at Agaune, whose abbot was actively engaged in forging links with many other European churches, and whose patrons, the

---

[97] S. J. Heathcote, 'The Letter Collection Attributed to Master Transmundus, Papal Notary and Monk of Clairvaux in the Twelfth Century', *Analecta Cisterciensia*, 21 (1965), 177 no. 18, 219–20 no. 177.

[98] P. Grosjean, 'Vies et miracles de S. Petroc', *Analecta Bollandiana*, 74 (1956), 174–88, esp. pp. 185–6, sent to the Breton monks who had originally stolen the body, providing a much more detailed account of an event also reported by Howden, *Gesta*, vol. I, pp. 178–80, whence *AS June*, 1:399–402.

[99] See, for example, the explanation given for the relatively private translation of the relics of Sainte-Geneviève at Paris in 1242: *RHGF*, 23, p. 141: 'ne prelati et nobiles de minutis ossibus et aliis ad sanctam pertinentibus aliquid importunitate, comminatione vel modo quocumque extorquere niterentur.' Bishop Sylvester of Worcester is said to have suffered divine vengeance for his decision to divide the relics of St Wulfstan, at his translation in 1218: H. R. Luard (ed.), *Annales Monastici*, 5 vols., RS (London, 1864–9), vol. II, p. 289, and see the remarks of Matthew Paris, *Chronica Majora*, vol. V, p. 113, on what he perceived to be the scandalous treatment of the relics of St Edmund at Pontigny. For a much earlier English example, see Rollason, *Saints and Relics*, p. 140.

[100] Stubbs (ed.), *Gervase of Canterbury*, vol. I, p. 249.

[101] Gerald of Wales, 'Gemma ecclesiastica', and 'De principis instructione', in Gerald, *Opera*, vol. II, pp. 104–5; vol. VIII, p. 233; *Vincenti Burgundi ex ordine praedicatorum venerabilis episcopi Bellovacensis speculum quadruplex*, 4 vols. (Douai, 1624), vol. IV, pp. 1199–200. According to Stubbs (ed.), *Gervase of Canterbury*, vol. I, pp. 369–70, it was the Viscount of Limoges who made off with the statue.

[102] *Reading Abbey Cartularies*, vol. I, pp. 75–6 no. 49, 188–90 no. 230.

counts of Savoy, had come to occupy a prominent position at the court of Henry III.[103]

For some idea of the sheer scale of such gifts, we can refer to a unique record of presents made to Henry III during the period from December 1234 to June 1235.[104] Amongst a great quantity of gold and silver plate, silk cloths, and even an ivory chess set[105] – revealing, incidentally, that kings, like saints, expected to receive very precious gifts – we find a quite extraordinary collection of relics. On 10 January 1235, a Franciscan gave the king a silver reliquary containing relics of St George, St Theodore and St Pantaleon, as well as a wooden case containing a spine from the Crown of Thorns.[106] At Dover, on 8 February, the king's brother, Richard of Cornwall, delivered a finger bone of St Augustine of Canterbury, and on 25 February, the Hospitallers offered not only a glass vase containing oil from the miraculous icon of Saidnaiya (*oleum de Sardenay*), north of Damascus, but also relics of St Jerome, of the golden gate of Jerusalem, of the Holy Sepulchre, of Calvary, of the altar upon which Christ had been presented in the Temple, and of the burning bush from which God had spoken to Moses.[107] On 6 March, the king took receipt of a leg bone of St Osyth, and on Easter Sunday (8 April), a gold cross containing

---

[103] For Henry III's gift of these and other relics to Westminster, see Flete, *History of Westminster*, pp. 69–72, 75. For the wholesale distribution of relics of St-Maurice and others of the Theban legion after 1225, see L. Dupont Lachenal, 'A Saint-Maurice au XIIIe siècle: l'abbé Nantelme (1223–1258) et la "révélation" des martyrs de 1225', *Annales Valaisannes*, 2nd series 31 (1956), pp. 393–444. In 1250, Henry III's uncle by marriage, Peter of Savoy, may have secured possession of St Maurice's ring: S. Guichenon, *Histoire généalogique de la royale maison de Savoye* (Lyons, 1660), part 6 (preuves), p. 73. For the persistence of an interest in St Maurice at the court of Edward I, see Taylor, 'Royal Alms and Oblations' (above n. 2), p. 102.

[104] PRO C47/3/4/1, whence the details supplied below. So interesting is this document, that I hope before long to prepare a proper edition.

[105] 'Die Iovis proxima ante festum sancti Mathie de dono prioris Ierl'io in Anglia, i. scaccarium de ebore cum scac(cariis) et tabellul' de eodem apud Straff'. Eadem die ibidem statim misit dominus Ysab(elle) sorori sue ipsum scaccarium cum sccacc(ariis) et tabbul'.

[106] 'i. almonera in qua continetur una capsa argent' cum reliquiis de sanctis Georg', Theodoro, Panteleun et aliis contentis et insertis eidem, et de spina corone domini in una capsa lignea.'

[107] 'De dono comitis Ric(ardi) i. iuncta de digito beati Augustini Angl(ie) apostoli... De dono Elye (?) homine fratris Iohannis de Mere' de domo hospitali i. vasculum vitreum cum oleo de Sardenay... est in parva ymagine argent' beate Marie, i. particulam de porta aurea Ierosol', i. particulam de sepulcro Domini, i. particulam de altari in qua Cristus fuit presentatus, i. particulam de rubo quo viderat Moyses, i. particulam de Sancto Ieronimo, i. particulam de Monte Calvar.' For the oil, see B. Hamilton, 'Our Lady of Saidnaiya: An Orthodox Shrine Revered by Muslims and Knights Templar at the Time of the Crusades', in R. Swanson (ed.), *The Holy Land, Holy Lands, and Christian History* SCH 36 (Woodbridge, 2000), 207–15; D. Baraz, 'The Incarnated Icon of Saidnaya Goes West', *Le Muséon*, 108 (1995), pp. 181–91. I am grateful to Bernard Hamilton and Colin Morris for their assistance here.

further relics.[108] If this represents a typical selection of the gifts made at court over one six-month period, and assuming that even a small number of these offerings remained in the king's possession, the Plantagenets would appear to have travelled with a relic collection that makes even those pious magpies, the fifteenth-century German princes, seem paupers by comparison.[109] Kleptomania, it would seem, is a very ancient characteristic of kings.

Much of Henry III's relic collection, we can assume, passed from his private chapel to the monks of Westminster. Just as Louis IX sought to transform his court chapel into a vast, architectonic reliquary, the Sainte-Chapelle, so at Westminster Abbey from the 1230s onwards, Henry III sought to establish a series of shrines fit to rival the greatest in Christendom.[110] The best known of Henry's gifts to Westminster, a portion of Christ's blood sent to the King from the Holy Land, was ceremonially processed through the streets of London before being deposited at the Confessor's shrine on 13 October 1247, the Confessor's feast day. Here we find the pilgrim king, processing barefoot, with his eyes fixed on the relic which he carried before him, walking beneath a pall borne on four spears, around both the abbey and the royal apartments at Westminster.[111] The pall should remind us, not just of the special solemnity of the occasion, but of the fact that in processing the Holy Blood, Henry was incidentally re-enacting his own coronation procession, in which the king walked under a pall borne on four spears before being anointed in Westminster Abbey.[112] When, some time afterwards,

---

[108] 'Apud Sanctam Osytham de dono abbatis loci i. os de tibia sancti Osythe'. Like most of these entries, this is followed by a note: 'in coffono relliquiar(um)', presumably to indicate that the gift had been deposited amongst the King's travelling relic collection. This should be contrasted with the fate of the more secular gifts recorded in the account, such as silver cups, most of which were distributed amongst Henry's family and courtiers immediately upon their receipt.

[109] For an equally remarkable consignment of relics, borrowed by Henry for his lifetime from the monks of Norwich in February 1234, see *Calendar of Patent Rolls 1232-47*, p. 39. At an earlier stage, however, it had been the monks of Norwich who are said to have petitioned the king for relics from the royal collection: A. Jessopp and M. R. James (eds.), *The Life and Miracles of St William of Norwich by Thomas of Monmouth* (Cambridge, 1896), p. 117. For the relic collection of the Anglo-Saxon kings, see Rollason, *Saints and Relics*, pp. 159–63.

[110] For comparison between the two projects, see P. Binski, *Westminster Abbey and the Plantagenets: Kingship and the Representation of Power 1200–1400* (New Haven, CT, 1995), esp. ch. 5.

[111] Pending the appearance of N. Vincent, *The Holy Blood: King Henry III and the Blood Relics of Westminster and Hailes* (Cambridge, 2001), see the written and pictorial records of this event by Matthew Paris, *Chronica Majora*, vol. IV, pp. 640–45; S. Lewis, *The Art of Matthew Paris in the Chronica Majora* (Aldershot, 1987), pl. 10, between pp. 290–1; R. Vaughan (ed.), *The Illustrated Chronicles of Matthew Paris: Observations of Thirteenth-Century Life* (Stroud, 1993), p. 38

[112] See the account of the 1189 and 1194 coronations of Richard I in Howden, *Chronica*, vol. III, pp. 10, 247–8.

the Blood worked its one recorded miracle, Henry commanded that all the bells in Westminster be rung and that the court participate in yet a further procession from Tothill to the abbey, where a new golden reliquary was presented to the monks.[113] What we find here is the court itself presented as a place of wonders, with the king very nearly usurping the role of high priest. That this was so should hardly surprise us. Although Henry III was informed in no uncertain terms that he was not a priest, and that his unction gave him no priestly authority; at mass, which we are told he attended more than once a day, he was accustomed to kiss the Holy Sacrament, and even to hold the priest's hand at the moment of consecration.[114] From at least the time of Henry II, the kings of England had commissioned the singing of the *Laudes*, the solemn acclamation of kingship, on major state occasions. From 1233 onwards, coinciding with the new image of kingship that was conveyed to him under the tutelage of Peter des Roches, Henry III greatly increased the regularity with which the *Laudes* were sung, sometimes as many as a dozen times a year.[115] A king who heard himself proclaimed as 'decked with all the pomp of Solomon . . . higher than the stars', might be excused for thinking himself more than just a cut above *hoi poloi*.[116] For all that we are more familiar with the image of Henry II seated on the ground amongst his courtiers in the hunting park at Woodstock, sending for a needle and thread to bandage his own injured finger; and for all that Walter Map may tell us that Henry, though dressed in the finest clothes, 'never vaunted himself above other men': the king was nonetheless the anointed of God, who in certain cases might elect to be buried in the cloth of unction that he had worn at his coronation.[117] Even John of Salisbury, or the otherwise undramatic Bracton, continued to write of the king as *Vicarius Dei in terris*, *Imago Dei*, *Vicarius summi regis*, or *Magnus Dominus noster*, titles inherited from the theocratic emperors of Rome.[118] Nor is it a point of purely diplomatic

[113] Oxford, Bodleian Library MSS Ashmole 842, fol. 80v; Ashmole 863, p. 436, as printed by Vincent, *Holy Blood*, p. 205.

[114] H. R. Luard (ed.), *Roberti Grosseteste episopi quondam Lincolniensis Epistolae*, RS (London, 1861), pp. 348–51, no. 124; Rishanger, *Chronica*, pp. 74–5; D. A. Carpenter, 'The Burial of King Henry III, the Regalia and Royal Ideology', in Carpenter, *The Reign of Henry III* (London, 1996), p. 437. For further discussion of Henry's well-attested devotion to the sacrament, see Vincent, *Holy Blood*, pp. 35–7.

[115] E. H. Kantorowicz, *Laudes Regiae: A Study in Liturgical Acclamations and Mediaeval Ruler Worship* (Berkeley, 1958), pp. 171–9.

[116] Ibid., pp. 171–2, citing the English form of the acclamations. For a suggestion of the particular significance that Henry may have attached to the figure of Solomon, see P. Binski, *The Painted Chamber at Westminster* (London, 1986), pp. 42–3; Binski, *Westminster Abbey and the Plantagenets*, pp. 61–2, 138–9.

[117] Adam of Eynsham, *Vita Sancti Hugonis*, vol. I, pp. 116–17, with perceptive commentary by Leyser, 'Angevin Kings', pp. 58–9; Walter Map, *De Nugis Curialium*, pp. 116–17: 'nec se supra hominem magnificat'. For the burial of Henry the Young King and probably of King John in the cloth of unction, see Carpenter, 'Burial of Henry III', pp. 434–7.

[118] F. Schulz, 'Bracton on Kingship', *EHR*, 60 (1945), 139, 147–9.

interest that from the spring of 1172, at precisely the time that he was reaching his settlement with the papal legates in Normandy, Henry II began to style himself king 'By God's grace' (*Dei gratia*). This change was not in any way haphazard, but the result of a carefully managed ruling to the chancery clerks, reflecting the King's desire to broadcast a new image of himself in the aftermath of the Becket conflict.[119]

Just as kings might approach the saints in tears and devotion, bearing special kingly gifts, so the king's subjects approached the king in a particular way, often on bended knee. As one recent writer has pointed out, there are remarkable similarities between the description of the penance of Henry II at the tomb of Becket in 1174, and contemporary descriptions of the penitential approaches made to Henry II by his repentant sons.[120] When cities or rebels surrendered to the king, they did so in fear and trembling, even going barefoot with ashes on their head, much as the king might put on penitential costume to seek pardon from the saints.[121] Finally, we cannot avoid the role that the king himself played as thaumatage. Whatever we make of the various claims as to the date at which touching for the King's Evil was introduced into England, there can be no doubt that, even at the court of Henry II, there were some who argued that the king's touch might bring healing.[122] Peter of Blois refers, merely as an aside, to this belief.[123] By the time of Edward I, touching for scrofula was a common practice, with as many as 1000 sufferers a year making their way to the king to be healed.[124] Much earlier, we have an account, written in the 1180s, of a woman, the close kinswoman of

---

[119] For recent discussion, building upon what was originally the discovery of the great Léopold Delisle, see N. Vincent, 'The Charters of King Henry II: The Introduction of the Royal Inspeximus Revisited', in M. Gervers (ed.), *Dating Undated Medieval Charters* (Woodbridge, 2000), pp. 98–9.

[120] J.-M. Moeglin, 'Pénitence publique et amende honorable au Moyen-Age', *Revue Historique*, 298 (1997), 225–69, esp. 236–8, 254–5, citing Howden, *Gesta*, vol. I, pp. 76–7, 82–3. Such examples of humble surrender before the king could be greatly multiplied.

[121] For ashes, see for example, the surrender of the men of Stirling in 1304: M. Haskell, 'Breaking the Stalemate: The Scottish Campaign of Edward I, 1303–4', M. Prestwich *et al.* (eds.), *Thirteenth Century England*, vol. VII (Woodbridge, 1999), p. 235. Moeglin cites the notorious case of Edward III and the burghers of Calais. For illuminating comparison with a much earlier period, see K. J. Leyser, *Rule and Conflict in an Early Medieval Society: Ottonian Saxony* (London, 1979), pp. 95–6; G. Koziol, 'England, France, and the Problem of Sacrality in Twelfth-Century Ritual', in T. N. Bisson (ed.), *Cultures of Power: Lordship, Status and Process in Twelfth-Century Europe* (Philadelphia, 1995), pp. 125–6; Koziol, *Begging Pardon and Favor: Ritual and Political Order in Early Medieval France* (Ithaca, 1992).

[122] For recent suggestions here, commenting upon the classic study by Marc Bloch, see F. Barlow, 'The King's Evil', *EHR*, 95 (1980), 3–27, with further, significant evidence that touching for scrofula was already known at the court of Henry II, in Koziol, 'The Problem of Sacrality', pp. 128–9, 139–40, citing *AS October*, 8: 575–6.

[123] Peter of Blois, as quoted by Barlow, 'King's Evil', 19.

[124] Prestwich, 'The Piety of Edward I' (above n. 2), pp. 124–6.

several powerful figures at court, whose extreme labour pains were reported to Henry II. There is no reference here to scrofula, or the king's
touch, but the king did send the woman various jewels that he believed to
be efficacious in childbirth.[125] Similar magic jewels are to be found at the
court of Henry III, including a great sapphire that King John is said to
have borrowed from the monks of Bury St Edmunds, and that Henry III
asked be lent to the Earl Warenne; and a stone, given to Henry by Master
Peter 'the surgeon', to be worn around the neck 'against thunder.'[126] One
such stone, supposedly inherited from his ancestors, is said to have been
especially treasured by King John, who wore it hung round his neck on a
golden chain, believing that it offered protection from the loss of any of
his lands: a hope in which the king was all too clearly deluded.[127]

Much has been made in recent years of the desacralisation of twelfth-
century kingship, stripped of its aura of holiness in the aftermath of the
investiture contest. Karl Leyser, for example, has suggested that the eagerness with which kings such as Henry II had recourse to the holy men
Hugh of Lincoln or Peter of Tarantaise represents an attempt on the
king's behalf to acquire, by association, a quality of holiness that the
king, in his own right, was increasingly perceived to lack.[128] More recently, Geoffrey Koziol has sought to demonstrate that this process of
desacralisation was the result, not only of changes in the relationship
between Church and State, but of the way that the Angevin kings perceived their own right to rule. Koziol draws a sharp distinction between the essentially desacralised, 'knightly' ethos of Plantagenet kingship, founded upon conquest, seeking bureaucratic safeguards against its
inherent instability, and bolstered by myths that traced the king's ances-
try to such 'chivalric' archetypes as king Arthur; as set against the sacral,
mimetic and largely unmilitary ethos of the Capetian kings of France.
According to Koziol, 'Something in the Anglo-Norman experience of
politics tended to desacralise political authority, rendering it fit for par-
ody and resistance, while in France something made it possible to adapt

---

[125] Kemp, 'Miracles of the Hand of St James', 16, no. 21.
[126] See, for example, Roger of Wendover, in Paris, *Chronica Majora*, vol. IV, p. 222; *Curia
Regis Rolls*, vol. VIII, pp. 35–6; *Calendar of Patent Rolls 1232–47*, p. 43. For the pendant
cure, see PRO C47/3/4/1: 'De dono magistri Petri Cyrurgici i. lapidem contra tonitura
in capsa argente cum ar . . . pendend' circa collum'. For thunder, and the fears to which
it gave rise, see V. Flint, *The Rise of Magic in Early Medieval Europe* (Princeton, 1993),
pp. 108–15.
[127] Adam of Eynsham, *Vita Sancti Hugonis*, vol. II, pp. 139–40, and note the tone of disapproval that this accounts adopts towards such kingly superstition. This is perhaps the
same stone later referred to by Wendover, in Paris, *Chronica Majora*, vol. IV, p. 222.
[128] Leyser, 'Angevin Kings', pp. 53–4, 72–3, and for Henry II's contacts with Peter of
Tarantaise, like St Hugh believed to have worked miracles in his own lifetime, see
Walter Map, *De Nugis Curialium*, pp. 134–7.

the old typologies that held political authority sacred.'[129] The argument here is a compelling one, but it should not be carried too far. Certainly, it would be absurd to suggest that the Plantagenets preserved the sacrality of the pre-Gregorian kings, or that they can be regarded simply as Ottonians with Pipe Rolls. Nonetheless, just because their sacrality was of a different or lesser order than that enjoyed by either their pre-Gregorian forebears or their Capetian contemporaries, we should not assume that the Plantagenets were perceived, or sought to be perceived, in an entirely secular light. Even in the thoroughly desacralised 1990s, a royal divorcee who dies as a result of drunk driving, chaperoned by the son of an Egyptian grocer, can achieve a cultic status that any sainted Anglo-Saxon princess would be hard put to match. How much more cultic potential there was to the lives and deaths of the Plantagenets can be gauged simply by counting the members of Henry III's extended family who at one time or another were credited with miracles from beyond the grave.

Henry's predecessors Edward the Confessor and Margaret of Scotland, not to mention a whole host of earlier Anglo-Saxon kings and princesses, were officially recognised as saints. The memory of the Saxon kings, whether sainted or not, was clearly cherished at the Plantagenet court. Early in the reign of Henry II, most probably in 1158, the bodies of those West Saxon kings and bishops buried at Winchester were translated by Bishop Henry of Blois, brother of king Stephen and close cousin of Henry II, placed in specially constructed lead coffers and ranged prominently on a wall around the high altar, close to the shrine of St Swithun.[130] A century later, Matthew Paris tells us that he was present in March 1257 when King Henry III reeled off a list of at least eleven of his sainted Saxon forebears.[131] Nor was it only from the distant past that the Plantagenets could lay claim to a tradition of royal sanctity. Henry III's uncle Henry the Young King, who had been buried in 1183 wrapped in the cloth of anointing that he had apparently carried with him from the time of his coronation thirteen years before, was believed, not only by his mother, Eleanor

---

[129] Koziol, 'The Problem of Sacrality', pp. 124–48, at p. 144.

[130] J. Crook, 'St Swithun of Winchester', in Crook (ed.), *Winchester Cathedral: Nine Hundred Years 1093–1993* (Chichester, 1993), pp. 60–3.

[131] Paris, *Chronica Majora*, vol. v, p. 617. For the ties of blood that bound a large number of the saints of medieval Europe to royal dynasties, see, for example, Chaney, *Cult of Kingship*, pp. 80–3; K. Hauck, 'Geblütsheiligkeit', in B. Bischoff and S. Brechter, *Liber Floridus. Mittellateinische Studien. Paul Lehmann zum 65 Geburtstag* (Saint-Ottilien, 1950), pp. 187–240. For an earlier instance of such devotion to Anglo-Saxon ancestors within the Plantagenet family, in which Henry III's aunt Matilda, daughter of King Henry II, had apparently specified the names of seven Anglo-Saxon royal saints worthy of veneration in her adopted realm of Saxony, see D. Ó. Riain-Raedel, 'Edith, Judith, Matilda: The Role of Royal Ladies in the Propagation of the Continental Cult', in Stancliffe and Cambridge (eds.), *Oswald*, pp. 223–4.

of Aquitaine, but by more humble pilgrims to have effected posthumous cures.[132] Henry III's half-brother Aymer de Lusignan, bishop-elect of Winchester, died in a most unexpected aura of sanctity in 1260, with cures being reported thereafter at his heart shrine in Winchester Cathedral.[133] Henry's cousin, William Longuespée, descended from a bastard son of Henry II, died a martyr's death at Mansurah in 1250, with Matthew Paris reporting the lights and wonders that were observed at his tomb.[134] Less well-known, on his mother's side, Henry was the grandson of Agnes de Courtenay, a direct descendant of the Capetian King Louis VI. Through her first marriage, Agnes was the stepmother of the blessed John de Montmirail, a knight and later monk, venerated as a saint at Longpont. By an extraordinary irony, it may have been over the relics of the blessed John that Louis IX sought, after 1242, to obtain a firm alliance with Henry III's mother and stepfather, Isabella and Hugh de Lusignan, recent defectors from an ill-fated alliance with the Plantagenets.[135] Henry's III's brother-in-law, Simon de Montfort, and Simon's first cousin John de Montfort, another victim of the crusade of the 1240s, were both to be venerated as saints: Simon as a martyr and warrior against the king whose cult the king sought actively to suppress; John as a confessor at Nicosia in Cyprus.[136] Henry III himself was to be credited with at least one posthumous miracle, albeit that the man who claimed to have been restored to sight at his tomb was later denounced as a fraudster whom Henry would rather have hung than cured.[137] On entering the nuns' church at Godstow in the 1190s, Bishop Hugh of Lincoln was shocked to discover the tomb of Henry II's mistress, Rosamund Clifford, placed in front of the high

[132] William of Newburgh, 'Historia Rerum Anglicarum', in Howlett (ed.), *Chronicles of the Reign of Stephen, Henry II and Richard I*, vol. i, p. 234, discounts the miracles, which are nonetheless favourably reported by Thomas Agnellus, 'Sermo de morte et sepultura Henrici regis iunioris', in J. Stevenson (ed.), *Radulphi de Coggeshall Chronicon Anglicanum*, RS (London, 1875), pp. 265–73. For Henry's burial, see above note 117.

[133] H. W. Ridgeway, 'The Ecclesiastical Career of Aymer de Lusignan, Bishop Elect of Winchester, 1250–60', in *The Cloister and the World* (above n. 86), pp. 174–5.

[134] S. D. Lloyd, 'William Longespee II: the Making of an English Crusading Hero', *Nottingham Medieval Studies*, 35 (1991), 41–69; 36 (1992), 79–125, esp. 65–6, and for further evidence of the posthumous veneration of Earl William, see the verses and verse 'mass' in William's honour preserved in Oxford, Corpus Christ College, MS. 232, fols. 64v–66v.

[135] N. Vincent, 'Isabella of Angoulême' (above n. 70), pp. 176, 212–13.

[136] For the posthumous cult of Earl Simon, see J. O. Halliwell (ed.), *The Chronicle of William de Rishanger . . . The Miracles of Simon de Montfort*, Camden Society 15 (London, 1840), pp. 67–110; J. R. Maddicott, 'Follower, Leader, Pilgrim, Saint: Robert de Vere, Earl of Oxford, at the Shrine of Simon de Montfort, 1273', *EHR*, 109 (1994), 641–53. For John de Montfort, see a forthcoming essay by Peter Edbury, in *Thirteenth Century England*, vol. viii.

[137] Rishanger, *Chronica*, p. 98, and for Henry's burial, and for the later anxiety of the nuns of Fontevraud to obtain a portion of Henry's body, see Binski, *Westminster Abbey*, pp. 101–2; Carpenter, 'Burial of Henry III' (above n. 117), pp. 427–59.

altar, draped with a pall, and with candles burning round about it: a privilege reserved for saints and kings, but only rarely accorded to the less exalted dead.[138] Not even the popes, for all their emphasis upon the sanctity of the successors of St Peter, could claim such a collection of miracle workers within one family and over so brief a period of time.[139]

With the one highly significant exception of their interest in St Edward the Confessor, and despite the role that Henry II is said to have played in persuading Frederick Barbarossa to obtain the canonisation of Charlemagne, the Plantagenets seem to have made no particular effort to foster a belief in their own family's sanctity.[140] It was Edward, Henry III's son, who is said to have been the first to scoff at the idea that his late father could work miracles. Not until the early fourteenth century do we read of any king of England showing an interest in the Three Kings of Cologne, that most remarkable of medieval cults to royalty.[141] The Plantagenet kings were neither saints nor priests. In some senses, however, they were approached by their subjects in the same way that pilgrims approached the saints. This not only casts yet further doubt upon the thesis advanced by Josiah Cox Russell, that sanctity was the preserve of the king's critics – a thesis that cries out for revision – but suggests that just as the king, with his itinerary of shrines, churches and saints, may be regarded as existing in a near permanent state of pilgrimage, so as king in his own right he could become the object of secular pilgrimage from his subjects.

No twelfth- or thirteenth-century king of England was officially canonised by the Church. No one, so far as we know, prayed for cures before the bodies of Henry II or Richard, even though those bodies were jealously guarded by the religious, keen to acquire some personal association with the king. Many voiced their conviction that certain members of the family, most notably King John, were destined to the fires of Hell. Many more wrote scurrilous stories against them. On occasion, the Platagenets themselves may have revelled in their own reputation for devilry, as when Richard I is said to have boasted of the legend that he and his family were

---

[138] Howden, *Chronica*, vol. III, pp. 167–8.

[139] For the deployment of papal sanctity in the propaganda of the investiture contest, see for example, H. E. J. Cowdrey, *The Age of Abbot Desiderius* (Oxford, 1983), pp. xii–xiii.

[140] For Henry II and Charlemagne, see Scholz, 'Canonization of Edward the Confessor', 53n; M. Appelt (ed.), *MGH Diplomata Regum et Imperatorum Germaniae*, vol. x, part 2 (*Die Urkunden Friedrichs I, 1158–1167*) (Hannover, 1979), pp. 430–33, no. 502; Ó. Riain-Raedel, 'Edith, Judith, Matilda', in Stancliffe and Cambridge (eds.), *Oswald*, p. 224.

[141] For an offering to the Three Kings at Cologne made by Edward I in 1306, see PRO E101/369/11 fol.30v, as noticed by Johnstone, 'Poor-Relief' (above n. 96), p. 151n. For the cult, established by the circle of Frederick Barbarossa, see B. Hamilton, 'Prester John and the Three Kings of Cologne', in Mayr-Harting and Moore (eds.), *Studies in Medieval History*, pp. 177–91; P. J. Geary, 'The Magi and Milan', in Geary, *Living with the Dead in the Middle Ages* (Ithaca, 1994), pp. 243–56.

descended from the she-devil Mélusine.[142] Nonetheless, we should not assume from this that, in the eyes of his subjects, the king had been entirely robbed of his sacral authority, or that the king and his court were regarded as a purely secular phenomenon. Chroniclers wrote beastly things of the Ottonians and the Carolingians, and Procopius was more damning of Justinian than ever Roger of Wendover was of King John, without this persuading us that Justinian, Charlemagne or Otto III were entirely divested of sacral mystique. Even by the death of Henry III, kingship was only part way advanced on the road to secular bureaucratisation. It is questionable whether even now it has fully travelled that particular road. I have shown, I hope, that there was ritual in plenty at the Plantagenet court, and that the Plantagenet kings took a keen interest in the saints, both living and dead. Ritual and relic-collecting are not the same as the sacrality of the early Middle Ages, which had been an indwelling quality and which had assumed the king's active, semi-magical participation in religious ceremonial.[143] Unlike the sacral kings of the past, Henry III, to borrow a phrase from Kantorowicz, pictured himself as a law-based rather than a Christocentric king. It was the wisdom of Solomon, and the Solomonic wisdom of Edward the Confessor, to which Henry aspired, not the divinity of Christ. Nonetheless, I would suggest that there is a point at which royal piety and religious ritual can come close to a convergence with the sacred. The Plantagenets – anointed with chrism, ruling by the grace of God, and buttressed by their devotions to their own particular saints, many of whose relics they carried around with them, packed up with the royal baggage – may well be considered to have dwelt somewhat closer to the frontier with the sacred than English historians have been inclined to suppose.

Just as the kings of Anglo-Saxon England had served as mediators between God and the people, making offerings to the Church *pro expiatione*

---

[142] Gerald of Wales, 'De principis instructione', in Gerald, *Opera*, vol. VIII, pp. 301–2, and for the circulation of this legend within the Plantagenet domain, see the remarkable essay by J. Le Goff, 'Mélusine maternelle et défricheuse', *Annales*, 25 (1971), 587–603, reprinted in Le Goff, *Pour un autre Moyen Age* (Paris, 1977), pp. 307–31.

[143] For a penetrating critique of the entire idea of royal 'sacrality', incidentally seeking to draw a distinction between the sacrality of pagan kings, which dwelt in their blood, and Christian royal sanctity, which had to be earned by good deeds and which, almost by definition, could only be obtained after death or abdication, see J. Nelson, 'Royal Saints and Early Medieval Kingship', *Sanctity and Secularity*, SCH 10 (1973), pp. 39–44; Rollason, *Saints and Relics*, pp. 127–8. By contrast, the model of 'sacrality' for which I would seek to find parallels at the Plantagenet court is that developed by Leyser, *Rule and Conflict*, ch. 3, p. 75ff (well summarised by Henry Mayr-Harting in his memoir of Karl Leyser, *Proceedings of the British Academy*, 94 (1996), pp. 614–16) and by Jacques Le Goff, 'Aspects religieux et sacrés de la monarchie française du Xe au XIIIe siècle', in A. Boureau and C.-S. Ingerflom (eds.), *La royauté sacrée dans le monde chrétien: Colloque de Royaumont, mars 1989* (Paris, 1992), pp. 19–28, esp. p. 20. This model is further considered in the conclusion to my forthcoming book, *The Holy Blood*, pp. 188–96.

nostrorum piaculorum, so elements of this role as mediator survived to their Plantagenet successors. Henry II, for example, in at least a dozen of his charters, made gifts to the Church, not merely for the sake of his soul and the souls of his family, but *pro stabilitate regni mei, pro stabilitate et pace regni Anglie (et Normannie)*, or *pro pace regni mei*, claiming a role for himself as intercessor in obtaining God's blessing upon the peace and tranquillity of England: a role that would have fitted quite comfortably with the sacral aspirations of his Anglo-Saxon ancestors.[144] Even at the court of Henry II there were those who cared to recall the old Saxon genealogies, according to which the Platagenets, as descended from the kings of Wessex, were direct successors to Woden, Noah and, via Noah, collateral kinsmen of Christ himself.[145] Those of us raised in the traditions of the Manchester school – of pipe rolls and close rolls, of Magna Carta and the birth of Parliament, more accustomed to reading of the Plantagenet court as a metaphor for Hell than of its kings as the vicars of Christ – would do well to take pause.[146] French and German historians, who know neither Manchester nor the pipe rolls, appear to find no problem in peopling the thirteenth century with kings who retained at least some element of sacrality.[147]

In one of his letters, Peter of Blois, a long-serving courtier of Henry II, sounds a warning against pilgrimage, using a phrase that must already have been clichéd by the 1190s, and that was to be echoed nearly three centuries later by Thomas à Kempis: *qui multum peregrinantur, raro sanctificantur*, 'Those who make many pilgrimages seldom find sanctity'.[148]

---

[144] See, for example, Delisle and Berger (eds.), *Recueil des Actes de Henri II*, vol. I, nos. 101, 117, 128; vol. II, nos. 529, 545. For the Saxon formula, see Chaney, *Cult of Kingship*, p. 72.

[145] For Woden and Noah, see Chaney, *Cult of Kingship*, pp. 41–2, and for the survival of this theme at the Plantagenet court, see Stubbs (ed.), *Radulphi Diceto*, vol. I, p. 299, rehearsing a genealogy of Henry II first proposed by Ailred of Rievaulx, in *PL*, 195, cols. 711–38 at col.717.

[146] For the Plantagenet court as a metaphor for Hell, see Harf-Lancner, 'L'Enfer de la cour' (above n. 12), pp. 27–50.

[147] The classic work here remains, of course, E. H. Kantorowicz, *The King's Two Bodies* (Princeton, 1957). For England, the essential point of departure is Marc Bloch, *Les rois thaumaturges* (Paris, 1924), reissued with an introduction by J. Le Goff (Paris, 1983). Various significant studies are to be found in the collection of essays edited by Boureau and Ingerflom, *La royauté sacrée dans le monde chrétien*. For an eastern European perspective, see also, G. Klaniczay, *The Uses of Supernatural Power* (Princeton, 1990), chs. 5–7, esp. pp. 93–4.

[148] Peter of Blois, urging Bishop Savaric of Bath to return from pilgrimage, in Peter of Blois, *Opera Omnia*, ed. I. A. Giles, 3 vols. (London 1846–7), vol. II, p. 78, also in *PL*, 207 col.439 no. 148, later employed by Thomas à Kempis, *Imitatio Christi*, 1.23.2, whence noticed by G. Constable, 'Opposition to Pilgrimage in the Middle Ages', *Studia Gratiana*, 19 (1976), 145, reprinted in Constable, *Religious Life and Thought (11th–12th Centuries)* (London, 1979), ch. 4.

Was this in fact true of the Plantagenet kings of England? Few, if any men made more pilgrimages. Whether in the process the Plantagenets enhanced their own royal status, participating as more than simple on-lookers in the cult of the saints, and gaining more from pilgrimage than a merely vicarious brush with sanctity, are questions to which we should not supply a simple, nor yet an entirely negative response.

2   The early imagery of Thomas Becket

Richard Gameson

Art played a crucial role in the cult of the saints and, by extension, in pilgrimage. It was above all the visual arts that defined and communicated the identity of a saint to the faithful as a whole; and individual communities immortalised their particular holy man or woman in paint, stone, wood, and precious metals as much as, if not more than in prose, verse, and prayer. Fairly plentiful examples from the eleventh and twelfth centuries survive, ranging from the carved capitals at Fleury with the miracles of St Benedict to the illustrated *vitae* of Ste Radegund of Poitiers.[1] Such works were key tools for perpetuating the community's view of, and relationship with the saint in question. Equally, art played a central part in projecting the majesty, numinism, and power of the saint and his or her relics. Imposing cult images such as that of Ste Foi provided a forceful reminder that the holy person in heaven was still very much a living presence on earth, above all at the centre that held the major relics;[2] while splendid reliquaries advertised and presented such 'treasures' in a fitting way, rendering bones and fragments of cloth majestic and eminently worthy of veneration.[3] Body-part reliquaries restored and amplified the relics themselves;[4] boxes or châsses concealed and re-presented them: in all such cases it was the reliquary rather than the relic that commanded attention.

Art determined the experience of the pilgrim. The majestic scale of the abbey church or cathedral as a whole; the impressive architectural setting of the shrine; the form and decoration of the reliquary; and the imagery round about – it was this above all that represented the climax of a pilgrimage. Bernard of Clairvaux († 1153) was in no doubt as to the

[1] E. Vergnolle, *Saint Benoît-sur-Loire et la sculpture du XIe siècle* (Paris, 1985), esp. pp. 248–57. Poitiers, Bibliothèque municipale, 250: R. Favreau (ed.), *La Vie de Sainte Radegonde par Fortunat* (Paris, 1995).
[2] J. Taralon *et al.*, *Les Trésors des églises de France* (Paris, 1965), cat. 534, pls. 34–5 + col. frontis.
[3] For a convenient conspectus of Romanesque reliquaries see A. Legner (ed.), *Ornamenta Ecclesiae: Kunst und Künstler der Romanik*, 3 vols. (Cologne, 1985), vol. III, pp. 19–183.
[4] Such objects are explored from different perspectives in *Gesta* 36:1 (1997).

overwhelming impact of such art on the faithful: 'The most beautiful image of some male or female saint is exhibited and that saint is believed to
be the more holy, the more highly coloured the image is. People rush to
kiss it, they are invited to donate, and they admire the beautiful more than
they venerate the sacred.'[5] He was equally clear that such sights encouraged monetary offerings: 'Wherever the more riches are seen, there the
more willingly offerings are made. Eyes are fixed on relics covered in gold,
and purses are opened.' At Canterbury from 1220 the centre-piece for
pilgrimage was the dazzling new shrine, of which some evocation remains
in a couple of panels of broadly contemporary glass,[6] and in the reports of
those who saw it: 'Notwithstanding its great size, it is entirely covered with
plates of pure gold. But the gold is scarcely visible beneath a profusion of
gems, including sapphires, diamonds, rubies and emeralds. Everywhere
that the eye turns, something even more beautiful appears; the beauty
of the material is enhanced by the astonishing skill of human hands.'[7] It
seems to have had the effect that St Bernard described: the income it generated was high (outstandingly so in the first year);[8] and in a reactionary
sermon responding to the beginnings of the Reformation, a Canterbury
Grey Friar exclaimed that when pilgrims saw 'the goodly jewels that be
there, how they think in their hearts "I would to God and that good saint
that I were able to offer such a gift" and by such good thoughts thousands
of souls are saved'.[9] This marvel was set in the magnificent gothic choir
and surrounded by brilliant windows that narrated Becket's life, advertised the efficacy of the shrine, and warned of dire consequences if one
reneged on one's obligations to it (see Plates 15–16 and 18–20).

Art fulfilled a correspondingly important role in the distribution of a
cult, and in what we might term the 'appropriation' of saints. The simplest and most common way in which individual shrines 'rewarded' the
deserving visitor, and distributed and publicised their holy man or woman

[5] *Apologia ad Guillelmum Abbatem: Sancti Bernardi Opera*, ed. J. Leclercq and H. M. Rochais,
  8 vols. (Rome, 1957–77), vol. III, pp. 80–108. The translation quoted here is that of
  C. Rudolph, *The Things of Greater Importance: Bernard of Clairvaux's Apologia and the
  Medieval Attitude Towards Art* (Philadelphia, 1990), pp. 280–1.
[6] M. H. Caviness, *The Early Stained Glass of Canterbury Cathedral* (Princeton, 1977), pp. 33–
  5 with fig. 164; *The Windows of Christ Church Cathedral, Canterbury* (London, 1981), p. 197
  with pl. 125.
[7] *An Italian Relation of England about the Year 1500*, ed. C. A. Sneyd, Camden Soc. 37
  (London, 1847), pp. 30–1.
[8] B. Nilson, *Cathedral Shrines of Medieval England* (Woodbridge, 1998), pp. 147–54. The
  glass in the Trinity Chapel, Canterbury Cathedral, includes images of the tomb with what
  appears to be a money box on it. The monetary offering of Jordan FitzEisulf is shown in
  Plate 20.
[9] *LP*, vol. VIII, 480. The sermon is put in context by G. R. Elton, *Policy and Police: The
  Enforcement of the Reformation in England in the Age of Thomas Cromwell* (Cambridge,
  1972), pp. 1–45.

was via pilgrim badges and the like.[10] At Canterbury, *ampullae* containing water that had been in contact with Becket's blood were available to the faithful within a few years of the murder. Even the simplest of these soon bore an image of Becket or of the martyrdom, while the grander examples were decorated with a couple of scenes from his life, and depictions of pilgrims and miracles at his shrine. The distribution of such objects, though impossible to chart in detail, was undoubtedly phenomenal. Moreover, by means of depictions, one could appropriate and possess any saint or biblical figure. Representations of one's preferred spiritual mentors and guardians could be included on anything from private jewellery to highly public sculptured portals. Thus was the company of heaven – which was in theory ever-present everywhere – made manifest according to the tastes and designs of man. The success or failure of a shrine like that of Thomas Becket as a centre of pilgrimage relied utterly on its fame and on that of its saint *outside* the town in question, and this was something to which art could make a major contribution.

With all this in mind, let us now consider the early imagery of Thomas Becket. Despite the general ravages of time and particular 'persecution' in England during the sixteenth century, a truly formidable number of images of Becket survive – in itself a measure of his standing.[11] We shall limit ourselves to those which were produced within a couple of generations of his death – before the translation of 1220 – and shall consider the material under three headings: distribution, 'internal' iconography, and 'external' iconography.

Distribution

Our notional map of the distribution of the early images is necessarily a minimalist view. The number of places that can be included on it has been dramatically reduced not only by the accidents of survival, but also by the fact that we are often ignorant of the early provenance of such movable items as remain. What a difference it would make, for example,

[10] See in general D. Bruna, *Enseignes de pèlerinage et enseignes profanes* (Paris, 1996); and, more particularly on Becket material, B. Spencer, *Pilgrim Souvenirs and Secular Badges, Medieval Finds from Excavations in London 7* (London, 1998), pp. 37–133 (pp. 37–52 for the early items).

[11] Although many of its dates and details can be improved, the fundamental study remains T. Borenius, *St Thomas Becket in Art* (London, 1932). This may be supplemented by his 'The Iconography of St Thomas of Canterbury', *Archaeologia*, 79 (1929), 29–54; 'Addenda to the Iconography of St Thomas of Canterbury', *Archaeologia*, 81 (1931), 19–32; and 'Some Further Aspects of the Iconography of St Thomas of Canterbury', *Archaeologia*, 83 (1933), 171–236 (note that the plates in *Archaeologia* are of a much higher quality than those in the monograph); and by several of the articles in R. Foreville (ed.), *Thomas Becket: Actes du colloque international de Sédières 19–24 Août 1973* (Paris, 1975).

if we could also include the original locations of the nearly fifty surviving Becket châsses.[12] Yet we know that key relics were given from an early date to the great and the good, abroad as well as at home,[13] and we can assume that if these were not already in suitable receptacles (quite possibly adorned with images of the saint), they soon would be. The extensive distribution of phials via pilgrims to the shrine was described by Garnier of Pont-Sainte-Maxence, writing *c.* 1174: 'Kings have sought [Becket] in pilgrimage, princes, barons, dukes with their nobles, strangers from foreign countries speaking many languages, prelates, monks, recluses, crowds of foot travellers. They take phials home with them as a sign of their journey. People bring a cross back from Jerusalem, a Mary cast in lead from Rocamadour, a leaden shell from St James: now God has given St Thomas this phial, which is loved and honoured all over the world. In the likeness of wine and water, God has his blood consumed throughout the world, to save souls; in water and in phials he has the martyr's blood taken all over the world to cure the sick.'[14] The surviving early visual evidence, such as it is, appears to correspond to this.

The outstanding examples in France are found at Chartres, whither Becket's friend and secretary, John of Salisbury, carried two phials of the martyr's blood when he became bishop there in 1176, and where they worked miraculous cures; and at Sens, Becket's home in exile from November 1165, and whose archbishop from 1168–77, William of Champagne, was an ardent promoter of his canonisation and cult. The cathedrals at both places boast elaborate accounts of Becket's life in stained glass (see Plates 11–14). Sens also possesses a mitre of English workmanship embroidered with the martyrdom, and a majestic sculptured panel of later twelfth-century date depicting a haloed archbishop who is generally thought to be Becket. It must, however, be admitted that although the mitre dates from *c.* 1200 and may well have been at Sens shortly thereafter, we do not know for certain when it got there;[15] while

---

[12] The provenances of the châsses are listed in S. Caudron, 'Les châsses reliquaires de Thomas Becket émaillés à Limoges: leur géographie historique', *Bulletin de la société archéologique et historique du Limousin*, 121 (1993), 55–82. This work is developed in her contribution to V. Notin *et al.*, *Valérie et Thomas Becket: De l'influence des princes Plantagenêt dans l'Oeuvre de Limoges* (Limoges, 1999), esp. pp. 58–65, where original location is inferred (sometimes rather daringly) from modern provenance.

[13] E.g., there were relics of Becket at Saint-Rémi, Reims, by 1175–6, being mentioned in a letter from the abbot, Peter of Celle (1162–81), to Benedict of Peterborough: *PL*, vol. 202, col. 594. For other cases see H. E. J. Cowdrey, 'An Early Record at Dijon of the Export of Becket's Relics', *Bulletin of the Institute of Historical Research*, 54 (1981), 251–3; and note 24 below.

[14] *Garnier's Becket*, trans. J. Shirley (Chichester, 1975), p. 157. Cf. Benedict of Peterborough, *Passio et miracula S. Thomae Cantuariensis*, vol. III, 22: *Materials*, vol. II, p. 134.

[15] A. G. I. Christie, *English Medieval Embroidery* (Oxford, 1938), no. 22 (pp. 61–2) with pls. XII and XV. It is documented at Sens in *s.* xvi.

the panel, which was discovered in the wall of a house in the old Place du cloître in 1897, is altogether more enigmatic.[16]

Also from France is the intriguing 'Saint-Fuscien' Psalter of late twelfth-century date, whose modest pictorial cycle includes a page devoted to Becket (Plate 8).[17] The manuscript was apparently made for an unidentified woman in the north of the country, subsequently passing to Saint-Fuscien, Amiens. In addition, it is likely that several Limoges châsses of early thirteenth-century date have been in France since their manufacture, and one might deduce their probable original home (or at least diocese) from their subsequent provenance. One châsse (which can no longer be identified) formerly belonged to the church of Saint-Thomas-du-Louvre in Paris, and was probably acquired shortly after the foundation of that institution by Count Robert de Dreux, the brother of King Louis VII, *c*. 1180.[18]

Scandinavia is represented by Lyngsjö in the south (Plate 10) and Nora in the north of Sweden, and by Bergen in Norway. The latter is particularly relevant to the issue of pilgrimage as the evidence takes the form of an *ampula*; and one remembers that a couple of Norwegians featured among the pilgrims mentioned by William of Canterbury.[19] A general context for the carvings in Sweden is provided by the continuing close relations between the Swedish and English churches, and by the fact that the first archbishop of Uppsala (Stephen) was a Cistercian of English origin who had been consecrated at Sens in 1164 by Alexander III. More particularly, William of Canterbury recorded the miraculous healing by Becket of a priest from Lund Cathedral, called Canon Sven; while there was a relic of the saint at Skåne in 1191. We may also note the Limoges châsse that is now at Trönö and was evidently in Scandinavia in the Middle Ages, and which may well have arrived there shortly after it was made.[20]

At the other end of Europe, in Italy, where several chapels and altars were dedicated to Becket before 1220, we have three Limoges châsses

[16] M. Beaulieu, F. Baron *et al.*, *Cathédrales: Sculptures, Vitraux, Objets d'art, Manuscrits des XIIe et XIIIe siècles* (Paris, 1962), no. 37.

[17] Amiens, Bibliothèque municipale, 19: V. Leroquais, *Les Psautiers manuscrits latins des bibliothèques publiques de France*, 3 vols. (Mâcon, 1940–1), vol. I, pp. 9–11 with vol. III, pls. XL–XLV; W. Cahn, *Romanesque Manuscripts: The Twelfth Century*, 2 vols. (London, 1996), vol. II, no. 136.

[18] Caudron, 'Châsses reliquaires'; Notin *et al.*, *Valérie et Thomas Becket*, p. 58.

[19] J. J. G. Alexander and P. Binski (eds.), *The Age of Chivalry: Art in Plantagenet England 1200–1400* (London, 1987), cat. 44. *Materials*, pp. 466–7.

[20] B.-M. Andersson, *Emaux Limousin en Suède: les châsses, les croix* (Stockholm, 1980), pp. 10–11 (where dated to *c*. 1210), with fig. 4. She further speculates (pp. 5, 8–10 and 32n. 4 with figs. 2–3) that the rather earlier Limoges reliquary châsse that still belongs to Uppsala Cathedral and which she dates to *c*. 1175–80 may have been commissioned to receive relics of Thomas Becket; however its iconography (Christ crucified and in majesty, plus apostles) offers no confirmation of this hypothesis.

that are probably still in the hands of their original owners – Lucca Cathedral, San Giovanni in Laterano, Rome, and Anagni Cathedral, south of Rome.[21] Anagni, which was consecrated by Alexander III in 1179 and where a chapel was dedicated to Becket, also possesses an early mitre showing the saint.[22] Further south, a small bust figure of Becket appears on a precious book-cover that is believed to have been given to Capua Cathedral by Archbishop Alfanus (implying a date no later than 1182) and whose manufacture has been ascribed to Palermo.[23] Be that as it may, an image of the saint is prominently placed in the programme of mosaic decoration that covers the main apse of Monreale Cathedral, Sicily, work that is probably datable to 1183–9. Beyond Sicily's general interest in the affairs of Thomas Becket, Pope Alexander III, and King Henry II, there are the specific connections at royal level. Margaret of Navarre († 1183), wife of William I of Sicily then regent for William II, had been given a pendant with relics of Becket by Bishop Reginald of Bath;[24] not to mention the fact that in 1177 William II had married the young Joan, daughter of Henry II of England and Eleanor of Aquitaine.

Correspondingly, the marriage of Henry II's daughter Eleanor to Alfonso VIII of Castille around the same time is perhaps part of the general context for early interest in the cult of Becket in Spain. She herself founded a chapel in his honour in Toledo Cathedral by 1174 , while her 'chaperone', Bishop Jocelyn, dedicated one in the Cathedral of Siguenza. In León the church of Palencia formerly had two Limoges châsses which were probably there from an early date.[25] Yet the case of Thomas Becket may have struck a more particular chord in Catalonia, whose primate, Hugo de Cervello, Archbishop of Tarragona, was assassinated in 1171; and it is from this region that the earliest certain visual evidence comes – the frescoes in the apse of the south transept of S. Maria at Tarrasa (Plate 1) near Barcelona (whose cathedral, incidentally had an altar dedicated to Becket by 1196). In addition, Tarragona Cathedral possesses a mitre dating from *c.* 1200 that shows the martyrdom, though when it arrived there is unknown.[26]

---

[21] The first (Notin *et al.*, *Valérie et Thomas Becket*, cat. 28) is seemingly documented at Lucca in an inventory of 1239. The other two are reproduced in U. Nilgen, 'La "Tunicella" di Tommaso Becket in S. Maria Maggiore a Roma: culto e arte intorno a un santo "politico"', *Arte Medievale*, 2nd ser. 9:1 (1995), 105–20, ills. 16–17.

[22] Christie, *English Medieval Embroidery*, no. 19, pl. XII.

[23] F. Steenbock, *Der kirchliche Prachteinband im frühen Mittelalter von den Anfängen bis zum Beginn der Gotik* (Berlin, 1965), p. 95, pls. 128–9; M. D'Onofrio (ed.), *I Normanni, Popolo d'Europa, 1030–1200* (Rome, 1994), cat. 333a–b.

[24] G. Zarnecki *et al.* (ed.), *English Romanesque Art 1066–1200* (London, 1984), cat. 303; M. E. Frazer, *Medieval Church Treasures* (= *Metropolitan Museum of Art Bulletin* separate issue) (New York, 1986), ill. 59.

[25] Cf. Notin *et al.*, *Valérie et Thomas Becket*, cat. 22.

[26] D. King, *Opus Anglicanum* (London, 1963), p. 15.

There is no doubt that Angevin family connections account for the earliest known example from Germany. The final decorated opening in the exceptionally lavish gospel book that was made by Herimann of Helmarshausen for Henry the Lion of Saxony and Bavaria around 1185–8 shows the duke and his duchess, Matilda, being crowned by Christ.[27] Both earthly personages are accompanied by their families, and behind Matilda we see her father Henry II, while above them in the ranks of heaven appears Thomas Becket, holding a martyr's palm. Another possible case, of slightly later date, is the mitre of English workmanship that belonged to the Cistercian Abbey of Seligenthal near Landshut (Bavaria) (Plates 3–4).[28]

Depleted in the extreme though it is, such visual evidence as remains leaves little doubt that images of Thomas Becket were distributed and, moreover, produced across the length and breadth of Europe at an early date. But what was it that was being thus diffused? What did the early images show; what messages did they convey? Let us first examine the depictions of Becket themselves (the internal iconography); we shall then consider, where appropriate, their broader visual setting (the external iconography).

Internal iconography

Formally the simplest images are the non-narrative standing, seated or bust-figures such as one sees on seals, on the book-cover at Capua, in the mosaics at Monreale, in the Gospels of Henry the Lion, and on a reliquary casket in New York.[29] Of such a type, too, was the painted figure that formerly decorated the vault in the Trinity Chapel of Canterbury Cathedral.[30] A modicum of visual identity is supplied by archiepiscopal

---

[27] Wolfenbüttel, Herzog-August-Bibliothek, Guelf 105 Noviss. 2°/Munich, Bayerische Staatsbibliothek, Clm 30055. Facs: *Das Evangeliar Heinrichs des Löwen*, ed. D. Kötzsche (Frankfurt am Main, 1989). More accessible are H. Fuhrmann and F. Mütherich, *Das Evangeliar Heinrichs des Löwen und das mittelalterliche Herrscherbild* (Munich, 1986); and E. Klemm, *Das Evangeliar Heinrichs des Löwen* (Frankfurt am Main, 1988).

[28] Munich, Bayerisches Nationalmuseum: Christie, *English Medieval Embroidery*, cat. 21, pl. xiv; King, *Opus Anglicanum*, cat. 13, pl. 1. It was reputedly given to Seligenthal by Duchess Ludmilla (*c*. 1170–1240).

[29] The last is H. C. Evans and W. D. Wixom (eds.), *The Glory of Byzantium* (New York, 1997), cat. 304; and Wixom (ed.), *Mirror of the Medieval World* (New York, 1999), cat. 116. See further Wixom, 'In quinto scrinio de cuprio: A Copper Reliquary Chest Attributed to Canterbury: Style, Iconography and Patronage', in E. C. Parker (ed.), *The Cloisters: Studies in Honor of the 50th Anniversary* (New York, 1992), pp. 194–227.

[30] See M. H. Caviness, 'A Lost Cycle of Canterbury Paintings of 1220', *Ant Jnl*, 54 (1974), 66–74, pl. xixc. London, BL, Seal lxviii.18 provides an example on a seal (that of London dating from *s*. xii^ex or xiii^in).

garb and, perhaps, a martyr's palm, but it is principally inscriptions that reveal that the figure in question is Becket.[31] (It is only at a later date that we find such figures distinguished iconographically by a sword or dagger in the head.) In these contexts it was Becket's eternal presence alongside other worthies and not the particular circumstances of his death (or life) that mattered, and a timeless persona that assimilated him to the ranks of saintly churchmen as a whole was ideal.

All the other works show events from Becket's life, and the irreducible minimum, the scene that occurs in every narrative depiction is, unsurprisingly, the martyrdom. This was the decisive moment that, alone, defined Becket's holy status; moreover, there was a very long-standing tradition for depicting martyrs at the moment of, or by allusion to their suffering and death.

The representation of the martyrdom at Tarrasa combines a number of unusual features and stands a little apart from the others (Plate 1).[32] In the first place, Edward Grim's role, holding on to Becket and receiving on the arm the first blow that touched the archbishop, is shown with unusual attention to detail. Secondly, the mortal archbishop has a halo. And thirdly, he is shown being cut down in an empty space and not in front of an altar; the ecclesiastical dimension of the event is indicated by Becket's crosier, nothing more. Virtually the only other early versions that lack an altar are those whose small scale required particularly streamlined compositions, such as the seals of Hubert Walter and Stephen Langton, a diminutive reliquary box (Plate 5),[33] and a tiny roundel within an illuminated initial (Plate 9).

Almost everywhere else, in defiance of the known fact that the struggle took place in the north transept of the cathedral, Becket is depicted beside an altar (see, e.g., Plates 3, 7, 8, 10, 12 and 17).[34] Edward Grim

---

[31] In the absence of which, a greater or lesser degree of uncertainty surrounds the identity of the figure, as is the case, e.g. for the high quality relief from Sens (see n. 16) and the low quality one from Godmersham, near Canterbury.

[32] Borenius, 'Addenda', 20–2; E. Junyent, *Catalogne Romane*, 2 vols. (St-Léger Vauban, 1961), vol. II, pp. 194–5 and 204–5; J. Ainaud, *Spanish Frescoes of the Romanesque Period* (Unesco, 1962), pl. 16; Ainand, *Romanesque Painting* (Amsterdam, 1963), pl. 134; P. de Palol and M. Hirmer, *Early Medieval Art in Spain* (London, 1967), pp. 182–4 and 486 with pl. XLVI; O. Demus, *Romanesque Mural Painting* (London, 1970), pp. 482–3, ill. 219; and J. Ainaud de Lasarte, *Catalan Painting* (Geneva, 1990), pp. 98–9.

[33] Borenius, *Thomas Becket in Art*, pl. XXVII (1 and 2); Zarnecki *et al.* (eds.), *English Romanesque art*, no. 302. On the ivory comb (Wixom [ed.], *Mirror of the Medieval World*, cat. 115), where space was at a premium, the altar was placed in a lozenge to the side of the main composition (see Plate 2).

[34] Most unusually, the Limoges châsse at Clermond-Ferrand, Musée des Beaux Arts, shows Becket beside a stylised architectural doorway, presumably representing Canterbury Cathedral: Notin *et al.*, *Valérie et Thomas Becket*, cat. 26.

1 Tarrasa, S. Maria, south transept, apse.

achieved the same effect in his account of the martyrdom by alluding to the geography of the cathedral in studiedly vague terms: 'He then turned aside to the right, under a pillar, having on one side the altar of the blessed mother of God, Mary-ever-Virgin, on the other that of the holy

confessor Benedict.'[35] John of Salisbury's manipulation of the truth
was more blatant: 'The martyr stood in the cathedral before Christ's
altar . . . ready to suffer: the hour of slaughter was at hand.'[36] This small
degree of artistic licence had very significant implications. It emphasised
the holiness of the saint; it underlined the sacrilege involved in his murder; and it highlighted the contrast between the secular knights with
their implements of violence and the holy archbishop with his tools of
peace, simultaneously making an implicit but telling contrast between
those who served the king of England on the one hand, and those who
served the king of kings on the other. The point is underlined visually –
again in defiance of reality – by the contrast between the violent movement of the knights and the serene deportment of Becket. He attends
to the altar, bows his head, holds a cross, or (as in the Lesnes Missal[37])
kneels in prayer. As a whole, the iconography parallels John of Salisbury's
rhetoric: 'Every circumstance in the archbishop's death agony conspired
to glorify the dying man for ever, to reveal the depravity of the assailants
and brand them eternally with shame . . . Take note too where his sacrifice was made. Yes in the church which is the kingdom's head, the
mother in Christ of all others in the kingdom, before the altar, among
his fellow priests and in the ranks of the monks whom the shouts of the
armed assassins had drawn together to witness the pitiful and tremen-
dous drama.'[38] This is taken a stage further on a superb ivory comb
dating from the beginning of the thirteenth century, where the martyrdom is explicitly visualised in terms of a conflict between good and evil.
An angel, holding a scroll, appears above the altar behind Becket and his
followers, while behind the four knights there is a devil clutching a book
(Plate 2).[39]

Furthermore, the inclusion of an altar drew an obvious and highly
resonant parallel between the sacrifice of Thomas Becket and the sacrifice
of Christ that was re-enacted at the altar, something that is underlined by

[35] D. C. Douglas and G. W. Greenaway (eds.), *English Historical Documents II, 1042–1189*, 2nd edn (London, 1981), p. 818.
[36] Ep. 305: W. J. Millor and C. N. L. Brooke (eds.), *The Letters of John of Salisbury*, 2 vols. (London–Oxford, 1955–79), vol. II, pp. 724–39 at 726–7.
[37] London, V & A, L.404-1916, fol. 18v: Borenius, 'Addenda', pl. XLIX(2). The image appears within the initial 'D' introducing the collect for the feast of St Thomas. The initial has suffered major losses of gilded surfaces, but it was never a masterpiece. Further on the manuscript see P. Jebb (ed.), *Missale de Lesnes*, HBS 95 (London: Henry Bradshaw Society, 1964). Cf. William FitzStephen's account of the death: *The Life and Death of Thomas Becket*, ed. G. Greenaway (London, 1961), p. 156.
[38] Millor and Brooke, *Letters*, pp. 730–1.
[39] Wixom (ed.), *Mirror of the Medieval World*, cat. 115.

2 New York, Metropolitan Museum of Art (Purchase, Rogers Fund and
Schimmel Foundation, Inc. and others, 1988). Ivory comb.

the chalice that is generally depicted thereon (see, e.g., Plates 3 and 7).[40]
The point is made explicit on one Limoges châsse where, most unusually,
the martyrdom is actually juxtaposed with the Crucifixion.[41] It is made
more subtly on the Seligenthal mitre via a dramatic spurt of blood issuing

[40] Some of the Limoges châsses (e.g. those in the Escorial, Lyon, and London, V & A)
have both paten and chalice; while, remarkably, that at Guéret shows the chalice covered
with a cloth. The font at Lyngsjö (Plate 10), which has both paten and chalice, shows
the dove of the Holy Spirit flying down above the latter. Unusually, no chalice is shown
in the Huntingfield Psalter (Plate 17), nor in the (very cramped) Lesnes Missal image.

[41] Only the front panel survives, in the Cleveland Museum of Art: W. D. Wixom, *Treasures
from Medieval France* (Cleveland, 1967), cat. III.36; also Notin *et al.*, *Valérie et Thomas
Becket*, p. 61, ill. 1. The juxtaposition reappeared at a later date on, e.g., a leaf from an
ivory diptych: Borenius, *Thomas Becket in Art*, pl. XXXI(3).

3 Munich, Bayerisches Nationalmuseum. Twill silk mitre.

from the saint's head, which echoes the familiar image of blood spurting from Christ's side and being collected in a chalice by Ecclesia (or an angel) (Plate 3).[42] It was doubtless also a visual reminder of the fact that

[42] Christie, *English Medieval Embroidery*, no. 21 (pp. 60–1), pl. xiv; King, *Opus Anglicanum*, cat. 13, pl. 1. For examples of relevant crucifixion iconographies see G. Schiller, *Iconography of Christian Art*, 2 vols. (London, 1971–2), vol. ii, ills. 357, 364–5, 367, 371–3, 424, 432, 446, etc.

4 Munich, Bayerisches Nationalmuseum. Twill silk mitre.

the blood of Becket was the principal disposable relic. Once again, the visual imagery parallels the language that was used by the early commentators. John of Salisbury declared that Becket 'had been accustomed to offer Christ's body and blood upon the altar; and now, prostrate at the altar's foot, he offered his own blood shed by the hands of evil men'.[43] Benedict of Peterborough proclaimed the view that St Thomas had been a perfect imitator of Christ in his life and passion, and that this parallelism continued after his death, for just as the blood of Christ nourished souls, so the blood of Becket was conducive to the health of the body.[44] One notes here how the nature of his death was used to redefine and enhance the spirituality of his life. Correspondingly, depictions of the martyrdom provided the most flattering view possible of Becket's spirituality.

A divergence in the way the murder itself was represented is also relevant in this context. While some of the Limoges châsses depict Becket receiving the sword blow on the top of his head,[45] many others clearly show the cut being made to his neck (Plate 7).[46] If the former was historically more accurate, the latter, with its implication of decapitation, assimilated the archbishop more directly to the early 'hero-martyrs' who, after improbably surviving varied torments, were inevitably dispatched thus.

A silver reliquary casket that was designed to contain phials of Becket's blood provides an example of a bi-partite depiction: the front shows the martyrdom (under a blessing angel), the back the burial with, above, an angel cradling Thomas's soul (Plates 5–6).[47] The same pair of principal scenes appears in the Harley 5102 Psalter;[48] and also on many of the

---

[43] Millor and Brooke, *Letters*, pp. 728–9.

[44] Benedict of Peterborough, *Passio et miracula S. Thomae*, vol. I, 12: *Materials*, vol. II, pp. 42–3: 'sicut beatum Thomam in uita et passione perfectissimum sui fecit imitatorem, ita ei et post mortem sui similitudinem admiranda perfectione concedere uoluit, ut quemadmodum Christi sanguis cum aqua transit ad uegetationem animarum, ita et serui sui sanguis cum aqua bibitus transeat in sanitatem corporum. Nec credimus aliquem hactenus exstitisse, cui Dei hanc similitudinis praerogatiuam concesserit; solius enim Agni Bethleemitici sanguis et cruor agni Cantuariensis in uniuerso mundo hauriri legitur.'

[45] E.g., those in Guéret, London (Society of Antiquaries), and Paris (Musée national du Moyen Age, inv. Cl. 23296): Notin *et al*, *Valérie et Thomas Becket*, nos. 27, 15 and 22. In the London example, Becket's head is inclined towards the knights. For other early depictions that clearly show the blow being made to the head see, e.g., ills. 2, 3, 5, 8–10 and 12.

[46] E.g., those in Clermont-Ferrand, the Escorial, Hereford, Cologne, Limoges, Liverpool, London (V & A), Lucca, Lyon, Oxford, Paris (Musée du Louvre), Paris (Musée national du Moyen Age, inv. Cl. 22596), and Sens. The fresco at Tarrasa (Plate 1) also seems to show a blow to the neck.

[47] Borenius, 'Addenda', pp. 27–8; Zarnecki *et al.* (eds.), *English Romanesque Art*, cat. 302; C. T. Little and T. B. Husband, *The Metropolitan Museum of Art: Europe in the Middle Ages* (New York, 1987), ill. 70.

[48] N. J. Morgan, *Early Gothic Manuscripts I: 1190–1250* (London, 1982), cat. 40; C. de Hamel and J. Backhouse, *The Becket Leaves* (London, 1988), pls. II–III. The psalter itself is of *s*. xiii[1]; the two miniatures (part of a series of five) are dated on stylistic grounds to *s*. xii[ex] and seem to have been inserted into it.

5 New York, Metropolitan Museum of Art, Gift of J. Pierpont Morgan, 1917. Silver reliquary casket.

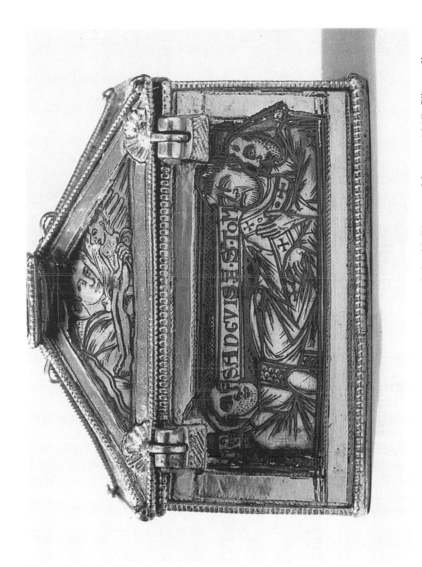

6 New York, Metropolitan Museum of Art, Gift of J. Pierpont Morgan, 1917. Silver reliquary casket.

7 London, Victoria and Albert Museum. Gilt copper and champlevé
enamel reliquary châsse

Limoges châsses, where both depictions are invariably on the same side of
the casket, inviting the beholder to consider them together. Here, therefore, there is a further image to counterpoise with the violence of the
soldiers against the living Becket, namely the care taken of his dead body
by the Church. Corresponding to reality, the little reliquary casket and
the miniature show Becket being consigned to the grave in full archiepiscopal regalia. The châsses, by contrast, generally depict him in a winding
sheet, conforming to the normal Limoges iconography for a holy burial.
A significant exception is the large châsse, now in the Victoria and Albert
Museum, where the body is robed (Plate 7).[49] The grief and attentiveness of the monks in the miniature are carefully shown by their gestures
and expressions. On the higher quality châsses the attentiveness of the
ministers is underlined by their actions: entombing the corpse, sprinkling
it with holy water and incense, as a bishop performs a requiem mass from
a service book – again paralleling the iconography of burial used on other

[49] Borenius, 'Addenda', pp. 28–30; Zarnecki *et al.* (ed.), *English Romanesque Art*, cat. 292;
P. Williamson (ed.), *The Medieval Treasury*, 2nd edn (London, 1998), p. 178, ill. 20.

Limoges works,[50] and echoing that of earlier pictorial hagiography.[51] Also on the châsses (though not the little reliquary casket, nor in the Harley 5102 Psalter) the sacred status of the body is shown by the fact that it has a halo. Interestingly, this is not a feature of the burial iconography on the broadly contemporary châsse of St Martial, the great local saint of Limoges. The ultimate iconographic parallel that springs to mind for this scene is, of course, the Entombment of Christ.

The second scene that appears on other Limoges châsses – echoing the lid of the little silver reliquary (Plate 6) – shows the saint's soul (again haloed) being elevated to heaven. Depictions of the elevation of saints were an established element of Romanesque visual hagiography and became part of the general Limoges repertoire. If the imagery used for Becket was less bombastic than that which had been deployed for St Omer and St Amand in their illustrated *vitae*,[52] it was nevertheless clear and – with its ultimate visual echoes of the Assumption of the Virgin[53] – highly charged. The châsse in the Victoria and Albert Museum (Plate 7) along with a slightly less grand one in Cologne[54] and a small one at Le Vigean[55] have both the entombment and the elevation, making the parallel with the

[50] E.g., cf. the châsses of Saint Martial and Saint Calmine: E. Taburet-Delahaye and B. D. Boehm (eds.), *L'Oeuvre de Limoges: Emaux du Moyen Age* (Paris, 1995), nos. 17 and 45.

[51] E.g., the entombments of SS Benedict (Vatican City, Biblioteca Apostolica Vaticana, lat. 1202, fol. 80r; *s.* xi[2]), Omer (Saint-Omer, Bibliothèque municipale, 698, fol. 28r; *s.* xi[ex]), Maur (Troyes, Bibliothèque municipale 2273, fol. 73v; *s.* xii[1]), Hadelin (Shrine in St Martin, Visé; *s.* xii[med]), and Heribert (Shrine in Deutz; *s.* xii[med]). See further, in general, B. Abou-El-Haj, *The Medieval Cult of Saints: Formation and Transformations* (Cambridge, 1994), pp. 46–55.

[52] Respectively, Saint-Omer, Bibliothèque municipale, 698, fol. 26r (col. pl. N. Delanne-Logié and Y.-M. Hilaire (eds.), *La Cathédrale de Saint-Omer* (Paris, 2000), pl. 16) and Valenciennes, Bibliothèque municipale, 501, fol. 31r (col. pl. A. Grabar and C. Nordenfalk, *Romanesque Painting* [Geneva, 1958], p. 187).

[53] E.g., cf. R. Kahsnitz, 'Koimesis-dormitio-assumptio: Byzantisches und Antikes in dem Miniaturen der Liuthargruppe', P. Bjurström, N.-G. Hökby and F. Mütherich (eds.), *Florilegium in honorem Carl Nordenfalk Octogenarii Contextum*, (Stockholm, 1987), pp. 91–122.
    The other scene on the ivory comb (see n. 39) has been identified as Henry informing Thomas that he is to be archbishop, an event that happened at Falaise. Although most unusual if this is indeed the case, it nevertheless has an obvious thematic logic: the cycle would thus encompass the whole of Becket's archiepiscopacy from nomination to martyrdom. The alternative possibility that the image was designed to show Henry and the four knights at Bur-le-Roi near Bayeux, though far less likely visually, cannot be entirely discounted since the four figures wearing sub-classical pallia owe more to a taste for classicising elements than to a wish to depict unambiguously the events of either 1162 or 1170.

[54] H. Schnitzler, *Das Schnütgen-Museum: eine Auswahl*, 2nd edn (Cologne, 1961), no. 38; A. von Euw, *Schnütgen-Museum, Köln* (Braunschweig, 1990), p. 41; Notin *et al.*, *Valérie et Thomas Becket*, cat. 16.

[55] Notin *et al.*, *Valérie et Thomas Becket*, p. 67, ills. 4–5. The same combination appears on other Limoges work, twice indeed on the back of the majestic Châsse de Saint Calmine: Taburet-Delahaye and Boehm (eds.), *L'Oeuvre de Limoges*, cat. 45.

early iconography of the Dormition and the Assumption of the Virgin especially striking. This is a particularly effective ensemble, amplifying the saint's martyrdom both with the reception of his soul into heaven and with his continued corporeal presence on earth – the two essential elements of his cult at Canterbury. In the London version all this is accomplished in the presence of the enthroned Christ, depicted on the surviving end of the casket.

It is the role of the archbishop as a conduit for divine power that is underlined in the Saint-Fuscien Psalter (Plate 8).[56] Here a depiction of the martyrdom is juxtaposed with an image of the haloed Becket enthroned, dressed in full pontificals, blessing three monastic figures. Though conceivably a stylised representation of the archbishop greeting the monks of Christ Church on his return to Canterbury at the beginning of December 1170 – or even of his ordaining clergy from his diocese on 20 December – the presence of the halo argues against this (particularly since he is depicted without a halo at the moment of his death in the scene above). The image was thus more probably designed to show how the martyred archbishop was a channel for divine grace to the faithful on earth – and it will be noted how his blessing hand echoes that of God in the superior register, and how, in both registers, the compartmentalisation of the ground distinguishes the 'heavenly' on the right from the 'earthly' on the left.

The châsses in London, Cologne and Le Vigean, though closely focused on the martyrdom and its implications, are effectively three-scene interpretations of the subject. Other three-scene versions relate a little more of the 'story'. Preceding the martyrdom and the image of the soul being carried up to heaven in the wall painting at Tarrasa, we are shown the soldiers surrounding Becket, a scene so conceived as to make allusion to the mocking of Christ (Plate 1). The magnificent initial 'I' that begins Book III in the Cirencester copy of Alan of Tewkesbury's edition of Becket's correspondence includes three roundels that show respectively: Becket at table confronting the knights, the martyrdom, and the entombed body attended by three monks (Plate 9).[57] A similar 'cycle' appears as a half-page miniature later in the book, standing between the end of Becket's own letters and John of Salisbury's *Ex insperato* (an account of the martyrdom): here we see the four knights arriving at the archiepiscopal

---

[56] See note 17 above.

[57] London, BL, Cotton Claudius B. ii, fol. 214v: C. M. Kauffmann, *Romanesque Manuscripts 1066–1190* (London, 1975), cat. 93; Zarnecki *et al.* (ed.), *English Romanesque Art*, cat. 72; A. Duggan, *Thomas Becket: A Textual History of his Letters* (Oxford, 1980), esp. pp. 100–29; M. Gullick, 'A Twelfth-Century Manuscript of the Letters of Thomas Becket', *English Manuscript Studies*, 2 (1990), 1–31. The letter invites comparison with the initial 'I's, containing the days of creation followed by the Crucifixion, that were becoming fashionable for introducing the Book of Genesis.

8 Amiens, Bibliothèque municipale, MS 19, fol. 8r (prefatory miniature
to the 'Saint-Fuscien' Psalter-hymnal).

9 London, British Library, MS Cotton Claudius B. ii, fol. 214v

palace, the martyrdom, and finally four figures prostrate before – or even under – a shrine, beside and on which are burning candles.[58] In both illuminations, the first scene with Becket at table is evocative of the Last Supper. The last scene in the miniature takes the story further than that of the initial, for the image of pilgrims at the (imaginatively conceived) shrine advertises the continuing spiritual significance of the events.

On the font at Lyngsjö, whose form permits a more continuous narrative, the cycle starts with an image of King Henry addressing one of the knights; a second knight hurries away, leading on to the two remaining knights who are actively cutting Becket down in front of an altar in the presence of Grim (whose wrist the first knight is slashing), not to mention the dove of the Holy Spirit (Plate 10); the final scene shows Christ welcoming Becket into heaven.[59] Here, as in the miniature, the extra narrative scene gives a little more emphasis to the human drama. Furthermore, the font introduces Henry II in a villanous role (the inscription *Rex Henricus* leaves no doubt that it is he). This is a theme that is taken up in more detail in one of the longer cycles, to which we now turn.

The westernmost window in the south-east apsidal chapel of Chartres Cathedral, dating from the early thirteenth century, is decorated with a lengthy cycle of Thomas Becket's life (Plates 11–12).[60] Although uncertainty surrounds the interpretation of the group of vignettes at the bottom of the window which may not pertain to Becket at all, there remain sixteen scenes that are unquestionably devoted to his story, beginning with his consecration and concluding with the martyrdom and a depiction of the infirm around his tomb.[61] As was commonly the case in glass, the cycle runs from the bottom upwards: the eye literally climbs towards the martyrdom – real space contributing a sense of apotheosis – and thence to the climactic scene at the top of the window that shows Becket's body laid out (Plate 12). Here the martyred archbishop is distinguished by a halo which, thanks to the medium (glass), literally glows. The theme of sacred and secular at the martyrdom itself is underlined by the juxtaposition directly above Becket's head of the sword wielded by the knight and the cross(staff) held by Grim. Equally, the cross advertises the Christocentric overtones of the archbishop's sacrifice. This resonant

[58] Fol. 341r: de Hamel and Backhouse, *Becket Leaves*, pl. I (incorrect foliation). The four pilgrims have sometimes been interpreted as the knights themselves.

[59] A. Anderson, *The Art of Scandinavia*, 2 vols. (London, 1970), vol. II, p. 239 with ill. 151; F. Nordström, *Medieval Baptismal Fonts: An Iconographic Study* (Stockholm, 1984), pp. 118–20 (their descriptions are contradictory in detail).

[60] Y. Delaporte and E. Houvet, *Les Vitraux de la Cathédrale de Chartres*, 4 vols. (Chartres, 1926), vol. I, pp. 247–54; vol. II, pls. LXIII–LXVI; L. Grodecki *et al.*, *Les Vitraux du Centre et des Pays de la Loire*, Recensement des Vitraux anciens de la France 2 (Paris, 1981), pp. 25–45, esp. 30 (where dated ?1215–25); and C. Manhes-Deremble, *Les Vitraux narratifs de la Cathédrale de Chartres* (Paris, 1993), esp. pp. 248–54 and 328–9.

[61] Notwithstanding the distance, the scenes are all clearly legible to the naked eye.

10 Lyngsjö, Sweden. Font.

juxtaposition, which features in certain other early depictions (notably those in the Harley 5102 Psalter and Alan of Tewkesbury's collection, as well as on the font at Lynsgjö: Plates 9–10), was something that the written accounts did not and could not parallel.

Yet notwithstanding the spiritually charged scenes that conclude the cycle at Chartres, this is very much an account of Becket's life – above

11 Chartres, Cathédrale de Notre-Dame. South-east apsidal chapel, westernmost window (*Corpus vitrearum*, baie 18, detail).

12 Chartres, Cathédrale de Notre-Dame. South-east apsidal chapel, westernmost window (detail).

all his journeys and meetings (Plate 11) – rather than of his death and afterlife. At one level, the cycle shows how little the acts of our archbishop had in common with the traditional life of a saint. At the same time, it stresses how his fate was intertwined with royalty. Becket emerges as a man who was hounded by the English – in particular by the two Henrys – but was favourably received by the pope and King Louis VII of France. *Rendez-vous* featuring kings and prelates articulate the narrative – we are shown Thomas meeting Louis VII at Soissons, Alexander III at Sens, and Louis VII and Alexander III at Bourges; Henry II in conference with an unidentifiable English bishop; and the young Henry refusing to speak to Becket – and the positive role played by the French king is underlined. Indeed there is a sharp contrast between the good French king, who is shown to be in harmony with the pope and the exiled archbishop, and the bad English kings who spurn and condemn Becket. The point is most apparent in the eighth and ninth scenes, where Becket's episcopal consecration is juxtaposed with an altercation between the archbishop and Henry II, into whose ear speaks a little devil.[62] This last iconography was redolent of that of the trial of Christ, or of some early martyrdoms where the scene of execution was presided over by the relevant king or emperor with a devil on his shoulder.[63] A demon incites Pontius Pilate in glass at Sens that is broadly contemporary with the nearby Becket window; while in the Huntingfield Psalter the martyrdom of Becket is juxtaposed with an image of Herod Agrippa I, urged on by a hairy devil, ordering the decapitation of St James.[64] Becket had himself exploited French political hostility towards Henry II; and Louis VII had made a pilgrimage to the martyr's tomb in 1179, an event that was perceived as crucial for the survival of his son, Philip Augustus, and hence for the Capetian dynasty as a whole. That the 'disreputable' nature of the English monarchy should have been stressed in a French context in the early thirteenth century when relations between the two countries were particularly tense, hardly requires explanation.[65] Moreover, the dispute over the nomination to Canterbury of Stephen Langton (an alumnus

[62] Delaporte and Houvet, *Vitraux de la Cathédrale de Chartres*, vol. II, pl. LXIV (the two lower quarters of the bottom roundel).

[63] E.g., the execution of Lawrence in the *s.* xi[med] Troper, London, BL, Cotton Caligula A. xiv, fol. 25r (E. Temple, *Anglo-Saxon Manuscripts* (London, 1976), cat. 97); and the execution of St James in the *s.* xii mural painting at the Priory of Saint-Jacques des Guérets (P.-H. Michel, *La Fresque romane* (Paris, 1961), pp. 80–1 and 151; R. Favreau *et al.*, *Peintures murales romanes*, Cahiers de l'Inventaire 15 [Paris, 1988], pp. 76–83).

[64] New York, Pierpont Morgan Library, M 43, fol. 25r (fourth scene).

[65] For a convenient summary of the relations between the English and French monarchy see R.-H. Bautier, 'Les Plantagenêts et le roi de France', D. Gaborit-Chopin and E. Taburet-Delahaye (eds.), *L'Œuvre de Limoges: Art et histoire au temps des Plantagenêts* (Paris, 1998), 109–22.

of Paris and a devotee of Becket) that resulted in the flight of the cathedral community to Saint-Omer (1209–13), the interdict on England, the excommunication of King John, and the exile of Langton (who settled at Pontigny) ensured that Becket and his myth remained a very live issue in gallic ecclesiastical circles at this time.

The designer of the broadly contemporary narrative window in the north ambulatory of the cathedral at Sens, which has particularly close artistic connections with the glass at Canterbury and might conceivably echo the cycle of Becket's life that has been lost therefrom, was less concerned to defame the king of England; however he still lauds the king of France (Plates 13–14).[66] Indeed, the first scene shows the reconciliation between Becket and Henry, mediated by Louis VII who holds centre stage. The eye then rises up through events to the climax of the martrydom, burial, and reception of the archbishop's soul by Christ at the top of the window (Plate 14). If the general arrangement of scenes is thus similar to that at Chartres, the emphasis in the cycle as a whole is rather different, for here it is Becket's role as pastor that is stressed. We see him received by clergy, preaching, saying mass, consecrating a church, and confirming the faithful. In scenes two to five he is accompanied by a group of acolytes, making the general effect reminiscent of Jesus and his disciples. In contrast to Chartres, where we are shown a cosmopolitan exile who is central to England's disgrace, at Sens it is the model cleric who is martyred. Indeed here, between the depiction of Becket receiving messengers from Henry and that of his martyrdom, we see not the king and his knights but rather Thomas consecrating a church and confirming the faithful – he is shown as the devoted churchman to the bitter end. This was the closest one could realistically get to depicting Thomas Becket as a saint in life.

The windows at Canterbury Cathedral itself, the last work we have to consider, would seem to have begun with a similar cycle of the archbishop's life, from which only one displaced panel remains.[67] Be that as it may, the programme as a whole was nevertheless quite different in emphasis.[68] The accent here was very much on the saint's afterlife – his

[66] J. Taralon, A. Prache *et al.*, *Les Vitraux de Bourgogne, Franche-Comté et Rhône-Alpes*, Recensement des Vitraux anciens de la France 3 (Paris, 1986), pp. 173–86, esp. 180 (where dated *c*. 1207 × 15). Colour reproductions: S. Brown, *Stained Glass: An Illustrated History* (London, 1992), p. 56 (whole window); M. Aubert, *Stained Glass of the XII and XIII Centuries from French Cathedrals* (London, 1951), pl. VII (lower half of window). The programme is compared with that of Chartres by Manhes-Deremble, *Vitraux narratifs*. The relationship between Sens and Canterbury is discussed by Caviness, *Early Stained Glass of Canterbury Cathedral*, esp. pp. 90–3; L. Grodecki and C. Brisac, *Gothic Stained Glass* (London, 1985), pp. 86–90 and 259–60 are more reserved on the connections. All the scenes (though not the inscriptions) are easily perceived by the naked eye.
[67] Fogg Museum, Harvard University: Caviness, *Windows of Christ Church Cathedral*, app. I, no. 5; Caviness, *Early Stained Glass of Canterbury Cathedral*, col. pl. IV.
[68] See further Caviness, *Early Stained Glass of Canterbury Cathedral*, pp. 105–6, 139–44 and 146–50, and *Windows of Christ Church Cathedral*, pp. 176–214.

13 Sens, Cathédrale de Saint-Etienne. North ambulatory (*Corpus vitrearum*, baies 23 and 21).

14 Sens, Cathédrale de Saint-Etienne. North ambulatory, westernmost window (*Corpus vitrearum*, baie 23).

posthumous miracles – to which at least ten of the twelve great windows in the Trinity Chapel ambulatory were devoted (Plates 15–16 and 18–20). Becket's life itself was profoundly lacking in the miracles and wonders that normally characterised the *Vita* of a saint (as the glass at Chartres shows only too clearly), and such an arrangement effectively redressed the balance. Simultaneously, it stressed the benefits of devotion to the saint and the power of the shrine itself. The Trinity Chapel windows are composed around divers series of self-contained mini-narratives, ranging in extent from as few as two scenes (Plate 16) to as many as nine (Plate 19), that recount the histories of those who were cured through Becket's intervention. The states of the individuals in question before and after the miraculous healing are juxtaposed, providing compelling visual testimony to the dead archbishop's power. Thus we first see Henry of Fordwich, his hands bound, ushered by two men who are beating him towards the tomb with its monastic attendant, under the inscription, 'Demented he approaches' (Plate 16).[69] He is then shown kneeling calmly in prayer, while the two secular figures and the monk gesture in acclamation, and the clubs and the rope that had formerly been used to restrain him, lie beside the tomb; the accompanying legend declares, 'He prays and goes away sound of mind'.[70] The cycle as a whole shows the full range of medieval society receiving the benefits of Becket's intervention; and if the presence of figures like Louis VII of France[71] and Matilda of Köln[72] illustrate the international dimension of the saint, the repeated appearance of the tomb itself underlines the particular efficacy of visiting the shrine at Canterbury. Indeed the saintly archbishop is shown to inhabit it in a very physical way.[73] There could hardly be a more overt example of the use of art in the service of pilgrimage.

External iconography

The miracle windows, situated below a monumental cycle of the ancestors of Christ, near to depictions of the lives of Becket's venerable predecessors, SS Dunstan and Alphege,[74] with further saints and kings on the vault, were a crucial part of the setting of the new shrine. This

---

[69] 'Amens accedit'.   [70] 'Orat, sanusq[ue] recedit'.

[71] Reproduced in colour: B. Rackham, *The Ancient Glass of Canterbury Cathedral* (London, 1959), pl. XI.

[72] Reproduced in colour: Caviness, *Windows of Christ Church Cathedral*, pl. XIV.

[73] E.g., see my Plate 15, topmost scene; reproduced in colour: Rackham, *Ancient Glass*, pl. XII.

[74] Who also accompany him, e.g., on a remarkable late twelfth-century pilgrim souvenir: Spencer, *Pilgrim Souvenirs*, pp. 45–7.

15 Canterbury Cathedral. Trinity Chapel ambulatory (*Corpus vitrearum* n. III, detail).

16 Canterbury Cathedral. Trinity Chapel ambulatory (*Corpus vitrearum* n. IV, detail).

leads to our next subject: the 'external' iconography, the broader visual context of the early images of Becket.

On the other work for which a Canterbury origin seems likely, the copper reliquary casket in New York, Becket appears in the company of Christ, Mary, Peter, Paul, and ten saints, four of whom were his predecessors at Canterbury: Augustine, Alphege, Dunstan, and Anselm.[75] He is thus shown as part of a local saintly lineage, and is paired, logically, with the other archbishop who was martyred, Alphege, to whom he is said to have likened himself in the sermon he delivered a few days before his death, and whose name, along with that of the great Parisian martyr, St Denis, was reputedly on his lips as he died.[76]

On the font at Lyngsjö (Plate 10), the story of Thomas Becket appears in the exalted company of Christ's baptism, his commission to Peter and Paul, his resurrection, and the Coronation of the Virgin. Be it by accident or by design, the martyrdom is thereby shown to be the modern counterpart of these highly charged spiritual events, and thus as a continuation of salvation history. Notwithstanding the loss of a couple of pages, it is clear that the same point was made more blatantly in the Saint-Fuscien Psalter, where the Becket scenes (Plate 8) accompany the Creation of Eve, the expulsion from the Garden of Eden, and a short cycle running from the Resurrection to the Last Judgement.[77] A similar theme features in a more general yet comprehensive way in the Huntingfield Psalter,[78] whose image of Becket appears after a lengthy cycle of Old and New Testament scenes as part of a set of martyrdoms (Plate 17). These are arranged four to the page, under arcades. The depictions, which invariably show the moment of death itself, are gratuitously violent; and the effect of eight such scenes of torment on an opening is gruesome. The slaughter of Becket appears at the extreme top left of an opening that also includes two crucifixions, one 'sagitation' (shooting with arrows), and four decapitations. Like his venerable predecessors, Becket is shown to be relatively serene, trusting in God, as the violence erupts around him – precisely the image of the archbishop on the point of death that contemporary written sources promulgated. The context for the depiction of Becket in the Gospels of Henry the Lion[79] is a representation of heaven, following a series of images devoted to the life of Christ. The celestial

---

[75] Frazer, *Medieval Church Treasures*, ill. 60; Wixom (ed.), *Mirror of the Medieval World*, no. 116.

[76] William FitzStephen, *Life and Death of Becket*, ed. Greenaway, pp. 147 and 156; Douglas and Greenaway, *English Historical Documents II*, p. 816.

[77] Leroquais, *Psautiers*, III, pls. XL–XLV.

[78] New York, Pierpont Morgan Library, M. 43: Morgan, *Early Gothic Manuscripts*, vol. I, no. 30.

[79] See note 27 above.

17 New York, Pierpont Morgan Library. M 43, fol. 24v.

realm is otherwise populated by two angels, and SS John the Evangelist, John the Baptist, Peter, Blaise, George, and Gregory. Both here and in the Huntingfield Psalter, Becket is by far the most recent figure: closest in date in the former is Edmund, in the latter, Gregory, characters who predeceased him by 301 and 566 years respectively.

At Monreale, as in the Gospels of Henry the Lion, Becket appears in a highly select and carefully selected company of saints, popes, and holy men as part of the celestial vision that occupies the place of greatest prominence in the cathedral – the central apse.[80] He is in the bottom register underneath the Virgin and child with apostles and angels, who are themselves below the imposing image of Christ pantocrator. The other saints in Becket's row are Stephen, Peter of Alexandria, Clement I, Silvester I, and Lawrence; Martin and Nicholas appear on the return; while Agatha, Anthony, and Blaise face Hilary, Benedict, and Mary Magdalene across the chancel. Becket is the 'youngest' of this gathering by over 600 years. Two general themes that his immediate companions raise are: resistance to temporal power, and martyrdom. Becket is paired with Bishop Peter of Alexandria († 311), who was also exiled from his see and returned to face martyrdom; while the next couple, Stephen and Lawrence, were of course the martyrs *par excellence*, and they had also defied the temporal powers of the day. In point of fact, Becket had further, more personal connections with both Stephen and Lawrence. The archbishop self-consciously allied himself with the former at the beginning of the conflict with King Henry; while shortly before his death he was offered relics of the latter (along with Vincent and Cecilia) by an obscure cleric from Chiddingstone at the prompting, the man asserted, of St Lawrence himself.[81] The particular relevance of Stephen and Lawrence as prototypes and points of reference for Becket is made explicit on the various mitres in which he is directly and exclusively juxtaposed with one or other of them (Plates 3–4). A more forceful declaration of the martyr of Canterbury's venerable credentials is difficult to imagine.

In the aforegoing examples, the visual context of the image has remained essentially unchanged; at Sens, unfortunately, the full early thirteenth-century setting is lost. Neverthelesss, there are three further, broadly contemporary windows in the north choir ambulatory, and the other one in this particular expanse of wall is devoted to the life of St Eustace, which has obvious parallels with that of Becket (Plate 13).[82]

---

[80] The fundamental discussion of these figures remains O. Demus, *The Mosaics of Norman Sicily* (New York, 1950), pp. 128–30.

[81] See F. Barlow, *Thomas Becket* (London, 1986), pp. 112, 231–2.

[82] Taralon, Prache *et al.*, *Vitraux de Bourgogne, Franche-Comté et Rhône-Alpes*, pp. 176 and 179. The window is much restored.

This legendary general of Trajan was converted by a miraculous vision of a crucifix between the antlers of a stag, and, after having led his troops to victory, was roasted to death by his master when he refused to honour the pagan gods.

At Chartres, by contrast, notwithstanding losses and alterations, the problem is the reverse: there is such a plethora of imagery with such a variety of themes, uncontrolled by an overarching design, that it is difficult to define the context of the Becket window in a brief compass. This is a useful reminder of the iconographic complexity of such monuments and of the variety and diversity of messages that they could convey. The setting of the Becket window is a visually self-contained one – a small chapel – but even here there is no obvious thematic logic, the other windows being devoted to the lives of SS Catherine, Margaret, Nicholas, and Remi.[83] On the other hand, considering the cathedral as a whole, the archbishop takes his place among the life of Christ, the Virgin, parables, and a panorama of the lives of saints, most of whom were widely culted. His more distinctive 'neighbours' include a couple of figures of largely local interest, such as SS Cheron and Lubin; and a series of characters with an obvious bearing on the issues of Christian kingship: St Silvester (who was credited with receiving the donation of Constantine), St Remi (who baptised Clovis), and Charlemagne, who had been canonised a mere five years before Becket's martyrdom. If these figures advertised positive relations between Church and State – two of them with reference to the Merovingian and Carolingian origins of France – plentiful saints alluded to the tension between the temporal and the ecclesiastical. Within such a context Becket offered an object lesson in how the English monarchy had – despite the efforts of the pope and the king of France – got it spectacularly wrong. Such a message was doubtless welcome in the realm of Philip Augustus, recently grown great at the expense of the Plantagenets.

It is appropriate to return in the last instance to the exceptional case of Canterbury Cathedral. Appearing in a context that included a lengthy genealogy, running from Adam to Christ, an elaborate sequence of biblical typology, and scenes from the lives of SS Stephen, Martin, Gregory, Dunstan, and Alphege – all in glass – Thomas Becket was presented as the contemporary climax to the long story of the Church. Yet, elevated though it is, such a characterisation fails to do justice to the extraordinary

---

[83] Delaporte and Houvet, *Vitraux de la Cathédrale de Chartres*, vol. I, pp. 254–72; vol. II, pls. LXVII–LXXIX; Grodecki *et al.*, *Vitraux du Centre*, pp. 28–30. The light that actually faces the Becket window is now a grisaille one of *s.* xiii^{ex}, into which an image of St Nicholas was set in 1417.

18 Canterbury Cathedral. Trinity Chapel ambulatory (*Corpus vitrearum* n. IV, III and II).

plethora and prominence of the Becket imagery. Not only was it remarkably extensive (with at least 180 scenes in the miracle windows alone),
it comprised virtually a self-contained complex that was the pinnacle of
the new Gothic structure. With a richly inlayed floor, painted vaults, and
enormous windows that extend most of the height of the walls recounting
Becket's life and miracles, the Trinity Chapel was, in effect, a massive,
highly opulent reliquary (Plate 18).[84] The experience it offered the pilgrim to the new shrine was, in consequence, uniquely highly charged.

Three general points arise from these examples. First, there is the ease
with which Thomas Becket fitted into the canon of saints and martyrs
as a whole, and how readily and universally he was envisaged as part
of the company of heaven. In part this was because of the obvious way
in which he echoed the earliest saints and martyrs, something that the
visual arts were particularly well equipped to bring out. This leads on to
the second point. Medieval hagiographers wrestled to project the sanctity
of their subject by showing how he or she echoed the earliest apostles,
saints and martyrs, but in the case of Becket this was self-evidently the
case. Whilst visual allusion might occasionally be made to Christ himself,
Becket's affinity to Stephen and Lawrence – not to mention the countless
other early martyrs who were finally beheaded after enduring lingering
torments – was patent, and easy to represent (Plates 3–4). Thirdly, Becket
typified the tension, real and potential, between Church and State. And if
his affinity to the earliest martyrs gave additional resonance to his status
in this respect, correspondingly, the presence of an image of Becket made
the political implications that were implicit in the images of the earliest
martyrs into a live issue.

Conclusion

The main points this chapter has underlined are: first, the quantity and
wide distribution of the early images of Thomas Becket; second, the comparative 'stability' of depictions of the key scenes (all the more notable in
view of their plethora) along with the great resonance of those iconographies; and third, the way in which context both enriched the iconography
and enabled it to convey subtly different messages and meta-messages.
There is every reason to believe that, had more material survived, each
of these points would be reinforced and amplified.

All cults promoted themselves visually; what is distinctive about the
case of Becket is how speedily and on how vast a scale this happened, and

[84] Cf. Caviness, *Windows of Christ Church Cathedral*, pp. 159–60.

the extraordinary extent to which centres outside Canterbury participated in the process. The imagery provides an important witness to set beside other sources, underlining the fact that Becket rapidly achieved a widely recognised status akin to one of the early martyrs or apostles, in whose company he was frequently depicted. It is true that the early years of a cult were generally the period when the greatest energy was put into it, and that we have therefore studied the imagery produced during the time of Becket's greatest celebrity apart from immediately after the translation of 1220; but this in no way alters the reality of the phenomenon. The spread of the imagery was part and parcel of the phenomenal growth of the cult as a whole.

The light the early imagery sheds on Becket himself is strictly limited. On the other hand, the contrast between the images and 'reality' – their very reticence in certain areas – both speaks volumes about the tensions he embodied, and illuminates the nature of sanctity at the time. Becket's life and deeds are exceptionally well documented (albeit generally in partisan sources); the issues he raised were exceptionally complex; and very little about his career as archbishop and the causes he stood for was straight-forward. Accordingly, outside his innermost circle, attitudes towards him in this phase of his life varied from hostility to reserve. His relationship with the community at Christ Church, for instance, was frosty at best,[85] while even King Louis VII of France and Pope Alexander III had good reason to hold back from giving him whole-hearted support. In the eight years of his archiepiscopate, Becket tied one gordian knot after another – which his martyrdom neatly cut. Artistic commemorations then carefully tidied up the events in question (defining the participants simply as good or bad) or – more frequently – swept them aside.

The narrative cycles of his life no less than the numerous images of the martyrdom underline the fact that, in contrast to most medieval saints, it was Becket's death alone that defined his sacred status. St Francis of Assisi († 1226), another high medieval holy man whose rise in popularity was meteoric, provides a very striking contrast, both in terms of the saintliness of his life, and with regard to his artistic commemoration.[86] If receiving the stigmata was regarded as the acme of his holiness, Francis's life as a whole was perceived to consist of a long series of spiritual incidents that

---

[85] Clearly brought out by R. W. Southern, *The Monks of Canterbury and the Murder of Archbishop Becket* (Canterbury, 1985).
[86] See G. Kaftal, *Saint Francis in Italian Painting* (London, 1950); K. Krüger, *Der frühe Bildkult des Franziskus in Italien* (Berlin, 1992); C. Frugoni, *Francesco e l'Invenzione delle Stimate* (Turin, 1993); and M. Feuillet, *Les visages de François de'Assise: L'iconographie franciscaine des origines 1226–1282* (Paris, 1997).

collectively comprised his sanctity: correspondingly, images of him often incorporated several of these scenes.

A general point that the case of Thomas Becket thus raises is that saints were, by and large, venerated less for their exemplary lives than for their ability to intercede with God and their power to affect everyday affairs – precisely the aspect of the archbishop that was stressed in the glass of the Trinity Chapel, Canterbury Cathedral. Text and image in the Lesnes Missal make the point even more directly. Becket is shown seemingly kneeling in the act of prayer as his head is being hacked by FitzUrse's sword, while the collect that this historiation introduces begs: 'O Lord, for whose church the glorious archbishop Thomas died by the swords of evil men, see to it, we beseech, that all who implore his assistance may enjoy the wholesome effect of their petition.'[87] Moreover, the diversity of the contexts in which Becket was depicted echoes his credibility, his popularity, and his versatility not only as a saint but also as an icon. Though particularly associated with Canterbury, the unusual circumstances of his life and his death made him a universal figure. He did not just represent the triumph of the Church over the State, nor of France over England – though he could stand for both. The fact that within four years of his martyrdom he was prepared to 'forgive' his arch-opponent Henry II, helping him to surmount the massive assault and rebellion of 1173–4, showed that he was ready to hear and to aid any sincere pilgrim[88] – as the windows of the Trinity Chapel underline. Correspondingly, a mere four years after this 'miraculous' turn of events, William of Scotland could dedicate an abbey (Arbroath) to Becket, the very saint to whom his recent defeat and capture had been ascribed!

At the same time, the evidence – greatly depleted though it is – leaves little doubt that the visual arts made their most important contribution to the cult of Becket through quantity not quality. The martyred archbishop may have inspired some highly prestigious works of superlative quality (which have inevitably attracted most attention from modern scholars), but ultimately it was the sheer number of depictions of him, many of very ordinary – even mediocre – quality that really spread his fame,

---

[87] 'Deus pro cuius ecclesia gloriosus pontifex Thomas gladiis impiorum occubuit, presta quesimus ut om[ne]s qui eius implorant auxilium, peticionis sue salutarem consequantur effectum.' For the manuscript see note 37 above.

[88] On the rapid adoption of Becket as a patron saint of the English Crown see, e.g., R. Foreville, 'Mort et survie de saint Thomas Becket', *Cahiers de Civilisation Médiévale*, 14 (1971), 21–38. Henry II is depicted (along with, perhaps, another king – this second figure is in large measure a restoration) adoring an imposing figure of Becket in the s. xiii glass at Nackington, just outside Canterbury: Borenius, 'Addenda', pl. LI(1); with Caviness, *Windows of Christ Church Cathedral*, p. 310 (refuting the view that this glass comes from Canterbury Cathedral).

19 Canterbury Cathedral. Trinity Chapel ambulatory (*Corpus vitrearum* n. II, detail).

making him a familiar, living presence throughout Christendom. The programmes of glass at Chartres, Sens, and, above all, Canterbury are deservedly famous, but it was competent mass-produced and widely distributed works such as the châsses, 'jobbing' images in liturgical books like the Lesnes Missal which must once have been legion, countless simple wall paintings and sculptures now lost, and, above all, the innumerable pilgrim souvenirs – it was all these that really fed the cult as a whole, and directly and indirectly powered its pilgrim trade.

To conclude, the plenitude of early images of Thomas Becket was simultaneously a by-product of his cult, and a major catalyst for its development. Indeed one might say that, along with FitzUrse's sword, it was at the cutting edge of the cult! The artworks we have surveyed and the numerous analagous items that have not survived were central to the veneration, projection, diffusion, and local appropriation of the martyr of Canterbury. Correspondingly, they both encouraged pilgrims to go to Canterbury and rewarded them when they got there. The windows in the Trinity Chapel (Plate 18) provided plentiful models for the good pilgrim, not least in depicting how those who received cures left offerings at the shrine, and they showed equally the terrible consequences of failing to fulfil one's obligations to the saint. The cycle devoted to Jordan FitzEisulf of Pontefract is a particularly dramatic case in point (Plate 19).[89] When his son was revivified through the water of St Thomas, Jordan promised to make a donation at the martyr's tomb but subsequently failed to honour his pledge (notwithstanding the monitions transmitted by a crippled leper). It was only once Becket – graphically depicted swooping, sword in hand, over the grieving family – had smitten the household, that the overdue offering was delivered, shown by the husband and wife placing money on his tomb (Plate 20). It is easy for the modern commentator to be cynical, and to interpret the phenomenon in terms of credulity and manipulation, and there is of course a measure of truth in this. However, the fact that we can perceive some such motives in the artistic commemoration and projection of Becket – as with any other saint – should not blind us to the profound spirituality that was at its heart. The business of the Church was to mediate between God and man, the place of the saint was as a conduit for that relationship, the function of pilgrimage was to enable the individual to benefit from such foci of holiness, and the role of art – the magnificent and humble alike – was to communicate and give reality to these beliefs and experiences. We began with St Bernard's pointed

---

[89] For a full description of the imagery (which is based on Benedict of Peterborough, *Passio et miracula S. Thomae*, IV, 63: *Materials*, vol. II, pp. 229 ff.) see Caviness, *Windows of Christ Church Cathedral*, pp. 197–9.

20 Canterbury Cathedral. Trinity Chapel ambulatory (*Corpus vitrearum* n. II, detail).

critique of art in the service of pilgrimage; it is appropriate to end with the more favourable view of such imagery proclaimed by the inscription around the image of Becket's martyrdom on the seal of Stephen Langton, archbishop of Canterbury 1206–28 and no less a theologian than Bernard: 'May the depiction of a death externally, be for you a life of love internally.'[90]

[90] 'Mors expressa foris tibi uita sit intus amoris': Borenius, *Thomas Becket in Art*, pl. xxvii(2).

3   Canterbury and the architecture of pilgrimage shrines in England*

Tim Tatton-Brown

The Trinity Chapel in the vast eastern arm of Canterbury Cathedral is arguably the finest space created in England for a 'pilgrimage shrine'. It was also the most popular and the most famous shrine in Britain, and its history is well known. Before looking at this space in more detail, I want briefly to try to set the architecture of pilgrimage shrines in a wider context.

With the arrival in England, in the summer of 1070, of Archbishop Lanfranc, a massive new campaign of church and cathedral building was put in hand, which reached its climax in the early to mid-twelfth century. During this period, however, the east ends of almost all the new churches (the chancel or sanctuary) were very small, and very simply constructed, either in an apsidal form or as a small square structure to house the principal altar. Even in the largest churches (cathedrals and Benedictine abbeys) the sanctuary areas were quite small and any relics that the church possessed were no doubt placed in unelevated structures associated with the high altar. These relics were probably not accessible to the layman, and any cults associated with the relics were relatively small 'private' affairs. These 'relic cults had little or no influence on architectural planning', as Dr John Crook has convincingly shown in his study of Romanesque shrines,[1] and five of the most famous shrines of the period, of St Augustine of Canterbury, St Swithun, St Alban, St Edmund, and St Cuthbert make this point very clearly. The relics of all these saints were translated by their episcopal and abbatial successors, and their associated Benedictine communities, to new containers in the eastern apses of their churches. The process is fully described in the well-documented account of the translation in 1091 by Bishop Gundulf (acting *in sede vacante*) of

* I am extremely grateful to Drs John Crook and Peter Draper for commenting most usefully on an earlier draft of this chapter, also to my wife Veronica for word-processing it, and to John Bowen for making the plan.

[1] In his Ph.D. thesis, and see now J. Crook, *The Architectural Setting of the Cult of Saints in the Early Christian West c. 300–1200* (Oxford University Press, 2000). It should perhaps be added that the present chapter was written before I had seen Ben Nilson's book, *Cathedral Shrines of Medieval England* (Woodbridge: Boydell, 1998).

the remains of St Augustine to a new tomb in the eastern apsidal chapel of the new Romanesque abbey church.[2] Two years after this, the remains of St Swithun were brought to the apse in Winchester Cathedral, and two years later the same thing happened at Bury St Edmund's Abbey. In all these cases the translation was from a tomb in an Anglo-Saxon church.[3] At Durham, the translation of St Cuthbert in 1104 was also to a simple new grave in the probably slightly raised floor in the eastern apse of the new cathedral, as John Crook has recently shown.[4] St Alban's Abbey had a very similar east end to Durham, and the central apse here probably received the remains of St Alban at about the same time.

With the building of the new 'glorious choir' at Canterbury Cathedral, in the early twelfth century, the situation starts to change and, although little is documented at this time about the tombs of St Dunstan and St Alphege, it seems likely they were given fairly prominent new positions on either side of the high altar just before the dedication ceremony of 1130. This 'glorious choir' was famous for its decoration, and William of Malmesbury tells us that:

Nothing like it could be seen in England, either for the brilliance of its glass windows, the beauty of its marble pavements, or the many coloured pictures which led the wandering eye to the ceiling.[5]

Recently Dr Christopher Norton has suggested that the great marble pavement in front of the later shrine of Thomas Becket (see below) was, in fact, an early twelfth-century pavement that originally lay in front of the high altar (and was flanked by the tomb-shrines of SS Dunstan and Alphege) in the 'glorious choir'.[6] This is a convincing suggestion, and it should be noted that immediately after the murder of Archbishop Thomas Becket on 29 December 1170, his mutilated body was placed for the night before the high altar and hence it perhaps lay on this very pavement. For this reason it may have been that the whole pavement would have been

[2] R. Sharpe, 'The Setting of St Augustine's Translation', in R. Eales and R. Sharpe (eds.), *Canterbury and the Norman Conquest* (London: Hambledon Press, 1995), pp. 1–13.

[3] J. Crook, 'St Swithun of Winchester', in J. Crook (ed.), *Winchester Cathedral, Nine Hundred Years, 1093–1993* (Chichester: Phillimore's, 1993), pp. 57–68, and J. Crook, 'The Architectural Setting of the Cult of St Edmund at Bury', in A. Gransden (ed.), *Bury St Edmunds, Medieval Art, Architecture, Archaeology and Economy* (Leeds: British Archaeological Association, 1998), pp. 34–44.

[4] J. Crook, 'The Architectural Setting of the Cult of St Cuthbert in Durham Cathedral (1093–1200)', in D. Rollason, M. Harvey and M. Prestwich (eds.), *Anglo-Norman Durham, 1093–1193* (Woodbridge: Boydell, 1994), pp. 235–50.

[5] N.E.S.A. Hamilton (ed.), William of Malmesbury, *Gesta Pontificum* RS, 52 (1870), vol. I, p. 138.

[6] In correspondence, and in a lecture on 7 November 1998 at a conference on the Westminster Cosmati pavements at the Courtauld Institute.

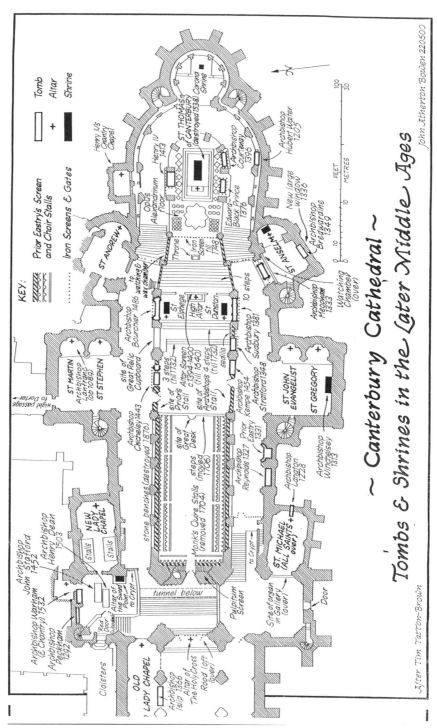

Figure 1 Plan of Canterbury Cathedral showing tombs and shrines in the later Middle Ages. Drawing by John Atherton Bowen.

taken up and relaid in the new Trinity Chapel in the early 1180s, as another relic of St Thomas.

This fine pavement, sometimes called (not very accurately) the *Opus Alexandrinum* pavement, still survives though it was fairly heavily restored in the later nineteenth century.[7] It is made of many small pieces of reused Roman 'marble' set in a geometric pattern within long thin strips of Purbeck marble. The commonest of the reused Roman materials, which must have been imported from Roman buildings in Italy, are purple and green porphyry, and paving of these very hard igneous rocks has only been found in England at a very small number of places, all of which were per-haps pavements close to shrines. Apart from Canterbury Cathedral, the one other place still to have *in situ* porphyry pavements is Westminster Abbey, where the Cosmati pavements laid in 1267–9 have recently been uncovered again, and are awaiting cleaning and conservation. The finest pavement, the 'great pavement', is a magnificent geometrical pavement in front of the high altar. Not only does it contain much red and green por-phyry and other precious materials set in a Purbeck marble matrix, but it was also covered in a whole series of inscriptions, made with 'brass' (lat-ten) letters.[8] Immediately to the east of this pavement, and surrounding the shrine of St Edward-the-Confessor, is another quite different geo-metric pavement, in which Cosmati work (also containing much purple and green porphyry) is inlaid into a Purbeck marble floor.[9]

All this sumptuous paving at Westminster Abbey survives *in situ*, and dates, as we have seen, from the later thirteenth century. At two other places loose fragments of purple and green porphyry have been found in contexts that suggest that they also originally came from pavements adjacent to shrines. At St Augustine's Abbey in Canterbury excavations in and around the ruined eastern crypt of the Abbey early in the twentieth century found over 100 loose fragments of purple and green porphyry.[10] These paving fragments may well have come from a new floor laid in front of the shrine of St Augustine which, we are told, was dedicated in 1221. Old St Paul's Cathedral in London was, of course, destroyed in the Great Fire of London, but William Harrison, the Elizabethan historian,

---

[7] T. Tatton-Brown, 'The Two Great Marble Pavements in the Sanctuary and Shrine Areas of Canterbury Cathedral and Westminster Abbey', in J. Fawcett (ed.), *Historic Floors: Their History and Conservation* (Oxford: Butterworth Heinemann, 1998), pp. 53–62.

[8] R. Foster, *Patterns of Thought, the Hidden Meaning of the Great Pavement of Westminster Abbey* (London: Jonathan Cape, 1991).

[9] T. Tatton-Brown, 'Canterbury Cathedral and Westminster Abbey', and Tatton-Brown, 'The Pavement in the Chapel of St Edward-the-Confessor, Westminster Abbey', *JBAA*, 153 (2000), 71–84 .

[10] D. Sherlock and H. Woods, *St Augustine's Abbey: Report on Excavations, 1960–78* (Maidstone: Kent Archaeological Society, 1988), pp. 135–7.

in his *Description of England* mentions a 'parcel of pavement of black marble spotted with a green similar to some at Westminster'. This was apparently in the floor of the huge late thirteenth-century presbytery (the 'New Work'), which had at its centre the shrine of St Erkenwald. It is, therefore, just possible that there was also a porphyry pavement associated with this shrine in St Paul's Cathedral. There may also have been a marble pavement at Glastonbury Abbey.

The other now destroyed cathedral that has provided clear evidence for an elaborate geometric pavement at the extreme east end of the cathedral is Old Sarum. Here excavations in 1913 uncovered the mortar bedding for this pavement, which was situated on the axis of the cathedral in front of an altar.[11] In a reassessment of the cult of St Osmund, I have recently suggested that this chapel also contained the tomb-shrine of St Osmund, where miracles are recorded as having taken place from about the 1180s.[12] The tomb-shrine, which still survives intact (a rare survival), was taken down to the new cathedral in 1226 in the expectation that Osmund would shortly be canonised. The canonisation and translation did not, in fact, happen until 1457.[13]

The tomb-shrine itself, which must have covered the stone coffin containing the body, is made of Purbeck marble, and has three round holes in each side. These were clearly for pilgrims to put their head or hands in, so that they could get as close as possible to the relics themselves. This indicates a new 'popular' phase for pilgrimage shrines, which seems to start in the middle of the twelfth century. One of the most famous examples of these tomb-shrines, now destroyed, but often depicted in contemporary stained glass, was that made to cover the original burial place of St Thomas in the crypt of Canterbury Cathedral.[14] This tomb-shrine, which was very like the surviving tomb-shrine in Salisbury Cathedral, must have been made soon after the canonisation of Thomas in 1173. The ultimate inspiration for these later twelfth-century tomb-shrines, with holes in their sides, was perhaps the newly built Tomb of Christ in the edicule at the centre of the rotunda in the Church of the Holy Sepulchre in Jerusalem.[15] This great church was completely rebuilt in the early to

---

[11] T. Tatton-Brown, 'Purple and Green Porphyry at Old Sarum Cathedral', *The Hatcher Review*, 5: 45 (1998), 33–8. See also the plan in A. W. Clapham, *English Romanesque Architecture after the Conquest* (Oxford University Press, 1934), p. 160.

[12] T. Tatton-Brown, 'The Burial Places of St Osmund', *Spire (65th Annual Report of the Friends of Salisbury Cathedral* (1999), pp. 19–25.

[13] A. R. Malden, *The Canonization of St Osmund* (Salisbury: Wiltshire Record Society, 1901).

[14] M. Caviness, *The Windows of Christ Church Cathedral, Canterbury CVMA*, vol. II (Oxford: British Academy, 1981), pls. 118–55 and XIV.

[15] M. Biddle, *The Tomb of Christ* (Stroud: Suttons, 1999), p. 86. See also my review in *Church Archaeology*, 3 (1999), 70–1.

mid-twelfth century (after the fall of Jerusalem to the Crusades in 1099), with a large new Augustinian Priory attached to it.[16] It then became the centre for a large influx of Western pilgrims until Saladin retook Jerusalem for the Muslims in 1187. Even after this, pilgrimage continued, and there is a famous request by Hubert Walter (bishop of Salisbury 1189–93, and archbishop of Canterbury 1193–1205) to Saladin in 1192, after they had concluded the truce:

> that at the tomb of the Lord, which he had visited and where the divine rites were only occasionally celebrated in the barbarous manner of the Syrians, the sacred liturgy be permitted to be celebrated somewhat more becomingly by two Latin priests and the same number of deacons, together with the Syrians, and that they be supported by the offerings of pilgrims.[17]

Saladin agreed to this, and now, over 800 years later, still no one Christian sect dominates the Church of the Holy Sepulchre.

This most famous of all shrines in Jerusalem must have greatly influenced the making of new shrines in England, and I would suggest that it had a strong influence on the building of the new raised shrines, often surrounded by new ambulatories, in England. Little is known of the new shrines at Winchester (1158),[18] Westminster Abbey (1163), Durham and St Albans (1170s), and St Frideswide's, Oxford (1181), but at Canterbury a really spectacular new Trinity Chapel was created in the early 1180s for the shrine of St Thomas.

The rebuilding of the eastern arm of Canterbury Cathedral, after the fire of 1174, is exceptionally well documented in Gervase's famous account, and this was brilliantly interpreted over 150 years ago by Professor Robert Willis in his seminal work *The Architectural History of Canterbury Cathedral*.[19] Since that time surprisingly little new architectural analysis has been undertaken, and a measured drawing of the fabric has yet to be carried out.[20] Despite this, it is very clear from the fabric that the design

[16] A. W. Clapham, 'The Latin Monastic Buildings of the Church of the Holy Sepulchre at Jerusalem', *Ant. Jnl*, I (1921), 1–18. Research, under the Israeli Antiquities Dept, is now once again being carried out on these buildings.

[17] F. E. Peters, *Jerusalem. The Holy City in the Eyes of Chronicles, Visitors, Pilgrims and Prophets from the Days of Abraham to the Beginning of Modern Times* (Princeton University Press, 1985), pp. 360–1.

[18] J. Crook, 'The typology of early medieval shrines – a previously unidentified "tomb-shrine" panel from Winchester Cathedral', *Ant. Jnl*, 70 (1990), 49–64. The later twelfth-century shrine of St Edward in Westminster Abbey also probably had 'portholes' in its sides, and they are clearly shown in the illustrations for 'La Estoire de Seint Aedward le Rei', Cambridge Univ. Lib. MS Ee. 3.59, fol.30.

[19] R. Willis, *The Architectural History of Canterbury Cathedral* (London: Longman & Co., 1845).

[20] Though see now P. Draper, '"Inter se disputandum" – interpretations of the rebuilding of Canterbury Cathedral, 1174–1186', *Jour. Soc. Archit. Historian*, 56:2 (June 1997), 184–203.

of the new eastern arm was evolving while it was being built. This is especially true for the new Trinity Chapel, and it is clear, from breaks and discontinuities in the fabric, that its final form was not worked out until building work had already started in the summer of 1180, just after the completion of the monks' choir.[21]

Most remarkable of all, a two-storied shrine was created with the original burial place in the crypt being surrounded by its own ambulatory, and a series of relatively high ribbed vaults. Above this a truly spectacular new raised shrine chamber (the Trinity Chapel) was completed, which incorporated the most costly materials available, including a unique purple to pink Belgian marble in the immediate surroundings of the shrine itself.[22] As well as this, magnificent new stained glass, depicting miracles relating to St Thomas, was installed in the huge lancets that surrounded the chapel and, as we have already seen, a spectacular marble pavement was laid (or relaid) in front of the shrine itself. To the east of the Trinity Chapel, yet another unique feature was created: the Corona. This was a circular chapel, made to contain the head-shrine of St Thomas. This chapel was at the far end of the pilgrims' route through the cathedral ambulatory, and it too was covered by magnificent octopartite vaults at both its principal and crypt levels. However, the Corona is also flanked on its north and south sides by two large spiral staircases, and it is clear that a second floor chamber in the round tower above the main vault was planned, that could be visited by the pilgrims. What was it for? Work on this final upper part of the new eastern arm was, however, rapidly stopped in 1184 and never completed. This was because of the appointment of a new Cistercian archbishop, Baldwin, as Gervase tells us.[23] After this, as is well known, several decades of great unrest followed, and it was not until 1220 that the interior work was completed, the shrine itself was built, and the translation of the relics of St Thomas took place. With this great event, popular pilgrimage was firmly put on the map.

This same year, 1220, saw the start of work on a completely new, very large building, Salisbury Cathedral, and it was at the east end of this new building that another Trinity Chapel was created (the whole cathedral was dedicated to the Virgin) almost certainly as the setting for a new shrine of St Osmund.[24] With the building of this chapel (finished in only five years, 1225) we enter a completely new 'Early Gothic' stage of

---

[21] Draper, *ibid.*

[22] Tatton-Brown, 'Canterbury and Westminster Abbey', and T. Tatton-Brown, 'The Trinity Chapel and Corona Floors', *Canterbury Cathedral Chronicle*, 75 (1981), 51–6. Only recently have the late Dr Freda Anderson and Professor John Prentice shown that this 'pink' marble came from the Tournai area.

[23] Willis, *Architectural History*, p. 62.   [24] Tatton-Brown, 'St Osmund'.

building that makes the shrine area a new focus in a greatly enlarged new eastern arm of the building, that is now very rectangular in plan, unlike anything in France, except perhaps Laon.[25] We should also, perhaps, bear in mind that at the beginning of the thirteenth century, under the great Pope Innocent III (1198–1216), canonisation became formalised, so that a much more bureaucratic and long drawn-out process was put in hand.[26] As a result, St Osmund was not canonised, as expected, in the 1220s and his remains were kept in the old tomb-shrine on the south side of the Trinity Chapel until 1457.

The first half of the thirteenth century was a period of unprecedented rebuilding of the chancels of parish churches, quite often with the addition of side-chapels. The chancel itself changed from a small Romanesque sanctuary into a much larger rectangular space that became the priest's domain. In the largest churches (cathedrals and abbeys) a magnificent new eastern arm was very often built at this time and, though it often incorporated a new Lady Chapel, and various other features, the focus was, in many cases, a magnificent new shrine for the local saint. Probably the earliest example of this, after Canterbury, is at Rochester Cathedral, where a very unusual new eastern arm, with secondary transepts, was built from c. 1180 to c. 1200. This was a very much smaller and cheaper version of the Canterbury rebuilding of a few years before. It was in the 'transitional' style and had as its focus the shrines of the early Anglo-Saxon bishops, Paulinus and Ithamar. Ironically, when the work was partly completed, a pilgrim from Perth, William, was murdered in 1201 outside Rochester, and a new secondary shrine was later created for him in 1256 in the centre of the already existing north-east transept.[27]

The earliest and most ambitious new eastern arm in the Gothic style was at Winchester Cathedral, where a remarkable new quasi-aisled hall was started to the east of the old apse.[28] This must have been intended as a grand new setting for the shrine of St Swithun. This building project, which was probably put in hand by Bishop Geoffrey de Lucy (1202–4), was never completed because its foundations started to give way during the building work. As a result, all the upper levels including a probable clerestory, and flanking towers, were never built. In 1476 it did, however,

[25] Whose design may have been influenced by its English bishop.

[26] E. W. Kemp, *Canonisation and Authority in the Western Church* (Oxford University Press, 1948).

[27] W. H. St John Hope, 'The Architectural History of the Cathedral Church and Monastery of St Andrew at Rochester', *Arch. Cant.*, 23 (1898), 243 and 310.

[28] P. Draper and R. K. Morris, 'The Development of the East End of Winchester Cathedral from the 13th to the 16th Century', in Crook (ed.), *Winchester Cathedral, Nine Hundred Years*, pp. 177–92.

eventually become the setting for the new shrine,[29] but the large open space here was soon filled up with several massive new chantry chapels.

At Worcester Cathedral a new eastern arm was built at about the same time as that at Salisbury. Like those at Canterbury and Rochester, it had twin shrines (of St Oswald and the newly canonised [1203] St Wulfstan), flanking the high altar. Also, like those at Canterbury, Rochester and Salisbury, it had secondary transepts for additional altars.[30] The earlier Romanesque shrine area at Worcester was also chosen as his place of burial by King John (who died in 1216), before the new work got under way, and it is interesting to note that no new shrines were built east of the high altar in the thirteenth century.

A highly unusual structure, which opened out the space around the shrine of St Cuthbert, was the 'Chapel of the Nine Altars' at the extreme east end of Durham Cathedral. Here a scheme was put in hand from about 1234 by Bishop Richard Poore who had been translated from the incomplete Salisbury Cathedral in 1228.[31] This new structure, with its row of extra altars, is in plan based on the greater transept at Salisbury. It was also, however, a fine new way of getting rid of the old enclosed apse around the Romanesque shrine (which had structural problems) and of opening up the whole area to pilgrims, from an ambulatory. Much of the paving within the original apse has survived, as well as the paving for the enlarged shrine platform.[32]

The two most spectacular thirteenth-century eastern arms were, however, those at Ely and Lincoln Cathedrals, and once again they were based around new shrines of St Ethelreda and St Hugh respectively. At Ely the magnificent 'new work', which was built from 1234 to 1252, is still intact, but its interior space and medieval liturgical topography was completely wrecked in the large-scale re-orderings of the later eighteenth and nineteenth centuries.[33] Ely is also very unusual (only Peterborough Abbey was similar) in having an almost detached large Lady Chapel to the north.

Lincoln Cathedral, by contrast, acquired a remarkable new east end in the years after 1192, perhaps based on that at Canterbury. Following Salisbury, the bishop and canons were seeking the canonisation of their

---

[29] Crook, 'St Swithun', p. 64.

[30] B. Singleton, 'The Remodelling of the East End of Worcester Cathedral in the Earlier Part of the Thirteenth Century', in *Medieval Art and Architecture at Worcester Cathedral* (Leeds: British Archaeological Association, 1980), pp. 105–16.

[31] P. Draper, 'The Nine Altars at Durham and Fountains', in *Medieval Art and Architecture at Durham Cathedral* (Leeds: British Archaeological Association, 1980), pp. 74–86.

[32] Crook, 'St Cuthbert', pp. 242–6.

[33] P. Draper, 'Bishop Northwood and the Cult of St Ethelreda', in *Medieval Art and Architecture at Ely Cathedral* (Leeds: British Archaeological Association, 1979), pp. 8–27.

early Norman bishop, Remigius, and this was actively pursued by their saintly bishop, Hugh of Avalon. This was not successful, but after his death, Hugh himself was soon canonised (in 1220) and from 1256 the cathedral was extended even further eastwards, probably to create the setting for his new shrine.[34] With the construction of this magnificent 'Angel Choir', as it is called, we move into a new era that was dominated by Henry III's total rebuilding of Westminster Abbey around his very grand new shrine for St Edward-the-Confessor. The area also, of course, became the burial place for the later Plantagenet kings,[35] and here is the one place in England where a magnificent medieval shrine can still be seen in its original setting.[36] Only one other building can have competed architecturally with Henry III's eastern arm at Westminster Abbey, an even more grand setting for a shrine, and this, alas, is the one great medieval building in England that has been totally destroyed, Old St Paul's Cathedral.[37] We do, however, have much visual evidence of the vast building, and this and the documentary evidence suggest that the 'New Work' here (the rebuilding of the eastern arm) was carried out between the 1250s and the first decades of the fourteenth century.[38] The new shrine for St Erkenwald was then made in the years around 1319, and the translation of the relics finally took place in 1326.

In the later thirteenth and fourteenth centuries a whole series of elaborate shrine-bases was made and, though they were all demolished in 1538 to 1539, fragments of many of them have been found, and some reconstructions have been attempted, most notably at St Alban's (SS Alban and Amphibalus), Chester (St Werburg) and St Frideswides (late Christ Church Cathedral) in Oxford. A most useful study of these fragments, and of the related visual and documentary evidence, has been made by Dr Nicola Coldstream.[39]

By the later Middle Ages, however, no entirely new architectural settings for shrines were being created and instead the shrine areas, within the buildings, were being remodelled. Most obviously this took the form

---

[34] P. Kidson, 'Architectural History', in D. Owen (ed.), *A History of Lincoln Cathedral* (Cambridge University Press, 1994), pp. 27–46.

[35] P. Binski, *Westminster Abbey and the Plantagenets* (New Haven, CT and London: Yale University Press, 1995).

[36] Though, of course, the Maryan rebuilding of the shrine was not done completely accurately see J. G. O'Neilly and L. E. Tanner, 'The Shrine of Edward the Confessor', *Archaeologia*, 100 (1966), 129–54.

[37] The one other major English building with an important shrine, which has also been almost completely destroyed, is Bury St Edmunds.

[38] R. K. Morris, 'The New Work at Old St Paul's Cathedral and its Place in English Thirteenth-century Architecture', in L. Grant (ed.), *Medieval Art and Architecture in London* (Leeds: British Archaeological Association, 1990), pp. 74–100.

[39] N. Coldstream, 'English Decorated Shrines', *JBAA*, 129 (1976), 15–34.

of enclosing the shrine, first with a large screen to the west, and then by putting up chantry chapels and screens or railings in the area around the shrine.

Today this process can, perhaps, best be seen at Winchester Cathedral, but several other large buildings, such as Westminster Abbey, St Alban's Abbey or Durham Cathedral, also show this well. In the mid or later fifteenth century, at Winchester and St Alban's, very tall new screens were put in that completely obscured the shrine from the west.[40] At about the same time large new chantry chapels were inserted into the arcades, which obscured the view of the shrine from the ambulatory. A similar situation happened at Salisbury, though most of the evidence for this was destroyed in *c.* 1790. Here a large screen was built behind the high altar with, immediately behind it, a long narrow vestry area, entered from the doorways that flanked the high altar on the north and south, exactly as at Winchester.[41] Because the early thirteenth-century Trinity Chapel at Salisbury was quite small, and with very small aisles and slender arcades, the chantry chapels had to be built outside the building. These too were demolished in *c.* 1790.[42]

The placing of reredoses and screens behind the high altar had, how-ever, started much earlier than this, in the thirteenth and fourteenth centuries, and one of the finest surviving early examples, completed in *c.* 1380, was the magificent Neville screen in Durham Cathedral. A short time after this (1394–8), an incredibly costly silver reredos, set in wood, in an iron screen, was built behind the high altar at Canterbury Cathedral, but sadly the reredos was completely destroyed at the Reformation.[43] Another costly screen was that placed between the high altar and the shrine of St Edward in Westminster Abbey. Only the very elaborately carved stone east face can be seen today, but its west face is clearly shown in the fine drawing, of the early sixteenth century, in Abbot Islip's funerary roll.[44] This screen was put up in the 1440s, and at about the same

---

[40] Draper and Morris, 'Winchester Cathedral' and E. Roberts, *The Hill of the Martyr, an Architectural History of St Alban's Abbey* (Dunstable: The Book Castle, 1993), pp. 136–8 and pp. 143–8.

[41] See the plan of Salisbury Cathedral, made in *c.* 1740, BL Maps, King's Top.Coll. XLIII, fol. 39.

[42] See plan above (Fig. 1), and the drawings of Schnebbelie (made in 1789), published in S. Brown, *Sumptuous and 'Richly Adorn'd'* (London: RCHM, 1999), pp. 20–25.

[43] The iron screen, called 'le Hake', survived for another two centuries, but the retable, which cost £3,428, was destroyed at the Reformation. It is documented in C. E. Woodruff, 'A Monastic Chronicle Lately Discovered at Christ Church, Canterbury', *Arch. Cant.*, 29 (1911), 71.

[44] Reproduced in J. Perkins, *Westminster Abbey, its Worship and Ornaments*, vol. I (London: Oxford University Press, 1938), p. 50. This is a unique drawing of a screen before the Reformation showing the Rood, High Altar and all the images intact. The famous thirteenth-century retable, which survives *ex situ*, may have been situated here.

time the exceptionally elaborate two-storied tomb and chantry chapel for Henry V was being made to the east of the shrine.[45] Most of the rest of the arcades around the shrine were, by this time, already filled with royal tombs, making it very difficult to see the shrine itself from the ambulatory. This was a common trend, so that in the late medieval and early Tudor period (before the destruction of the shrines in 1538–9) almost all of the pilgrims will only have been able to glimpse the shrines that they had come to see through the railings, tombs and chantry chapels. Only the especially privileged would have been admitted to the shrine area itself.

This leads me back to where I began, the shrine of St Thomas Becket in Canterbury Cathedral, which was visited by Erasmus and his friend, Dean Colet of St Paul's, about twenty-five years before its destruction in 1538.[46] Their well-known 'VIP' tour with the prior, Thomas Goldstone II, has often been quoted,[47] but I want to conclude this chapter by briefly taking a contemporary tour of the eastern arm of Canterbury Cathedral to see what survives within the building that relates directly to the late medieval and early Tudor pilgrimage route.

By about 1500 the rebuilding of Canterbury Cathedral was complete,[48] and the whole cathedral had just been capped with its magnificent new two-storied crossing tower, known as 'Bell Harry', a gift from Cardinal Morton.[49] The pilgrim entered the cathedral through the southwest porch, and above his head as he entered he would have seen a fine early fifteenth-century relief carving of the murder of Thomas Becket. The figures on this relief panel above the porch archway must have been destroyed in 1538, but a fine depiction of the Martyrdom altar, known as the 'altar of the swordpoint', with the broken sword beneath it, still survives.

---

[45] Heavy iron grilles were put into the lower stage around the tomb. See W. H. St John Hope, 'The Funeral Monument and Chantry Chapel of Henry V', *Archaeologia*, 65 (1913–4), 129–86, and Jane Geddes, *Medieval Ironwork in England* (London: Society of Antiquaries, 1999), pp. 345–8.

[46] D. Erasmus, *Pilgrimages to St Mary of Walsingham and St Thomas of Canterbury*, trans. J. G. Nichols (2nd edn, London, 1875).

[47] Starting perhaps with A. P. Stanley's bestselling *Historical Memorials of Canterbury* (London: John Murray, 1875).

[48] For this rebuilding see T. Tatton-Brown, 'The Rebuilding of the Nave and Western Transepts', in K. Blockley, M. Sparks and T. Tatton-Brown (eds.), *Canterbury Cathedral Nave, Archaeology, History and Architecture* (Canterbury: Canterbury Archaeological Trust, 1997), pp. 128–46.

[49] It was paid for by Archbishop John Morton who had acquired his cardinal's cap in 1493, and had the tower covered externally in his rebuses and red hats. Initially only a lantern tower was intended. See C. Hewett and T. Tatton-Brown, 'New Structural Evidence Regarding Bell Harry Tower and the South-east Spire of Canterbury Cathedral', *Arch. Cant.*, 92 (1976), 129–36.

The south-west porch leads directly to the quite small, but spectacularly tall nave of the cathedral, which had been rebuilt in the finest
Perpendicular architecture at the end of the fourteenth century. Between
some of the piers of the nave, the pilgrim would have seen the chantry
chapels (on the north) of Bishop Buckingham and Archbishop Arundel
(destroyed in *c*. 1540) and the table-tombs of Archbishops Whittlesey
and Islip (destroyed in 1787), but most strikingly the east end of the nave
would have been dominated by the great Rood above the altar of the
Holy Cross. This Rood was of course destroyed in 1548 (and briefly re-
instated under Queen Mary), but the iron screen beneath it, with its two
iron gates, survived until 1748, and parts of this screen still exist today,
reused in the west and south porches of the cathedral.[50] By examining
today the inner faces of the western crossing piers, one can see where the
screen was fixed and the wear patterns in the first step behind the screen
also show the site of the two doorways. Above the iron screen was a large
Rood-loft, and the moulded outline of its front face, as well as its fixings,
can still be seen on the upper faces of the piers. The blocked-up holes for
the Rood beam itself are also visible.[51]

Canterbury Cathedral is unusual in having several openwork iron
screens and gates in the cathedral, and this was clearly a deliberate policy
to allow the pilgrim to glimpse the great elevated shrine of St Thomas
from a distance. Standing at the east end of the nave, one would have
looked first through the Rood screen (above the Holy Cross altar), then
through the iron gates in the Pulpitum screen,[52] and in the far distance
the top of the shrine was probably visible through and above the iron
screen, called 'le Hake', above the high altar.[53]

From the nave there was only one way for the pilgrim to start his 'tour'
of the eastern arm of the cathedral, and this was through another iron gate
into the south transept at the east end of the south aisle. Until the mid-
fifteenth century the east end of the north aisle was taken up by the Lady
Chapel and, even after this was removed, there was no direct way into
the north transept or 'Martyrdom' until after the Dissolution. This was
because the monks came into the choir during the day from the cloister
by the processional doorway in the west wall of the transept. From here
they went up the northern crossing steps, and entered the choir through
the door in the large pulpitum screen. By the later fifteenth century the

[50] The screen is shown *in situ* in J. Dart, *The History and Antiquities of the Cathedral Church of Canterbury* (London, 1726), pl. 28.

[51] See T. Tatton-Brown, 'The Rood-Screen and Loft in Canterbury Cathedral', *Canterbury Cathedral Chronicle*, 84 (1990), 26–9.

[52] These gates were made in *c*. 1304–9 and reset in *c*. 1450, when the Pulpitum was rebuilt. For all the iron gates and screens see now Geddes, *Medieval Ironwork*, pp. 308–10.

[53] See note 43 above.

crossing area, and probably the north choir aisle, were almost certainly the exclusive domain of the monks. At the west end of the north choir aisle a special 'bridge' connected it with the crossing steps, and into the north choir aisle came the monks' night passage from the cloister (via the north-east transept). At the extreme east end of the north choir aisle was the entrance to the vestry and treasury on the north and, to the south, the steps down into the wax chamber (candle store) below the archbishop's throne. This remarkable vaulted chamber still survives and is now the Vesturer's (head verger's) office.[54] It also acted as the watching chamber to the crypt shrine. The north choir aisle also contained the great relic-cupboard (under the arcade, east of Archbishop Chichele's tomb),[55] and though important pilgrims like Eramus and Colet may have been taken through the north choir aisle, it is likely that it was not a 'pilgrims' route' in the late Middle Ages. In the thirteenth and fourteenth centuries, before the making of the crossing tunnel and other changes, it was, however, probably used by pilgrims.

If we return now to the south transept, we can see how this area was the starting point for a tour of the various shrines associated with St Thomas. As well as the door in the south nave aisle, access to the south transept could be gained directly from a door in its south wall which lead into the lay cemetery. From the south transept the pilgrims could not go into the crossing area, which by the later fifteenth century was walled off.[56] Instead they went through a barrel-vaulted tunnel, below the upper crossing platform, which leads directly to the 'altar of the swordpoint', the place in the north transept where Becket was actually murdered. Today there is a free-standing modern altar here, but immediately to the east of it, and just above ground level, one can see how the early Norman plain chamfered plinth was cut into for the new altar in the late twelfth century, and how this was, in turn, 'made good' after the altar was destroyed in 1538. On the north side of the altar the broken-off end of an iron fixing is also visible. This was presumably for an iron railing, or some other fixing beside the altar.

The north transept of the cathedral was completely remodelled in the mid to later fifteenth century, with the vault above being finally completed in the later 1470s and the huge new great north window glazed in the early 1480s.[57] The latter was paid for by King Edward IV. From this time until the Dissolution this area was a favourite place for burial for archbishops and priors, with Archbishop Warham cutting a hole in the north wall of

---

54 For drawings of this chamber see Draper, 'Inter se disputandum'.
55 The site is now occupied by Archbishop Howley's monument.
56 The narrow steps up to the crossing used by modern tourists are post-medieval.
57 For the details of the rebuilding see Tatton-Brown, 'Rebuilding of the Nave'.

the transept for his own tomb and chantry chapel in 1507, long before his death in 1532.[58] To the east of the Martyrdom the new Lady Chapel was built in 1448–55, while the western part of the area, from the bottom of the crossing steps, was walled off. This was to give the monks private access from the cloister door to the crossing and choir, as we have already seen. There was, however, a door in this wall, known as the 'Red Door', that could be opened to allow the monks access to the Lady Chapel.

The pilgrims left the Martyrdom area, and the 'altar of the sword-point', by going down the steps in its south-east corner to the fine mid-twelfth-century northern entrance to the crypt. From here they would perambulate along the north aisle of the great western crypt until they reached the eastern crypt, in the centre of which was the original burial place of St Thomas.[59] They could then continue around the ambulatory, past the corona undercroft, and return along the south aisle passing the wonderful early Perpendicular chantry chapel of the Black Prince.[60] In the centre of the great crypt was the Chapel of Our Lady of the Under-croft, and this was remodelled in the later fourteenth century, in part as a burial place for the Black Prince.[61] This chapel was then used (from 1396) as a chantry for Lady Joan de Mohun, and from 1500 as the burial place of Archbishop John Morton. His monument was built nearby in the south arcade, and this massive twelfth-century arcading used to contain a later medieval iron screen which ran all the way around the eastern apse and returned northwards just to the west of Morton's monument.[62] Unfortunately this screen has now disappeared, but its fixing points can still be seen. Once again an iron screen was used to allow the pilgrims to glimpse this magnificent and highly decorated chapel, while at the same time protecting it and its very valuable contents.

The pilgrims departed from the crypt by the south-west door, and after climbing the steps, found themselves back in the south transept. From here they climbed up a parallel stone staircase to the north that took them into the south choir aisle, and one bay along this aisle was another iron screen and gate to close off the area beyond. Unfortunately this has also been destroyed, but it survived until the mid-eighteenth century, and

[58] For details see J. Wickham and W. H. St John Hope, *Inventories of Christchurch, Canterbury* (Westminster: Archibald Constable & Co., 1902), pp. 138–47.

[59] It is overlooked from the west by the windows of the wax chamber, see note 54 above. The burial place is now roughly marked in a modern concrete floor.

[60] This chapel is now screened off, and used by the French Protestant church in Canterbury.

[61] Although after his death in 1376, his wishes were overruled, and he was buried 'upstairs' in the Trinity Chapel.

[62] For full details of these see C. E. Woodruff, 'The Chapel of Our Lady in the Crypt of Canterbury Cathedral', *Arch. Cant.*, 38 (1926), 153–71, with a useful plan.

is therefore shown in several early paintings.[63] Just beyond the gate the pilgrim would have passed the tombs of Archbishop Reynolds and Prior Henry of Eastry in the south wall before entering the larger open area of the south-east transept with its altars of St John and St Gregory. In the centre of the south wall of this transept was the tomb of Archbishop Winchelsey who died in 1313. This tomb soon became another unofficial shrine so that, at the Reformation, it too was destroyed.[64] The transept also contained, according to Gervase, the relics of four pre-Conquest archbishops.[65]

If the pilgrim continued along the south aisle, he would have been able to see something of the presbytery area to the north by looking through the iron gates and the fine tombs of Archbishops Kempe, Stratford, and Sudbury. The last two tombs were also protected by iron screens and through them one could see the presbytery steps, and immediately to the north of Sudbury's tomb the shrine of St Dunstan. As we have seen, this was one of a pair of shrines that flanked the High Altar. The northern shrine, of St Alphege, had (from 1486) the magnificent tomb of Archbishop Bouchier alongside it on the north. Behind the nearby High Altar was the reredos and screen, already discussed, and beyond this were ten more steps leading up to the archbishop's fine Purbeck marble throne.[66]

At the end of the south aisle, yet another iron screen and gate was reached which still survive at the foot of the steps leading up to the Trinity Chapel. Just before this, on the south where the aisle begins to curve northwards, is the entrance to the beautiful chapel of St Anselm.[67] The shrine and altar of St Anselm were always thought to have been in the fine eastern apse of this chapel, and as such were destroyed at the Reformation.[68] However, across the entrance to the chapel is the remarkable tomb of Archbishop Simon of Meopham (died 1333) which looks much more like a shrine than an 'ordinary' archiepiscopal tomb.[69] The main elements are made from Tournai marble, a very unusual material

---

[63] See W. D. Caröe, 'Canterbury Cathedral During the Commonwealth', *Archaeologia*, 62 (1911), 353–65.

[64] For this cult see C. E. Woodruff, 'The Miracles of Archbishop Winchelsey', *Trans. St Paul's Eccles. Soc.*, 10, pt.iv (1938), 111–23, and J. H. Denton, *Robert Winchelsey and the Crown 1214–1313* (Cambridge University Press, 1980), p. 15.

[65] Gervase, *Historical Works*, vol. I, pp. 15, 24.

[66] This throne was probably made in the early thirteenth century.

[67] Originally this was the chapel of SS Peter and Paul.

[68] A translation of St Anselm's relics to a new shrine seems to have happened in the 1160s, and it is just possible that this new shrine was already on the Meopham tomb site.

[69] The tomb of Archbishop Bredwardine (died 1349), in the south wall of the chapel, was also apparently destroyed after the Reformation.

for this time,[70] and the shrine tomb structure is built into a wide screen with doors on either side. The whole structure was, of course, very visible from the main aisle, but this would not have been the case for the shrine and original altar in the apse. Is it possible that we are dealing here with a new shrine of the 1330s that was being made for St Anselm, but that for some unknown reason was not completed. It was then used for Archbishop Meopham. Or just possibly it became both a new shrine to St Anselm *and* Meopham's tomb.[71] In this context it is worth noting that a very fine new large 'Decorated' window of five lights was put into the south wall of the chapel in 1336 to light the chapel and tomb.[72]

The pilgrim now came to the final climax to his visit, the ascent of the steps into the Trinity Chapel,[73] to see the great shrine of St Thomas. The shrine itself was completely demolished in 1538, but the three steps of the podium for it were taken apart and laid flat on the floor.[74] Around this, however, the original flooring still survives, and on this were placed the magnificent tombs of the Black Prince, King Henry IV and his queen, and Archbishop Courtenay.[75] The horseshoe-shaped (in plan) ambulatory around the Trinity Chapel also still retains its original Wealden marble floor, and around the edge of this is a thin wall passage flanked by Purbeck marble and pink Belgian marble bases and shafts. It is very noticeable indeed how polished and worn the bases are,[76] and this can only have been caused by the deliberate rubbing of them by countless pilgrims. At the end of the ambulatory is the Corona, which once contained the head-shrine of St Thomas,[77] and here again much of the original floor survives in and around the two steps of the podium on its east side.[78] Remarkably, much of the early medieval glazing still survives in the Trinity Chapel and

---

[70] Tournai marble was only otherwise used at Canterbury in the mid-twelfth century. Is it possible that the original twelfth-century shrine of St Anselm was made of Tournai marble?

[71] For a fuller description of the tomb see C. Wilson, 'The Medieval Monuments', in P. Collinson, N. Ramsay and M. Sparks (eds.), *A History of Canterbury Cathedral* (Oxford University Press, 1995), p. 466.

[72] Willis, *Architectural History*, pp. 115–17.

[73] Situated above St Anselm's chapel, and overlooking the steps, was the main watching chamber for the shrine. It has a very good view of the Trinity Chapel area.

[74] See Tatton-Brown, 'The Trinity Chapel'.

[75] Courtenay's burial here was ordered by Richard II. For all these tombs, see Wilson, 'Medieval monuments'.

[76] The Belgian marble, being much harder, is less well-worn. See also note 22 above.

[77] The pink Belgian marble base for the head-shrine is perhaps the object that now lies at the base of the stairs inside the dormitory doorway (now the stairs up to the Cathedral Archives).

[78] E. C. Norton and M. C. Horton, 'A Parisian Workshop at Canterbury, a Late Thirteenth-century Tile Pavement in the Corona Chapel and the Origins of Tyler Hill', *JBAA*, 134 (1981), 58–80. On either side of the head-shrine were the relics of St Odo (south) and St Wilfred (north), see Wickham and Hope, *Inventories of Christchurch*, p. 34.

Corona windows, set in its original iron *ferramenta*,[79] and on the north side of the ambulatory, the small chantry chapel for King Henry IV still survives built between two external buttresses. It was made in 1438–9, and has an almost flat vault. In front of the chapel is a contemporary wooden screen. All of these are mere fixtures and fittings when compared to the architecture of the Trinity Chapel itself, which is perhaps the finest architectural setting for any pilgrimage shrine in Christendom.

[79] See Caviness, *Windows of Christchurch*. The *ferramenta* have, however, suffered during recent restoration work.

4   Curing bodies and healing souls: pilgrimage and the sick in medieval East Anglia[1]

Carole Rawcliffe

A certain well-known man of Norwich had himself phlebotomised on a particular occasion. But he neglected to take the necessary measures for post-operative care; and as a result found it impossible to sleep ... By and by, his muscles contracted; he grew pale and lean and shrivelled, and his mouth was all discoloured; and those who beheld him seemed able to count all the bones in his body ... In the seventh year of his misfortune, when the relics of St Bartholomew's hospital church were brought and placed in the oratory of St Nicholas's church in Yarmouth, this man approached them devoutly, and meekly prostrating himself asked and sought remedy ... Grovelling on the ground, he increased his prayers and began to sleep. And after he had slept for a long time, he arose whole, and went back home, giving thanks to God who mortifies and revives, smites down and heals.[2]

So runs a twelfth-century account of one of the many miracles vouch-safed to the pilgrims who flocked in large numbers to venerate the relics of St Bartholomew's priory as they were exhibited around England for the benefit of searchers after physical and spiritual health.[3] In this tale we find all the elements that make the subject of pilgrimage so fascinating to the medical historian: the deployment of relics as the focus of a healing cult; the apparent risks and inadequacies of earthly medicine; despair in the face of a debilitating, but otherwise unspecific, disorder of the kind likely to be psychogenic or self-limiting; and, above all, a conviction that God alone, through the medium of his Son or of his saints, could alleviate suffering. The close connection between the Church and healing, as intimate as that deemed to exist between the body and the soul, constitutes one of the most salient features of medieval medical practice, and is nowhere more striking than in the context of pilgrimage.

[1] The author wishes to thank the Wellcome Trust, whose support made possible the research undertaken in writing this paper.
[2] N. Moore (ed.), *The Book of the Foundation of St Bartholomew's Hospital*, EETS, 163 (1923), p. 27.
[3] The practice of sending such relics 'on tour', usually to raise money, was quite common: B. Ward, *Miracles and the Medieval Mind* (Aldershot, 1987), pp. 134–42.

Figure 2 Major healing shrines of medieval East Anglia.

East Anglia, with its profusion of shrines, from the great international centres at Walsingham and Bury St Edmunds, to the smaller, more localised cults at Woolpit, Bawburgh and Hautbois, offers outstanding material for a regional study. At least twenty important healing shrines have been identified in Norfolk alone during the later Middle Ages, their presence suggesting that – in theory at least – the sick pilgrim had as much choice in this regard as he or she did when selecting a physician, surgeon, wise woman, herbalist, midwife, phlebotomist, empiric, bonesetter or apothecary.[4]

In an age without antisepsis, antibiotics, blood transfusion, reliable anaesthesia or any of the other advances in clinical science and technology readily available in the West today, God and his saints dominated this variegated hierarchy of medical resort.[5] From the cradle to the grave, men and women were urged to enlist their help, rather than relying upon secular practitioners, however accomplished:

As Christians we know that there are two kinds of medicine, one of earthly things, the other of heavenly things . . . Through long experience, earthly doctors learn the powers of herbs and the like, which alter the condition of human bodies. But there has never been a doctor so experienced in this art that he has not found some illnesses difficult to cure and others completely incurable . . . The author of heavenly medicine is Christ, who could heal the sick with a command and raise the dead from the grave.[6]

Theologians, from St Augustine onwards, described Christ as a heavenly physician, *Christus Medicus*, who eradicates the cancer of sin in all diseased souls, as well as curing the physically sick and disabled.[7] Exposed to the quotidian miracle of transubstantiation, whereby bread and wine turned into the body and restorative blood of Christ, the medieval parishioner was schooled to venerate the Host for its healing powers and accept – indeed expect – divine intervention in the crises and misfortunes of daily life. Spectators of the celebrated East Anglian *Play of the Sacrament* could, indeed, see such miraculous cures enacted on stage, while also enjoying knockabout farce at the expense of the medical profession, in the person of an inebriated and incompetent quack.[8] The *topos* of the divine healer, with its attendant corpus of specialist terminology, is recurrent in the context of medieval pilgrimage. In the popular English version of Guillaume de Deguileville's meditation on 'Le Pèlerinage de l'Ame', for example, Grace Dieu advises the pilgrim soul to 'shewe thy sore to me, that am thy leche, and I the shal awoyden of thy flythe, receyuynge the anon vnder my cure'.

---

[4] R. Hart, 'The Shrines and Pilgrimages of Norfolk', *Norfolk Archaeology*, 6 (1864), 277–94; R. Taylor, *Index Monasticus: The Abbeys and other Monasteries . . . in the Diocese of Norwich* (London, 1821), p. 66.

[5] For the place of religion in the hierarchy of resort, see N. Siraisi, *Medieval and Renaissance Medicine: An Introduction to Knowledge and Practice* (Chicago, 1990), pp. 17–47.

[6] An eleventh-century hymn to St Pantaleon: K. Park, 'Medicine and Society in Medieval Europe', in A. Wear (ed.), *Medicine in Society* (Cambridge, 1992), p. 64. See also, S. R. Ell, 'The Two Medicines', *Janus*, 68 (1981), 15–23.

[7] R. Arbesmann, 'The Concept of *Christus Medicus* in St Augustine', *Traditio*, 10 (1954), 1–20. For the overlap between medical and theological discourses, see J. Ziegler, *Medicine and Religion c. 1300: The Case of Arnau de Vilanova* (Oxford, 1998), notably ch. 4.

[8] N. Davis (ed.), *Non-Cycle Plays and Fragments*, EETS, supplementary text, 1 (1970), pp. 58–89; C. Rawcliffe, *Medicine for the Soul: The Life, Death and Resurrection of an English Hospital* (Stroud, 1999), pp. 103–5.

Despite his Nonconformist credentials, the 'Antient and well approved Physician', Mr Skill, who treats John Bunyan's young sinner with a purge 'ex Carne et Sanguine Christi' diluted by tears of repentance, boasts a long and distinguished pedigree.[9]

But might the work of necromancers and wise women be easily confused with sacred medicine? As Benedicta Ward has emphasised, the Church's 'need to distinguish Christian miracles from pagan magic was a powerful incentive to find authentication in recognised patterns for the miracles of later saints'.[10] This problem continued to exercise the ecclesiastical authorities throughout the Middle Ages: an examination held in Norwich at the close of the fifteenth century of one Marion Clerk, who claimed to have received 'the art of healing people ... from God and the Blessed Virgin and the gracious fairies', resulted in a series of public ceremonies of recantation and penance in pilgrim centres across the region.[11] From the *miracula* of St Ireneus in the second century to the late medieval vernacular verses describing cures at Walsingham and Bawburgh in Norfolk, the vocabulary and references are biblical, the model unmistakably that of *Christus Medicus*:

> Many seke ben here cured by oure ladye's myghte
> Dede agayne revyved of this is no dought
> Lame made hole and blynde restored to syghte ...
> Defe, wounde and lunatyke that hyder have fought
> And also lepers here recovered have be
> By oure lady's grace of their infirmyte.
> Folke that of fendys have had acombraunce
> And of wycked spyrytes also moche vexacyon
> Have here be delivered from every such chaunce...[12]

Such 'accepted principles of sanctity' were no less important to the pilgrims themselves. A fourteenth-century hagiographical compilation recounting *The Life, Passion and Miracles of St Edmund, King and Martyr*

[9] R. Potz McGeer (ed.), *The Pilgrimage of the Soul: A Critical Edition of the Middle English Dream Vision* (New York, 1990), p. 36; John Bunyan, *The Pilgrim's Progress*, ed. R. Sharrock and J. B. Wharey, 2nd edn (Oxford, 1975), pp. 228–30.

[10] Ward, *Miracles and the Medieval Mind*, pp. 100–1, 168. See also M. E. Goodich, *Violence and Miracle in the Fourteenth Century* (Chicago, 1995), pp. 6–14.

[11] C. Harper-Bill (ed.), *The Register of John Morton, Archbishop of Canterbury, 1486–1500*, vol. III (Canterbury and York Society, 2000), pp. 106–7. The need to distinguish between 'magic' and 'religion' occasioned, and still occasions, debate at Lourdes: R. Harris, *Lourdes: Body and Spirit in a Secular Age* (London, 1999), pp. 282–3, 290; J. Eade and M. J. Sallnow (eds.), *Contesting the Sacred: The Anthropology of Christian Pilgrimage* (London, 1991), pp. 64–5.

[12] The 'Pynson Ballad' of 1465, is printed in H. M. Gillett, *Walsingham, the History of a Famous Shrine* (London, 1950), p. 84. Similar verses were displayed at St Walstan's shrine, Bawburgh: M. R. James, 'Lives of St Walstan', *Norfolk Archaeology*, 19 (1917), 238–67.

records, for instance, the case of a young woman with a swelling on her breast who elected, after conventional medical treatment had exacerbated her condition, to invoke the *Celestus Medicus*. He, in turn, referred her to the shrine of 'the glorious martyr', St Edmund, at the Benedictine abbey in Bury, an endorsement eagerly reported by the chronicler.[13] On many occasions the saints themselves are described as *medici*, sharing Christ's gift of healing. One twelfth-century pilgrim from Middleton in Suffolk experienced a vision in which the two physicians, St Edmund and St Thomas Becket, warned him in the course of a joint consultation about the dangers of man-made potions and medicaments.[14] *Ampullae* containing sacred water from Canterbury tinged with Becket's blood, which were believed to protect pilgrims from disease, bore the legend 'Thomas is the best physician of the worthy sick [optimus egrorum medicus fit Thoma bonorum]'.[15] Nor was he the only saint to resent the competition offered by earthly practitioners. A salutary case in the twelfth-century *vita* of William of Norwich (d.1144), recounts how the sacrist of Norwich Cathedral Priory was obliged to renounce all physical cures before the boy martyr would consent to treat him. A relapse, when 'he yielded to the advice of physicians and sought refuge in the deceits of medicine', was punished by death.[16]

In *The Canterbury Tales*, Geoffrey Chaucer draws attention to the academic credentials of his physician-pilgrim, which derive from classical medical authorities and the Arab and Hebrew scholars who wrote commentaries upon them. Well versed in the texts of Hippocrates, Galen and Avicenna, he is thus essentially a theoretician, who exercises his art through the careful management of each patient's diet and lifestyle according to ancient ideas about human physiology.[17] With its emphasis on moderation and the need for a careful balance of the bodily humours, the traditional *regimen sanitatis* accorded well with the teachings of the Church and may, in certain circumstances, have helped to preserve health. But once a patient fell ill, treatment could be protracted, unpleasant and unpredictable.[18] The risks and limitations of earthly medicine were exploited by shrine-keepers and chroniclers, such as those who recorded the *miracula* of St Edmund at Bury. All too often the saint himself was

---

[13] T. Arnold (ed.), *Memorials of St Edmund's Abbey*, 3 vols., RS (London, 1890–96), vol. I, p. 374. Her own physician is described, unusually, as a '*prudentus medicus*' because he recognises the limitations of his art.

[14] *Materials*, vol. I, pp. 184–7.

[15] J. Alexander and P. Binski (eds.), *Age of Chivalry: Art in Plantagenet England 1200–1400* (London, 1987), pp. 218–20.

[16] Thomas of Monmouth, *The Life and Miracles of St William of Norwich*, ed. A. Jessopp and M. R. James (Cambridge, 1896), pp. 174–7.

[17] F. N. Robinson (ed.), *The Works of Geoffrey Chaucer* (Oxford, 1970), p. 21.

[18] C. Rawcliffe, *Medicine and Society in Later Medieval England* (Stroud, 1995), pp. 105–24.

called upon to rectify serious errors of professional judgement: dropsical patients had, for example, been made worse through the prescription of an unsuitably phlegmatic diet (fish) or regimen (cold baths), while others had been given life-threatening medication.[19] The cost of treatment and the avariciousness of practitioners, topics embraced by satirists as well as theologians, likewise served as a valuable weapon in the Church's armoury. The Benedictine Thomas of Monmouth, a tireless propagandist in this regard, refers repeatedly to the money spent by sick pilgrims before they recovered their health at St William's shrine in Norwich. Women, in particular, poured good money after bad, being 'mocked and left destitute by physicians', whose remedies proved as costly as they were worthless. But here, too, we encounter a biblical model. The case of Agnes, wife of a local cowherd, physically weakened by her 'issue of blood' and bled dry by medical practitioners replicates in every detail one of Christ's most celebrated miracles (Mark vi. 25–34).[20]

High-quality medical care was certainly expensive. A glance at the obedientiarics' accounts of Norwich Cathedral Priory shows that the monastic community spent quite heavily on the provision of drugs and the services of trained professionals: during a bout of illness in 1356–7, for instance, Brother William Dersingham alone cost the precentor 30s., a sum which clearly lay beyond the means of ordinary men and women. The court physician, Roger Marshall, who attended the future duke of Norfolk's first wife for a few days as she lay dying in 1465, charged a consultation fee of 53s; his apothecary's bill came to almost 60s.; and other incidental costs sustained locally, in Ipswich, exceeded 20s.[21] But not all practitioners charged so much. One of the most striking features of medieval healing is the wide range of treatment, from herbal medicine to geomancy, available at a price to suit almost every pocket. Thus, for example, John Crophill of Wix, on the border between Suffolk and Essex, asked only a few pence for casting the horoscopes and examining the urine of his rural patients during the 1470s, while the barber-surgeons of Ipswich maintained a sliding scale of fees, calculated in shillings rather than pounds.[22]

[19] Arnold (ed.), *Memorials of St Edmund's Abbey*, vol. I, pp. 200–1, 374; *Materials*, vol. I, pp. 184–7.

[20] Thomas of Monmouth, *St William*, pp. 132–3, 169–70, 192–3 (where the woman's complaint, 'universa profecto que habui in medicos expendi, et nihil profeci', reiterates the words of the Gospel), 248. For William's cult see G. I. Langmuir, 'Thomas of Monmouth: Detector of Ritual Murder', *Speculum*, 56 (1984), 820–56; Ward, *Miracles and the Medieval Mind*, pp. 68–76; and Finucane, *Miracles and Pilgrims*, pp. 118–21.

[21] Rawcliffe, *Medicine for the Soul*, pp. 160–61; A. Crawford (ed.), *The Household Books of John Howard, Duke of Norfolk, 1462–1471, 1481–83* (Stroud, 1992), part I, pp. 303–9.

[22] L. J. Ayoub, 'John Crophill's Books: An Edition of British Library Ms Harley 1735', Ph.D thesis, University of Toronto (1994), pp. 4, 196; Suffolk Record Office, Ipswich, C5/3 (Petty Pleas, 15–16 and 34–5 Edward I), 8 (3 and 8 Henry IV), 9 (2–3 Henry V).

Nonetheless, if physic offered scant hope of recovery, surgery, as we have already seen, constituted even more of a gamble. Routine procedures, of which bloodletting was by far the most common, could result in serious complications. Many presumed miracles concerned the restoration to health of patients who had been incompetently or excessively phlebotomised. One such was John de Kirkby, bishop of Ely, who apparently lost his senses in 1290 after being bled too heavily by a barber. St Etheldreda, whose shrine lay in the cathedral, took pity upon him and effected a cure, but his vicious lifestyle brought divine retribution in the end.[23] Aware of the risk of accidental homicide and the threat thus posed to their immortal souls, medieval surgeons were reluctant to 'carve' their patients, and thus eschewed more serious operations in favour of diet and medication. Guild and civic regulations endorsed the view, reiterated in medieval surgical texts, that terminal or otherwise problematic cases, such as breast cancer, internal injuries and 'dropsy' (retention of fluid), should be avoided. Contrary to the impression conveyed by shrine-keepers and the collectors of *miracula*, caution and restraint remained the hallmarks of a successful practitioner. Nor was it deemed advisable to subject the young, the old, or the otherwise enfeebled to the trauma of the lancet, cautery or knife, especially when the cure seemed likely to prove worse than the disease. 'O thou wrecchid leche, that for a litil money puttist a mannes liif in perel of deeth', warned one surgical treatise, recommending 'goddis merci' as a preferable alternative.[24] For many pilgrims, such as the woman from Thornage in Norfolk who 'got no aid from doctors' for an apparently cancerous breast, an appeal to the saints was, of necessity, a first rather than a last resort.[25]

It would, however, be unwise to take the apparent dichotomy between secular and sacred medicine at face value, since, in practice, the two more often formed part of a seamless web, complementing rather than competing with each other. 'Gretly expert in crafft off medycyne', and one of the most eminent physicians of his age, Abbot Baldwin of Bury St Edmunds had first come to Suffolk from France in 1065 to treat his sick predecessor. He numbered both Edward the Confessor, himself destined to become the focus of a healing cult, and William the Conqueror among his many patients.[26] His cauteries healed the penitent Bishop Herfast, who travelled as a repentant pilgrim to the abbey after being injured in the eye,

[23] Bartholomew Cotton, *Historia Anglicana*, ed. H. R. Luard, RS (London, 1859), p. 174.

[24] R. von Fleischhacker (ed.), *Lanfrank's 'Science of Cirurgie'*, EETS, 102 (1894), pp. 166, 272–3. Lanfrank advised the surgeon 'loue he noon harde curis, and entremete he nought of tho that ben in dispeir': *ibid.*, p. 9.

[25] Thomas of Monmouth, *St William*, pp. 266–7.

[26] C. H. Talbot and E. A. Hammond, *The Medical Practitioners in Medieval England* (London, 1965), pp. 19–21.

21 Horning, Norfolk. Pilgrim Hospital of St James. Founded by the monks of the Abbey of St Benet Hulme, on a causeway leading to their house, the Hospital was one of many refuges for the sick pilgrims who crossed East Anglia in large numbers during the Middle Ages.

made a public confession of sins and was duly restored to sight. Since this particular cure was considered beyond the skill of either Hippocrates or Galen (an analogy usually reserved for the most desperate of cases), Baldwin was seen as an instrument of St Edmund, and the wound itself as condign punishment for Herfast's previous attempts to undermine the authority of his spiritual sons.[27] During this period the abbey became a centre of medical excellence: a century later, the almoner, Brother Walter, was able to rebuild its 'ramshackle' wooden almonry in stone with the profits made from his lucrative medical practice in the town. Activities of this kind, which might so easily be pursued for selfish gain or other worldly ends, prompted a series of conciliar decrees prohibiting the religious from studying or practising medicine *outside* the cloister. That they would, however, continue to learn the art within the safe confines of the monastery was understood, as was their responsibility to tend the poor 'who are abandoned by the ordinary physicians and surgeons'.[28] There is thus a strong possibility that pilgrims travelling to shrines in the larger monastic houses actually received some basic medical treatment, as well as sharing whatever doles of food may have been distributed by the almoner. The undernourished, in particular, probably derived considerable benefit from the largesse of strangers, not least in the many hospices which sprang up across the region.[29]

Shrine-keepers, who may themselves have been accorded the best care then available to a medieval patient, none the less avidly reported botched phlebotomies and other failed attempts at treatment, as they constituted such effective propaganda. But celestial practitioners were not always infallible: just like their earthly counterparts they could misdiagnose symptoms or bungle operations, in which case it seemed legitimate to solicit a second opinion. The sick templar who dreamt that the Virgin Mary, St Leonard and St Edmund performed thoracic surgery on him in his sleep ('dolorem quem patiebar de meis praecordis abraserunt') reported how St Thomas Becket managed to eliminate the corrupt matter they had missed.[30] Displaying a robust pragmatism somewhat at odds with

[27] Arnold (ed.), *Memorials of St Edmund's Abbey*, vol. I, pp. 62–5.
[28] Jocelin of Brakelond, *Chronicle of the Abbey of Bury St Edmunds*, ed. D. Greenway and J. Sayers (Oxford, 1989), p. 85; D. W. Amundsen, 'Medieval Canon Law on Medical and Surgical Practice by the Clergy', *Bulletin of the History of Medicine*, 52 (1978), 23–43, notably 38.
[29] C. Rawcliffe, *The Hospitals of Medieval Norwich*, Studies in East Anglian History 2 (Norwich, 1995), pp. 135–46.
[30] *Materials*, vol. I, p. 440. Dreams, in which divine acts of healing (including abdominal surgery) were performed, constituted a significant feature of Asklepian medicine at Epidauros in Ancient Greece: H. King, *Hippocrates' Woman: Reading the Female Body in Ancient Greece* (London, 1998), p. 102.

their apparent credulity, medieval pilgrims were quite prepared to 'shop around' in the saintly as well as the medical marketplace, visiting one centre after another until they experienced some improvement. The hagiographers who recorded their experiences shared with the authors of medieval medical and surgical texts an understandable, if less bombastic, pride in successful cures achieved at the expense of competitors. Both were, moreover, prone to exaggerate the odds against recovery, thus heightening the dramatic effect.[31] It is easy to imagine the delight at the comparatively modest shrine of St Walstan at Bawburgh, just outside Norwich, when a Canterbury weaver who had repeatedly but unsuccessfully begged St Thomas Becket to cure his lameness was finally able to discard his crutches as he travelled to Norfolk in pursuance of a vow made to the East Anglian confessor.[32] The monks of Bury were no less jubilant when, in about 1095, a local man who had been struck down with paralysis on returning from a pilgrimage to Rome, and had actually received the *viaticum*, was restored to health after calling upon their very own St Edmund.[33] Alarmed at the immediate and dramatic popularity of St Thomas Becket's cult, the Benedictine monk, Thomas of Monmouth, closed his account of William of Norwich's miracles in 1172 with the story of a Canterbury man who experienced acute facial swelling after the extraction of three teeth. During his all-night vigil before the archbishop's shrine, he had a vision in which Becket advised him to make a model of his jaw with hot wax (which eased the inflammation) and then take the *ex voto* to Norwich, as a tribute to the saint who had cured him. He was miraculously transported there by Saints Thomas and Edmund, who thus endorsed and, implicitly, deferred to the boy martyr.[34]

The anthropologists, Edith and Victor Turner, have described pilgrimage as a liminoid experience, whereby participants traverse the margins of society to experience a personal and collective epiphany before returning to the 'nagging guilts' and burdensome minutiae of daily life.[35] Although their interpretation has been criticised as unduly monolithic, it

---

[31] Fleischhacker (ed.), *Lanfrank's 'Science of Cirurgie'*, pp. 69–70, 102–3, 138–9; P. Murray Jones, 'Thomas Fayreford: An English Fifteenth-Century Medical Practitioner', in R. French *et al.* (eds.), *Medicine from The Black Death to the French Disease* (Aldershot, 1998), p. 169; John of Arderne, *Treatises of Fistula in Ano*, ed. D. Power, EETS, 139 (1910), pp. 3, 44–6, 49.

[32] James, 'Lives of St Walstan', 262–3. See also C. Twinch, *In Search of St Walstan* (Norwich, 1995), *passim*, and E. Duffy, *The Stripping of the Altars: Traditional Religion in England c. 1400–c. 1580* (New York, 1992), pp. 200–5.

[33] Arnold (ed.), *Memorials of St Edmund's Abbey*, vol. I, pp. 160–62.

[34] Thomas of Monmouth, *St William*, pp. 289–94.

[35] V. Turner and E. Turner, *Image and Pilgrimage in Christian Culture* (Oxford, 1978), pp. 2–5. But see also Eade and Sallnow, *Contesting the Sacred*, pp. 4–10.

22 London, British Library. The shrine of St Edmund at the Abbey of Bury St Edmunds, from Harley MS 2278, fol. 106. The illumination is from the history of the martyr's shrine by John Lydgate, a member of the Benedictine community in the fifteenth century. It shows how richly decorated and impressive the structure must have appeared to pilgrims.

offers some interesting insights so far as the medical aspects of pilgrimage are concerned. Since the sick were widely perceived as liminal beings, inhabitants of an earthly purgatory somewhere between life and death, their ambivalent status must have seemed all the greater once they put on a pilgrim's robes and embarked on the quest for healing. For the Turners the journey marked the first stage of separation 'from the ingrown ills of home'. Highly ritualised from the outset, this voluntary *via crucis* carried a powerful freight of spiritual meaning. In a pre-Cartesian world, where body and soul appeared inseparably joined, the one determining the health of the other, what might today be loosely described as psychosomatic disorders responded especially well to the cathartic experience of pilgrimage and its attendant rituals. The belief that sin could, and frequently did, cause physical suffering exercised a powerful hold on the medieval mind. A dissolute knight tormented by skin disease was urged to confess his sins and make a penitential pilgrimage to St Edmund's tomb at Bury, as it was only through the restoration of his *spiritual health* that the fires of lust would cease to inflame his body.[36] One of the most celebrated decrees of the fourth Lateran council of 1215 insisted upon confession *before* the start of medical treatment in order to eliminate the cause of disease: as many physicians observed, the ensuing sense of relief could alone expedite recovery. For devout Christians, whose experiences inevitably dominate the written record, confession and absolution were essential precursors to pilgrimage, which required a clean soul and a contrite heart.[37] If the sick pilgrim returned home as ulcerated, feverish or lame as he or she had started out, there was, at least, some prospect of health in the world to come. A woman from Cambridge who had not yet confessed 'the sins and crimes and all the enormities' of her life was repulsed from the tomb of William of Norwich by an unseen hand until 'repentance with floods of tears had washed away the stains' that defiled her.[38] Thomas Becket's ability to cure leprosy – itself, as his *miracula* show, often seen as punishment for sexual depravity – provided an earthly reflection of Christ's power to eradicate 'that leprosy which pollutes the soul'. Herein lay the ultimate miracle, as another knightly pilgrim proclaimed when entreating St Edmund to free him from the shackles of temptation, just as he released others from bodily pain.[39]

The more immediate possibility of a physical cure, effected at long distance, while the pilgrim was still on the road, helped to mobilise the sick and disabled. One of the most poignant miracles attributed to St Edmund recounts how an old man from Northumberland, blind from his youth, travelled to Bury with friends and neighbours. Some distance from the town, but within sight of the tall bell-tower, they *knelt to pray*, at which point the man's sight was restored and he, rather than his servant,

---

[36] Arnold (ed.), *Memorials of St Edmund's Abbey*, vol. I, pp. 187–8; Ward, *Miracles and the Medieval Mind*, p. 114. The ritual attending a pilgrim's departure is described in D. Webb, *Pilgrims and Pilgrimage in the Medieval West* (New York, 1999), pp. 21–2.

[37] R. Palmer, 'The Church, Leprosy and Plague in Medieval and Early Modern Europe', in *The Church and Healing*, Studies in Church History 19 (Oxford, 1982), p. 86; N. Tanner (ed.), *Decrees of the Ecumenical Councils*, 2 vols. (Georgetown University Press, 1990), vol. I, pp. 245–6 (where the confessor is compared to 'a skilled physician'). See also, Turner and Turner, *Image and Pilgrimage*, p. 15.

[38] Thomas of Monmouth, *St William*, pp. 279–83.

[39] *Materials*, vol. I, pp. 333–4, 340; Arnold (ed.), *Memorials of St Edmund's Abbey*, vol. I, pp. 187–8, 204–7.

was able to lead the party towards the abbey.[40] Such tales, carefully recorded and no doubt embellished by the shrine-keepers, were a potent stimulus to pilgrimage. For the journey itself constituted a profession of faith or personal offering, and thus constituted a crucial stage in the process of spiritual healing. Personal histories of fortitude in face of suffering added, moreover, to that sense of pathos, expectation and drama which rendered the final outcome all the more impressive.[41] Pilgrims welcomed a change of scenery, the companionship of the road and a break from the pressures of daily life. Yet, as Eamon Duffy reminds us, comparatively few were as active and carefree as Geoffrey Chaucer's fictional band of travellers.[42] Many were seriously incapacitated and dogged by pain: conventional iconography, from Walsingham to Marburg, shows them bent over crutches or supporting themselves on hand-held trestles.[43] Several such cases are itemised among the miracles of William of Norwich. Even allowing for the customary rhetoric and exaggeration, they reveal a commitment born of desperation. One concerns an acutely disabled woman who reputedly dragged herself on trestles over twenty-five miles from Langham (near Holt) to the martyr's tomb in the cathedral. She had previously been carried to shrines by her vicar, slung over the back of his horse, but on this occasion she sought to prove her devotion by proceeding unassisted. Another cripple, 'very weak throughout his body', travelled on foot over 180 miles from York 'as best he could and, journeying slowly, spent many days over his long pilgrimage, supported on the way by faith and drawn on by hope'.[44]

Close physical proximity to the saint's earthly remains was the ultimate goal of these pilgrims, who hoped that a touch or kiss would infuse their bodies with healing grace. Now at the very boundary where the sacred and the temporal met, the pilgrim sought, through prayer, ritual and gesture, to harness these awesome intercessionary powers.[45] According to Thomas of Monmouth, the aura of sanctity which surrounded William of Norwich's tomb seemed almost palpable. As soon as her bare knees

---

[40] Arnold (ed.), *Memorials of St Edmund's Abbey*, vol. I, pp. 371–2. Cures accomplished in transit were regularly reported: R. Finucane, *The Rescue of the Innocents: Endangered Children in Medieval Miracles* (New York, 1997), pp. 56, 226.

[41] Ward, *Miracles and the Medieval Mind*, p. 35; B. Nilson, 'The Medieval Experience at the Shrine', in J. Stopford (ed.), *Pilgrimage Explored* (York, 1999), pp. 95–122.

[42] Duffy, *Stripping of the Altars*, p. 199.

[43] BL, Add. Ms 42, 130, fols. 104v, 186v; J. Lang and H. N. Loose, *Elisabeth von Thüringen: Eine Bildbiographie* (Basle, 1993), p. 103.

[44] Thomas of Monmouth, *St William*, pp. 242–4, 271. See also the case of the woman from Bury St Edmunds who walked to Norwich, 'bent double...with trestles held in her hands', having implicitly failed to win the favour of St Edmund: *ibid.*, pp. 105–6.

[45] A. Dupront, *Du sacré: croisades et pèlerinages, images et langages* (Paris, 1987), pp. 88–9, 398–9.

came in contact with the stone and her eyes had been wiped by the altar cloth, Godia the wife of Copman was able to see and walk again.[46] Women, in particular, experienced miraculous cures upon kissing the sepulchre or handling its cover; children, the paralysed and those who had been restrained were laid upon it; others pressed their diseased or painful limbs against the sides. A young woman with an ulcerated breast had experienced some relief after modelling an *ex voto* offering out of warm wax, and thus applying a soothing poultice to the sores, but did not recover fully until her flesh actually touched the martyr's tomb.[47] At the ornate shrine of St Edmund in Bury, where the head of the decapitated Anglo-Saxon martyr lay miraculously attached to its body, sick pilgrims participated in a more elaborate ritual, being additionally offered holy water from the saint's cup. This they drank in three sips, invoking the protection of the Trinity, as well as the intercession of St Edmund, and, significantly, replicating the gestures and language so often adopted in healing charms. The eucharistic resonances were even stronger at the tomb of Thomas Becket, 'the lamb of Canterbury', whose blood was reputedly mixed in the water given to pilgrims.[48]

The high Middle Ages witnessed an almost insatiable demand for water in which the relics of saints or other sanctified objects had been diluted, powdered or immersed, since it could be more widely deployed for prophylactic or healing purposes.[49] In this regard, as in so many others, shrine-keepers were more likely to indulge the rich and powerful. If, as the Turners argued, pilgrimage broke down the traditional hierarchies of the *communitas*, this new society of believers could none the less prove as class-ridden as the old. In return for valuable support given to the nascent cult of William of Norwich, the Lady Mabel de Bec was permitted to remove a small portion of his tomb. Once ground into powder, the stone could be mixed with water for internal or external use in medical emergencies.

This she was careful to guard with the utmost diligence, since she thought it likely to produce often for herself and her children a fruitful outcome of her faith. And as she so confidently hoped, so it happened, for whenever she or her children experienced any inconvenient complaint, she resorted at once to the remedy in which she had confidence and which her faith had provided for her.[50]

[46] Thomas of Monmouth, *St William*, pp. 216–17.
[47] *Ibid.*, pp. 129, 132, 149–50, 154–5, 159, 169–71, 194, 217–18, 222–3, 249, 253–4.
[48] Arnold (ed.), *Memorials of St Edmund's Abbey*, vol. I, pp. 191, 374; Ward, *Miracles and the Medieval Mind*, p. 102.
[49] J. Sumption, *Pilgrimage: An Image of Medieval Religion* (London, 1975), pp. 82–3.
[50] Thomas of Monmouth, *St William*, pp. 135–6. For similar cases from Lincoln and York, see Nilson, 'Medieval Experience', p. 104.

23 York Minster. The healing of a female leper at the shrine of
St William of York, in the St William window, n. VII 22c. The ability
to heal leprosy, as Christ had done, constituted a special proof of a saint's
intercessionary powers.

Less influential pilgrims were given 'dust scraped from the slab of the
sepulchre mixed in holy water' for immediate consumption.[51] Although
such practices may appear literally as well as figuratively distasteful to
present-day readers, it is important to remember that the medieval phar-
macopoeia utilised a wide variety of animal and mineral components,
such as hair, human milk, powdered stones, urine and faeces. Men and
women whose medication might well contain the blood and body parts
of birds, dogs, cats and other fauna were generally less squeamish in such
matters. Given the widespread belief in sympathetic medicine – that one
might thus absorb the virtues or attributes of the beast in question – to
ingest the sacred must have seemed all the more beneficial.[52]

[51] Thomas of Monmouth, *St William*, pp. 128, 150, 189–91.
[52] See, for example, W. R. Dawson (ed.), *A Leechbook or Collection of Medical Recipes of the
Fifteenth Century* (London, 1934), *passim*; and generally, P. Camporesi, *The Incorruptible*

Even so, towards the close of the medieval period a greater sensitivity with regard to the consumption of human detritus became apparent. As religious experience grew increasingly introspective, men and women sought consolation in graphic depictions of Christ's suffering, while also enlisting the intercessionary powers of his mother, the Virgin Mary.[53] Since both had already ascended to heaven, leaving little in the way of physical remains, shrines displaying sacred artifacts associated with their persons and miracle-working images assumed cult status. Although, in theory, illness constituted a divine blessing for those who sought to identify more perfectly with Christ, the quest for healing lost none of its intensity, fuelled from the 1350s onwards by fear of plague. Not surprisingly, fragments of the True Cross were deemed especially potent. One such belonged to St Bartholomew's Priory, and would almost certainly have been venerated by the Norwich pilgrim whose journey to Yarmouth is described at the start of this chapter. Another was acquired after the sack of Constantinople by the Cluniacs at Bromholm on the Norfolk coast. The chronicler Roger of Wendover recounts a catalogue of miracles whose biblical antecedents guaranteed authenticity. With accustomed predictability 'the dead came alive, the crippled recovered their mobility, the flesh of lepers was cleansed, the possessed were freed of their demons, and every single individual who approached the said wood [of the Cross] with faith withdrew again whole and well'.[54] Here, significantly, 'the multitude who resort from afar to [the] church' were provided, from 1401 onwards, with a 'fit priest' to hear their confessions and grant absolution *before* they approached the shrine, 'it sometimes happening that some, their sins...being the cause, are unable perfectly to look upon the said piece, thereby sometimes incurring infirmities of divers sorts'.[55]

The proliferation of pilgrimage centres dedicated to the Virgin Mary reflects the growing popularity of her cult throughout East Anglia. Her earthly remains were confined to tears and milk, such as the suspiciously chalky-looking matter that Erasmus found on display at Walsingham

---

Flesh: Body Mutilation and Mortification in Religion and Folklore (Cambridge, 1988), pp. 10–19; L. B. Pinto, 'The Folk Practice of Gynaecology and Obstetrics in the Middle Ages', *Bulletin of the History of Medicine*, 47 (1973), 513–23; and D. Jacquart, *La médecine médiévale dans le cadre Parisien* (Paris, 1998), pp. 505–6 and ch. 5.

53 Sumption, *Pilgrimage*, pp. 82–3.

54 Roger of Wendover, *Flores Historiarum*, ed. H. G. Hewlett, 3 vols., RS (London, 1886–98), vol. II, pp. 274–6; F. Wormald, 'The Rood of Bromholm', *Journal of the Warburg Institute*, 1 (1937–38), 31–45.

55 *Calendar of Papal Letters, 1396–1404*, p. 432.

24 Long Melford, Suffolk. The Lady/Pilgrim Chapel, Holy Trinity Church. Completed at the close of the fifteenth century, this chapel, with its lavishly decorated images of the Virgin Mary, was intended to attract pilgrims *en route* to more established healing shrines.

shortly before the Dissolution.[56] But statues or pictures of her as a me-
diatrix on behalf of sinful humanity or as a nursing mother could alone
become the focus of popular enthusiasm. Hoping to attract some of the
lucrative international pilgrim traffic bound for Walsingham, clergy at
Woolpit in Suffolk and the Cluniacs of Thetford on the Norfolk border exploited this trend. The latter assembled a remarkable collection of
relics, which included a piece of Christ's robe, as well as fragments of
his sepulchre and the manger in which he had been laid as an infant,
and these, too, drew crowds in search of healing miracles.[57] Pilgrims may
also have been attracted to the Lady Chapel built and adorned in 1496 by
the more affluent parishioners of the church of the Holy Trinity at Long
Melford in Suffolk, which was approached by a wide ambulatory or 'processional way' allowing ample space for circulation. Did the residents
hope to divert traffic on its way to the region's more famous centres?
In 1529 the statue of the Virgin there was festooned with votive offerings, including rings, enamelled and bejewelled girdles, rosaries of silver,
coral and jet, brooches and buckles set with precious stones, and velvet,
damask and satin vestments, which suggests an auspicious beginning.[58]
In an attempt to counteract the declining appeal and material value of
St William's remains, the Benedictine monks of Norwich set up three such
Marian shrines in the cathedral during the fourteenth century. Neither
they, nor any of the other relics purchased at this time, however,
drew the sick or their donations in significant numbers: although it
might be nurtured from above, the response had to come freely from
below.[59]

Many of the men, women and children who set out each year on pilgrimages would be clutching, or would purchase on arrival, wax images of
diseased body parts as *ex voto* offerings, pledged to the saint either in the
hope of a cure or because one had already taken place. The Canterbury
weaver, whose recovery on the road to Bawburgh is noted above, felt

[56] Desiderius Erasmus, *Colloquies*, in C. R. Thompson (ed.), *Collected Works of Erasmus, XL* (University of Toronto Press, 1997), pp. 632–3.

[57] G. McMurray Gibson, *The Theater of Devotion: East Anglian Drama and Society in the Late Middle Ages* (Chicago, 1989), p. 213 n14; D. Dymond (ed.), *The Register of Thetford Priory, I*, Norfolk Record Society 59 (1994), pp. 30–31, 63; T. Martin, *History of Thetford* (London, 1779), app. XVIII, pp. 81–5.

[58] D. Dymond and C. Paine (eds.), *The Spoil of Long Melford Church: The Reformation in a Suffolk Parish* (Ipswich, 1992), pp. 13–14, and map p. 27; N. Pevsner, *The Buildings of England: Suffolk* (London, 1991), pp. 345–6. Eamon Duffy has suggested to me that the Lady Chapel was built as a speculative venture on the Walsingham model.

[59] J. R. Shinners, 'The Veneration of Saints at Norwich Cathedral in the Fourteenth Century', *Norfolk Archaeology*, 40 (1987), 138.

constrained to fulfil his promise of an *ex voto*:

> A leg of wax he did make . . .
> In his arme he did it beare
> To the towne of Bawburgh, and there it layd
> Before Saint Walston, and heartily prayd.
> Many folkes seing when he did depart,
> Both leg and body hale and querte.[60]

As we have already seen, the application of warm wax to aching limbs or ulcers could prove extremely therapeutic. Wax was a basic ingredient in many 'entretes' or poultices, one such, known significantly as *gratia Dei*, figuring prominently in several late medieval remedy books. Sore breasts and lips were conventionally treated in this way: the celebrated English physician, Gilbertus Anglicus (fl. 1207), recommended the practitioner to 'melte wex and oile of violet or oile de olyf togedir, and put therto the poudir of mastike and olibanum togedir and ther with anoynte the soor'.[61] The *miracula* of William of Norwich vouchsafe a striking example of yet another woman diagnosed as suffering from cancer of the breast (perhaps mastitis) who recovered, or at least obtained temporary respite from pain, after two protracted applications of wax for the modelling of *ex voto*s, while a lame pilgrim from Yorkshire reported that 'as soon as the wax had covered my swollen limbs . . . the swelling subsided so entirely that on removing [it] not a trace was to be seen'.[62] Although they clearly recognised the practical value of such procedures, many sick pilgrims still viewed the preparation of *ex voto*s in a sacred, quasi-magical light. For some it constituted a more personal type of exorcism, whereby 'the disease of the afflicted member is handed over, in an extroversion of deliverance to the healing power'.[63]

That the offering constituted a bargain, or pledge, which the patron saint could not honourably refuse, can hardly have escaped men and women raised in a society of clientage and obligation. For reasons of status as much as desperation, wealthier pilgrims might wish to present their 'good lord', or spiritual benefactor, with a silver, gold or bejewelled *ex voto* or a candle of considerable size instead. The shrine of the Blessed

[60] James, 'Lives of St Walstan', 262–3.
[61] BL, Sloane Ms 521, fols. 266r–66v, 271v–72r; Dawson (ed.), *Leechbook*, pp. 117–19 (for *gratia Dei*), 109–13, 271, 281, 287–9; F. Getz (ed.), *Healing and Society in Medieval England: A Middle English Translation of Gilbertus Anglicus* (Madison: Wisconsin University Press, 1991), pp. 88–9.
[62] Thomas of Monmouth, *St William*, pp. 195–6, 266–7. See also *ibid.*, pp. 250–51, 289–94.
[63] Dupront, *Du sacré*, p. 404; D. Gentilcore, *From Bishop to Witch: The System of the Sacred in Early Modern Terra d'Otranto* (Manchester, 1992), p. 8.

Virgin at Walsingham dripped jewels and shone with the glow of candlelight on plate, so lavish was the patronage bestowed upon it. As the carefully measured wick burned slowly to the base, it must have seemed that the affliction, too, would begin to retreat. When John Paston fell ill in London in 1443, his mother-in-law despatched what was evidently a second (or even third) 'ymmage of wax' of his exact weight to Walsingham, while his wife arranged to make a pilgrimage there on his behalf.[64] On arriving at the same shrine a decade later to pray for an heir, Margaret of Anjou, queen to Henry VI, presented 'a tablet of gold garnished at the borders . . . with ten tronches of pearl, five sapphires and five spinel rubies of rose-red, with an angel in the middle having at the head a cameo . . . and holding between its hands a cross garnished with a ruby and nine oriental pearls'.[65] At the shrine Margaret encountered Cecily, duchess of York, whose repeated and difficult pregnancies proved an even greater cross to bear than the queen's childlessness.[66] Some royal pilgrims, such as Robert Bruce, king of Scotland (d.1329), who reputedly visited Walsingham under safe conduct during his last illness, were as desperate for healing miracles as their subjects, having exhausted all the possibilities of medical science.[67]

Although it appealed to a regional rather than an international clientage, the shrine of St Walstan, a king turned ploughman who had allegedly given all his wealth to the poor, underwent a similar transformation. Its holy well and association with animals suggests an ancient site traditionally connected with pre-Christian rituals of healing, or at least the existence of a popular cult maintained by local people. So numerous were the offerings made at Bawburgh church in the thirteenth century that by 1309 there were sufficient resources to rebuild and lavishly to adorn the chancel, providing space for six chantry priests to celebrate mass for pilgrims.[68] Whether crafted out of wax or solid gold, a notable

---

[64] N. Davis (ed.), *Paston Letters and Papers of the Fifteenth Century*, 2 vols. (Oxford, 1971–6), vol. I, p. 218; Nilson, 'Medieval Experience', p. 107. Finucane, *Rescue of the Innocents*, p. 14, argues that the practice of 'substituting' a candle as a surrogate offering to a saint in cases of illness was confined to children but the practice was ubiquitous: see Rawcliffe, *Medicine and Society*, pp. 22–4.

[65] A. R. Myers, 'The Jewels of Queen Margaret of Anjou', *Bulletin of the John Rylands Library*, 42 (1959–60), 115, 124; J. C. Dickinson, *The Shrine of Our Lady of Walsingham* (Cambridge, 1956), pp. 38–9.

[66] Rawcliffe, *Medicine and Society*, p. 179.

[67] Gillett, *Walsingham*, p. 31. Scottish pilgrims frequently visited Walsingham: Webb, *Pilgrims and Pilgrimage*, pp. 213–14.

[68] G. Jones, 'Authority, Challenge and Identity in Three Gloucestershire Saints' Cults', in D. Mowbray, R. Purdie and I. P. Wei (eds.), *Authority and Community in the Middle Ages* (Stroud, 2000), pp. 126, 127; Twinch, *St Walstan*, pp. 62–4.

proportion of these gifts were a tangible manifestation of human pain and the continuing quest for the miraculous. Yet comparatively few shrines enjoyed more than strictly local appeal for very long. As one declined in popularity, another took its place, sometimes under questionable circumstances.[69] This pattern of change and diversity reflects shifting trends in popular piety, as well as the constant search for health, often born of disappointment and desperation, by individuals whose opportunities for long-distance travel might be limited as much by disability as financial hardship. A conviction that, once arrived in heaven, holy men and women would immediately provide a conduit of healing grace to the sick on earth remained strong. The relics or images of recently deceased individuals of great piety, such as Walter Suffield the saintly bishop of Norwich (d.1257), inevitably attracted attention, although reports of their healing miracles were often short-lived.[70] The case of Richard Caister (d.1420), the 'good vicary' of St Stephen's, Norwich, whose tomb became the centre of a healing cult immediately after his death, provides a good example of the speed with which reputations were established. Margery Kempe had known him as a confessor, and later made a pilgrimage of some forty-five miles to his shrine in thanks for the deathbed recovery of her amanuensis from 'gret sekenes'. It was through men of his sanctity, she reflected, that 'God shewyd mercy to hys pepil'.[71] Inspired by a national rather than a local cult, the miraculous image of King Henry VI (d.1471) at the Benedictine cell of St Leonard's, just outside Norwich, was also reputed to possess curative powers.[72] Prayers to the Lancastrian martyr figure prominently in a book of hours belonging to the Finchams of Norfolk, suggesting that members of the East Anglian gentry commonly invoked his assistance in times of physical and spiritual malaise:

> Feyth full in Cryst enoyntyd Kyng
> Restiryng *bodely helthe* to me
> In disese paynfull languishyng
> Shew gostly helthe thro thi pete
> Disposyng my sowle dewout to be
> Everlastyng helthe to hawe in blys . . . [73]

[69] Duffy, *Stripping of the Altars*, pp. 190–200.
[70] Bartholomew Cotton, *Historia Anglicana*, p. 394.
[71] N. Tanner, *The Church in Late Medieval Norwich* (Toronto, 1984), pp. 231–2; S. B. Meech (ed.), *The Book of Margery Kempe*, EETS, 212 (1940), pp. 147–8; B. Spencer, *Medieval Pilgrim Badges from Norfolk* (Norfolk Museums Service, 1980), p. 25.
[72] Rawcliffe, *Hospitals of Medieval Norwich*, p. 142.
[73] C. F. Richmond, 'Margins and Marginality: English Devotion in the Later Middle Ages', in N. Rogers (ed.), *Endland in the Fifteenth Century* (Stamford, 1994), p. 247.

Hagiographers and shrine-keepers provide valuable evidence of medieval attitudes to sickness and the strategies deployed by men and women in a world beset by pain and loss. Thomas of Monmouth records the arrival of anguished parents with their paralysed children on litters and stretchers and even in wheelbarrows.[74] He itemises almost 120 cases of heart failure, dropsy, blindness, deafness, toothache, constipation, dysentery, cancer, fever, demonic possession, convulsions, epilepsy, sore eyes, insomnia, deformity, ulcers and wasting sickness that were miraculously healed through William's intervention. Such cures appeared all the more remarkable in a society whose understanding of physiology seems so different from our own. It was, for example, hard to determine the extent or seriousness of internal injuries, and, by extension, to distinguish between life and death. Notwithstanding the availability of medical tracts describing the signs of impending mortality, superficial appearances could be misleading. One of the keepers at Thomas Becket's shrine in Canterbury observed laconically that in England resurrections from the dead were common within three days, but comparatively rare after a week.[75] The East Anglian chronicler, John Capgrave (d.1464), believed that almost forty such miracles had occurred at Bromholm, alone, but in the popular imagination even relatively minor saints were held, like Christ, to possess power over death itself. St Walstan of Bawburgh was, for example, said to have breathed life into a thatcher whose body had been placed before his shrine to await burial after it had lain, apparently lifeless, for two days in a shallow pond.[76]

Thomas Gatele, an early fifteenth-century sub-prior of Walsingham, claimed as a boy to have fallen down one of the shrine's two sacred wells, and to have been brought back from the dead through the good offices of the Virgin.[77] His experience was by no means unusual. Accident victims of all ages, apparently stillborn infants, and adults who had collapsed without warning might also be transported to the nearest shrine, where recovery would inevitably be seen as miraculous. The most spectacular cures associated with the 'new painted and new ornamented' image of the Virgin at Thetford Priory concerned lifeless children, one of

---

[74] The scene at Lourdes before 1883 offers a striking analogy: Harris, *Lourdes*, p. 266.

[75] Finucane, *Miracles and Pilgrims*, p. 74. The anatomist, J. B. Winslow, *The Uncertainty of the Signs of Death* (London, 1748), p. 3, describes cases that in an earlier age would have seemed miraculous.

[76] J. Capgrave, *Nova Legenda Angliae* (Wynkyn de Worde, 1516), fol. cviii verso; James, 'Lives of Saint Walstan', 261.

[77] Dickinson, *Our Lady of Walsingham*, p. 12.

25 London, British Library. A sick pilgrim being transported in a wheelbarrow, from Add MS 42130, fol. 186v. Assisted by friends (one of whom carries coins to offer to the shrine) this incapacitated pilgrim makes a difficult journey.

whom had, indeed, already been pronounced dead by a highly respected local surgeon. In cases of this kind the skill, rather than the customary incompetence, of practitioners served to underscore the hopelessness of the situation and the power of the saint. Since it was, moreover, customary on such occasions to invoke a healing saint and sprinkle the body with holy water of the sort Lady Mabel de Bec kept about her person, resuscitations did not even have to occur at a shrine for the keepers to proclaim a miracle.[78] Men, women and children who were fortunate enough to recover quickly from concussion following falls, industrial injuries and traffic accidents also seemed touched by God: an understandable reaction in an age when surgical intervention under such circumstances was actively discouraged. One striking anecdote concerns the courtier, Sir James Berners, who was travelling to Walsingham on a pilgrimage with Richard II, in 1383, when the royal party encountered a thunderstorm at Ely and he was struck by lightning. Since the tomb of St Etheldreda lay nearby, Richard immediately ordered all the clergy to process to 'the shrine of the great virgin' in the cathedral, where his favourite, 'blind and half-crazed' by a vision of the Last Judgement, regained his faculties.[79]

Cases of this type offered dramatic and apparently incontestable proof of divine healing. Yet most reputed miracles seem, on close inspection, to have been neither so clear-cut or immediate. Two important considerations need to be borne in mind when we examine medieval attitudes to spiritual as well as earthly medicine. First, expectations were generally far lower than they are in the West today. Evidence from the numerous medical malpractice cases to survive from the later Middle Ages confirms that the boundary between sickness and health was at best ill-defined and fluid: the restoration of limited mobility or lessening of pain was often all a patient hoped for. One case, heard in the petty pleas at Ipswich in 1415, involved a failed attempt to treat blindness, the criterion for success established at the outset being that the plaintiff would be able to distinguish one colour from another.[80] It is, of course, quite possible to do this while still remaining visually impaired. Success was entirely subjective, and might prove short-lived. Chronic toothache and constipation, ubiquitous features of medieval life, clearly fell into this category, as did malaria (endemic throughout the fen and marshland areas of East Anglia) and other

---

[78] Martin, *History of Thetford*, app. XVIII, pp. 93–4. See Finucane, *Rescue of the Innocents*, pp. 101–49, for *miracula* following childhood accidents.

[79] L. C. Hector and B. F. Harvey (eds.), *The Westminster Chronicle 1381–1394* (Oxford, 1982), p. 43.

[80] 'Ita quod discerneret unum colore ab alio infra octo dies tunc proxima': Suffolk Record Office, Ipswich, C5/9 (Petty Pleas, 2–3 Henry V).

diseases liable to periods of remission. Even when the process of canonisation was involved, no sustained attempt was made to monitor the pilgrim's progress after he or she had returned home. Secondly, we should remember the derivation of the word 'patient'. Living as they did in a world of pain, disease and death, medieval men and women were accustomed – but hardly any less sensitive – to physical discomfort, and rarely expected instant results. Human suffering was, after all, an inevitable condition of life after the Fall, to be accepted and endured in the hope of redemption. Nor did they possess a keenly developed sense of time. Pilgrims were prepared to trudge from one shrine to the next, in the hope that one day their faith would be rewarded and they would be deemed worthy of a cure. On arrival they settled down to wait, perhaps for days on end. Not surprisingly, those with self-limiting complaints often experienced some improvement as, no doubt, did many victims of psychosomatic disorders. The less fortunate were advised to accept God's will with humility, lest they incur further punishment for questioning the divine physician.[81]

Because medieval ideas about the aetiology of disease and the terminology used to describe it were so very different from our own, most attempts at retrospective diagnosis remain impressionistic and are generally best avoided altogether.[82] Shrine-keepers and hagiographers derived their understanding of human physiology from classical medical theory, with the result that, in the relatively few cases where physical symptoms are recorded in any detail, the explanation hinges upon humoral imbalances or blockages, which the saint miraculously dispels. In some of St Edmund's miracles these noxious humours are described in language that clearly invites comparison with sin, creeping through the body and overwhelming its defences.[83] By and large, however, chroniclers employ an unspecific and limited vocabulary, without much in the way of elaboration: pilgrims are blind, or crooked, possessed by demons, palsied, feverish, dropsical or afflicted with sores. The frame of reference, as we have seen, is consciously and deliberately biblical, conforming to a predetermined model. The ubiquity of pathological conditions likely to disappear or enter periods of remission during the pilgrimage season in spring and summer is, none the less, striking.[84] St Walstan, a king turned ploughman, placed 'mowers and sythe [*sic*] followers' under

[81] T. F. Crane (ed.), *The Exempla of Jacques de Vitry* (Kraus reprint, 1967, of Folk Lore Society 26, 1890), no. ccliv.

[82] M. MacDonald, 'Anthropological Perspectives on the History of Science and Medicine', in P. Corsi and P. Weindling (eds.), *Information Sources in the History of Science and Medicine* (London, 1983), p. 71.

[83] As e.g. Arnold (ed.), *Memorials of St Edmund's Abbey*, vol. I, pp. 191, 200, 374.

[84] See King, *Hippocrates' Woman*, p. 100, for classical analogies.

his special protection, and many of his miracles did, indeed, concern crippled farm-workers, who welcomed warmer weather and a rest from heavy labour before the harvest.[85] Far more common than it is today in the West, and ubiquitous in the records made by shrine-keepers, blindness was often a result of poor nutrition, parasitic infections and dirty, smoke-filled domestic surroundings. In many cases a simple change of diet or living conditions would alone have occasioned a noticeable improvement. Xerophthalmia, which in its early stages causes temporary or partial visual impairment, arises from a lack of retonil (from vitamin A or compounds such as beta-carotene) and must have dogged rural communities whose winter diet consisted largely of cereals and root vegetables.[86] Crowded and unhygienic living quarters provided ideal conditions for the spread of trachoma, another eye disease initially characterised by intermittent bouts of disability, discomfort and scarring identical to those described with such regularity in the surviving sources. Among the miracles attributed to St Edmund was the cure of a three-year-old girl from Colchester who had been blind for five weeks, and of a young man whose sudden *malus in oculo* was regarded as a punishment for blasphemy, but probably had more to do with diet or infection. In the latter case, we are told that the charms and mutterings of old women proved powerless to help him, which serves as a reminder that most people's first resort was to a wise woman or herbalist.[87]

Seasonal changes in diet must also have had a beneficial effect on the boils, running sores and other debilitating – often pre-scorbutic – skin conditions loosely described by shrine-keepers as 'ulcers'. Contaminated or adulterated food gave rise to intestinal problems at all levels of society, but especially among the poor. It has been convincingly argued that some of the more spectacular cases of violent dementia, where the sufferer was dragged bound and chained to church, were, in fact, the result of ergotism, which is caused by poisoned rye. But to contemporaries be-haviour of the kind displayed by the son of Richard de Needham before the shrine of William of Norwich offered indisputable evidence of de-monic possession, which only God or his saints could bring to an end.[88]

[85] James, 'Lives of St Walstan', 238–67.

[86] Finucane, *Miracles and Pilgrims*, pp. 106–7, offers this interpretation. For supporting evidence, see C. E. West, 'Vitamin A and Carotenoids', in J. Mann and A. S. Truswell (eds.), *Essentials of Human Nutrition* (Oxford, 1998), p. 179.

[87] Arnold (ed.), *Memorials of St Edmund's Abbey*, vol I, pp. 83–4, 145–6. See also *ibid.*, pp. 77–8, 91–2, 160, 181–2. John Capgrave recorded nineteen cures of blindness at Bromholm: *Nova Legenda*, fol. cviii verso.

[88] Thomas of Monmouth, *St William*, pp. 203–5, 223–4; Finucane, *Miracles and Pilgrims*, pp. 107–8. See also Ward, *Miracles and the Medieval Mind*, pp. 142–3, and V. H. Bauer, *Das Antonius-Feuer in Kunst und Medizin* (Berlin, 1973), pp. 73–4.

William's equally spectacular 'cure' of the deranged Sieldeware of Belaugh, who was brought in fetters on an eight-mile pilgrimage to Norwich, recalls the two detailed descriptions of dementia later provided by Margery Kempe in her autobiography. Both of these cases followed childbirth, and may perhaps have resulted from puerperal psychosis, although we should remember that Margery regarded her own mental collapse as divine retribution for failing to make a full confession, and her cure as the work of *Christus Medicus*.[89] In an intense, claustrophobic atmosphere, heady with the smell of incense and the shimmer of candles, outbreaks of mass hysteria cannot have been uncommon. In his *Dialogue Concerning Heresies*, Thomas More describes how the adolescent daughter of Sir Roger Wentworth was apparently released from demonic possession before a large crowd at the famous shrine of the Blessed Virgin in Ipswich:

beyng brought and layde before the ymage of our blessyd lady, [she] was there in the syght of many worshypfull people so greuously tourmented and in face, eyen, loke and countenaunce so grysely chaunged, with her mouthe drawen asyde and her eyen layde out vpon her chekes, that it was a terrible syght to beholde. And, after many merueyllous thynges at the same tyme shewed vpon dyuers persones by the deuyll, thorowe goddes sufferaunce, as well all the remenaunt as the mayden her selfe in the presence of all the company restored to theyr good state perfytely cured and sodeynly.[90]

For all its immediacy and circumstantial detail, More's account replicates set-piece descriptions of exorcisms to be found centuries earlier.

An analysis of English shrines and their clientele undertaken by R. C. Finucane, in his important study of *Miracles and Pilgrims*, shows that, generally speaking, rich pilgrims were less likely to display symptoms of diseases associated with hard manual labour, dietary deficiencies and squalid living conditions, while poor women, not surprisingly, were the most vulnerable of all.[91] They were also the group most likely to invoke the cult of saints at an early stage in the hierarchy of resort, while elite males (including monks) would, as we have seen, almost certainly turn first to earthly medicine or surgery. The threat to health of repeated pregnancies and the very real possibility of death in childbirth loomed large over all medieval women, whether queens or paupers, although malnutrition, deformity and squalid surroundings, sometimes shared with domestic

---

[89] Thomas of Monmouth, *St William*, pp. 226–7; Meech (ed.), *Book of Margery Kempe*, pp. 6–9, 177–9. M. MacDonald, *Mystical Bedlam: Madness, Anxiety and Healing in Seventeenth Century England* (Cambridge, 1981), pp. 198–217, offers a valuable survey of early ideas about dementia.

[90] T. M. C. Lawler (ed.), *The Complete Works of Saint Thomas More, VI* (New Haven, CT: Yale University Press, 1981), p. 93.

[91] Finucane, *Miracles and Pilgrims*, pp. 130–51.

animals, inevitably worsened the plight of the female poor.[92] The risks increased during periods of high population density. An examination of skeletal material from one of the more deprived areas of late eleventh-century Norwich, for example, reveals that adult women were then lucky to reach the age of 33, dying, on average, some three years later than men, who were exposed to an unusually high level of physical injury during their twenties. Children were even more vulnerable. Infant mortality, clearly affected by maternal health, was there running at about 63 per cent, and around 50 per cent in similar communities in medieval York.[93] The case of Gurwain the Tanner, who made a pilgrimage to William of Norwich's tomb in the hope of saving the only one of his six sons to survive infancy, was all too typical.[94] Standards of living may have improved among those who survived late medieval outbreaks of plague, but life seemed no less transitory. In the Clopton family chantry at Long Melford, a few yards from the Lady Chapel with its lavish *ex voto* offerings, were painted verses by the Bury St Edmunds monk, John Lydgate. These served to warn the fifteenth-century pilgrim that time in this vale of tears was short:

> Tarye no lenger toward thyn herytage
> Hast on thy weye and be of ryght good chere,
> Go eche day onward on thy pylgrymage,
> Thynke howe short tyme thou hast abyden here.[95]

As St Augustine had reminded his readers, the discomforts of pregnancy, suffering in childbirth, miscarriage, the loss of infants and maternal mortality were a bitter legacy, bequeathed by Eve to each of her daughters. Yet redemption might be achieved through the agency of Christ and his saints, to whom women turned, with optimism as well as fear, at this potentially dangerous time. Being herself without sin, the Virgin Mary had given birth without pain, and thus seemed to offer special protection.[96]

During the sixteenth century English reforming bishops, who were responsible for the licensing of midwives, sought to prevent them from

---

[92] For a broader discussion of these problems see Finucane, *Rescue of the Innocents*, pp. 17–53; H. Leyser, *Medieval Women: A Social History of Women in England 450–1500* (London, 1995), pp. 122–33; D. Jacquart and C. Thomasset, *Sexuality and Medicine in the Middle Ages* (Oxford, 1988), pp. 168–88.

[93] B. Ayers (ed.), *Excavations within the North-East Bailey of Norwich Castle*, East Anglian Archaeology, 28 (Norwich:1985), pp. 49–58; J. D. Dawes and J. R. Magilton, *The Cemetery of St Helen on the Walls, Aldwark* (York Archaeological Trust, 1980), p. 63.

[94] Thomas of Monmouth, *St William*, p. 167.

[95] McMurray Gibson, *Theater of Devotion*, p. 89. The verses may still be seen in the Clopton Chantry: Pevsner, *Suffolk*, p. 347 and pl. 16b.

[96] Recourse to saints during childbirth was not, however, gender specific, as Becket's recorded miracles reveal: Finucane, *Rescue of the Innocents*, pp. 17–53.

encouraging women in labour to enlist the help of saints or relics, such as the numerous holy girdles that decorated miraculous images of the Virgin or St Mary Magdalen (one of each being kept, respectively, at the priories of Bromholm and Thetford) and were occasionally hired out by shrine-keepers for royal or aristocratic women to wear during their confinements.[97] The less well-connected made do with paper rolls, bearing representations of the *arma Christi* and other sacred objects, which they may already have seen and venerated in person on antenatal pilgrimages.[98] Many wore *ampullae* containing holy water or cheap metal pilgrim badges depicting the Virgin and Child, the Annunciation or the Holy House of Walsingham (a wooden replica of the dwelling in Nazareth where medieval men and women believed the Incarnation had begun) throughout pregnancy and during labour.[99] As an elderly woman, Margery Kempe, herself the mother of fourteen children, travelled further afield to Cologne in 1433 to see 'owr Ladys smokke', which was thought to assist women in childbirth. She may well have returned with a badge depicting the *sancta roba*, Virgin and Child similar to one fashioned into an ornate pendant recently unearthed in Pottergate, Norwich.[100] Devices of this kind provided valuable aids to meditation in an age of growing lay spirituality. They were also powerful symbols of fertility. Despite the obvious risks of childbirth, failure to conceive or produce a living heir weighed heavily with women from all social classes, as we have seen in the case of Margaret of Anjou. To look upon and wear such auspicious images promised a more hopeful outcome than the various potions and *regimina* recommended by practitioners 'ad conceptum'. Indeed, since medical authorities maintained that conception and the ensuing health of the embryo could be affected by whatever thoughts and images impressed themselves upon the mother's mind, pilgrimage and its artifacts here marched in step with scientific theory.[101] Surviving

---

[97] PRO, SP1/102/112; Martin, *History of Thetford*, app. XVIII, p. 85; Rawcliffe, *Medicine and Society*, pp. 96, 180. The silver and enamel girdle on a green fabric given by 'Madam Broke' and the red girdle with a cross attached presented by 'Madam Tye' to the statue of the Virgin at Long Melford were probably available for similar purposes: Dymond and Paine, *Spoils of Melford Church*, p. 13.

[98] One such roll, Wellcome Institute Library, London, Western Ms 632, depicts the instruments of the passion on one side, and promises a safe delivery on the other: 'Yf a woman travell [travail] wyth chylde gyrdes thys mesure abowte hyr wombe and she shall be safe delyvyrd wythowte parelle [peril]'.

[99] Spencer, *Medieval Pilgrim Badges*, pp. 10–19.

[100] Meech (ed.), *Book of Margery Kempe*, pp. 237, 346–8; S. Margerson, *Norwich Households: The Medieval and Post-Medieval Finds from Norwich Survey Excavations 1971–1978*, East Anglian Archaeology 58 (Norwich, 1993), p. 8.

[101] Pinto, 'Folk Practice of Gynaecology', 520; J. Musacchio, *The Art and Ritual of Childbirth in Renaissance Italy* (New York, 1999), pp. 127–39, 144; J. C. Bologne, *La naissance interdite: sterilité, avortement, conception au moyen âge* (Paris, 1988), pp. 107–37; J. Cadden,

26 Norwich, Norfolk Museum Service. Copper alloy badge from Cologne showing the *Sancta roba*. Excavated at Pottergate, the badge depicts the Virgin Mary, the Christ Child and the Holy Robe, a celebrated relic deemed to help women at various stages of conception, pregnancy and labour.

depictions of the Annunciation and of members of the Holy Family (notably the thrice-married St Anne) in churches at East Barsham,

Meanings of Sex Difference in the Middle Ages: Medicine, Science and Culture (Cambridge, 1993), pp. 243–53; Jacquart and Thomasset, *Sexuality and Medicine*, p. 83. The stigma of childlessness is discussed by Goodich, *Violence and Miracle*, pp. 88–9, and Finucane, *Rescue of the Innocents*, pp. 18–23. Typical recipes 'for to gete a knaue chylde' may be found in BL, Royal Ms 17 A VIII, fols. 63v–65r.

Bale and Houghton on the approaches to Walsingham should remind us of this important aspect of pilgrimage. So too should the golden image of St Margaret, patron saint of women in childbirth, which flanked that of the Virgin Mary at the shrine itself and was despoiled at the Dissolution.[102]

In 1538, the evangelical bishop of Salisbury, Nicholas Shaxton, who became master of the Great Hospital, Norwich, warned the midwives in his diocese to cease urging women 'in travail to make any foolish vow to go in pilgrimage to this image or that image', but he faced an uphill struggle.[103] Obstetrics, as the fourteenth-century French surgeon Guy de Chauliac scornfully noted, was a 'field haunted by women', where the arrival of the male practitioner almost invariably spelt death and dismemberment.[104] In this respect, as in so many others, pilgrimage was comfortably absorbed into an ancient, pre-Christian tradition of folk-healing through the use of amulets, incantations and sacred objects, which the medieval Church attempted to harness for its own purposes of social control. Although the fifteen days' labour reputedly endured in 1144 by the wife of a Norwich cook was far from typical, her resort to the occult power of relics and plants associated with the recently martyred William reflects widespread contemporary practice. In reducing tension, offering solace and helping the mother overcome her fear, such measures may have proved beneficial.[105] However much learned authorities such as de Chauliac, who was himself a papal chaplain, may have disparaged the invocation of saints and use of charms in healing, the boundaries were inevitably blurred. Recourse to prayer and other aspects of sacred medicine was often the first response of the practitioner, whatever his background, in any medical emergency, when the patient seemed likely to bleed to death or was gripped by a violent seizure. Although medieval physicians attempted to treat epilepsy through the use of medication and humoral

---

[102] C. L. S. Linnell, 'The Commonplace Book of Robert Reynys of Acle', *Norfolk Archaeology*, 32 (1961), 126.

[103] W. H. Frere and W. M. Kennedy (eds.), *Visitation Articles and Injunctions*, 3 vols. (London, 1910), vol. II, p. 58. See also D. Cressy, *Birth, Marriage and Death: Ritual, Religion and the Life Cycle in Tudor and Stuart England* (Oxford, 1997), pp. 22–3, 64.

[104] M. S. Ogden (ed.), *The Cyrurgie of Guy de Chauliac*, EETS, 265 (1971), p. 530. Two of the miracles attributed to William of Norwich concerned women with 'an issue of blood', probably from *fistulae* sustained in childbirth, while another involved a woman traumatised by a difficult labour: Thomas of Monmouth, *St William*, pp. 133, 169–70, 206.

[105] Thomas of Monmouth, *St William*, pp. 78–9; F. Harris Stoertz, 'Suffering and Survival in Medieval English Childbirth', in C. Jorgensen Itnyre (ed.), *Medieval Family Roles* (New York, 1996), pp. 101–20, notably 112–13.

management, most recognised that, in the last resort, a higher power alone could protect the patient from harm.[106] The charms, prayers and incantations deployed on such occasions were not only highly ritualised, with regard to the gestures (repeatedly making the sign of the Cross) and repetitions (usually multiples of three) involved, but also referred constantly to past miracles, thus giving the patient the same reassuring sense of divine order or integration into a 'collective mythology' as that experienced by the sick pilgrim on her or his arrival before a shrine.[107] John Crophill of Wix, for instance, recorded charms for wounds and childbirth in a commonplace book which also included abstracts of scientific texts on uroscopy and the lunar cycle.[108] Such eclecticism seemed entirely natural, reflecting the rich diversity of medieval medical practice, of which pilgrimage constituted a crucial part.

Whether their search was for physical or spiritual health, medieval men and women drew comfort and reassurance from their communion with the saints. Pilgrimage offered a sense of purpose and personal empowerment in an uncertain world, a 'mental mechanism' for 'disciplining the archaic forces of the cosmos'.[109] Energetically promoted by the Church and a fundamental part of religious life at all levels of society, it bestowed sufficient tangible benefits to occupy a prominent place in the lives of the sick and disabled throughout the Middle Ages and beyond, not least because it drew upon and reinforced popular traditions of healing. Nor, in a society convinced of the symbiotic relationship between body and soul, could the physiological effects of spiritual medicine and the power of belief be lightly dismissed.[110] We should not, however, assume that every pilgrim approached shrines encumbered by guilt or burdened by sin. Indifferent to, or ignorant of, the niceties of medieval theology, the majority of medieval East Anglian pilgrims – like their counterparts in twentieth-century rural France – regarded saints as potent forces for healing or destruction, who were to be propitiated through the

---

[106] Jones, 'Thomas Fayreford', 175–7; Jones, 'Harley Ms 2558: A Fifteenth-Century Medieval Commonplace Book', in M. R. Schleissner (ed.), *Manuscript Sources of Medieval Medicine* (New York, 1995), pp. 47, 50–51; Rawcliffe, *Medicine and Society*, pp. 94–9.

[107] E. Bozóky, 'Mythic Mediation in Healing Incantations', in S. Campbell *et al.* (eds.), *Health, Disease and Healing in Medieval Culture* (New York, 1992), pp. 84–92; Jacquart, *Médecine médiévale*, p. 440. For examples see T. Hunt (ed.), *Popular Medicine in Thirteenth-Century England* (Woodbridge, 1990), pp. 78–99.

[108] Ayoub, 'John Crophill's Books', pp. 214–32. See also BL, Sloane Ms 3548, a collection of medical, chemical and religious tracts, which includes an account of the miracles of the Virgin (fols. 7r–7v) alongside standard texts on herbal medicine and uroscopy.

[109] Dupront, *Du sacré*, pp. 451–2.   [110] Harris, *Lourdes*, pp. 304–19.

appropriate rituals.[111] But as well as being stern judges and harsh lords, they appeared, like Christ and his mother, as physicians and nurses, anxious to ameliorate the lot of suffering humanity. 'Be of good cheer, brother, your recovery is at hand', William of Norwich reassured one of his patients, demonstrating an exemplary bedside manner of the kind each and every medieval practitioner was urged to emulate.[112]

[111] S. Wilson (ed.), *Saints and their Cults: Studies in Religious Sociology, Folklore and History* (Cambridge, 1983), pp. 29, 39. A. Bensa, *Les saints guérisseurs du Preche-Gouet* (Paris, 1978), pp. 231–4, provides modern analogies.

[112] Thomas of Monmouth, *St William*, p. 191; M. McVaugh, 'Bedside Manners in the Middle Ages', *Bulletin of the History of Medicine*, 71 (1997), 216.

5   Pilgrimage to Jerusalem in the late Middle Ages

Colin Morris

> Some people rather foolishly suppose . . . that there is no other country
> than the one where they were born. Some again, although they know that
> other countries exist, are like a mother who with unmeasured affection
> always says that her children are the most beautiful, and they say that
> their own land is like shining day compared with the gloominess of
> night.[1]

With these words, Anselm Adorno began the dedication of his account of
his pilgrimage to the Holy Land in 1471. He was offering it to King James
III of Scotland, with whom he had close connections, and he proceeded to
rehearse the names of famous men who, throughout history, had travelled
the world.

As we have seen in the Introduction, most pilgrimage was local pilgrimage, but the great continental routes were also frequented by English
travellers. Chaucer's Wife of Bath had been to Rome, to Compostela and
(three times) to Jerusalem. Fewer English people went to Jerusalem than
to the other two, but the pilgrimage to the Holy Land nonetheless deserves
our attention because it presents us with a dimension of travel different
from journeys within Western Europe, and even more from those within
England. Travel to Jerusalem was hugely more expensive and more dangerous. It also had a special quality in terms of devotion. The intense
attachment to the crucified humanity of Jesus that was so characteristic
of the later Middle Ages has been called 'a mysticism of the historical
event', and the place of that event was Jerusalem.[2] In these respects, the
Jerusalem pilgrimage stands out among the others. English evidence is
less abundant than that on the continent. The greater distance that had
to be covered, and the relative accessibility of Compostela as a goal for
English pilgrims, discouraged large-scale travel to Palestine. The English

---

[1] J. Heers and G. de Groer (eds. and trans.), *Itinéraire d'Anselme Adorno en Terre Sainte
(1470–1)* (Paris: ECNRS, 1978), p. 26.
[2] The phrase is that of Ewert Cousins, 'The Humanity and the Passion of Christ', in
Jill Raitt (ed.), *Christian Spirituality: High Middle Ages and Reformation* (London: SCM,
1987), p. 383.

experience has to be understood within the total European pilgrimage to Jerusalem, but within that framework it has some special features to offer.[3]

The fall of Acre in 1291 had made it much more difficult to visit the Holy Land. Once the Franciscan community was established on Mount Sion by 1336, however, a regular system for pilgrimage was rapidly created, which remained remarkably stable for two centuries. One or two pilgrim galleys sailed from Venice each year, and the transport was carefully regulated by the Republic. There is no proper way of estimating numbers, which obviously varied from time to time, but it is safe to say that during the last two medieval centuries a yearly average of something like 300 pilgrims sailed by the dedicated galleys from Venice. This rather small figure does not include people who made their own arrangements to travel on merchant shipping by other routes, or who hired their own vessel, and it may not take proper account of accompanying retinues or of the poor who travelled on charity. If English pilgrims were less numerous than those from Italy or Germany, they nonetheless included people from influential sections of society. A future king, Henry of Bolingbroke, paid a brief visit to Jerusalem in 1393 after his journey to Prussia. The exiled Thomas Mowbray, duke of Norfolk, died in Venice on his way back in 1399. Prominent men often travelled with a substantial retinue: 50 went with Bartholomew Burghersh in 1348, 30 with Hugh Neville in 1349. We also find occasional references to English travellers who are otherwise unrecorded, some of whom were clearly influential and interesting people. In 1467, Sir Arthur Ormesby, a rich landowner, devout and well read, resolved 'to visite the holy citte of Jherusalem and also other holy places to the same adioinyng'. He made provision 'to scole a pour child born in North Turkey whose name was Miter afore he resceived the sacrament of Baptisme and of my goodnes he was brought into this land . . . whiche child is called Hugh Arthur'.[4] We encounter two more Englishmen, anonymous this time, in the narrative of friar Felix Fabri, when in 1480 he found they were the only available companions for a pilgrimage to Mount Sinai. Since, true to the genius of their island race, they

---

[3] Surveys of the pilgrim literature as a whole are limited in number. Among the best are D. R. Howard, *Writers and Pilgrims: Medieval Pilgrimage Narratives and their Posterity* (Berkeley University Press, 1980), and J. Richard, *Les récits de voyages et de pèlerinages*, Typologie des sources du moyen âge occidental, fasc.38 (Turnhout: Brepols, 1981). Otherwise, the main studies have been in German. U. Ganz-Blättler, *Andacht und Abenteuer: Berichte europäischer Jerusalem- und Santiago-Pilger (1320–1520)* (Tübingen: Jakobus Studien, 1990) provides an impressive analysis, with discussion of, and references to, earlier work.

[4] J. C. Challenor Smith, 'A Note on the Brass to Philip Carew, 1414', *Surrey Archaeological Collections*, 43 (1935), 53–60. I am grateful to Matthew Groom for supplying this reference.

spoke no language other than their own, he postponed the expedition.[5] Quite apart from actual travellers, England displayed a high level of interest in the Holy Land: written descriptions were in demand and a sense of responsibility for its well-being continued to exist in royal circles. In 1395, Philippe de Mézières described it to Richard II as the king's 'propre heritage', purchased by Christ's passion.[6]

Apart from the Franciscan house on Mount Sion, there were no Latin communities of clergy in the holy places that would be visited in the East. Indeed, most of these shrines were actually in ruins. Hence, there are virtually no local accounts of visits, and as a result records of miraculous healings, so important in the records of Western shrines, are so rare that they can effectively be ignored. There are indeed stories of what we might call institutional miracles: marvels attached to holy places that are repeated throughout the centuries. The wonderful lighting of the holy fire at the Sepulchre each Easter eve is the most obvious of these.

These stories are preserved within a remarkable set of sources, essentially peculiar to the Holy Land tour: the pilgrim narratives. By themselves, they constitute a major literary genre. They continued in high demand in the early days of printing, and the more influential ones were still being read well into the modern period. Any calculation of the number of these works must be a matter of convention, since it is far from clear (within a genre in which borrowings, translations, and free adaptations are common) just what should be deemed to be an independent composition. Ursula Ganz Blättler estimates 262 composed in the two centuries after 1320, with more than half of them falling between 1440 and 1500.[7] The density of the occurrence of these works can be startling: there are, for example, six accounts of the 1458 pilgrimage, while that of 1483 produced three of major importance. For a long time these books were discounted because they were regarded as repetitive. Scholars as prominent as Röhricht and Sonnenfeld suggested that they had been based on a guidebook or Baedecker, which could be purchased at Venice, and attempts have even been made to reconstitute the precise text of this missing book.[8] It is perfectly true that there is a great deal of common material, especially in the descriptions of the visits to holy places. A large proportion of the authors included details of the indulgences available at each of the sites, which so strongly attracted the traffic of pilgrims, and – a little

[5] A. Stewart (trans.), *The Wanderings of Felix Fabri* (London Palestine Pilgrims Text Society, 1887–97, reprint 1971), vol. I, p. 24.

[6] For references, see C. Tyerman, *England and the Crusades* (London: University of Chicago Press, 1988), pp. 280–7.

[7] Ganz-Blättler, *Andacht und Abenteuer*, pp. 39–40.

[8] See especially J. Brefeld, *A Guidebook for the Jerusalem Pilgrimage in the Late Middle Ages* (Hilversum: Neth, 1994).

more surprisingly – they were fond of giving details of the various types of Christian community represented in Palestine. The most likely source of this common information are the Franciscans, who, soon after their arrival on Mount Sion, established a series of brief tours around Mount Sion itself, the church of the Holy Sepulchre, the streets of Jerusalem, the Mount of Olives, and the surrounding districts. These tours did not vary much over the centuries, and the lists of them, with brief explanation of the sites, had a huge amount in common. In addition, writers borrowed heavily from each other, normally without acknowledgement. Felix Fabri, whose huge account of his travels in 1480–3 is perhaps the most interesting example of this whole literature, is an exception here: he was learned in the past literature of the Holy Land, and on occasions was painstaking about citing his references. He tells us, for example, that in describing the Holy Sepulchre itself he used the account of Hans Tucher of Nuremberg, who had spent a long time there in 1479, and whose work he had brought with him on his journey. The English writers show the usual pattern of mutual dependence. Thus, Richard Torkyngton in 1517 closely followed some of the descriptions in the anonymous account of the pilgrimage of Sir Richard Guylforde in 1506.[9]

Throughout Western Europe, authors tended to combine the framework of a diary with a list of the 'pilgrimages' conducted by the Franciscans around Jerusalem. In the most elaborate accounts, that structure might be concealed within a more extensive narrative: among others, brother Felix tells us more than once how he made daily notes of events and place-names on his wax tablets. Several of the English narratives retained this sort of diary format, but described what happened in an exceedingly sober manner. The writer of the Guylforde narrative recorded events day by day, and provided the conventional list of pilgrim visits, with a few descriptive notes. He noted that the 'temple of the Holy Sepulchre', as he called it, is made 'after the fourme and makynge of the Temple at London, saffe it is fer excedynge in gretenesse'. He included a few judicious reflections designed to be of use to later travellers. He warns them that his party had a particularly awful return voyage, because they had started too late from Venice, 'by reason whereof we had no tyme to perfourme our pylgrymage and retourne to Venyce before the comyng of ye deed wynter season'. He recorded conventional expressions of devotion, telling us how the party thanked 'Almighty God with all our hertes of ye

[9] Stewart (trans.), *The Wanderings of Felix Fabri*, vol. I, pp. 403–4; W. J. Loftie (ed.), *Ye Oldest Diarie of Englysshe Travel, being the hitherto unpublished Narrative of the Pilgrimage of Sir Richard Torkyngton to Jerusalem in 1517* (London, 1884); Henry Ellis (ed.), *The Pylgrymage of Sir Richard Guylforde to the Holy Land, A.D. 1506* (London: Camden Society, 1851).

grete grace that he gave unto us to se and vysyte the sayde blessyd places and holy cytie ones in our lyves or thanne we dyed'; but as a whole he displayed a remarkable lack of feeling. The death of Sir Richard Guylforde, the senior member of their party, was simply recorded as a fact, essentially without any profession of regret.[10] The author, like Brygg (1392) before him, and Torkyngton (1517) after him, belongs to the most sober and factual diary tradition. Whatever one's doubts about national characteristics extending through the centuries, these solemn English travellers do make one think of the stiff upper lip of the imperial future.

The outstanding writer in this group was Mr William Wey, a Fellow of Eton, and subsequently an Augustinian canon of the rich house of Edington in Wiltshire. He visited Compostela in 1456, and Jerusalem twice in 1458 and 1462. He was exceptional in the breadth of the information that he offered. At his death, he left to Edington what is essentially a collection of papers, a file rather than a composed book. These papers are directed to both devotional and practical needs, and show a concern for a wide range of pilgrims. The extent of the influence of the collection is more doubtful: there is only one manuscript, and the only text that seems to have drawn from it was the short and anonymous *Informacion for Pylgrymes*. The collection, as it stands, launches first into a list of the comparative value of Mediterranean currencies, and advice where you should select your berth on the ship: 'the lawyst under hyt ys ryght smolderyng and stynkyng'. On no account plan to land at Famagusta in Cyprus, he warns his readers, 'for meny Englysch men and other also have dyde'. There is a long list of the 'holy places in the stations of Jerusalem', and another, separately, of the 'holy stations'. The prevailing usage throughout the late Middle Ages was to describe these tours as 'pilgrimages'. Liturgically these pauses for prayers were 'stations' in the course of a procession, and William's usage is interesting because later 'the stations of the cross' became a standard term to describe the stops along the route that Christ took to Calvary. He seems to be the first witness to its use. The writer then proceeds to a Latin narrative of his two itineraries to the Holy Land. There are other memoranda, too: an English–Greek lexicon, a list of the ten reasons for going to the Holy Land, and a number of queries about the holy places. Most of this is in Latin, and is evidently designed to provide information to readers who are in charge of a pilgrimage.

At the same time, William Wey provided an English verse account of the Holy Land, which is presumably directed to less learned circles. It possesses little poetic quality, but provides instruction in the sort of basic

---

[10] Ellis, *The Pylgrymage of Sir Richard Guylforde*, pp. 24, 40, 56.

devotion enjoined by the pilgrim narratives:

> And, when wee be passyd that place,
> We schal se Jerusalem in short space.
> Then knele we downe upon our kne,
> When we that holy cyte see:
> For to all that thydyr come
> Is yeve and graunt ful remyssioun.[11]

The works which we have considered so far were focused almost exclusively on Jerusalem. There were, however, others that associated a visit to Jerusalem with wider travels, and with a keen curiosity about unfamiliar topography, climate, customs and animals. It is sometimes supposed that literature of this sort, which ranged widely beyond a specific devotion to the holy places, indicates the advent of the Renaissance.[12] Without any question, some writers were aware of the contrast between devotion and curiosity as motives for travel. Santo Brasca advised his readers

to make the journey solely with the intention of visiting, contemplating and adoring with great effusion of tears those most holy mysteries... and not with the intention of seeing the world or from ambition and pride to say, 'Been there! Seen that!'.[13]

But Brasca was a noble at the court of Milan in 1480, and might conventionally be counted less as a champion of the old ways than as a Renaissance man. In reality, pilgrimage and travel stories had been combined more than a century previously. The accounts of journeys into Asia, written by friars and by the famous Marco Polo, had created a taste for compendious travel literature early in the fourteenth century. Thereafter, visits to more distant shrines such as St Catherine's in Sinai or Sardenay near Damascus were combined, in some writers, with much more ambitious journeys and with reports of the lands that they had visited. William of Boldensele (1334–6) was one of the first representatives of this new approach. Niccolò of Poggibonsi (1346–9) travelled widely in Egypt and the Middle East. The Spaniard, Pero Tafur (1435), visited Egypt, contemplated a journey to India, and came back via Constantinople and Germany. Bertrandon de la Broquière (1433–8) also made the perilous journey through the Ottoman dominions, in spite of serious warnings

---

[11] B. Bandinel (ed.), *The Itineraries of William Wey* (London: Roxburgh Club, 1856), pp. 1, 4–5, 9, 20; see also G. H. Freeling (ed.), *Informacion for Pylgrymes unto the Holy Londe* (London: Roxburgh Club, 1824), and the discussion in D. R. Howard, *Writers and Pilgrims*, ch. 1.

[12] This view is argued by F. Tinguely, 'Janus en Terre Sainte: la figure du pèlerin curieux à la Renaissance', *Revue des Sciences Humaines*, 245 (1997), 51–65.

[13] Cited Ganz-Blättler, *Andacht und Abenteur*, p. 233.

and in Eastern dress. These examples of wide-ranging travel all antedate the middle of the fifteenth century. England has a peculiar involvement in this scene. The greatest travel book of the Middle Ages was written, so its author claimed, by an English knight, Sir John Mandeville, who left England in 1322, spent three decades in journeys to all the known world, and wrote his *Travels* about 1357. The book was immensely influential. There are about 300 existing medieval manuscripts (about four times as many as for Marco Polo) and numerous printed editions, and it can be found, during the late Middle Ages, in ten languages. Mandeville, if we may give him this name, sometimes claims personal knowledge of what he records, and at times also he shows special knowledge of England. Quite a number of modern writers have accepted his claim to be a great English traveller: he would satisfy any fourteenth-century equivalent of the Tebbit test of Englishry. But the work is basically a combination of two major continental authors: William of Bodensele (for the Jerusalem pilgrimage) and Odoric of Pordenone (for the travels in Asia). These works showed a good deal of discursive curiosity, and between them they provided a narrative into which extracts from a wide range of other writers could be inserted. The author was impressively well read, but there is no convincing evidence that he travelled anywhere except to a good library. Iain Higgins has observed with justice that '*The Book* makes no significant use of Sir John's "national identity", rather offering a Latin Christian's view of the world. The Knight's Englishness is ... almost without relevance to a reading of the text.'[14] It seems that a French writer, a knight or more probably a monk, adopted the invented personality of a fictitious Sir John Mandeville. Nevertheless, England is abundantly represented in the surviving manuscript tradition. The educated classes there were its eager readers.[15]

The Book of Sir John Mandeville was not a single work. Just as the original compiler rewrote and adapted his sources, so translators and copyists produced different versions in English, French and German.[16] There was no single programme behind this mass of writing, which incorporated a

---

[14] I. M. Higgins, *Writing East: The 'Travels' of Sir John Mandeville* (Philadelphia: Pennsylvania University Press, 1997), p. 43.

[15] The modern literature is vast. Among discussions during the past twenty years are C. Deluz, *Le livre de Jehan de Mandeville: une 'géographie' au XIVe siècle* (Louvain: Institut d'études médiévales, 1988); M. C. Seymour, 'Sir John Mandeville', in his *Authors of the Middle Ages* (Aldershot: Variorum, 1994); and G. Milton, *The Riddle and the Knight: In Search of Sir John Mandeville* (London: Alison and Busby, 1996).

[16] On the German versions, where the difference is particularly marked, see K. Ridder, *Jean de Mandevilles 'Reisen': Studien zur Überlieferungsgeschichte der deutschen Übersetzung des Otto von Diemeringen*, Texte und Untersuchungen zur Deutschen Literatur des Mittelalters 99 (Munich, 1991).

variety of opinion and imagination, was variously interpreted by its different editors, and which pointed, Janus-like, at once to past and future. The *Book* began with an emphatic affirmation of the significance of the Holy Land, and then expanded to become a record of travels to almost all known countries, similar in a sense to the massive collections of travel manuscripts that were made for monastic libraries and royal courts. There is some truth in the view that it tended to displace Jerusalem from its centrality in geography and in culture. Yet this was clearly not the intention: in the version closest to the original, the author made deliberate attempts to establish the primacy of Jerusalem among all the regions that he was describing. It was, he said, 'the best, the most virtuous and the most worthy [region] in the world; for it is the heart and the middle of all the land of the world'.[17] He proclaimed the qualities of Western Christendom above those of any other culture (on the whole, this literature is virulently anti-Jewish); and yet appreciated good men of other religions, and spoke of the need for reform in the Western Church. The Mandeville literature held up a mirror to the people of the late Middle Ages that reflected their aspirations and fears of the mysteries of the holy places and of Asia, indeed of 'the East', which at the time virtually meant the rest of the world.

Friar Felix Fabri has some affinity with this wider pilgrimage tradition, in that he shared a delight in strange places and an interest in the unfamiliar: 'something new is always happening', he observed of his desert journey, 'to fill a man with admiration'.[18] At the same time, he also observed that self-knowledge was one of the blessings that comes from pilgrimage. The journey of pilgrimage was both outside and within the self. It was quite rare for people to record their inward response to a visit to the holy sites in a personal way. True, it was common to speak of the excitement of pilgrims on approaching the coast, and of the *Te Deum* sung on the ship. Sometimes there is a mention of the prayers and antiphons at the various shrines, although only Felix Fabri and Santo Brasca (1480) report them in any detail. There are, too, descriptions of the overflowing emotions at the Holy Sepulchre in particular: 'verily', wrote Niccolò of Poggibonsi (1346), 'there is no-one so hard who can here withhold his tears, who does not cry aloud, when he enters inside this most holy chapel'.[19] Yet few writers went beyond a description of behaviour to speak of an

[17] See, in particular, I. M. Higgins, 'Defining the Earth's Centre in a Medieval "Multi-Text": Jerusalem in *The Book of John Mandeville*', in S. Tomasch and S. Gilles (eds.), *Text and Territory: Geographical Imagination in the European Middle Ages* (Philadelphia: Pennsylvania University Press, 1998), 29–53.

[18] Stewart, *The Wanderings of Felix Fabri*, vol. II. p. 512.

[19] T. Bellorini and E. Hoade (trans.), *Fra Niccolò of Poggibonsi, A Voyage Beyond the Seas* (Jerusalem: Studium Biblicum Franciscanum, 1945), p. 15 (xix).

inner experience. The omission is curious, because they were writing in centuries in which personal piety was growing strongly, and the Franciscans were the champions of this type of devotion. One of the reasons may be that, under the pressure of unsympathetic Muslim authorities, the Franciscans were at times surprisingly casual guides. Pietro Casola (1494) complained that no prayers or antiphons were said as they went round, and that the fathers 'only explained in Latin and in the vulgar tongue what those places were and nothing else'.[20] We must remember, too, that the aim of most writers was not self-expression. They were concerned to guide later travellers and to help those at home to see the holy places in their mind's eye, since 'what we see by eye moves us most strongly'.[21] In itself, that was not new: the holy places had inspired visitors to see in imagination the historical events ever since Paula, the companion of Jerome. But such a spirituality now corresponded more directly with the new fashions in devotion in the West. These had their proper place in mystical works rather than in guidebooks. Deeply personal reactions hardly fitted into the accepted format of a travel journal.

For real inwardness of feeling, we must go to an English writer, Margery Kempe. She dictated her memoirs shortly after 1436. Her importance lies, not in her influence, since the one surviving manuscript was unknown to other travel writers, but in her intensely personal expression of pilgrim devotion. She is the polar opposite of Mandeville: Dame Margery only took an interest in what was important to her own spiritual life. Her meditation was rigidly centred on the sufferings of Christ. She defined her motivation for her Jerusalem journey in 1414 as 'a desire to see those places where [our Lord] was born, and where he suffered his Passion, and where he died, with other holy places where he was in his life, and also after his Resurrection'. In the church of the Holy Sepulchre, she 'wept and sobbed as plenteously as though she had seen our Lord with her bodily eye, suffering his Passion at that time'. The intensity of the emotion produced in her a new physical phenomenon: 'she had such great compassion and such great pain, at seeing our Lord's pain, that she could not keep herself from crying and roaring though she should have died for it. And that was the first cry that ever she cried in any contemplation.'[22]

[20] M. M. Newett (trans.), *Canon Pietro Casola's Pilgrimage to Jerusalem in the Year 1494* (Manchester University Press), pp. 246–7.
[21] 'Les choses veues a l'oeil plus fort nous esmeuvent': Nicolas Le Huen (1487), cited in Tinguely, 'Janus en Terre Sainte', p. 62.
[22] W. Butler-Bowdon (ed.), *The Book of Margery Kempe (1436): A Modern Version* (London, 1963), p. 107. Critical editions of the text are by S. B. Meech and H. E. Allen (eds.), *The Book of Margery Kempe*, EETS 212 (London, 1940) and L. Staley (ed.), *The Book of Margery Kempe* (Kalamazoo: Medieval Institute Publications, 1996).

These dramatic manifestations were unwelcome to her fellow-travellers, and they win little sympathy in our present secular age. Margery Kempe was, however, closer to the main line of late medieval spirituality than is sometimes supposed. One of the reasons for her travels was her desire to interview holy men and women, and her range of contacts included preachers, monks and hermits, among them some learned churchmen. Her eccentricities caused some people to suspect her of Lollardy, but – according to herself or her secretary – most of her advisers were supportive.[23] Dame Margery was influenced by the distinctive tradition of hermit spirituality in fourteenth-century England. It has been rightly observed that 'Margery and her scribe supply a dimension to late medieval English spirituality which is suggested in the prayer books of the period, but recorded from experience in no other place'.[24] She bridges the gap between outward pilgrimage and inner experience. Outside England, she found a special affinity with St Birgitta or Bridget of Sweden. In spite of their great differences (Margery was descended from a burgess family in an English port, whereas Birgitta's royal birth made her a major player on the European political scene), their piety was deeply connected with the Jerusalem pilgrimage. For Margery, it was a turning-point: for Birgitta, her visit at the end of her life in 1372 was a longed-for culmination. Each records her visit, not in a pilgrim narrative of the usual kind, but within their spiritual histories: the *Revelations* of Birgitta and the *Book* of Margery Kempe.[25]

Among the writers of journals of the voyage the nearest parallel to Margery is a very different personality who was her close contemporary, Mariano da Siena. Unlike Margery's, his account follows a strict framework of dates, but he concentrates on his own experience. His editor describes the work as a 'narrazione-confessione' rather than a 'narrazione-storia'. Mariano recorded his third visit to the Holy Land, which took place in 1431, and spoke of his desire to return one final time and to die at the Holy Sepulchre. His experiences were in a number of ways like those described by Margery. Just as she seemed to see the crucified Jesus before her, Mariano said at Bethlehem that 'I seemed to have that lovely child before my eyes'. The language is much more personal and emotional than in the majority of accounts. At the first sight of Jerusalem, it

[23] See David Knowles, *The Religious Orders in England* (Cambridge University Press, 1955), vol. II, pp. 198–202.

[24] J. C. Hirsch, *The Revelations of Margery Kempe: Paramystical Practices in Late Medieval England* (Leiden: Brill, 1989), p. 87.

[25] S. Schein, 'Bridget of Sweden, Margery Kempe and Women's Jerusalem Pilgrimages in the Middle Ages', *Mediterranean Historical Review*, 14 (1999), 44–58.

seemed that his soul left his body, and he could not wait to visit the city where 'the beloved Jesus' had suffered. When he entered Jerusalem, it was 'in the name of the suffering and beloved Jesus'. He tells us of 'the burning love and charity of sweetness that we felt at Calvary'. Mariano was very much more learned than the illiterate Margery, but he stood in a not dissimilar spiritual tradition that was strong in cultivated circles in Siena. His writing is sometimes reminiscent of the great preacher Bernardino, and his vocabulary is often close to that of St Catherine. Like Margery Kempe he linked with his pilgrimage a strongly personal devotion to the humanity of the suffering Jesus, which one suspects was shared by a lot of sincere pilgrims, but which rarely receives expression in accounts that follow more conventional lines.[26]

'What we see by eye moves us most strongly.' I have already quoted these words of Nicolas Le Huen (1487).[27] In much of Western Europe, during the fifteenth and sixteenth centuries, there was a determined effort to make the holy places, and the saving events that had taken place there, tangible to believers. The role of images as the books of the illiterate was famous throughout the Middle Ages, but appropriate illustrations could function just as well for cultivated worshippers: the art of memory turned essentially on the creation of images of time and place.[28]

It is quite wrong to suppose that interest in creating memorials of the Holy Sepulchre in the West was waning towards the end of the Middle Ages. On the contrary, after a period in the late fourteenth and early fifteenth centuries, when I believe that such 'copies' were less frequently built, there was a great surge of interest. Anselm Adorno, whose travels extended from Scotland to Jerusalem and who provided the warm commendation of internationalism that stands at the head of this lecture, was associated with one major project of the sort. The Adorno family originated in Genoa, but had long been domiciled in Flanders. They owned an important property in the Peperstraat at Bruges, and here they built a set of almshouses. In 1427 the building of a chapel, dedicated to the Passion of Christ and the Holy Sepulchre, was authorised. It received its final form, which it still almost exactly preserves, as the Jerusalem Church, after the pilgrimage of Anselm and his son John in 1470–1. It was a private chapel, as indeed it legally still is, and it formed the centre of devotion to the Passion and the Holy Sepulchre. Given the dedication

---

[26] For discussion and references, see P. Pirillo (ed.), *Mariano da Siena: Viaggio fatto al Santo Sepolcro* (Pisa: Ospedaletto, 1996), pp. 84, 109, 116 and introduction.

[27] See note 21.

[28] J.-P. Antoine, 'Mémoire, lieu et invention spatiale dans la peinture des XIIIe et XIVe siècles', *Annales: Société, Economie, Civilisation*, 48 (1993), 1447–70.

Ecclesia Hierosolymitanae BRUGENSIS.

Praetorium Familiae Adorniorum.

27 Bruges, Belgium. The Jerusalem Church, *c.* 1480, completed by Anselm and John Adorno, who visited Jerusalem in 1470–1. Anselm had close links with the Scottish royal court. The tower is apparently a commemoration of the dome above the Holy Sepulchre at Jerusalem. From Sanderus, *Flandria illustrata*, Keulen, 1641.

and the popular name of the church, it seems safe to assume that the highly distinctive design of the large octagonal tower was intended to be a reminiscence of the dome over the Holy Sepulchre at Jerusalem, although no one could conceivably claimed that it is an accurate imitation. The altarpiece of the main body of the church, probably constructed at the time Anselm was buried there in 1483, depicts the hill of Calvary, with the emblems of the Passion. The crypt contained a fragment of the wood of the cross, and a small chapel was subsequently added to represent the Holy Sepulchre. Once again, this is not accurate, for it was designed in the form of a sarcophagus. It is tempting to link its construction with the foundation of a Jerusalem brotherhood at Bruges about 1520, which survived until 1628. On the eve of the Reformation, pilgrim devotion in fact was not dying away, but expanding into new forms.[29]

The Bruges Jerusalem Church belonged to a wave of pilgrim reminiscence and piety. Some of the designs were highly imaginary, while some, almost for the first time in Western Europe, showed an anxiety for accuracy. Thus at Görlitz there was a highly distinctive set of monuments, completed apparently by 1504. Like Bruges, these brought together reminiscences of the holy places associated with the Passion in the chapel of the Holy Cross, but they were much closer to being copies. The bürgermeister Georg Emerich, who had been created a knight of the Holy Sepulchre on the occasion of his visit there in 1465, sponsored the building of a chapel of the Holy Sepulchre that was based quite precisely on the measures and appearance of the edicule at Jerusalem.[30] Westerners did now have a much better idea of what the sepulchre really looked like, because a few wealthy pilgrims had taken artists with them. Particularly important was Erhard Reuwich, who travelled with the dean of Mainz, Bernhard of Breydenbach, and whose accurate engravings of Eastern scenes illustrated Breydenbach's somewhat pedestrian account of his travels.[31]

Images of the holy places such as those at Görlitz are reminiscent of the *sacri monti* that now began to be created. At San Vivaldo in Tuscany an elaborate imitation of Jerusalem was set out on a hillside location, designed to provide access to the various pilgrimage sites – thirty-four of them, apparently, by 1516. The design seems to have been the inspiration of the Franciscan Brother Thomas of Florence from 1499 onwards. He had worked in Crete, and certainly knew Jerusalem, the topography of

[29] J. Penninck, *De Jeruzalemkerk te Brugge* (Bruges: Koninklijke Gidsenbond, 1986).

[30] H. Möbius, *Passion und Auferstehung in Kultur und Kunst des Mittelalters* (Vienna: Tusch, 1978), pp. 78–82, pls. 119–24; G. Dalman, 'Das heilige Grab in Görlitz', *Neues Lausitzisches Magazin*, 91 (1915), 198–243; E.-H. Lemper, 'Die Kapelle zum Heiligen Kreuz beim Heiligen Grab in Görlitz', in *Kunst des Mittelalters in Sachsen: Festschrift Wolf Schubert* (Weimar, 1967), pp. 142–57.

[31] M. Biddle, *The Tomb of Christ* (Stroud: Sutton, 1999), figs. 36–7.

which is fairly accurately represented. As time went on pilgrims were invited to enter into an imaginative relationship with the events by seeing a group of realistic figures representing the original partakers within the setting: a holy Madame Tussaud's, except that the material consisted of terracotta and fresco rather than waxworks.[32]

Spiritual theme parks of this description were much more elaborate than early Western shrines had been. So were the representations of the stations of the cross that now began to be provided for the access of local pilgrims. An early version had been created outside Nuremberg by Adam Krafft between 1490 and 1508. At Seville, Don Fadrique returned from the Holy Land in 1519 and commemorated his pilgrimage by marking his magnificent palace with Jerusalem crosses. It was called the Casa de Pilatos, and supposed to be a memorial of Pilate's tribunal at Jerusalem. In reality, it is unlike any form that that building could have taken, even supposing that its location could be identified; but it marks the beginning of a set of stations of the cross that were laid out through the streets of the city in 1521. In all these cases, not only was the Holy City being evoked, but the plans were based on the reports of returned pilgrims or on information specially secured from Palestine.

Imagery and visual expression were fundamental to late medieval spirituality, and much of the imagery in use referred to Jerusalem. Some of it was embodied in the age-old recollection of the holy sites. Virtually all Crucifixions were represented on a hill, derived from the site which had been identified as Calvary. Mrs C. F. Alexander might well have been startled to hear that her 'green hill far away' owed more to Constantine than to the Gospels. Sometimes the influence was far more contemporary: an altar-piece might contain a direct reference to pilgrimage to the Holy Places. A triptych by Campin, dated about 1410 and now in the Courtauld Gallery, shows the donor, who has just arrived to worship at the Entombment. He has come down a country lane, wearing travelling clothes and accompanied by his dog. Unfortunately he cannot be identified, and we cannot be sure whether this is a recollection of a real pilgrimage or a reference to a spiritual one.[33]

Conversely there were differences between imagery in the West and the pilgrim experience at Jerusalem. Pilgrimages, as conducted by the Franciscans on site, normally began at the church of the Holy Sepulchre, and therefore did not follow the *via dolorosa* in sequence from Pilate's

---

[32] L. Vaccaro and F. Ricardi (eds.), *Sacri Monti: Devozione, arte e cultura della Controriforma* (Milan: Jaca, 1992).

[33] M. Botvinick, 'The Painting as Pilgrimage: Traces of a Subtext in the Work of Campin and his Contemporaries', *Art History*, 15 (1991), 1–18. A. Chatelet had denied the pilgrim reference in *Robert Campin: le Maître de Flemall* (Antwerp: Mercator, 1996), no. 3, pp. 284–5.

judgement seat to the cross, as it came to be incorporated in Western Calvaries. Thomas Brygg's account of his pilgrimage in 1392 is typical in following *sanctum circulum,* 'the holy circuit', as he calls it, from the Holy Sepulchre to the houses of Pilate, Herod and finally Simon the Leper, 'where Christ remitted the sins of Mary Magdalen'. The sites he visited included 'the house of the rich man who denied a portion of bread to Lazarus', the place 'where the blessed Virgin met Jesus carrying the cross', and 'the school where the Blessed Virgin learned to read'. Such episodes either had no basis in the Gospels, or (in the instance of Lazarus) treated a parable as if it were a historical episode.[34] Some of these supposed events formed the basis for a rich development in the West, notably the encounter between Jesus and his mother, the *madonna dello spasimo* of Italian devotion.

In many cases, we cannot be sure where a particular image originated. A good example of the interchange between pilgrim experience and the devout imagination is Birgitta's vision of the Nativity at Bethlehem in 1372, recorded in book VII of her *Revelations.* She saw the Blessed Virgin kneeling in devotion, and not, as in the standard picture, lying down. That Birgitta realised that this was an innovation is indicated by the fact that the Virgin assured her that what she was seeing was indeed the true picture. This experience was followed almost immediately by the appearance of new-style representations of the Nativity, with the kneeling Virgin, in Naples and Orvieto, spreading within a generation to Birgitta's native Sweden. Undoubtedly, Birgitta's reputation helped to spread the new iconography, but we have no means of knowing whether it originated with her experience at Bethlehem, or whether she had taken there in her imagination a striking new image that she had seen in Italy.[35]

Other images of major importance were definitely made in the West. Eucharistic devotion was immensely productive of symbols of the Passion.[36] Another dramatic example was the Entombment of Christ, where the dead body is surrounded by Joseph of Arimathea, Nicodemus, the Blessed Virgin, Mary Magdalen and angels, all represented by life-sized stone figures. In its completed form it was a fifteenth-century

---

[34] P. Riant (ed.), 'Voyage en Terre-Sainte d'un maire de Bordeaux au XIVe siècle', *Archives de l'Orient Latin,* 2 (1882), 378–88.

[35] See the discussion in B. Morris, *Saint Birgitta of Sweden* (Woodbridge: Boydell, 1999), pp. 133–9.

[36] This has been the subject of so much distinguished recent work that it would be impossible to consider it adequately here. Recent discussions include M. Rubin, *Corpus Christi: The Eucharist in Late Medieval Culture* (Cambridge University Press, 1992); S. Beckwith, *Christ's Body: Identity, Culture and Society in Late Medieval Writings* (London: Routledge, 1993); G. J. C. Snoek, *Medieval Piety from Relics to the Eucharist: A Process of Mutual Interaction* (Leiden: Brill, 1995); and J. F. Hamburger, *Nuns as Artists: The Visual Culture of a Medieval Convent* (Berkeley University Press, 1997).

devotion: we hear that in 1421 the bishop of Langres 'caused to be constructed a commemoration of the Sepulchre of our Lord Jesus Christ in great images', and a splendid set of such figures survives from some ten years later in Freiburg in Switzerland. Nothing in the Gospels supports such a representation: it is probable that here currents from the Jerusalem pilgrimage, the Good Friday ceremony of the *depositio*, and perhaps the guild plays in the cities, have come together.[37] The emergence of the pietà theme affords another example of a powerful image that had no basis in the Gospels or, in this case, in the experience of pilgrims.[38] Even allowing for such purely Western elaborations of the Passion theme, the Jerusalem influence on its evolution was strong in much of the West.

The power of these devotions, and of the pilgrimages with which they were linked, can be demonstrated in most of continental Europe. It is more difficult to speak with confidence of England. The medieval artistic heritage in this country has been particularly depleted, with the exception of alabaster figures; otherwise, there is more late medieval art at Cologne than in the whole of England. Even more seriously, the Reformation drew a line under the evolution of medieval religion. There is no substantial continuity in pilgrimage or imagery. That makes it peculiarly difficult to decide whether the Jerusalem pilgrimage was as significant here as on the Continent, or whether the tides of its influence were washing these distant shores more weakly than elsewhere. English churches, like those on the Continent, had a developed cult of the Holy Sepulchre. In many churches there was a specially built Sepulchre, normally located to the north of the high altar, for use in the Easter ceremonies. These might be elaborately designed, with the figures of the sleeping guards, angels and holy women. Famous examples are those in Lincoln Cathedral, Hackington (Lincolnshire) or Patrington (Yorkshire), carved primarily between 1290 and 1350. On Good Friday, the dead Christ was placed in the Sepulchre, in the form of a crucifix and the sacramental Host, was honoured by vigils and lights, and was removed, in a reminiscence of the Resurrection, on Easter morning. The lights and hangings were often presented by lay patrons or provided by a guild of the Holy Sepulchre. We simply do not know how many of the patrons of these Sepulchres had been on the Jerusalem pilgrimage, and there are also reasons for thinking that in late medieval England Easter Sepulchres, although certainly very numerous, were less elaborate than on the Continent. The structures themselves became simpler after 1350: characteristically, the later medieval Sepulchre

[37] See W. H. Forsyth, *The Entombment of Christ: French Sculptures of the Fifteenth and Sixteenth Centuries* (Cambridge, MA, Harvard University Press, 1970); V. Beyer, *La sculpture strasbourgoise au XIVe siècle* (Strasburg/Paris, 1955).

[38] J. E. Ziegler, *Sculpture of Compassion: the Pietà and the Beguines in the Southern Low Countries c. 1300-c. 1600* (Turnhout: Brepols, 1992).

28 Lincoln Cathedral. The Easter Sepulchre or Tomb of Christ, *c.* 1300. There would originally have been an image of the Risen Christ and angels above the surface of the tomb.

29 Heckington, Lincolnshire. The Easter Sepulchre, *c*. 1345, containing all the characters of the Easter story. The aperture is intended for
the deposit of the sacrament, and the shrine would have been the goal
of Easter processions and local pilgrimages.

was a tomb which often doubled for that of the donor. This was probably the result of the somewhat simpler form of the Easter ceremonies in England. The Sarum rite did not include the *visitatio* ceremony, that is the enactment of the visit of the holy women seeking the body of the risen Lord. If England ever developed the great Entombment groups in the French manner, we do not know of them, apart from the life-size figure of the dead Christ found concealed within the fabric of the Mercers' Hall in London, and even this shows French or Burgundian influence in its composition.[39] We do know, however, that on the flyleaf of the *Itineraries* of Mr William Wey there is a list of his goods left at Edington 'to the chapel made to the lyknes of the sepulkyr of our Lord at Jerusalem'. This was clearly a promotion on a large scale. There were hangings, including 'a clothe stayned with the tempyl of Jerusalem, the Mounte of Olyvete, and Bethlehem'. He gave relics, including a crucifix from Jerusalem and stones from many of the holy places. There was a map, presumably the large one that still survives; boards containing measures taken from the Holy Sepulchre itself; and a further series of boards that appear to be models of the chapel of Calvary, the church of Bethlehem and other places. The original chapel of the Holy Sepulchre, sadly, cannot be identified at Edington. Presumably this was an unusually elaborate chapel, because of Wey's commitment to the Holy Land. There is no reason to suppose that it was unique, although the evidence for the existence of Easter Sepulchres within their own chapel is very limited in England.[40]

It may be the relative difficulty of travel to the Holy Land that created an interest among English poets and thinkers in 'spiritual pilgrimage', the conviction that meditation on the holy places was as effective as a physical visit, and moreover that the Jerusalem pilgrimage provided a model for understanding the spiritual life as a whole. Not that this was peculiar to England. Such thinking went back to Bernard of Clairvaux and long before him, and its most elaborate statement was in the trilogy by the French Cistercian, Guillaume de Deguileville, written in the years after 1330, partly translated into English by Lydgate.[41] This was a persistent theme in English spirituality. Walter Hilton used the image of a pilgrim

[39] P. Sheingorn, *The Easter Sepulchre in England* (Kalamazoo: Medieval Institute, 1987); E. Duffy, *The Stripping of the Altars* (New Haven, CT: Yale University Press, 1992), esp. pp. 28–35; and J. Evans and N. Cook, 'A Statue of Christ from the Ruins of Mercers' Hall', *Archaeological Jnl*, 111 (1954), 166–80.

[40] Bandinel (ed.), *The Itineraries of Mr William Wey*, pp. xxviii–xxx; P. Sheingorn, *Easter Sepulchre*, pp. 344–6; R. Röhricht, 'Die Palästinakarte des William Wey', *Zeitschrift des Deutschen Palästina-Vereins*, 27 (1904), 188–93 and map. Apart from the chapel in Winchester Cathedral, which was of earlier origin, Sheingorn is able to note only a small number of other chapels that probably contained representations of the Holy Sepulchre.

[41] There is a good account by E. Faral, *Histoire littéraire de la France*, vol. xxxix (Paris: Imprimerie Nationale, 1952), pp. 1–132, and a more favourable assessment by

who wished to set out to Jerusalem, which 'be tokenyth contemplacyoun in parfyte love of God'. The presence of the idea in Chaucer's *Parson's Tale* confirms that it was widespread:

> And Jhesu, for his grace, wit me sende,
> To shewe yow the way, in this viage,
> Of thilke parfit glorious pilgrimage
> That highte Jerusalem celestial.[42]

The 'pilgrimage for truth' became a central feature in *Piers Plowman*:

> 'And I shal apparaille me', quod Perkyn, 'in pilgrims wise,
> And wende with yow I wil, til we fynd Truthe.'

Even actual pilgrims to Jerusalem entered into this spirituality. When Margery Kempe hoped to return to the Holy Land, she was assured,

Daughter, as oftentimes as thou sayest or thinkest, 'Worshipped be those holy Places in Jerusalem that Christ suffered bitter pain and passion in', thou shalt have the same pardon as if thou wert there with thy bodily presence, both to thyself and to all that thou wilt give it to.[43]

If we accept the view of David Aers that this tradition represents a different attitude to the humanity of Christ, in contrast with the intense devotion to his suffering and the eucharistic body that came to dominate in fifteenth-century England, the spiritualisation of pilgrimage would offer a major alternative to the prevalent orthodoxy; but that is a large topic that cannot be explored here.[44] In any event, it had a special significance for England, because it continued beyond the Reformation within Protestant spirituality, and led to the creation, in Bunyan's *Pilgrim's Progress*, of the greatest literary expression of spiritual pilgrimage.

It is curious to notice that, in face of the Henrician government's attack on English shrines, one dissenting preacher at Christmas 1538 urged his hearers to go to Jerusalem, 'seeing that Our Lady of Walsingham, Our Lady of Grace, and Thomas Becott were put down'.[45] Inevitably, post-Reformation England had little interest in narratives of pilgrimage to

J. M. Keenan, 'The Cistercian pilgrimage to Jerusalem in Guillaume de Deguileville's *Pèlerinage de la vie humaine*', in J. R. Sommerfeldt (ed.),*Studies in Medieval Cistercian History*, vol. II (Kalamazoo: Cistercian Publications, 1976), pp. 166–85.

[42] The Prologue to *The Parson's Tale*, lines 48–51.

[43] W. Butler-Bowdon (ed.), *The Book of Margery Kempe (1436)*, p. 117. For other references in this paragraph, see E. Zeeman, 'Piers Plowman and the Pilgrimage to Truth', *Essays and Studies*, 11 (1958), 1–16.

[44] D. Aers and L. Staley (eds.), *The Powers of the Holy: Religion, Politics and Gender in Late Medieval English Culture* (Philadelphia: Pennsylvania University Press, 1996); E. M. Ross, *The Grief of God: Images of the Suffering Jesus in Late Medieval England* (Oxford University Press, 1997).

[45] J. Gairdner and R. H. Brodie (eds.), *LP*, vol. XIV.1, 32. I am grateful to Dr Peter Roberts for this reference (see below, p. 229).

Jerusalem. There is nothing like Feyerabend's massive German *Reyszbuch desz heyligen landes* of 1584, with its eighteen classic narratives of the Palestine pilgrimage. Nor could there be a recrudescence of interest in pilgrim literature, like the one that was so evident on the Continent after the middle of the sixteenth century. This was the form taken in Catholic Europe, and indeed in some Protestant societies, by the demand for meditation on Christ and the Holy Land: 'the book, a substitute for the journey, was from then on the instrument for prolonged meditation'. For this outpouring of literature and publication, England had no equivalent.[46]

There was, nevertheless, a different sort of cultural continuity within England. The country no longer had the same reverance for pilgrimage to the Holy Land, and even more than France or Germany its geographical interests were being shaped by voyages on the great oceans. Richard Hakluyt, when he prepared the first edition of *The Principall Navigations* (1589), was aware of standing on the brink of a new age of geographical knowledge.[47] He recorded how, when he was a young man, his cousin 'began to instruct my ignorance, by shewing me the division of the earth into three parts after the old account, and then according to the latter and better distribution into more'. He was conscious, too, that until very recently the English had not been prominent in exploration, and that they were despised 'for their sluggish security, and continuall neglect of the like attempts'. *The Principall Navigations* stood between the old and new geographies. It presented English exploration as being rooted in the former world of pilgrimage: 'I find that the oldest travels as well of the ancient Britons, as of the English, were ordinarie to Judea which is in Asia, termed by them the Holy Land, principally for devotions' sake according to the time.' The collection began with records of early travels to Palestine, from the time of 'Helena the Empress, daughter of Coelus king of Britain' and Constantine, and it continued with some brief accounts of English crusaders. Hakluyt did not include any of the English pilgrimage narratives, which one suspects had been lost to view by this time. The bulk of the first section came from Mandeville, in the abbreviated Latin version then in common use. Curiously, it was the only Latin material not provided with a translation. It is worth remembering that Mandeville's work contained material of genuine geographical value, for it was based on travels to the Near East and further Asia, even if the author was in fact not the traveller. In the second edition of 1598–1600 Hakluyt omitted Mandeville without apology or explanation. He substituted some other early accounts of travel to the same regions, but the collection no longer

---

[46] On this whole subject, see M.-C. Gomez-Géraud, *Le crépuscule du Grand Voyage: les récits des pèlerins à Jérusalem (1458–1612)* (Paris: Honoré Champion, 1999).

[47] Richard Hakluyt, *The Principall Navigations, Voiages and Discoveries of the English Nation*, imprinted at London, 1589. (Facs. edn, Cambridge 1965.)

began with them. The emphasis on exploration had shifted significantly from its original roots in the Holy Land to the increasingly successful oceanic voyages.

By then, the Jerusalem pilgrimage had diminished in numbers and importance. One of the reasons was undoubtedly the increasing danger of the route, although that was hardly new. In 1480 the pilgrims on Felix Fabri's first expedition were warned not to continue beyond Venice because of Turkish naval activity, and those who travelled had a perilous time. While the Ottoman conquest of Jerusalem in 1516 and of Rhodes in 1522 made matters worse, the pilgrimage was still held in esteem. Ignatius Loyola (1523) was such a devotee of Jerusalem that he wanted to settle there, until he was ordered by authority to return to the West. Guilds of the Holy Sepulchre in some towns in the Netherlands were extremely rich and influential. At Utrecht, Jan van Scorel, a pilgrim himself in 1520, founded a tradition of group portraits of visitors to the Holy Sepulchre, incorporating details of their lives and pilgrimages. They were presumably designed to hang in the local chapel of the Holy Sepulchre. The pilgrims are shown carrying their palms of Jericho, and one portrait includes an accurate drawing of the Sepulchre itself – one supposes that it was sketched by Scorel when he was there.[48]

Greffin Affagart was a noble from Maine, and a lover of the old way. His main purpose in writing a full account of his visit to the Holy Land, and long stay there, in 1533, was to persuade his readers to support the continuation of the pilgrimage:

A great many people of status used to go, such as bishops, abbots, dukes, counts, barons and other people of standing, who paid for the ship, so that poorer travellers could go more cheaply and easily. But since that wicked rogue Luther has been in power with his accomplices, and also Erasmus – who in his *Colloquies* and *Enchiridion* attacked pilgrimages – many Christians have withdrawn and grown cold. This is specially true of the Flemings and Germans, who used to be more devout in travelling than all the others.[49]

Affagart was right about the effect of Protestant critics. They did not object only to uncritical and superstitious attitudes to relics (as, for that matter, did many Catholic thinkers). They also rejected a theology that

---

[48] As late as 1544, Scorel's pupil Antonis Mor painted two of the canons of Utrecht who had made the journey in 1520 and later. See J. Woodall, 'Painted Immortality: Portraits of Jerusalem Pilgrims by Antonis Mor and Jan van Scorel', *Jahrbuch des Berliner Museums*, 31 (1989), 149–63; *Kunst voor de Beeldenstorm: Noordnerderlandse Kunst 1525–80,* 2 vols. (The Hague: Staatsuitgeverij, 1986), vol. II. p. 185; J. D. Bangs, *Cornelis Engebrechtsz's Leiden: Studies in Cultural History* (Assen: Van Gorcum, 1979), pp. 68–9; and, on the importance of the guilds, W. Schneider, *Peregrinatio Hierosolymitana* (Münster, 1982).

[49] J. Chavanon (ed.), *Relation de Terre Sainte (1533–4) par Greffin Affagart* (Paris: Lecoffre, 1902), pp. 20–1.

saw God as manifested in the special sanctity of particular places and things. They taught 'a different doctrine of the power of God. No earthly thing contained, or received delegated to it, one jot of the sovereign power of the Divine providence.'[50]

The Jerusalem pilgrimage was also being reshaped within Catholicism into a contemplation of the mysteries of Christ's life. The huge indulgences, which are listed by almost all the narratives, and which during the last two medieval centuries had been a major attraction to the Holy Land, were readily available nearer home: at first at Rome, then at pilgrimage centres whose altars represented Rome or Jerusalem, as S. Stefano Bologna claimed to do; and then simply as a reward for spiritual exercises. Books now guided the faithful on their imaginary pilgrimages, as they had once done in Palestine. Thus at a site full of reminiscences of the Passion Francesco Patricelli published in 1575 *The chronicle of the mysterious and holy church and monastery of S. Stefano at Bologna, traditionally called Jerusalem*, to guide his readers on their way round the church and inform them about its abundant indulgences.[51] Even less physically demanding was the hugely popular *Spiritual Pilgrimage* published at Louvain in 1563 by Jan Pascha, the prior of the Carmelites there. His readers are provided with an imaginary pilgrimage to the Holy Land, with spiritual reflections, covering each day for the whole of a year.

The West never totally lost interest in visiting the Holy Land. In 1604 a treaty signed between France and the Ottoman government provided for the protection of French pilgrims at Jerusalem and of Latin clergy at the holy places there, and this was the first of a series of agreements that contained clauses safeguarding the handful of people who still made the journey. These negotiations reflected a new situation, not the continuation of an old one. The annual pilgrim galleys from Venice sailed no longer, the Franciscan position at Jerusalem was insecure, and indulgences (for those who valued them) were to be earned by spiritual pilgrimage in the West. The great narrative sequences were being republished, and other accounts were newly published; but they no longer reflected the reality of ships full of pilgrims who regularly attended the shrines. The journey to Jerusalem, which had persisted with remarkable stability for more than two centuries, had, in its old form, come to an end.

---

[50] The contrasting theologies are analysed in an important articule by Euan Cameron, 'For reasoned faith or embattled creed? Religion for the people in early modern Europe', *TRHS*, vi.8 (1998), 165–87. The article is not primarily concerned with pilgrimage, but its conclusions are very relevant.

[51] F. Patricelli, *Cronica della misteriosa e devota chiesa e Badia di S. Stefano in Bologna* (Bologna, 1575); G. Fasoli, 'Storiografia Stefaniana tra XII e XVII secolo', in G. Fasoli (ed.), *Stefaniana: contributi per la storia del complesso di S. Stefano in Bologna* (Bologna, 1985), pp. 27–49.

6   The dynamics of pilgrimage in late medieval England

Eamon Duffy

In 1986 work to strengthen the south-east tower pier in Worcester Cathedral uncovered a shallow late-medieval grave. It contained the skeleton of a stocky man who had died in his sixties, still clad in a lined woollen tunic and thigh-length walking-boots. By his side was a stout metal-shod wooden staff, once painted bright red, and a pierced cockle-shell, the conventional sign of a late medieval pilgrim.[1] The whole burial and not just the shell was clearly self-consciously symbolic: the expensive walking-boots had been almost new when they were slit along their lengths to dress the corpse, the metal double-spike which shod the staff showed little sign of wear. The state of the skeleton's knee- and hip-joints, by contrast, suggested a man who had walked long and far, and archaeologists concluded that the boots, staff and shell represented a deliberate evocation of one or more pilgrimages that had retained deep significance for the dead man and those who buried him.

The symbolic language here is plain: death itself is being presented as the last long pilgrimage, the culmination of the Christian life conceived as a journey away from the familiar towards the divine. Such symbolism had its biblical sources in Abraham's abandonment of his homeland at the command of God in Israel's journeyings in the wilderness, in the biblical idealisation of the holy city of Jerusalem, and in Christ's homeless wandering with nowhere to lay his head. All this was evoked in the liturgy of death itself – *Proficiscere anima Christiane, de hoc mundo* [Go forth Christian soul, go from this world], and in the very name given to the dying Christian's last communion – *viaticum*, journey-money.

Understandably, this is the set of resonances and associations that have found most favour in modern discussion of the symbolic meaning of late medieval pilgrimage, and that in fact were to survive the practice of pilgrimage in England to re-emerge as a literary metaphor in the hands of writers like Bunyan. The work of the social anthropologist Victor Turner in particular has encouraged historians to think of pilgrimage as

---

[1] Helen Lubin, *The Worcester Pilgrim* (Worcester, 1990).

a 'liminal' phenomenon, a religious rite that temporarily liberates pilgrims from the constraints and boundaries of the familiar by removing them physically and socially from their normal environments, across geographical and social thresholds, and that thereby creates a new and wider *communitas* in which social class, wealth and a convention give way to a wider common identity and equality. As Patrick Geary has written:

Christians have gone out into the wilderness, that is they have left their familiar locales, their normal social positions and their accustomed activities in favour of the ambiguous, ill-defined liminality of the pilgrim in order to seek a variety of persons and things. For some, the life of the pilgrim itself was the goal: as the Christian is a stranger and a wanderer in this world until he reaches the heavenly kingdom of the next . . . .[2]

Or, as the *Pilgrimage of the Lyfe of the Manhood* expressed it 'alle, as seith Seynt Paul, be thei riche, be thei poore, be thei wise other fooles, be thei kynges other queens, alle thei ben pilgrimes'.[3]

Yet all this raises questions for the historian aware that the single most important energy in late medieval English religious practice was its drive towards localism. The defining institutions of fifteenth-, and early sixteenth-, century Christianity in England were the parish and the guild, and the English laity lavished their devotion and their excess wealth in the construction of local religious identities in the elaborate reconstruction and furnishing of their parish churches. There is, of course, no contradiction here: no religion is monovocal, and every religious system holds a range of often divergent energies in creative tension. So medieval people inhabited both their localities, and a wider world. But they were not schizophrenic, and we need an account of the popularity of pilgrimage that brings it into some sort of intelligible relation with this drive towards the local.

In this chapter I do not want to challenge the value of the rich and suggestive notion of 'liminality' as a tool in teasing out the meaning of medieval pilgrimage in general: I do want to suggest, however, that there are crucial aspects of late medieval pilgrimage that it obscures rather than illuminates.[4] For many medieval Christians, going on pilgrimage was, it seems to me, not so much like launching on a journey to the ends of the

---

[2] Patrick Geary, 'The Saint and the Shrine: The Pilgrim's Goal in the Middle Ages', in L. Kriss-Rettenbeck and G. Mohler (eds.), *Wallfahrt Kennt Keine Grenzen* (Zurich, 1984), p. 265. For a discussion of the specific applicability of Turner's model to late medieval English pilgrimage, see J. M. Theilmann, 'Communitas among Fifteenth-century Pilgrims', *Historical Reflections*, vol. XI (1984), pp. 253–70.

[3] A. Henry (ed.), *The Pilgrimage of the Lyfe of the Manhood*, EETS (1985), p. 1

[4] For criticism of the 'liminality' account of pilgrimage from alternative anthropological perspectives, see J. Eade and M. J. Sallnow (eds.), *Contesting the Sacred: The Anthropology of Christian Pilgrimage* (London and New York, 1991).

earth, as of going to a local market town to sell or buy geese or chickens: shrines were features by which they mapped the familiar, as much as signposts to other worlds and other social realities; a local, not a liminal, phenomenon.

There were, of course, national shrines like Walsingham or Canterbury drawing visitors in their thousands from all over England and a steady stream of English men and women made their way even further afield to Rocamadour and Compostela, Jerusalem and Rome. But most fifteenth-century pilgrimages were to sacred sites within one's own region, journeys that might take one no further than the next parish, and rarely further than the nearest market town.[5] When John Baylis of Rolvenden's wife went to her own parish church on Relic Sunday 1511 to gain the annual indulgence for venerating the parish's relics, she described herself as going on 'pilgrimage at the relics'. She applied the metaphor of journeying to her stroll to the parish church, recalling that 'the parson declarid and said for every foote that a man or a woman sett to the reliques he shal have great pardone'. Nevertheless, it makes very little sense to try to force Mistress Baylis' steps towards her parish church into a model emphasising a perilous and disorienting venture into the unknown. It is this perception that I shall try to explore in this chapter, which will focus on the phenomenon of local pilgrimage.

The first thing to grasp about late medieval pilgrim centres is that they were legion, and that most of them were localised or regional in their appeal. Pressure of space means that I can look at just one such shrine, the pilgrimage to the East Anglian local saint St Walstan, a cult unmentioned in any surviving liturgical book or calendar, and initially confined, like so many of these popular cults, to the immediate hinterland of the saint's burial place at Bawburgh. Till the end of the fifteenth century none of the standard collections of *vitae* of British saints has any mention of Walstan. By 1516, however, Walstan's cult had become sufficiently important for a fairly full legend to be included in Wynken de Worde's printed edition of John Capgrave's *Nova Legenda Anglie*. This had thirteen new lives of saints not included in any of the manuscript versions, half of whom can be associated more or less directly with new or newly flourishing cults: a couple with fifteenth-century English canonisations – John of Bridlington

---

[5] For some other accounts of late medieval English pilgrimage, see R. Finucane, *Miracles and Pilgrims: Popular Beliefs in Medieval England* (London, 1977); E. Duffy, *The Stripping of the Altars, Traditional Religion in England c. 1400–1580* (New Haven, CT and London, 1992), pp. 155–205; R. Whiting, *The Blind Devotion of the People: Popular Religion and the English Reformation* (Cambridge, 1989), pp. 54–9; B. Nilson, *Cathedral Shrines of Medieval England* (Woodbridge, 1998); G. W. Bernard, 'Vitality and Vulnerability in the Late Medieval Church: Pilgrimage on the Eve of the Break With Rome', in J. L. Watts (ed.), *The End of the Middle Ages* (Stroud, 1998), pp. 199–233.

and Osmund of Salisbury – the rest with popular English shrines, like that of Joseph of Arimathea at Glastonbury, or St William of Rochester, or the East Anglian shrine of the True Cross at Bromholm, with which I think the life of St Helena should be associated. The life of St Walstan falls into this cluster of shrine legends.[6] Its outline is as follows.

Walstan is a Saxon prince, son of Benedict and Blida, born in 'the southern part of Great Britain'. At the age of twelve he renounces his right to royal succession, and with his parents' reluctant agreement leaves home, travelling north to Taverham in Norfolk, where he settles to a life of virtuous labour and poverty, working on the land as a paid man and giving away his food and even his shoes to the poor. His mistress, angered by such ostentatious goodness, spitefully sends him barefoot into the woods to load a cart with thorns and thistles, but Walstan is unharmed, and his mistress is converted by this miracle. His childless lord and lady offer to make him their son and heir: he refuses.

After a life of virtuous toil, Walstan is eventually warned by an angel of his imminent death – he dutifully seeks *viaticum* and anointing. On the Saturday before his death he throws his scythe away at the hour of noon, since work done after this hour profanes the sabbath. Walstan duly dies while at work in the meadow on the following Monday, first asking that any labourer who comes to his shrine driven by any necessity may receive help and healing, and that his intercession will also be accepted for ailing farm animals. His body is taken in an ox-cart to Bawburgh for burial: *en route* the oxen stop twice and where they stop miraculous wells spring up. The legend concludes by emphasising the saint's chastity, self-mortification and charity to the poor, and his humility in renouncing royal authority to bind himself to 'simple rural people'. The reader is assured that Walstan's power is effective even for men and beasts who have actually lost organs, such as their eyes or genitals: he is declared to have died on 30 May 1016.

Two distinct elements seem to be combined in this Latin *vita*. At one level is the story of an aristocratic youth who renounces wealth and security to take up a life of self-denial and labour, whose life is attended both by persecution and by miraculous signs of divine favour, and who becomes an intercessor for farm labourers and sick animals, what Andre Vauchez calls 'a saint of charity and labour'. Overlaying these elements is a lightly priggish and decidedly clericalist picture of a devout and obedient parishioner anxious to make a good ending in devout penitence, concerned about sabbath observance and the evil of servile work in the fields carried out on a Sunday.

[6] C. Horstmann, *Nova Legenda Angliae*, 2 vols. (London, 1901), vol. II, pp. 412–15.

The legend of St Walstan survives, however, in another greatly expanded form which was printed in 1917 by M. R. James.[7] The original source was a pinnacled triptych panel make of wainscotting about three feet high, and covered with the verse legend written on parchment, formerly in Bawburgh Church. It is clear from internal evidence that it had hung near the shrine for the information and edification of pilgrims.

This Walstan verse legend is written in a rather spavined Rhyme Royal, made up of seven decasyllabic lines rhymed *ababbcc*. This was an established verse-form for saints' lives, with a particular East Anglian pedigree established by Lydgate and others. The language of the Walstan legend suggests that it was written around the turn of the fifteenth and sixteenth centuries, and as it happens the first decades of the Tudor century saw a spate of such verse legends, most of them appearing under the auspices of the publisher, Richard Pynson.[8]

Several of these early Tudor legends were clearly commissioned to promote pilgrimage to particular shrines, a fact which itself throws an interesting light on the management of pilgrimage in late medieval England, and the adaptation of new technologies to promote it. The legends all follow a common pattern, first narrating the story of the shrine's foundation or the life of the saint, then going on to give details of miracles performed there and encouraging the reader or hearer to come and test the power of the place for themselves. Pynson's legend of the Holy Blood of Hailes falls in this category,[9] as does his legend of Walsingham, published in the late 1490s and perhaps the most likely direct model for the Walstan poem,[10] and the Glastonbury legend of Joseph of Arimathea.[11]

The Walstan shrine legend is a thoroughly clericalised production. It beings with an elaborate theological reflection on the mystery of predestination.

> Almightie God in his eternall majestie
> disposing all things by his providence
> some he chooseth, some reproved be
> Scripture holy testifieth in sentence;
> Jacob elect was, Esau rejected by his power immense
> ye apostle called, not all chosen, I wys,
> some to damnation and some to eternal bliss.

[7] M. R. James (ed.), 'Lives of St Walstan', *Norfolk Archaeology*, 19 (1917), 238–67.

[8] Duffy, *Stripping of the Altars*, pp. 78–9.

[9] The sole surviving copy of the Holy Blood poem is missing from the Gloucester Public Library, where it was on deposit: we now rely on the account in J. C. T. Oats, 'Richard Pynson and the Holy Blood of Hayles', *The Library*, 5th series, 13 (1958), 269–77.

[10] Printed in J. C. Dickinson, *The Shrine of Our Lady of Walsingham* (Cambridge, 1956), pp. 124–30.

[11] J. A. Robinson, *Two Glastonbury Legends* (London, 1926); R. F. Traherne, *The Glastonbury Legends* (London, 1967).

The poem follows the basic pattern of the Latin *vita*, but incidental detail is elaborated – the harsh mistress is not only pierced with compunction on seeing Walstan's miracles, but physically torn with the thorns she had hoped would pierce the saint; the theme of Walstan as a figure promoting fertility, hinted at in the *vita*, is spelled out in the verse legend. Holy Walstan

> goth forth to semination.
> The angell above his head by multiplication
> Corn in his seedlepe make to increase.

The poem also greatly elaborates the theme of Walstan's royal birth, and the account of Walstan's life closes with the arrival of the bishop of Norwich for the funeral: the people tell him of the dead man's miracles; the result is an official local canonisation:

> The Bishop layd ear and harkened soore
> And allowed him a saint for ever more.

The second half of the poem is devoted to an account of eleven miracles performed at the shrine. They are a pretty standard set – a manacled lunatic restored to sanity, the cure of a woman wounded by an arrow, a priest with a perforated hernia restored by bathing in the holy water placed on the tomb, a drowned man raised to life after his body was laid before the shrine – and so on. Most of these miracles are local – four in Bawburgh itself, three for people from villages within a ten-mile radius. The only remote cure is that of a Canterbury weaver who had vainly gone to Becket's shrine on crutches and, on the advice of a Norfolk man whom he met there, had sought instead St Walstan, who succeeded where Becket had failed. But Sir Gregory Lovell, an identifiable person healed of 'bone ache' who died in 1507,[12] lived thirty miles from the shrine, and there is a miracle for labourers in the Flegge, twenty-five miles the other side of Norwich. The legend summarises many miracles

> done in this place
> of Men also women, wch to him will sue...
> Good folks cease not, devoutly seeke and pray
> yee shall be succoured and comforted ere yee gang away.

The author provides a prayer to Walstan to be recited even

> though ye be unlearned nor can read nor spell,

---

[12] His will is in PCC Adeane 23, PRO Prob 11/15 LH 187: there is no mention of Bawburgh or St Walston.

and the poem ends with another polysyllabic theological meditation on God's power and love:

> Omnipotent God and nature doth werke
> neither frustratory nor vainly, but to an end,
> as the Philosopher wch is called a Clerke
> testifieth ready is to defend;
> and yet could not the first cause perfectly comprehend
> which is the will of God and create all things,
> but stood and abideth in himself musing.

Even more than in the Latin *vita*, two divergent energies are evident in the Walstan verse legend. On the one hand there is the fairy-tale story of the secret prince, the king's son who makes himself humblest of the humble, and whose touch brings renewal, fruitfulness and healing. But this is framed within a theological grid in which a nervous desire to provide official episcopal credentials for the saint's status is in evidence, in which marvellous tales of atrocious wounds healed and the dead raised are topped and tailed by abstract meditation on the sovereignty of God. And as in the *vita*, the picture of the wonder-working prince is overlaid by the virtues of a good Tudor parishioner, elaborately respectful of a strict sabbatarianism, conscientiously performing the corporal works of mercy, seeking the last sacraments from his parish priest as death approaches. A popular saint's life has been pressed into a moralising clerical mould and more than that, the piety of pilgrimage is clearly being assimilated to the localised parochial piety that was the heart of late medieval religion.[13]

It seems clear that Walstan's cult was gathering momentum in the later fifteenth century. Badges of Edward IV on the nave roof suggest that the body of the church was rebuilt in the 1460s or 1470s and in 1460 Thomas Easthawe, a former vicar, left 20 shillings to the building of St Walstan's chapel. By the early 1470s parishioners were leaving bequests to this chapel, by 1496 there was a Walstan guild, which over the next decade was itself the recipient of small bequests ranging from one to twelve shillings, and the shrine had joined the list of local and national shrines – Walsingham, Woolpit, Master John Schorne and King Henry – to which routine mortuary benefactions might be left.[14]

The shrine was clearly booming by this stage. Blomefield claims that there were six chantry priests working at St Walstan's altar, a figure he

[13] Duffy, *Stripping of the Altars*, p. 204.

[14] These details are from: F. Blomefield and C. Parkin, *An Essay towards a Topographical History of the County of Norfolk* (London, 1805–10), vol. I, pp. 641–5. M. Gill, 'The Saint with a Scythe', *Proceedings of the Suffolk Institute of Archaeology*, 38 (1993), 245–54; Colin Richmond, 'Religion', in R. Horrox (ed.), *Fifteenth-Century Attitudes* (Cambridge, 1994), p. 187.

seems to have plucked from the air. But chantry chaplains there certainly were, and by the end of the fifteenth century the parochial incumbent was routinely a graduate, a sign of the prosperity that pilgrimage had brought to the parish. By the early years of the sixteenth century local clergy and lay people regularly bequeathed their souls not only to God and the company of heaven, but in particular to St Walstan.

This evident growth of devotion and of devotional infrastructure in the parish was reflected in the appearance of devotional imagery further afield. Traces of nine images of Walstan appear on Norfolk screens, the best of them at Sparham, at Barnham Broom, at Ludham, at Litcham All Saints, and at Burlingham Saint Andrews. On several of these screens Walstan keeps company with other East Anglian pilgrimage saints, suggesting the location of his cult within a generally vigorous interest in the shrines of the region and beyond – at Ludham with St Edmund of Bury but also Henry VI, at Litcham with St Edmund, St William of Norwich and (probably) St Etheldreda of Ely. St Etheldreda occurs again at Beeston, and both St Etheldreda and St Withburge of East Dereham at Burlingham St Andrews and at Barnham Broom: in both these cases St Withburge holds her shrine church in her hand. The Burlingham screen also carries images of Edward the Confessor and Thomas Becket. The earliest datable of these images is the one at Ludham, painted in the mid-1490s or soon after; Litcham and Sparham probably date from about the same time; the screen at Barnham Broom probably dates from the second decade of the sixteenth century; while the latest is certainly that at Burlingham St Andrews, completed in 1536 after the break with Rome. The geographical scatter of these images, contrary to my own earlier impressions, suggests a thriving cult of Walstan well outside the immediate area of his burial place, borne out by the statement of the East Anglian Protestant polemicist, John Bale, who declared that Walstan was 'after the maner of Priapus the God of theyr fieldes in Northfolke and gyde of theyr harvests, al mowers and scythe folowers sekyng hym once in the Yeare'.[15] Outside the county, there is a wall-painting of Walstan with clients, which I have not seen, at Cavenham in Suffolk; he is carved on the hammerbeam roof at Earl Stonham, painted on the screen at Foxearth, Essex, and there was a chapel dedicated to him in St Mary's, Bury St Edmunds.[16]

I have dwelt at length on the cult of Walstan because it provides a comparatively full case-study of one of late medieval England's myriad local shrines. But many, perhaps most, of these local shrines were centred not on a body, as at Bawburgh, but on an image, and it was the

---

[15] Blomefield and Parkin, *Topographical History of Norfolk*, vol. I, p. 642.
[16] Gill, 'The Saint with a Scythe', p. 248.

multiplication of images in the later Middle Ages that made possible the multiplication of shrines. Image shrines could, of course, loom just as large and serve the same function as grave shrines: Rocamadour and Walsingham were image shrines. Below these great international image shrines were thousands of lesser images that themselves attracted local loyalty. The good rood of the North Door of St Paul's, or the Rood of Boxley, were matched by hundreds of lesser roods, niched or tabernacled above side-altars in country churches – like the 'Good Rood upon the northseyde' of Blythburgh Church to which John Brown left 40 shillings in 1533 'to make hym a new cote', or the good rood on the north side of Bramfield Church whose decorated niche is still visible.[17] The cluster of shrines to which the early fifteenth-century Alice Cooke of Horstead declared 'I will have a man to go . . . pilgremages' – Our Lady of Reepham, St Spirit of Elsing, St Parnell of Stratton, St Leonard without Norwich, St Wandred of Byskeley, St Margaret of Horstead, Our Lady of Pity of Horstead, St John's head at Trimingham, and the Holy Rood of Crostwight – were all local image shrines, some of them known only from this single mention.[18] All over late medieval England the local shrines of the Virgin were based on images, some of which achieved a regional status that put them on a par with more famous shrines.

Our Lady of Woolpit in Suffolk was an image in a chapel on the north side of Woolpit Church.[19] By the early thirteenth century the offerings of pilgrims were significant enough for Bury Abbey to demand a share: by 1286 a fair had sprung up, held on the main pilgrimage day, 8 September, the feast day of the Nativity of the Virgin. By the fifteenth century local people were lavishing gifts on the shrine, like the diamond ring bequeathed by Dame Elizabeth Andrews of Baylham in 1473, one of a pair, the other of which went to Our Lady of Walsingham, or the 'pair of beads of thrice sixty garnished with silver and three gold rings set thereto, with a cross and heart of silver' offered to the shrine by Robert Reydon of Creeting in 1505, on condition that they remained always round the neck of the image of Our Lady of Woolpit. From the 1450s to the late 1520s local wills from many of the surrounding villages and towns – Thorndon, Thurston, Otley, Gislingham, Wetheringsett, Kelsale, Fornham – make arrangements for pilgrimages on behalf of the dead to Our Lady of Woolpit, and the shrine had clearly become a focus of regional identity. Lord John Howard of Stoke-by-Nayland, future duke of

[17] NCC Punting 31r.
[18] R. Hart, 'Shrines and Pilgrimages of the County of Norfolk', *Norfolk Archaeology*, 6 (1864), 277.
[19] For what follows on Woolpit, C. Paine, 'The Chapel and Image of Our Lady of Woolpit', *Proceedings of the Suffolk Institute of Archaeology*, 38 (1996), 8–12.

Norfolk, made several benefactions of money, lights and silver-gilt votive images to our Lady of Woolpit in the early 1480s, and Woolpit was one of the five East Anglian shrines (alongside our Lady of Walsingham, Ipswich, Sudbury and Stoke by Clare) to whom Queen Elizabeth sent a pilgrim to pray for her in Lent 1502. As all this suggests, local shrines certainly helped focus and express the regional sensibility of lay elites. In the same year that Queen Elizabeth's pilgrims toured their shrines, the prosperous Norfolk grazier William Atereth commissioned a painting of St Helena for his parish church of Cawston: she is depicted holding the reliquary of the True Cross from the East Anglian shrine of Bromholm. Twenty years or so earlier a replica of a pilgrimage souvenir card from Bromholm, containing an indulgenced hymn and prayers to the Cross, like the one pasted into the Lewkener Hours at Lambeth, was carefully bound into an East Anglian Book of Hours which shows other signs of a self-conscious interest in local shrines, such as St Edmund's at Bury. The devotions of the shrine were thus transplanted into the daily piety of the book's owner.[20]

Shrines might help define and sustain the boundaries of regional identity in other ways. In 1499 a group of parishioners from the village of Great Ashfield, four miles from Woolpit, were found guilty of magical practices. They were required to perform public penance not only in their parish church, but at Norwich Cathedral, Bury St Edmunds marketplace, and during the procession at the shrine of Our Lady of Woolpit, where they were required to offer candles to the image of St Mary in the chapel.[21] The shrine and its liturgy were therefore felt to provide a suitable and conspicuous regional forum for the exemplary punishment of religious deviants. Other shrines were used in this way throughout the late Middle Ages. In 1411 the bishop of Salisbury required the rector of Ramsbury, convicted of fornication, to make a pilgrimage to Salisbury to offer a pound of wax to the image of the Virgin.[22] In 1486 the bishop of Hereford required a group of parishioners from Bosbury who had

---

[20] For the Cawston screen, E. Duffy, 'The Parish, Piety and Patronage in Late Medieval East Anglia', in K. L. French, G. C. Gibbs and B. A. Kumin (eds.), *The Parish in English Life* (Manchester, 1997), pp. 145–6; Fitzwilliam Museum Mss 5, Horae *c*. 1480, fol. 57b. Such gestures are extensions of the devotional vogue for pilgrim badges and tokens. These were widely believed to retain and transmit some of the power of the shrine itself, so that even bulky lead badges were sometimes pinned or glued into Books of Hours: see pl. 1, p. 148 in B. W. Spencer, 'Medieval Pilgrim Badges', in *Rotterdam Papers: A Contribution to Medieval Archaeology* (Rotterdam, 1968). (Replicas of pilgrim badges painted in the margins of a Flemish Book of Hours in Sir John Soane's Museum, Ms 4 fol. 122v.)

[21] P. Northeast, 'Superstition and Belief: A Suffolk Case of the Fifteenth Century', *Suffolk Review*, n.s., 20 (1993), 44–6.

[22] J. M. Horn (ed.), *Register of Robert Hallam, Bishop of Salisbury 1407–17* (Torquay, 1982), p. 215.

attacked a local cleric to make a pilgrimage to the shrine of St Thomas Cantilupe in Hereford Cathedral.[23]

Salisbury is twenty-five miles from Ramsbury, Hereford is fifteen miles from Bosbury: the penitential elements of distance, inconvenience and expense were clearly part of the point of these pilgrimages of reparation. But once again the notion of 'liminality' does not seem an altogether helpful analytical tool. These penitential pilgrimages were indeed part of the process by which deviants might be restored to the wider *communitas* of the Church. In many cases, however, and certainly that of the magicians of Great Ashfield, the penitents were sent to their regional shrines not to lose or submerge their individuality in a wider *communitas*, but precisely so that their specific misdemeanours might the better be made excruciatingly public: the pilgrimage was designed to endorse and enforce rather than to dissolve the values of the local community.

In any case, the distance these reluctant pilgrims were obliged to travel mattered not because it sent them on a journey beyond the familiar, but because it put them to trouble. Pilgrimage was a labour, an arduous and expensive work – the Kentish Lollard, John Franke, considered that 'pilgrimages to holy and devoute places be not necessary nor meritorious for mannys soule, but that money and labor doon and spent therabout is all in vain'.[24] This emphasis on 'doing', 'labouring' and 'spending' was not the isolated perception of heretics: testators making provision for surrogate pilgrimages to be made on their behalf as a form of post-mortem intercession stipulated payments to those making the pilgrimages 'for their labours'.[25]

Provisions for these surrogate pilgrimages were extremely common, and they illustrate further the problematic character of the concept of liminality as a tool for interpreting late medieval local pilgrimage. The devotee who pays someone else to go on pilgrimage is clearly happy to dispense with the symbolic value of journeying, of abandoning the safe and familiar things of home, in favour of a transaction in which a transferable benefit is secured. The point of the pilgrimage is not the journeying but the pardon it secures, and the pilgrimage is simply one means among many of gaining a desired spiritual benefit. Even the pilgrimage to Rome might be viewed in this way. Thomas Herynge of Walsingham left money in 1504 so that 'as sone as my executor may

---

[23] A. T. Bannister (ed.), *Registrum Thome Myllyng, Episcopi Herefordiensis 1474–92* (London, 1920), p. 107.

[24] N. Tanner (ed.), *Kent Heresy Proceedings, 1511–12* (Kent Records, 1997), p. 4, 90: D. P. Wright (ed.), *The Register of Thomas Langton, Bishop of Salisbury, 1485–93* (Canterbury and York Society, 19-), p. 72.

[25] L. L. Duncan (ed.), *Testamenta Cantiana: West Kent* (London, 1906), pp. 271, 348.

know that any troste man that is a preste of this cuntre have any eryn
to Rome, that he shall gyve unto him a certeyn money, to synge for my
soule and for the soules of my good benefactors, v massys at Rome,
at such places as moste mede is at'.[26] The priest here, we note, is to
be chosen because he already has an errand at Rome: what Herynge
wants is masses at powerfully privileged altars, for which the journey itself has no apparent significance. Even pilgrimage literature might present
the benefits of pilgrimage in this resolutely sedentary and unadventur-
ous way. William Brewyn's guide to the Roman pilgrimage, listing the
indulgences available at the Lateran, made the conventional comment
that 'if people only knew how great are the indulgences of the Lateran
church, they would not think it necessary to go across the sea to the Holy
Sepulchre'.[27]

The role of indulgences as a motive for pilgrimage in late medieval
England hardly needs demonstration. The whole pilgrim-literature genre
represented by *The Stacyons of Rome* turned on it – all such books were
essentially trainspotter's guides to the best and most powerful relics and
indulgences.[28] One of the spiritual privileges Christ granted Margery
Kempe when she desired to go again to Jerusalem was a dispensation
from the *need* to travel: 'Dowtyr, as oftyn-tymes as thu seyst or thynkyst
"Worshepyed be alle tho holy placys in Ierusalem that Crist suffyrde bitter
peyn and passyon in", thu schalt have the same pardon as gyf thu wer
wyth thi bodily persens bothyn to thi-self & to alle tho that thu wylt
gevyn it to'.[29] The same eagerness for indulgences motivated local
pilgrimage. The episcopal registers of Edmund Lacy provide dozens of
examples of indulgences granted to local chapels, hospitals and churches
to help defray the costs of building or repair work: donors wanting the
indulgence had to go to the parish in question 'devote causa perigrina-
cionis', penitent, confessed and contrite, and make an offering.[30] 'Gostly
helth'[31] rather than physical healing was the object of such pilgrimages
(which perhaps formed the majority of pilgrimages in fifteenth- and
sixteenth-century England). In them, pilgrims were primarily interested

---

[26] H. Harrod (ed.), 'Extracts from Early Norfolk Wills', *Norfolk Archaeology*, 1 (1847), 257.
[27] C. E. Woodruff (ed.), *A XVth Century Guide-Book to the Principal Churches of Rome
Compiled c. 1470 by William Brewyn* (London, 1933), p. 25.
[28] F. J. Furnivall (ed.), *The Stacyons of Rome* (London, 1867).
[29] S. B. Meech and E. H. Allen (eds.), *The Book of Margery Kempe*, EETS 212 (1940),
p. 75.
[30] J. H. Parry (ed.), *Register of Edmund Lacy, Bishop of Hereford, 1417–20* (London, 1918),
pp. 21, 24, 28; G. R. Dunstan (ed.), *The Register of Edmund Lacy, Bishop of Exeter 1420–
1455* (Torquay, 1963), vol. I: pp. 51, 107, 300, 306, 315; vol. II: pp. 25, 314, 403;
vol. III: pp. 14, 38, 39, 136, 210.
[31] Meech and Allen (eds.), *Book of Margery Kempe*, p. 22.

in the spiritual benefits of an indulgence, and the consequent reduction of time spent by the devotee in purgatory after death.

The association with indulgences was an important aspect of the integration of pilgrimage into the soteriology of late medieval Christianity, in which grace and obligation were finely balanced. The arrangements made by Henry VII's queen Elizabeth of York for pilgrimages to be made on her behalf in Lent 1502 to shrines all over the country have often been noted, and I have already mentioned them here. It is not usually noted, however, that the payments to the two pilgrims concerned are for exactly forty days' journeying in total – a *lent* of pilgrimages, carried out during lent of that year, and a very clear signal of the assimilation of pilgrimage to other forms of penitential observance.[32]

The same processes of assimilation are evident in the management of vows of pilgrimage. Pilgrimages might be taken as the result of pure devotion, or as the consequence of a vow. Vows of pilgrimage were by and large treated very seriously, and promises of pilgrimage to the major shrines of Rome, Compostela and Jerusalem could be dispensed only by the pope himself.[33] Pilgrimage vows might be undertaken as an act of devotion to a saint or to secure help or healing in emergency. When the ship in which the Norfolk priest Sir Richard Torkyngton was travelling back from the Holy Land was caught in a January storm, the crew and passengers pledged themselves to pilgrimage, 'sum of us pylgrymages to or blyssed lady of Lorett in Ytalya, and sum to or Lady of Walsyngham and sum to Seynt Thomas of Caunterbury we that war Englyshmen'. The captain of the ship clinched all these vows by taking a collection to offer at the shrine of the three kings of Cologne, patron saints of travellers.[34] Vows of this sort had to be fulfilled one way or another, and if sickness or circumstances prevented it, then it had to be done by proxy. William Couper of Stone in Oxney asked his executors in 1517 to make provision for someone to perform four pilgrimages 'undone in my life'.[35] Agnes Parker of Keswick in Norfolk told her executors in 1507 that 'I owe a pilgrimage to Canterbury; another to St Tebbald of Hobbies, and another to St Albert of Cringleford'.[36] Margaret East, widow of the parish of St Martin in the Bailey, made arrangements for her executor, her 'right

---

[32] N. H. Nicholas (ed.), *Privy Purse Expenses of Elizabeth of York* (London, 1830), pp. 3–4.

[33] The faculties given to private chaplains licensed at Rome routinely specify the power to dispense all pilgrimage vows except those to these greater sites: e.g., J. A. Twemlow (ed.), *Calendar of Entries in the Papal Registers Relating to Great Britain and Ireland: Paper Letters*, vol. xiv (London, 1960), pp. 189, 255.

[34] R. B. Wheeler (ed.), 'Torkington's Pilgrimage to Jerusalem in 1517', *Gentleman's Magazine*, 82 (1812), 313.

[35] Duncan (ed.), *Testamenta Cantiana: West Kent*, p. 326.

[36] Hart, 'Pilgrimages of the County of Norfolk', p. 277.

trusty and well beloved cosyn Thomas Thurkell, shoemake in Berstrete' to go on her behalf:

steyn [certain] pylgremage, that is to sey, in my lyf to the holy St Wandrede, and after my dissease he xall go unto Seynt Thomas of Canterbury, and there to prey for me to release me of my vowe which I made thyrdyr myself. And from thens the same Thomas sall go for me on pylgrymage unto the Abbey of Chelkey (Chertsey) ther as Kyng Henry lyth, yf my goodys wyll stretch so fer for his costs. And so be hys pylgrimages that I may be relesyd of myn avowes.[37]

The argument of this paper has been a modest and simple one. Much of the most interesting recent work on late medieval religion has emphasised the central place of the local in it, and we have become intensely aware of the importance of community and community formation in the religious priorities of the late medieval laity. Much recent discussion of pilgrimage, by contrast, has emphasised the solvent and 'liminal' character of the practice of pilgrimage, and its power to remove Christians from their local contexts and integrate them into a wider and more anonymous *communitas*. I have argued that in practice late medieval pilgrimage tended to be assimilated to the locality and to community formation in the narrower and more specific sense: going on pilgrimage is a liminal phenomenon only if, and to much the same extent, that going to market was a liminal phenomenon. Pilgrimage *might* take one beyond the familiar, and might dissolve the ties that bound. But we should not be mesmerised by Margery Kempe. Most late medieval pilgrims were consolidating, not dissolving, their social and religious world.

[37] Harrod (ed.), 'Early Norfolk Wills', *Norfolk Archaeology*, 4 (1855), 338.

Michael Bush

Thanks to the Dodds, the northern risings of October 1536 and the Lincolnshire rebellion of the same month are usually seen as interlinked components of the pilgrimage of grace.[1] Yet this is somewhat misleading. Although connected in motive and organisation, the two insurrections differed in certain vital respects. The government's relationship with the Lincolnshire rebels was quite unlike the one it had with the pilgrims of grace, since the former submitted unconditionally while the latter were granted a promise of parliamentary remedy and a complete pardon for every participant.[2] More to the point, the Lincolnshire rebellion did not claim to be a pilgrimage. The term 'pilgrimage of grace' only came into use after the Lincolnshire uprising had collapsed. The concept of revolt as a pilgrimage first surfaced on 13 October in Yorkshire when two practising London lawyers – Robert Aske and William Stapulton – both of them younger sons of Yorkshire gentry families, met on Weighton Hill, each in command of a rebel army. At the meeting Aske declared that they were all pilgrims and had 'a pilgrimage gat to go'.[3] This analogy must have occurred to him within the previous two days since it failed to receive any mention in a proclamation that he issued on 11 October, announcing a muster on Skipwith Moor.[4]

Having taken York on 16 October, Aske produced, over the next two days, a number of manifestos that presented the revolt as a pilgrimage: notably a proclamation addressed to the northern gentlemen and signed by Aske 'in the name of all pilgrimage and commonalty'; an order for religious houses dissolved, issued 'by all the whole consent of all the headmen of this our pilgrimage for grace'; and an oath for swearing the gentlemen which mentioned 'our pilgrimage of grace for the commonwealth'. The latter cited the title of the uprising in full. First, the term 'pilgrimage

---

[1] See M. H. Dodds and R. Dodds, *The Pilgrimage of Grace, 1536–1537 and the Exeter Conspiracy, 1538*, 2 vols. (Cambridge University Press, 1915), chs. 5 and 6.

[2] M. Bush, *The Pilgrimage of Grace: A Study of the Rebel Armies of October 1536* (Manchester University Press, 1996), pp. 13, 16, 393–4.

[3] *LP*, vol. XI, 828/xii, p. 327.   [4] Bush, *Pilgrimage of Grace*, p. 8 and n15.

for grace' came into use which, following the addition of 'for the commonwealth', was altered to 'pilgrimage of grace' in order to avoid a repeat of the preposition 'for'. Aske soon afterwards revealed the meaning of the term.[5] Meeting the royal messenger, Lancaster Herald, in Pontefract Castle on 21 October, he announced that 'he and his company would go to London, of pilgrimage to the king's highness, and there to have all vile blood of his council put from him, and all noble blood set up again; and also the faith of Christ and his laws to be kept and full restitution of Christ's church of all wrongs done unto it; and also the commonty to be used as they should be'.[6] At his examination in April 1537, Aske shed further light on the term's meaning, remarking that the revolt was 'for grace by petition to [the king] for remedy for their faith'.[7] The uprising, then, came to be conceived as a pilgrimage typically designed to invoke grace. Yet the grace sought appeared to be that of the king. Moreover, rather than relying upon God's grace to persuade the king to extend his favour, the rebels took the precaution of backing up their supplication with an impressive show of military force. Appropriately for a pilgrimage, the rebels were on a religious mission. Their aim was to persuade the king to end his pact with heresy: in other words, to undo the religious changes that he had authorised in the previous three years. But they also wanted him to respect the commonwealth, essentially by complying with the abiding principles of the society of orders.[8]

Presenting a rebellion as a pilgrimage seemed to be the clever invention of Robert Aske, conceived in reaction to the royal injunctions of the previous August that had ordered priests to discourage pilgrimages on the grounds that the practice caused people to venerate the saints as gods. To attribute it to certain elderly former crusaders – such as Lord Darcy, Sir Robert Constable and Sir Ralph Ellerker, who had participated in the holy war against the Moor of 1511 – is wrong, simply because the idea of presenting the insurrection as a military pilgrimage had been implanted prior to their involvement. Nor does there seem to be any connection between Reginald Pole's call for a crusade in his work *De Unitate* and the form the rebellion took. It is faintly possible that Aske was inspired to coin the phrase by current talk in London – of the sort that the imperial ambassador, Eustace Chapuys, relayed to Charles V – but this concerned an internal revolt in conjunction with the emperor's conquest of England; whereas the pilgrimage of grace rose simply to call the government to

---

[5] *Ibid.*, pp. 8–9, 11.   [6] *SP Henry VIII*, I, pp. 486–7 (*LP*, vol. XI, 826).
[7] M. Bateson (ed.), 'The Pilgrimage of Grace and Aske's Examination', *EHR*, 5 (1890), 571.
[8] Bush, *Pilgrimage of Grace*, pp. 102–11.

order and made no attempt to link up with foreign powers. If the pope had proceeded in 1536 to excommunicate Henry VIII and to order the Catholic powers to conduct a holy war against England, the plans relayed by Chapuys might have appeared more credible; but this did not happen until two years later.[9]

Yet it would be wrong to attribute the pilgrim idiom simply to Aske. Its usage also derived from a 'captain poverty movement'. A great deal of the north, notably the uplands, rose independently of Aske but, nonetheless, still subscribed to a sense of pilgrimage, for they saw themselves led by Captain Poverty, an embodiment of the commons and Christ and seemingly drawn from the literary tradition of Piers Plowman.[10] William Langland's late fourteenth-century poem appeared to provide the northern rebels of October 1536 with a guide to revolt, explicitly in books five and six [B text], and again in book nineteen [B text]. Thus, 'a thousand of men thronged together' and appealed for grace to Christ and his mother. Their plan was to go on a pilgrimage in search of St Truth, but they had no idea of where to go, until, that is, they met Piers, a ploughman, who declared that he was familiar with this particular saint and prepared to lead them to him. But work had to come first. Before Piers could take them, he needed to plough and sow his half acre of land. And so the pilgrimage was left in prospect and, then according to book seven [B text], called off on the grounds that one could get much closer to St Truth by staying at home and following the example of Do Well.[11] Yet the pilgrim story is taken up again in book nineteen [B text] where the allegorical figure of Grace came to Piers, advising him 'the commons to summon' and offering him 'weapons to fight with that will never fail'.

[9] For Robert Aske, see *ibid.*, pp. 10–11. For its attribution to former crusaders, see C. Tyerman, *England and the Crusades, 1095–1588* (University of Chicago Press, 1988), p. 343. All were members of the peace party in October that was responsible for pressing a non-military solution. See Bush, *Pilgrimage of Grace*, p. 379. Constable only became an advocate of war in December after learning that, in breach of the terms of the Truce, Cromwell was planning to establish garrisons in the north, notably at Scarborough. See J. C. Cox (ed.), 'William Stapleton and the pilgrimage of grace', *Transactions of the East Riding Antiquarian Society*, 10 (1903), 104–5. For his support of a peaceful solution in October, see PRO SP1/119, f. 7 (*LP*, vol. xii(1). 1022), *LP*, vol. xi. 1300, *LP*, vol. xii(1), 1225. He reverted to this approach following the December agreement when with Aske he opposed further revolt. See M. Bush and D. Bownes, *The Defeat of the Pilgrimage of Grace* (Hull University Press, 1999), p. 349. Tyerman relies too much on what was imparted by Chapuys and Pole (see pp. 359–60). For obvious reasons, this cannot be taken as good evidence of the rebels' intent

[10] M. L. Bush, 'Captain Poverty and the Pilgrimage of Grace', *Historical Research*, 65 (1992), 17–36. For some intimation of the sixteenth century's familiarity with Langland, see H. C. White, *Social Criticism in Popular Religious Literature of the Sixteenth Century* (London: Macmillan, 1944), ch. 1.

[11] W. W. Skeat (ed.), *The Vision of William Concerning Piers the Plowman*, 2 vols. (Oxford University Press, 1886), vol. i, pp. 178, 180–224, 226.

At this point, then, the plan to go on a pilgrimage was revived specifically in the military form of a crusade to destroy the agents of anti-Christ: 'the false prophets, flatterers and glozers [i.e. glossators]' who insert themselves as 'the curators over kings and earls'. But before this can happen the poem is abruptly ended as Conscience, having resolved to become a pilgrim in order to search out Piers Plowman, the archetypal commoner, the earthly embodiment of Christ and the most appropriate leader for this crusade, wakened Langland with a cry for grace, thus terminating his poetic dream.[12]

The northern risings of October 1536 became an uncanny fulfilment – perhaps a deliberate enactment – of Langland's proposed pilgrimage. Captain Poverty first appeared in Richmond on 15 October. On that day, a rebel gathering was held in the town and John Dakyn, acting archdeacon of Richmond, claimed to have 'heard a very simple poor man, whose name I know not whom they named Lord Poverty, say amongst the tumult he would die in the matter'.[13] Soon afterwards, letters circulated in the upland north signed by Captain Poverty or some variant, such as Lord of Poverty, Master Poverty or Brother Poverty – stating the rebel cause and calling upon the commons to rise in its support as 'the brethren of Christ'. The purpose was to defend the border against Scottish incursion while demanding religious and political reforms from Henry VIII and agrarian reforms from local landlords. Dispatched into Durham and Northumberland, and across into Cumberland, Westmorland, Lancashire and the West Riding, the letters caused armies to form with the aim of going on a crusade to destroy heresy and to protect the commons.[14] Some of them (notably the two hosts recruited from Durham and the North Riding) joined Aske in order to march on London; others (notably the two hosts recruited from Cumberland and the barony of Westmorland) went to defend the border; yet more (notably the host recruited from Kendal and Dent, and another recruited from Percy Fee in Craven) sought to pin down northern magnates who had remained loyal to the Crown: that is, the earl of Derby operating from Preston, and the earl of Cumberland based at Skipton.

The northern rebels subscribed to other rituals and procedures redolent of the pilgrim tradition. In the pilgrim manner, they took vows, in the form of an oath. This came in several forms, but mostly it obliged the sworn 'to be true to God, the king and the commonwealth' or 'to be true to God, the king and the commons'.[15] Gentlemen and clerics swore individually on a missal, while the commons took the oath *en masse* with a

---

[12] *Ibid.*, pp. 562, 600.
[13] Bush, 'Captain Poverty', 147; PRO SP1/117, fol. 207 (*LP*, vol. XII(1), 786/ii).
[14] Bush, 'Captain Poverty', 18–26.   [15] Bush, *Pilgrimage of Grace*, p. 12.

roar of approval.[16] Crosses, moreover, were very much to the fore, usually borne by priests. It was felt that the rebel armies should proceed behind the cross of Christ. The oath composed by Aske urged his supporters to 'take afore you the cross of Christ'.[17] And when his army went on its first march, from Skipwith Moor to Market Weighton, it did so behind the cross of Howden Minster. The practice was not simply created by Aske. The Cumberland rebels, who developed their own 'captain poverty' procedures, had a designated cross-bearer who accompanied the four captains of Penrith – named, in recognition of Langland's poem, Charity, Faith, Poverty and Pity – as they mustered the county.[18] In Halifax, before Aske had influenced those parts, John Lacy ordered the inhabitants to don harness and march behind its parish church cross into Lancashire.[19] By 15 October cross-bearing was a well-established practice, so much so that from Pontefract a loyalist gentlemen, who had taken refuge there, reported that the rebels 'doth daily increase fast of every parish [and] the cross goeth afore them'; and on 26 October the pilgrim host stood arrayed outside Doncaster behind a cross; for attached to its main banner, the standard of St Cuthbert, was an actual cross with miraculous powers.[20] Clerics were needed to carry the crosses. George Lumley, whose task was to raise support from a number of religious houses, specifically ordered from each 'two monks with the best crosses to come forward'.[21] Yet the clergy were not always ready to oblige. Having been called upon to carry the cross before the Percy host – when, on 20 October it marched through York to join Aske at Pontefract – William Thorneton, abbot of York St Mary, initially and presumably under pressure complied, but then made his getaway, leaving his cross behind him.[22]

Furthermore, in the manner of pilgrims, the northern rebels saw themselves as going on a remedial journey. This was clearly in Aske's mind when, on 21 October, he told Lancaster Herald, who wished to hear the rebels' resolutions, that the very first was to go to London. To do so, he claimed, the people were 'all of one accord'.[23] The point was substantiated by others, notably Harry Sais who, about this time, was captured by a band of commons in the region of Ferrybridge and heard them say 'that they would come forward towards London, as far as they be suffered'.[24]

[16] *Ibid.*, pp. 114, 227–8, 345.
[17] T. N. Toller (ed.), *Correspondence of Edward Third Earl of Derby*, Chetham Society, n.s. 19 (1890), pp. 50–1.
[18] Bush, *Pilgrimage of Grace*, p. 333.
[19] SP1/117, fol. 193 (*LP*, vol. xii(1), 784); PRO E36/122, fol. 28 (*LP*, xii(1), 853).
[20] SP1/110, fol. 47b (*LP*, vol. xi, 729). For the cross attached to the banner, see below, note 38.
[21] SP1/115, fol. 212b (*LP*, vol. xii(1), 369).
[22] SP1/115, fols. 260b–161 (*LP*, vol. xii(1), 393 (2)).
[23] *SP Henry VIII*, i, p. 486 (*LP*, vol. xi, 826).
[24] SP1/109, fol. 203b (*LP*, vol. xi, 879/ii).

Thomas Percy made the same point, alleging that the commons 'thought to have come towards London and to take up the country by the way and afterwards to have spoken with the king and to sue to his grace to have certain statutes revoked and to have them punished that were the causes of the making thereof'.[25] The basic rebel aim, then, was to win the government over by directly threatening it with military force. All this was in keeping with earlier pilgrimages, especially the crusader journeys to the Holy Land or to Albigensian France or to Moorish Spain and Africa or to the Ottoman Front.

In the traditional pilgrim way, the northern rebels were bedecked with declaratory banners and badges that overtly declared a religious cause. Until the Truce of 27 October, many rebels wore, front and back, the black cross of St Cuthbert. However, this came to be confused with the red cross of St George as worn by the king's army. A terrible incident, in which the rebels killed one of their own through mistaking his black cross for a red one – thus causing the only death to occur in combat during the whole revolt – led to a change of badge. Thereafter, the pilgrim troops sported either the badge of the five wounds or the badge of Christ's name.[26] The five wounds badge was something the rebel leader Lord Darcy had brought back from crusading against the Moor and which he pressed upon Aske after finding a supply in Pontefract Castle. This badge was prominently displayed when the pilgrim host stood outside Doncaster on 26 and 27 October.[27] Moreover, in the interval between the October Truce (the result of the first appointment between the duke of Norfolk, the king's lieutenant, and the rebel leadership) and the December agreement (the result of the second appointment with Norfolk), more elaborate badges of the five wounds were made, to be worn by the rebel delegates when treating with the representatives of the Crown. It was these badges that the delegates dramatically tore off on 8 December in Norfolk's presence to signal that the pilgrimage was over.[28] As for the rebels' banners, the main one was St Cuthbert's. Loaned to the rebels by the monks of Durham Priory, it was brought to the front by the Durham men and placed in front of the pilgrim host at Doncaster.[29] A second banner, a depiction of the five wounds, was furnished by Lord Lumley, another rebel with crusader interests, this time associated with the cult of St George. However, this particular banner only surfaced in

[25] SP1/115, fol. 261 (*LP*, vol. xii(1), 393 (2)).

[26] Bush, *Pilgrimage of Grace*, p. 182; Bateson (ed.), 'Pilgrimage of Grace', 511–12, 571–2.

[27] Bateson (ed.), 'Pilgrimage of Grace', 555, 571–2; and evident in Latimer's St Paul's Cross sermon of 29 October (quoted in Tyerman, *England and the Crusades*, p. 344).

[28] Bush, *Pilgrimage of Grace*, p. 405.

[29] *LP*, vol. xiii(1), 946 (118); Bateson (ed.), 'Pilgrimage of Grace', p. 336; R. W. Hoyle, 'Thomas Master's Narrative of the Pilgrimage of Grace', *Northern History*, 21 (1985), 71; Bush, *Pilgrimage of Grace*, pp. 379–80.

December when, coming down from Durham to take part in the second appointment, Lumley displayed it outside his lodgings in Pontefract.[30]

Finally the northern rebels had their own pilgrim songs: one, composed by Friar Pickering of Bridlington; another, by a monk of Sawley Abbey. The former urged 'O faithful people of the boreal region' to 'boldly go forward in our peregrinatio' to destroy 'the cursed Cromwell' who was presented, in crusader terms, as one of 'those southern Turks perverting our laws [and] spoiling Christ's church'.[31] The latter song proposed something similar: guided by Christ, the commons should go on a pilgrimage. However, its emphasis was upon obtaining the grace of God. 'Through God's grace', the aim was to secure for the spirituality 'old wealth and peace'. The Church had been 'robbed, spoiled and shorn', it declared. By committing this act of sacrilege, the government had exceeded natural limits and therefore had behaved tyrannically. In the circumstances, the commons had no choice but 'to mell/To make redress' and to go on 'this voyage/And pilgrimage of young and sage/In this country'. In return, the ballad promised that God would reward the pilgrims with 'wealth, health and speed', plus salvation.[32]

Besides involving a journey, true pilgrims needed a spiritual goal: either to persuade saints to intercede with God for the benefit of themselves and their relatives, alive and dead; or to defend a holy place or institution in order to demonstrate their worthiness. Although termed a pilgrimage of grace for the commonwealth, and therefore charged with a strong secular purpose, the northern revolts of 1536 also had genuine religious aims. Especial sources of objection were the dissolution of monasteries, the abrogation of holy days and the introduction of a new order of prayer. In this respect, the pilgrimage of grace sought to undo certain radical changes in religion, all of them authorised by recent legislation: notably the parliamentary act dissolving the lesser monasteries, as well as the acts of convocation that had reduced the number of saints' days, banned prayers for the pope and his cardinals and ended the practice of listing in the church service the offences punishable by damnation.[33] In rebel eyes, responsible for these religious changes was not simply the greed of a government eager to annex the wealth of the Church but also certain

---

[30] *LP*, vol. XI, 1253; M. E. James, *Family, Lineage and Civil Society* (Oxford University Press, 1974), p. 48.
[31] SP1/118(*LP*, vol. XII(1), 1021 (5)).   [32] Bateson (ed.), 'Pilgrimage of Grace', 344–5.
[33] For pilgrims' religious grievances, see C. S. L. Davies, 'The Pilgrimage of Grace Reconsidered', *Past and Present*, 41 (1968), 54–76 and his 'Popular Religion and the Pilgrimage of Grace' in A. Fletcher and J. Stevenson (eds.), *Order and Disorder in Early Modern England* (Cambridge University Press, 1985), pp. 58–91. For government's religious measures, see E. Duffy, *The Stripping of the Altars* (New Haven, CT: Yale University Press, 1992), ch. 11.

heretical beliefs, notably the wish to restrict the divine to what was authorised by scripture, and the view that Christ was the sole intermediary between man and God. Central to these objectionable beliefs was the dismissal of purgatory as a medieval invention. The concept of purgatory had been sustained by saint-worship; while saint-worship had been promoted by the practice of pilgrimage. Thus, compelled by its disbelief in purgatory and by its belief in Christ as man's only hope of God's grace, the government took action against the practices associated with the saints' traditional function as intercessors with God.

In defence of the saints, the rebels deeply resented the abolition of holy days. St Luke was central to revolt in the Barony of Westmorland which broke out on 15 October when the curate of Kirkby Stephen parish church did not announce the forthcoming St Luke's Day, due on 18 October, but was then obliged to do so by the menace of a murmur from the congregation. On St Luke's Day itself, the men of the East Ward gathered in Kirkby Stephen, sending out parties to bring others in. Having formed a host, they marched to Penrith, raising revolt *en route*.[34] St Wilfred was associated with disturbances in the East Riding and probably others in the West Riding wapentake of Claro. His day fell upon 12 October. On the previous Sunday, the priest of Watton parish church had failed to announce the fact, causing the congregation to object. Then, on St Wilfred's Day itself a large assembly met at Hunsley Beacon, with the men from Beverley and the surrounding townships, including Watton, coming together to form an army under William Stapulton. As Hallom, a rebel leader from Watton, put it: 'Everyone that was able to bear a staff went forward towards Hunsley'.[35] The Cumberland rebels also objected to the abolition of saints' days, producing, on 20 October, a proclamation that ordered priests to 'bid holy days and beads after the old custom'.[36] The same issue had surfaced in Richmondshire five days earlier when a leading cleric of the region, John Dakyn, the same person who had borne witness to the creation of Lord Poverty, attended a rebel assembly in the town of Richmond and was threatened by a certain Thomlynson of Bedale for being a 'putter down of the holy days'. This particular uprising appeared to begin on St Wilfred's Day at the horse fair held in Ripon. According to Dakyn, the abrogation of holy days was something 'the people did murmur at'. Aggression was shown towards him because he and other high-ranking clergymen had authorised it in convocation.[37] The more familiar grievance, the dissolution of the lesser monasteries,

---

[34] Bush, *Pilgrimage of Grace*, pp. 292–3, 299.   [35] *Ibid.*, pp. 34–5.
[36] SP1/117, fol. 55 (*LP*, vol. xii(1), 787 (2)).
[37] SP1/117, fol. 216 (*LP*, vol. xii(1), 789). For Ripon origins of Richmondshire uprising, see Bush, *Pilgrimage of Grace*, p. 148.

was, of course, also associated with saintly intercession, since their principal spiritual function was to offer up prayers for the dead, and monks, moreover, had the duty of caring for shrines and their saintly relics, as Robert Aske indicated in his address to the lords in Pontefract Castle on 19 October; a point he repeated under examination in April 1537. On both occasions he claimed that, among other things, the Dissolution was found objectionable because it had led to the violation of such relics. The pilgrims' reverence for saintly relics was also evident in the importance they attributed to the banner of St Cuthbert, attached to which and held in a pocket sown to the banner cloth was, along with a cross, part of the saint's winding sheet.[38]

Besides seeking to defend saint-worship, the northern rebels had a broader religious aim, which also fell within the pilgrim tradition. It was to defend the Church itself. The enemy was heresy which was seen as bent on terminating its basic beliefs and practices, confiscating its wealth and suppressing its privileges. The pilgrimage of grace thus became a crusade to preserve a holy institution against the barbaric designs of an alien sect. In performing this role it suffered a fatal weakness. This lay in the ambivalent regard of both the pilgrim clergy and the pilgrim gentlemen for the rebels' religious cause. The clergy, as an order, had already accepted the major changes in religion. Having approved them in convocation and in the Lords, it was now weakly placed to oppose them with any credibility. The same could be said for the gentlemen who had accepted, with little evident dissent, the same reforms in parliament, and who were easily swayed by plans to confiscate ecclesiastical wealth through having so much to gain from its redistribution, especially at a time when inflation and the widespread existence of customarily fixed rents and dues were depreciating their landed revenues. Such a situation – which encouraged the commons to suspect the clergy and gentlemen of betraying the cause – led to further revolts early in 1537 that represented, quintessentially, a pilgrimage against the 1536 pilgrimage, with a rebellious commons spurning the non-military policies the pilgrim leaders had adopted the previous December in the conviction that the pilgrimage of grace could only achieve its goal by a march on London. They emphasised the importance the pilgrims attached to stopping the Dissolution and restoring the traditional service – with its prayers for the pope and its listing of the damnable offences – but also made the point, in no uncertain way, that the northern rebels had political and economic complaints as well.[39]

[38] Bateson (ed.), 'Pilgrimage of Grace', 335, 561. For relics attached to the banner, see M. Bush, *Durham and the Pilgrimage of Grace* (Durham County Local History Society, 2000), pp. 13–14.

[39] For these uprisings, see Bush and Bownes, *Defeat of the Pilgrimage of Grace*, p. 26 and ch. 7.

The pilgrimage of grace directly engaged very few women and children but large numbers of men: something like 50,000 in October 1536.[40] These pilgrims were carefully selected troops, not just anyone wishing to take part, and served properly harnessed and weaponed, in accordance with what the regulations for mustering the militia normally required. Following instructions, committed communities provided well-armed troops and supplied them with sufficient money to meet their travelling expenses.[41] In other words, the northern revolts of October 1536 qualify as a pilgrimage only in resembling a crusade.[42] Yet it was an odd sort of crusade, not only because it was an act of civil disobedience but also because the impetus came essentially from below. It began as a series of popular movements that sought to enlist the rest of northern society. Presenting themselves as risings of the commons, they subscribed to a genre of revolt that reached back to at least 1381 but was especially prevalent under the early Tudors (occurring in 1489, 1497, 1513, 1525, 1536 (twice) and 1549 (twice)).[43] Although the pilgrimage of grace managed to engage support from the whole range of society – enlisting at least seventy gentlemen and over forty clerics – and therefore appeared to represent the whole northern community, its driving force remained the commons.[44] Clerics and lords concentrated on steering it in what they felt to be the right direction: that is, to treat with Norfolk in Doncaster, not to confront the king in London.[45] Crusades were not normally organised in this manner. As military operations, they were intent on conquest and capture; and, rather than driven from below, they simply followed the rules laid down by the social order of the time.

Furthermore, although the pilgrims of grace sported the miraculous banner of St Cuthbert, they appeared, untypically, to have no expectation of miracles. This was fortunate since the two that occurred in the course of revolt – the sudden rising of the River Don on 26 October that prevented the pilgrim host from proceeding southwards, and the extremely cold weather in the winter of 1536/7 that discouraged further rebel mobilisations – favoured the government.[46] In contrast to the normal pilgrimage, sorrow for sin, the need for atonement, and the search for salvation played little ostensible part in recruiting support. In late

---

[40] Bush, *Pilgrimage of Grace*, pp. 375–6 and app. 1.   [41] *Ibid.*, pp. 407–8.

[42] Tyerman, *England and the Crusades*, ch. 13.

[43] See M. Bush, 'The Risings of the Commons in England, 1381–1549', in J. Denton (ed.), *Orders and Hierarchies in Later Medieval and Renaissance Europe* (London: Macmillan, 1999), ch. 7.

[44] For their names, see Bush and Bownes, *Defeat*, p. 391 and app. 2.

[45] *Ibid.*, pp. 12–15. But it would be wrong to think that the war party was simply the commons. See Bush, *Pilgrimage of Grace*, pp. 378–9, 389–91.

[46] For miraculous rising of the Don, see Bush, *Pilgrimage of Grace*, p. 380. For miraculously cold winter, see Bush and Bownes, *Defeat*, p. 27.

October a muster proclamation, calling for an assembly at Hawkshead, threatened hell-fire for those who failed to respond; about the same time, Christopher Howden, the vicar of Clapham, in a sermon to the rebels gathered in Kendal promised certain salvation for those who perished in the struggle; and the Sawley ballad offered the pilgrim rebels 'joy endless/ When they be dead'. But many participants were impressed to take part by cadres of armed men and the threats of reprisal they issued against those who held back. Initially, these military cadres were small groups of mounted men, of between 20 and 300; eventually large forces, comprised of thousands of troops, went on recruitment campaigns, notably the army from Richmondshire which marched into Durham, and the two Westmorland hosts, one of which marched into Cumberland and the other into Lancashire.[47] What is more, because the grace the pilgrims sought was Henry VIII's, they did not need to invoke the saints to pluck at God's sleeve but simply had to ensure that their complaints, set out in a lengthy petition of twenty-four articles, were properly presented to the king. These complaints were only partially in accord with a true pilgrimage: for many were unrelated to religion and beyond spiritual relief. Remedy lay in persuading the government to alter its ways by parliamentary enactment, not in travelling to a devotional place and receiving as a result the grace of God.

The northern rebels placed their grievances in two basic categories. One related to the subversion of Christ's faith; the other, to the decay of the commonwealth. This was made evident in Aske's first proclamation of 11 October, an address to the commons of the wapentake of Ouse and Derwent that exhorted them both to stop the spoliation of the Church and 'to be ready upon pain of death for the commonwealth'.[48] A second proclamation of 17 October, an address to the gentlemen of Yorkshire, followed suit, complaining of 'sundry new inventions', which were, on the one hand, 'contrary to the faith of God' and, on the other, 'contrary . . . to the commonwealth of this realm'.[49] The same duality was found in the two petitions that the northern rebels sent to the king, the one in October, the other in December. The first, having advocated the preservation of Christ's faith, demanded the common law and the commonwealth to be restored to the state in which they were found on Henry VIII's accession.[50] In November, Aske referred to 'our petition on faith

---

[47] For promises of salvation, see Toller (ed.), *Correspondence of Derby*, pp. 49–50; *LP*, vol. XII(1), 914; Bateson (ed.), 'Pilgrimage of Grace', 344–5. For process of impressment, see Bush, *Pilgrimage of Grace*, pp. 37–40, 94–5, 114–15, 145, 149–50, 152, 228, 230, 252–4, 298–300, 345.

[48] SP1/107, fol. 116 (*LP*, vol. XI, 622).   [49] *SP Henry VIII*, I, p. 467 (*LP*, vol. XI, 705 (2)).

[50] SP1/ 109 (*LP*, vol. XI, 902(2)).

and commonwealth'.[51] In formulating the December petition – which was meant to detail what the October petition had set out in general – the rebels were fully aware of its dual task: the pilgrim council summoned to York in November followed a plan, according to Aske, 'to agree upon certain articles as well touching our faith as the commonwealth'.[52] Moreover, the pilgrim council held at Pontefract in December, to decide which articles to include in the petition, ordered the clergy 'to study for the articles ... of the church' and instructed 'wise men' to seek 'remedy of evil laws for the commonwealth for the commodity of this country'.[53]

The term 'commonwealth' meant something of great importance to the rebels. Besides featuring in the title the rebels gave to their revolt ('our pilgrimage of grace for the commonwealth'), and in the rebels' oath, which, in one of its forms, obliged those taking it to be true to God, the king and the commonwealth, the term served to indicate a main category of grievance. But what did it mean precisely? Some rebels, as in Richmondshire, used it to signify 'the weal of us all'.[54] On occasions, it was used to denote the wealth specifically of the commons: Aske, for example, referred to 'the commons and their wealths', and both Darcy and Bigod wrote of 'the commons' wealth'.[55] The rebels also used the term to distinguish the wealth of subjects from the personal wealth of the king, as was evident in the distinction a rebel leader made between a 'council for his person', which would essentially promote the prosperity of the king and his family, and the more commendable 'council of the commonwealth', which would concentrate on safeguarding the prosperity of the realm.[56] Two usages of the term had emerged in the late Middle Ages: one was distinctly radical and proposed 'a commonwealth' to signify a society in which all was held in common; the other conservatively proposed that a true commonwealth would result from the proper operation of the society of orders. Although the former usage was imputed to the rebels in various reports – notably from Westmorland and Cumberland where the local gentlemen overreacted to peasant demands for agrarian reform there is no reason to believe that this was the pilgrims' intent. After all, the rebel emphasis was on the preservation of a commonwealth, not its establishment. Undoubtedly inciting the rebels to reiterate the term was the blatant manner in which Thomas Cromwell and other ministers of the

[51] SP1/111, fol. 117 (*LP*, vol. XI, 1079).   [52] E36/122, fol. 61b (*LP*, vol. XI, 1128).
[53] Bateson, 'Pilgrimage of Grace', 339.
[54] According to Thomas Percy: see SP1/115, fol. 258b (*LP*, vol. XII(1), 393 (2)).
[55] SP1/107, fol. 116 (*LP*, vol. XI, 622); SP1/106, fol. 286 (*LP*, vol. XI, 563 (2, article 1));
SP1/114, fol. 205 (*LP*, vol. XII(1), 147).
[56] *LP*, vol. XI, 1244. This appeared in a statement of grievances submitted to the pilgrims' council at Pontefract in early December. It has been attributed, originally by the Dodds, to Sir Thomas Tempest. In all probability, it was by Sir Robert Constable.

Crown used 'the good of the commonwealth' to justify their policies. In this respect, the rebels were pursuing a counter-argument to demonstrate that these policies had produced just the opposite of what they were meant to achieve.[57] The commonwealth complaints were directly, if not exclusively, concerned with material matters. They focused upon the threat of impoverishment and its social repercussions. At the root of these complaints was the belief that a greed for wealth and power within the realm was upsetting two of its basic institutions: the body politic and the society of orders. The malefactors were identified as within the government, especially Thomas Cromwell, and as landlords who held the custom of tenant right in contempt.

In rebel eyes, the government was planning, through exaction and appropriation, a major onslaught upon the wealth of the realm, as Cromwell sought to fulfil his boast of making Henry VIII the richest prince in Christendom.[58] The Lincolnshire rebels – whose petition to the government the pilgrims employed in the early stages to voice their own complaints – had led the way in formulating this grievance.[59] They had communicated it to the government first in a letter of 3 October, a composition of the captured subsidy commissioners, and, a few days later, in a petition comprised of six articles.[60] The letter concentrated upon the issue of exaction and complained of 'enhancements and other importunate charges which they were not able to bear by reason of extreme poverty'. These included the peace-time subsidy and a number of rumoured indirect taxes on sacraments, foodstuffs, livestock and ploughs. Of the six articles in the petition the Lincolnshire rebels presented to the king, three related to objectionable taxes: the fifteenth-and-tenth without the traditional rebate for poverty, the first fruits and tenths newly imposed on the clergy, and the fiscal feudalism unleashed by the Statute of Uses. These tax grievances the pilgrims adopted.[61] Although the government backed off, suspending all attempts at collection during the period of insurrection, and also vigorously denied the rumours relating to the new indirect taxes, the pilgrims never lost sight of the fiscal issue, condemning most of these measures in their December petition.[62] The rebels argued that,

[57] Bush, 'Risings of the Commons', pp. 118–19; Bush, *Pilgrimage of Grace*, pp. 11–12.

[58] See *LP*, vol. xi, 1244.

[59] M. L. Bush, ' "Up for the Commonweal": The Significance of Tax Grievances in the English Rebellions of 1536', *EHR*, 106 (1991), 302–5.

[60] For letter of 3rd October, see SP1/106, fol. 250 (*LP*, vol. xi, 534). For petition to king, see Bush, 'Up for the Commonweal', 303, n. 4.

[61] Bush, 'Up for the Commonweal', 305–7.

[62] For suspending subsidy collection, see Bush, *Pilgrimage of Grace*, p. 386. For government denial of rumoured taxes, see M. L. Bush, ' "Enhancements and Importunate Charges": An Analysis of the Tax Complaints of October 1536', *Albion*, 22 (1990), 408. For tax complaint in December petition, see Bush, 'Up for the Commonweal', 312–13.

of the taxes they found objectionable, all featured fiscal innovations that, if allowed to stand, would sweep away the protective rights that subjects had traditionally enjoyed and expose them, in the near future, to a tax burden of unprecedented and crippling weight.[63] Their fiscal concern, however, was not simply a materialistic one. Widely rumoured in the north at the time was a government plan to levy 6s. 8d. upon all baptisms, marriages and burials, exactions that threatened both to tax the poor heavily and to disgrace those unable to pay for these vital sacramental services.[64] Although these indirect taxes failed to feature in any petition submitted to the government, they undoubtedly represented an important grievance. On 21 October Lancaster Herald, as he travelled to Pontefract to negotiate with the rebels, met a band of armed peasants who told him they had risen 'for the commonwealth'. In the grievances they cited, they mentioned, along with a tax on unmarked beasts, that 'no man should bury nor christen nor wed . . . but that the king would have a certain sum of money'.[65] This particular grievance was circulated in the north through bills passed by hand or nailed to church doors. One bill was appended to the already-mentioned muster proclamation summoning men to Hawkshead in late October. The proclamation presented the contents of the bill as being 'to the utter undoing of the commonwealth'. The bill declared that 'no infant shall receive the blessed sacrament of baptism unless a tribute be paid to the king', with the implication that failure to pay would condemn the child to limbo, thus denying it the chance of salvation.[66] However, it is far from certain that the objection to these sacramental taxes was on these grounds. Usually, it was listed with other complaints against taxes on basic foodstuffs, livestock and ploughs. The implication was that these taxes would fall heavily either upon the poor or upon communities – such as those in the border counties – that had been traditionally exempted from taxation, thanks to having a military obligation to resist the Scots. These new taxes, it was thought, would harm those whom the tax system had formerly and justifiably protected, and were therefore unacceptable.[67]

According to the pilgrims, a government led astray by greed was also committed to a programme of confiscation – a reasonable assumption in the light of the lesser monasteries recently suppressed. Such a programme, it was feared, would not stop at monasteries but include parish churches: with all deprived of their treasures and some razed to the ground. It could easily be seen as trampling on religious beliefs, but the

[63] Bush, 'Enhancements', 404–12.   [64] *Ibid.*, 408–10.
[65] *SP Henry VIII*, vol. I, p. 485 (*LP*, vol. XI, 826).
[66] Bush, 'Enhancements', 408–9; Toller (ed.), *Correspondence of Derby*, pp. 49–50 (*LP*, vol. XI, 892).
[67] Bush, 'Enhancements', 410; Bush, *Pilgrimage of Grace*, pp. 111, 282–3.

rebels' objection also sprang from material considerations. Besides weakening the means of intercession, the replacement of silver and gold censers, plate, processional crosses and chalices with replicas of little worth could be regarded as an attack on the wealth of the community, since parish church treasures usually resulted from donations made by the congregation.[68] The importance of the material consideration was evident in the way some congregations from the mid-1530s disposed of their church treasures in order to forestall the government's suspected plan of appropriation.[69] The suppression of religious houses was also resented for material as well as religious reasons. The Lincolnshire petition had explicitly objected to it on the grounds that not only 'the service of God is . . . minished' but also 'the poorality of your realm be unrelieved, the which as we think is a great hurt to the commonwealth'.[70] Taken up by Aske, this material objection to Dissolution figured strongly in the pilgrimage of grace. For example, on 19 October, in his address to the lords who had taken refuge in Pontefract Castle, Aske neatly established a connection between exaction and appropriation when he warned them that the Dissolution would make the tax reforms more oppressive since 'much of the relief of the commons was by succour of abbeys'.[71] In his Examination he emphasised how the dissolution of religious houses 'was greatly to the decay of the commonwealth of that country' and that therefore subjects 'of all degrees grudged at the same'.[72] He defined the material impact of the Dissolution in terms of a loss of charity as the poor ceased to receive alms; of a loss of waged employment as tenants ceased to be required for monastic service; of a loss of hospitality as the gifts of meat and cloth traditionally dispensed by the monks to the local community ceased to be handed out; and of a withdrawal of coin out of the north as the rents of the dissolved houses were diverted southwards into the coffers of the king and his court favourites. Yet Aske failed to identify the whole range of material concern associated with the Dissolution. The manner in which it was done offended local communities because the goods confiscated from the dissolved houses were sold to strangers.[73] It was also feared that the transfer of monastic wealth into lay hands would raise rents and dues. Dissolution therefore became linked to a prevalent conviction in the upland north – the country susceptible to Captain Poverty – that the beneficial custom of tenant right was under attack as gressums

---

[68] Bush, 'Captain Poverty', 31.
[69] R. Whiting, *The Blind Devotion of the People: Popular Religion and the English Reformation* (Cambridge University Press, 1989), ch. 9.
[70] SP1/108 (*LP*, vol. XI, 705).   [71] Bateson, 'Pilgrimage of Grace', 335–6.
[72] *Ibid.*, 561–2.
[73] *LP*, vol. XII(1), 138. For analysis of this bill, see Bush and Bownes, *Defeat*, pp. 151–3.

(i.e. entry fines) were exorbitantly raised and commoning rights on the waste were restricted by enclosure.[74]

The commonwealth was regarded by the rebels as in peril, then, because of policies of spoliation conducted both by the Crown and by harsh landlords. Another perceived danger was the way the Crown was extending its authority at the expense of the constitution. Disturbing enlargements of the royal prerogative were taking place, it was felt: represented, for example, by the Act of Succession which allowed the king, in the absence of direct heirs, to will the Crown to whoever he liked; by the Act of First Fruits and Tenths which had imposed upon the clergy in perpetuity a regular tax on income; by the Subsidy Act of 1534 which had granted a subsidy not, in the normal manner, for purposes of war but simply in peace time, thus opening the way to regular direct taxation of the laity; by the Act of Supremacy which enabled the king not only to assume the headship of the English Church but also to delegate it to a layman; or the Treason Act which extended the offence from deeds to words.[75] In addition, the rebels felt the government was annexing new powers simply by unchallenged acts of self-assertion: for example, in controlling parliamentary business through packing the Commons with its officers and agents, and by blatantly committing perjury, as in the Wycliffe case of 1536, when it sought to persuade a Yorkshire jury of arraignment to change its verdict, and then punished the non-compliant members with a summons to London and the imposition of a heavy fine.[76]

Manorial lords were thought to be practising the same sort of high-handedness, through extending their proprietorial rights at the expense of the customary tenures.[77] The rebels saw these accretions of power as responsible not simply for the exploitation of the realm but also for a distemper in the body politic. They also found them objectionable as expressions of contempt for the society of orders in the sense of maltreating its component parts: notably the royal family, through the bastardisation of Mary; the nobility, through replacing them in the service of the king by men of villein blood, evident in the proceedings recently taken against the great northern families of Percy and Dacre and in the recent elevation of Thomas Cromwell to the peerage; the clergy, through undermining it by seizing its wealth and reducing its liberties and privileges; and the

---

[74] This is dealt with in my forthcoming study of the northern rebels' grievances, entitled *The Pilgrims' Complaint.*

[75] Bush, *Pilgrimage of Grace*, pp. 112, 166.

[76] For Wycliffe case, see *ibid.*, pp. 166–7. For management of parliament, see *ibid.*, pp. 112, 168.

[77] For agrarian issues at stake, see M. L. Bush, 'Tenant Right Under the Tudors: A Revision revised', *Bulletin of the John Rylands Library*, 77 (1995), 161–88; Bush, *Pilgrimage of Grace*, pp. 170–3, 256–60, 309–14, 337–41.

commons, through oppressing them with fiscal novelties and raised rents and dues. The rebels feared that, abused in this way, the orders would not be able to fulfil their complementary functions: that is, for the nobles, politically, to fight and govern, the clergy, religiously, to administer the faith, and the commons, economically, to generate the wealth upon which the system depended.[78] Some of this commonwealth complaint related to matters spiritual, since the point was made that the Church needed its wealth to perform its pastoral functions properly; but mostly it expressed temporal concerns far removed from the pilgrim tradition.[79] The latter had undoubtedly served economic and political ends, but not ostensibly: the declared purpose of pilgrimages had to be religious just as the expected remedy had to be of supernatural provenance.

Viewed as a pilgrimage, then, the northern revolts of October 1536 were distinctly peculiar. The closer one looks the more they seem a pilgrimage in name only. Subjected to close analysis, their pilgrim characteristics become less certain. The bearing of the crosses, for example, partly derived from fear of their confiscation, the practice being drawn from the non-pilgrim Lincolnshire rebellion that began with Thomas Foster, a yeoman of Louth, shouting out at the Sunday service: 'Go we to follow the crosses, for, if they be taken from us, we be like to follow them no more'.[80] It was also a means of finding an explicit function for the rebel clergy who mostly refused to serve as soldiers and who were therefore suspected by the pilgrim commons and gentlemen of having no more than a luke-warm commitment to the cause.[81]

As for the pilgrim's vow, this was an oath of allegiance designed to mirror the one the Succession Act of 1534 had required of every subject to test their acceptance of the king's divorce from Catherine of Aragon and the rejection of the papal supremacy. As a counter to this royal oath, the rebels created a commons oath. The latter was adopted from the Lincolnshire revolt, and had featured in earlier risings of the commons.[82] As for the pilgrims' marching song – the work of Friar Pickering – this was not an integral part of the march to Doncaster but was composed after the Truce.[83] The banner of St Cuthbert was used because of its long and lucky military associations, typically in the wars against Scotland.[84] Furthermore, the banner of the five wounds was first used by the

---

[78] Bush, 'Risings of the Commons', p. 118; Bush, *Pilgrimage of Grace*, pp. 103–12.

[79] A rebel bill proposed 'to maintain the profit of holy church which was the upholding of the Christian faith'. See SP1/114, fol. 201 (*LP*, vol. xii(1), 163).

[80] *LP*, vol. xi, 828/iii(1).

[81] For suspicion held of the clergy, see Bush, *The Pilgrimage of Grace*, pp. 181, 213–14, 349, 352, 361, 409.

[82] Bush, *Pilgrimage of Grace*, p. 12.   [83] *Ibid.*, p. 198.

[84] *Ibid.*, p. 182; G. Bernard, 'Vitality and Vulnerability in the Late Medieval Church', in J. L. Watts (ed.), *The End of the Middle Ages?* (Stroud: Sutton, 1998), pp. 215–16.

non-pilgrim Lincolnshire rebels.[85] And as for the crosses the pilgrims wore back and front, this was the normal device in the early sixteenth century for denoting troops on public, as opposed to private, service. For instance, they were also worn by the royal army mobilised to resist the pilgrimage of grace.

Although certain strands of revolt undoubtedly opposed the removal of holy days and others showed concern for sanctuaries which, like that of Durham, centred on the protection offered by a saint, the rebels of October 1536, as professed pilgrims, appeared remarkably detached from saint-worship. The pilgrimage of grace, in fact, could be regarded as part of a movement within the late medieval Catholic church that had shifted away from the saints to establish an exclusive relationship with Christ – a movement abruptly stopped when that idea was adopted as the central belief of Protestantism.[86] Significantly, the northern rebels did not demand the restoration of abrogated holy days in their petition to the king; nor was it demanded in 1537 by further protest in support of grievances that had been omitted from the December petition. In December 1536 and January 1537 a good deal of congregational opposition was directed against the new order of prayer in Yorkshire and Westmorland (for example, in Kendal, Arncliffe and other parishes in Percy Fee, Brough and parishes about, and Richmond), but the reason given was not the order's failure to announce holy days but its failure to offer prayers for the pope and his cardinals and to list the damnable offences.[87] The pilgrimage of grace was distinctly christocentric. The rebels referred to themselves as 'brethren in Christ' or as 'Christ's soldiers'. Captain Poverty, as previously shown, was a conjunction of the commons and Christ. Their banners and badges, apart from that of St Cuthbert, were assigned directly to Christ.[88] Langland made Piers say he would not give a farthing to Becket, and allowed Reason to offer the following advice to those caught up in saint-worship: give up the search for St James and the saints of Rome and instead 'Seeketh St Truth for he may save you all'.[89] This advice the northern rebels appeared to follow. They took oaths to be true to the king, as well as seeking, through their petitions and representations, to show him the Truth, in return for which they hoped remedy would result from royal grace and parliamentary statute.

The northern revolts only qualify as a pilgrimage in the form of a crusade to rescue the Church from the heretic. But among the rebels was

[85] *LP*, vol. XI, 828/i (2), 828/ii.

[86] See R. Pfaff, *New Liturgical Feasts in Late Medieval England* (Oxford University Press, 1970), chs. 4 and 5.

[87] Bush and Bownes, *Defeat*, pp. 111, 150, 243, 264–5. For sanctuaries issue, see Bush, *Durham and the Pilgrimage of Grace*, pp. 35–31.

[88] Bush, 'Captain Poverty', 36.   [89] Skeat, *Vision of William*, pp. 128–9, 184.

a great unwillingness to go all the way, militarily. In fact, the rebels who were naturally expected to lead a crusade – the lords and clergy – were mostly intent on avoiding military conflict. In retrospect, the raising of the pilgrim host seemed no more than a diplomatic device. The lords and clergy got what they wanted in late 1536, from both the Crown and commons; but their achievement was wrecked by a revival of the plan to march on London early in 1537, which, by dividing the pilgrims into two opposed parties, allowed the government to reclaim control in the north.[90] As for the general pardon that the rebels demanded in 1536, this was a natural consequence of their exposure to the charge of treason rather than the pilgrim desire for some sort of plenary indulgence.[91] Finally, the journey taken by the pilgrims of grace – not to a place of devotion but to the seat of government – was arguably a response to another tradition: for the risings of the commons in 1381, 1450 and 1497 had featured a march on London in order to present grievances directly to the king and to destroy the evil ministers who had led him astray.[92]

In the history of the pilgrimage of grace two remarkable events get overlooked: one was the meeting of the pilgrim leaders with the king in late December and early January; the other was the pilgrim council held in the town of Richmond on 5 February 1537. At the former – first with Aske over the Christmas holidays and finally on 14 January, when the pilgrim leaders agreed to wear the red cross of St George – the king personally offered them his grace. Previously, it had only been imparted by Norfolk at Doncaster and by the general pardon proclaimed on 9 December. The one condition of the king's grace was the non-resumption of revolt. The pilgrims present found this acceptable upon learning from Henry's own mouth that a parliament and convocation would be held in York to consider their December petition and to enact appropriate remedy.[93] However, in the north the December petition itself became a major source of complaint, largely because of the grievances it had omitted or misrepresented; so much so that disgruntled pilgrims summoned a council at Richmond in February 1537 for the purpose of identifying and presenting the missing grievances.[94] The Richmond council was a fiasco; and so were the rebel attempts to renew the pilgrimage in 1537. Fearful that further revolt would destroy the December agreement, many pilgrims – gentlemen, clerics and commoners – came to the king's aid in putting it down.[95] In fact, the second pilgrimage was largely suppressed by the supporters of the first: not because they had undergone a change of heart but because they wished to preserve the king's grace. In the circumstances – with

[90] See Bush and Bownes, *Defeat*, chs. 9 and 10.   [91] *Ibid.*, ch. 1.
[92] Bush, 'Risings of the Commons', pp. 109–11.   [93] Bush and Bownes, *Defeat*, p. 24.
[94] *Ibid.*, pp. 105–108.   [95] *Ibid.*, ch. 9.

revolts breaking out in the East Riding, the North Riding, Durham and Cumbria – they could hardly expect it to remain intact. Yet the king's grace was not totally withdrawn. The December pardon held firm. The royal repression fell largely upon those who had repudiated its terms. Moreover, in the following years a partial acceptance of the pilgrims' grievances was evident: for example, in the restoration of all seven sacraments in the Bishops' Book of 1537; in the establishment that same year of the Council of the North, which met the pilgrims' complaint 'that no man upon subpoena is from Trent north to appear but at York'; in the replacement of arbitrary by fixed customary dues; in the Statute of Wills which mostly undid the Statute of Uses; in the abandonment of peacetime subsidies and of fifteenth-and-tenths without the rebate for poverty; in the governmental onslaught upon heresy that was implemented by the royal proclamation of November 1538 and the Act of Six Articles of 1539; in the removal of Cromwell in 1540; in the restoration by statute of Mary to the succession in 1544; in the admission made in the same Act that the king's authority to determine his successor by will – granted in 1536 in the event of an absence of direct heirs and strongly opposed by the pilgrims – should be tempered by the subjects' right to consent to the king's nominated successor.[96]

The overall story of the pilgrimage of grace went as follows: alienated by government policy and licensed to take action by disaffected gentlemen and clerics, the commons of the north went on a journey under the name of a pilgrimage. The principal purpose was to reveal to the king the truth: that, because a heretic of base blood had charge of government policy, the faith of Christ was in danger and the commonwealth exposed to decay. Making the journey were not humble pilgrims peacefully carrying staffs and scrips and dressed distinctively in tunics, cloaks and broad-brimmed, badge-decorated hats, but a formidable military force, well equipped with salets, jacks, bills, bows, bucklers, swords and the occasional pole-axe, that easily outnumbered the opposed army royal. With many of its troops horsed, a rapid march to London was a distinct possibility. This did not disqualify the uprising from being a pilgrimage but defined it as a crusade. As a crusade, however, it was far from typical: first in taking the form of a rebellion; secondly in being driven from below.

As a result of the rebels' obvious military superiority, an agreement was reached at Doncaster, originally on 27 October and confirmed on 8 December, to pardon every pilgrim and, in return for a demobilisation of rebel and government troops, to apply remedy.[97] Thereafter, everything

---

[96] *Ibid.*, pp. 398–400; Bush, 'Up for the Commonweal', 314–16; Bush, 'Tenant Right Under the Tudors', 186–8. For Succession Act, see 35 Henry VIII, c. 1.

[97] Bush, *Pilgrimage of Grace*, ch. 10 and app. 1.

fell apart. What is more, no miracles occurred to reward the pilgrims' valiant effort. From the religious point of view, the outcome was a disaster: in 1538 pilgrimages were banned and their normal destinations, the saintly shrines, abolished; and, by 1540, the traditional curators of saintly places and relics, the monasteries, had all gone. Essentially, the pilgrimage of grace was no such thing. In reality, it was yet another uprising of the commons. Within this genre of revolt, it was distinguished by the prominence of religious grievances and the capacity to enlist support from the upper ranks of society. But these distinctive features had nothing to do with the claim to be a pilgrimage. After all, they were shared by the Lincolnshire rebellion of October 1536, another commons' revolt but one with no pilgrim pretension.

8 Politics, drama and the cult of Thomas Becket in the sixteenth century*

Peter Roberts

> There was much discussion among the people, some simple folk saying
> that he was a holy and saintly man, others that he was a wilful traitor to
> his king...[1]

The debate about the reputation of Thomas Becket at the Reformation, the popular manifestation of which was recorded by the soldier Elis Gruffydd in his Welsh chronicle, is a subject that has commanded little attention in recent revisionist writings on Tudor England. A modest start could be made in compensating for this relative neglect by exploring the respective roles of Henry VIII, Thomas Cromwell and Archbishop Cranmer in the sequence of events that culminated in the destruction of the shrine at Canterbury and the end of medieval pilgrimage in England. The reverence in which St Thomas's name was held became the target of official censure somewhat late in the campaign against the veneration of saints and images that was launched in the mid-1530s. The representation of Thomas of Canterbury as a pseudo-martyr, which had begun with the Lollards and been continued by the early 'Protestant' reformers, was overtly countenanced by authority in 1538. The official attack on Becket was all the more fierce for the perception that he symbolised the triumph of papal over regal jurisdiction in a notorious quarrel over jurisdictions, and yet it came about some time after the definitive break with Rome. The circumstances that led to the final decision to impugn the cult in a political *coup de théâtre*, together with the role of drama in its suppression and later revival, are related subjects that deserve closer attention than they have received in traditional accounts of the English Reformation.

One reason for the delay in suppressing the cult is hinted at in the item that appeared as early as 1533 in Thomas Cromwell's 'remembrances':

* I am grateful to Dr Margaret Aston, Professor Patrick Collinson, Professor Nora Johnson,
Dr David Potter and Dr Richard Rex for their valuable comments on earlier versions of
this chapter. Thanks are also due to Professor J. B. Trapp and Dr Thomas Freeman for
generously sharing with me their insights into the writings of Sir Thomas More and John
Foxe respectively.

[1] Translated from the Welsh: NLW, Mostyn MS 158, fol. 527.

'What the kynges highnes wooll have done with them that shall go to Canterburye to doo penance'.[2] The more immediate problem of what punishment should be meted out to Elizabeth Barton, 'the nun of Kent', and her accomplices for their contumacy was dealt with within a year. It took five years for the minister to elicit a decision from Henry on the more momentous question of what was to be done about the penitential element in pilgrimage. The campaign against the veneration of saints and images, which gathered momentum in 1535 under Cromwell's aegis, received at first but a hesitant endorsement from Henry, who evidently held back on doctrinal grounds from authorising the iconoclasm of the reformers. The repudiation of the abuses involved in image-worship and the practice of pilgrimage did become a consistent element in the official pronouncements on the faith issued in 1536 and 1537, though it fell short of a complete prohibition. Henry's vacillation during these years seems to have proceeded as much from policy – the need to placate his foreign enemies and rebellious subjects – as from genuine reluctance to break completely with traditional religious observances. In May 1536 the papal nuncio in France reported that Henry, in making overtures to the emperor, was prepared to rein in the reform of purgatory, saints' cults, and pilgrimages. He was evidently not prepared to make such concessions to his daughter Mary, for in the next month, after a period of recalcitrance, the princess obediently agreed to submit to her father's guidance on these points. But the reforms were not immediately enforced, and the outbreak of the pilgrimage of grace later in the year led to further procrastination.[3]

Henry's equivocation lasted until a sustained onslaught on false relics began early in 1538. By the time the second injunctions to the clergy were presented to him later in the year, he had become convinced that firmer action had to be taken against the adoration of images. His priorities shifted so that the political motives for discrediting St Thomas of Canterbury came to outweigh the theological objections that had deterred him from abolishing the cult. He had special reasons to object to the honour accorded to England's foremost saint, but before he could act upon his conviction on that score he had first to overcome his scruples about challenging the role of penitence in motivating pilgrimages to holy sites. Even then, it was only after the authenticity of the saint's 'miraculous

---

[2] Henry's hesitancy on this point was quite independent of the vexation caused by Elizabeth Barton: further down the list of desiderata Cromwell added a separate note, to find out 'the kynges plesure ffor sendyng the non to Canterberye, and whether she shall retorne'. BL Cotton MSS, Titus Bi, fol. 461; *LP*, vol. VI, no. 1382.

[3] The bishop of Faenza, papal nuncio, with the French court at Montbrison, to Mgr. Ambrogio, 8 May 1536: *LP*, vol. X, no. 831. Mary to Cromwell [23 June] 1536: *LP*, vol. X, no. 1186. For the impact of the pilgrimage of grace on the king's plans, see Michael Bush, Chapter 3 above, pp. 190–93.

blood' had been called in question that he authorised the desecration of Becket's shrine at Canterbury. St Thomas was then decanonised in official propaganda aimed at defusing potential resistance to the king's actions, in themselves irreversible, as Henry assumed a more conservative position on other matters of doctrine. The adoration of saints' images and relics was not only anathema to the reformers but was also deemed to be incompatible with the tenets of the Henrician Church in its 'reactionary' phase. In so far as the cult of Becket in particular was a symbol of the Roman obedience, its suppression was necessary for the consolidation of the royal supremacy. That it finally required such resolute action to bring this about may be construed as a tacit acknowledgement by the regime that the Canterbury pilgrimage was still a vital component of English religious life.

In the early sixteenth century St Thomas's memory was still revered by the leaders of the Church in England. During the debate on the Submission of the Clergy in the House of Lords in March 1532, Archbishop Warham prepared a speech in which he invoked Becket's defence of the liberties of the Church and quoted at length from the saint's life. The legislation that had precipitated Thomas More's resignation of the great seal was compared to the Constitutions of Clarendon, the crucial articles of which had been renounced by Henry II at the martyr's tomb. In response to the charge of *praemunire* and the order to find sureties for his appearance, Warham warned that this offence to Holy Church would incur an interdict.[4] But the clergy had already acknowledged the royal supremacy; if Warham thought of casting himself in the martyr's role, the moment soon passed, for the speech was not delivered.

The English religious dissidents, on the other hand, objected to the cult of Becket on the grounds of doctrine as much as jurisdictional rights. St Thomas had long been a *bête noir* of the Lollards: in 1464 one of them had declared that pilgrims to Canterbury committed their souls to the Devil, and similar sentiments were still being expressed by those identified as Lollards in the 1520s and early 1530s.[5] The English Lutheran reformers took up the refrain in the same decade, and it became a significant theme in their repertory of arguments against the abuse of clerical privileges. The first of these dissidents to attack Becket, it appears, was the turncoat religious, William Barlow, whose tracts, prohibited by the bishops in 1529, included 'a convicyous dyaloge withowt any tytle, specyally against Saynt Thomas of Canterburye'. This was not printed or

---

[4] J. Moyes, 'Warham, an English Primate on the Eve of the Reformation', *The Dublin Review*, 114 (1894), 390–420, esp. 407–14. M. Kelly, 'The Submission of the Clergy', *TRHS*, 5th ser., 15 (1965), 103.

[5] *HMC IXth Report* (2 parts, London, 1883–4), vol. I, App., p. 155.

openly publicised, as he assured the king in 1533 in a recantation that ensured his rehabilitation and rapid promotion in the Henrician Church.[6]
William Tyndale in *The Practise of papistical Prelates* discredited Becket
on two counts: not only had 'he dyed for the liberties (to do all mischief
unpunished) and privileges of the Church', but he was a violent man of
war who had struck the first blow in the skirmish in the cathedral.[7] At his
trial for heresy in April 1532, the lawyer James Bainham spoke in much
the same vein in discrediting the martyrdom of Becket. He confessed to
having read *The Practise* as well as other forbidden tracts, though Tyndale
may not have been his immediate source. He had been convinced, he
said, by what he had read in 'an olde history' that Becket was not a saint
but a traitor.[8] Hugh Latimer tried to dissuade Bainham from sacrificing
his life for such a cause, 'for it maie be a lie, as well as a true tale, and
in suche a doutfulle matter yt were mere madness for a man [to] ioparde
his lif.'[9] Bainham refused to recant his heretical opinions and went to the
stake in the following year.

In 1530 William Umpton, formerly a groom of the king's chamber,
was clapped in irons and kept prisoner in the Tower for over two years
for having asked 'why St Thomas was a saint rather than Robin Hood'.[10]
There is no evidence that the king himself was entertaining such questions

---

[6] Barlowe recanted his errors and sued for pardon, and as a protégé of the Boleyns became
bishop of St Asaph and then of St David's in quick succession in 1536, and was translated
to Bath and Wells under Edward VI. *DNB*; Thomas Wright (ed.), *Three Chapters of Letters
Relating to the Dissolution of the Monasteries*, Camden Soc., vol. XXVI (1843), p. 6.

[7] Tyndale was not altogether consistent: at another point in the tract he used the parallel
with Becket to censure Wolsey rather than the saint: 'where St Thomas of Canterbury
was wont to come after, Thomas, cardinal went oft before, preventing his prince and
perverting the order of that holy man'. Cited in D. Daniell, *William Tyndale: A Biography*
(New Haven, CT and London, 1994), p. 203.

[8] This may have been a Lollard tract: a (manuscript?) 'book against St Thomas of
Canterbury' was burned at Paul's Cross late in 1531. Bainham may have derived his
knowledge of the murder in the cathedral from his own selective reading of the lives of the
saint preserved in the 'First' *Quadrilogus* (Paris, 1495). J. F. Davis, 'Lollards, Reformers
and St Thomas of Canterbury', *University of Birmingham Hist. Jnl*, 9 (1963), 8–12. John
Bale draws attention to the denial by Baynham (misnamed George) of the doctrine of
purgatory and the sainthood of Becket, in *The epistle exhortatory of an Inglyshe chrystian*
(?Antwerp, 1544), fol. 13v.

[9] BL Harleian MS 422, fol. 90; *LP*, nos. 24, 30. The main charges of heresy against
Bainham were that he had distributed prohibited books and had denied the sacrament
of the Eucharist, on which points Foxe's narrative is silent. The account of the interview
appears among Foxe's papers but was not included in his *Acts and Monuments*, perhaps
because it cast Latimer in an unfavourable light. For another possible significance of the
omissions, see T. S. Freeman, 'The Importance of Dying Earnestly: the Metamorphosis of
the Account of James Bainham in "Foxe's Book of Martyrs"', in R. N. Swanson (ed.), *The
Church Retrospective* (Bury St Edmunds, 1997), pp. 283–4. Cf. R. M. Fisher, 'Reform,
Repression and Unrest at the Inns of Court, 1518–1558', *HJ*, 20 (1977), 791; A. G.
Chester, *Hugh Latimer, Apostle to the English* (Philadelphia, 1954), pp. 82–3.

[10] *LP*, vol. v, no. 1271.

much before 1533.[11] Becket could not have been far from his mind when in March of that year Henry informed the imperial ambassador, Chapuys, that he was determined to correct the mistakes made by his predecessors, Henry II and King John, who had made England and Ireland tributary to the papacy.[12] He threatened to confiscate all the property that the Church had over the centuries misappropriated from the Crown. The appeal to history served the immediate purposes of diplomacy and cannot be taken to represent a settled attitude on his part: he was later to reduce his demands in negotiations for concessions from Rome before proceeding to the final schism.[13]

George Bernard has recently argued that Henry VIII was consistent in his piety; his hostility to the religious orders developed early in his reign, and 'Henry was a rare pilgrim'.[14] The king's early devotion to the saints may have been conventional, and it is true that it cannot be documented much after 1520, when it was displayed on an occasion of state, the visit of Charles V to Canterbury. At Whitsuntide in that jubilee year the king and the emperor processed under a canopy into the cathedral to say their prayers and make their oblations at the shrine of St Thomas.[15] While Henry may have been Laodicean in these observances, he certainly did not begin to countenance the attack on images and pilgrimages until some time after his final challenge to papal supremacy. The king had then to be persuaded of the dangerous superstition of 'idolatry', and Cromwell and Cranmer were instrumental in bringing him to this frame of mind. Once convinced, he did not relent.

Iconoclasm was rife in London by October 1533 but was still decried as vandalism by the authorities. There was an ominous intimation of Henry's detachment from the cult of Becket when, on his visit to Canterbury in

---

[11] P. W. White claims that Henry's hostility to Becket is reflected in 1532 in a letter to the authorities at York to suppress a religious interlude of St Thomas, but this was not Becket. A rising had broken out at York at the instigation of 'the seditious conduct of certain papists' preparing to perform an interlude on St Thomas the Apostle. Henry intervened directly to prohibit the performance of any enactment based on any part of the Bible from using language 'which may tend to excite those who are beholding the same to any breach of the peace'. J. O. Halliwell-Phillipps (ed.), *Letters of the Kings of England*, 2 vols. (London, 1846), vol. I, p. 354. P. W. White, *Theatre and Reformation: Protestantism, Patronage and Playing in Tudor England* (Cambridge, 1993), pp. 28 and 197 n. 60.

[12] He went on to say that he was bound by his coronation oath to recover for the Crown the goods that churchmen held of it and that had been unlawfully alienated by his precedessors. Chapuys to Charles V, 15 March 1533: *LP*, vol. VI, no. 235.

[13] A. F. Pollard, *Wolsey* (London, 1929), pp. 356–7.

[14] G. Bernard, 'The Piety of Henry VIII', in N. S. Amos, A. Pettegree and H. van Nierop (eds.), *The Education of a Christian Society: Humanism and Reformation in Britain and the Netherlands. Papers Delivered to the Thirteenth Anglo-Dutch Historical Conference, 1997* (Aldershot, 1999), pp. 63–88, esp. pp. 74–6.

[15] J. G. Russell, *The Field of Cloth of Gold* (London, 1969), app. C.

30 Corpus Christi College, Cambridge. MS 298, fol. 2r, from the English verse translation by Laurence Wade of the Becket *vita*, 1497. The words 'saint' and 'martyr' are blotted out throughout the manuscript, which bears Cranmer's autograph on the first leaf.

that year, he neglected to enter either of the two great monastic houses. This may have been intended as a calculated snub to the monks of Christ Church priory for their involvement in the sedition of Elizabeth Barton. The 'holy maid of Kent' riposted with the comment that the king was so abominable in the sight of God that he was not worthy to tread on hallowed ground.[16] St Thomas of Canterbury had appeared in her visions, and her criticism of the king's 'divorce' and remarriage had been publicised by Dr Edward Bocking, the cellarer of the priory. Bocking was accused of encouraging her visions of the Blessed Virgin Mary, which were no more than a deception undertaken for the purpose of attracting pilgrimages and lucrative offerings to the image in the Lady Chapel of the cathedral. The indictment denounced the blasphemy of Elizabeth Barton's hypocritical sanctity and feigned miracles, whereby many were incited to idolatry and sedition. She was executed at Tyburn on 20 April 1534.[17] While the episode must have hardened Henry's attitude to idolatry and pilgrimage, he would have had another compelling reason for avoiding the cathedral in 1533. The inscription on the shrine – 'pro iusticia et iure ecclesie dei conserviando'[18] – was a standing rebuke to the denial of Roman jurisdiction in the Act of Appeals. Henry may have spared himself the embarrassment of confronting these words, but no attempt was made then, or even after the passing of the Act of Supremacy in 1534, to subject the abuse of images to general censure. Nor was there at this stage an outright attack on the veneration of saints by the other reformers to match Latimer's vehement opposition. Copies of Robert Barnes's *A supplicatyon ... vnto the most excellent and redoubted prince henrye the eyght* (Antwerp, 1531) had been brought to Cromwell's attention by Stephen Vaughan. In the second edition, printed in London in November 1534, Barnes toned down its Lutheran position, allegedly at Cromwell's instigation, to make it more palatable to the king. The revision entailed the removal of a section denouncing idolatry that was presumably considered to be unacceptable to Henry at this time.[19] Even after the official

---

[16] *LP*, vol. VI, no. 1468 (p. 588). It may be doubted whether this incident in itself supports Professor Dobson's conclusion that the king had already been convinced by Cromwell, Cranmer, and others 'that the cult of Becket was worse than superstitious: it was politically dangerous too.' B. Dobson, 'The Monks of Canterbury in the Later Middle Ages, 1220–1540', in *Hist. Canterbury Cath.*, p. 150.

[17] T. Wright (ed.), *Dissolution*, pp. 16–34; R. Rex, 'The Execution of the Holy Maid of Kent', *Historical Research*, 64 (1991), 216–20.

[18] 'The Customary of the Shrine of St Thomas Becket': BL, Additional MS 59616, fols. 1–11.

[19] S. E. Lehmberg, 'The Religious Beliefs of Thomas Cromwell', in R. L. DeMolen (ed.), *Leaders of the Reformation* (London and Toronto, 1984), pp. 40–2.

campaign against the abuse of images was unleashed in 1535, Henry continued to hold to the belief in the efficacy of prayers to the saints in the salvation of souls.

The cult of Becket became potentially dangerous to the king with the challenge posed by the refusal of Bishop John Fisher and Sir Thomas More to subscribe unconditionally to the oath of supremacy. Fisher had already offended the king by his indulgent attitude to the nun's visions, and More narrowly escaped being implicated in the affair. After these three trials and executions, it was hardly to be expected that a tradition that sustained the memory of the defiance of royal authority in a historic quarrel with Rome would be suffered to continue; yet it was left undisturbed for another three years. If the problem inherent in this political embarrassment was not immediately addressed in Cromwell's propaganda, it was because Henry balked at questioning the reputation of the most pre-eminent English martyr-saint.

Thomas More's devotion to Becket, his name saint along with Thomas the Apostle, is well attested. When in 1530 he was received into the confraternity of Christ Church Canterbury, it was a recognition of his reverence for its patron saint and not, at least in More's own eyes, a merely conventional honour bestowed upon a newly appointed lord chancellor. As a relentless persecutor of heretics, More was moved to defend Archbishop Becket's good name against the irreverence of the reformers. He was particularly incensed at the heretical insertion of another 'St Thomas' in the calendar. In *The Confutation of Tyndale's Answer* (1532) he inveighs against the errant priest, Thomas Hitton, who was burned for heresy at Maidstone in 1530, 'the dyvyls stynkyng martyr of whose burnynge Tyndale maketh boast'. More also denounced the reformer George Joye for *his* contumely in depicting Hitton as another sainted Thomas.[20]

More's identification with Becket became close as his personal crisis intensified. His last extant letter, written in the Tower to his daughter Margaret on 5 July 1535, expresses his longing for death on the morrow, 'a day very mete and conveniente' for him to go to God, 'for it is S. Thomas evin and the vtas of Sainte Peter'.[21] The order duly came for his execution on that day, the significance of which could not have been lost on the king. He would hardly have wished to make a martyr of More, and if there

---

[20] *The Complete Works of Thomas More*, ed. A. Schuster *et al.* (New Haven, CT, 1963–) vol. VIII, pp. 31207–8 (*Confutation*); vol. IX, pp. 355, 361 (*Apology*). In his *Dyaloge* (London, 1530) More defended the traditional teaching of the Church on the veneration of images and relics, praying to saints and going on pilgrimage. *Ibid.*, vol. VI, pt 1: *A Dialogue against Heresies*, esp. pp. 90, 185.

[21] BL, Royal MS. 17D XIV, fols. 426v, 427.

was an inwardness in the choice of date on Henry's part, the intention may have been to damn his former chancellor by association with another notorious traitor to a king of England. We cannot tell whether his hostility to More was increased at any stage in the proceedings by an intimation of the latter's devotion to Becket. As it turned out, the layman most closely associated with the cult of Becket, and the one most likely to have served as a focus for discontent at the king's actions, was out of the way long before it was extinguished.

More's predecessor as chancellor, Thomas Wolsey, had already been depicted by contemporary critics as another Becket. To Tyndale the cardinal's life was but a counterfeiting of Thomas of Canterbury, who had been 'made a saint for his worshipping of the holy seat of St Peter... the *Cathedra Pestilentiae*'.[22] No reformer at the time seemed to have pointed to the more obvious comparison between Becket and More on these grounds to discredit More, at least in print, until John Bale in 1544 linked their names in a list of false martyrs, both historical and contemporary, who had died rather for the 'ryches and proude mayntenance of theyr holye whorysh churche'.[23] The parallel between More and Becket as champions of papal jurisdiction against the pretensions of English kings was drawn by a later generation of Catholic hagiographers; it was not openly discussed at the time. For that matter, it should not be assumed that the Vatican consistently recognised the martyrdom of St Thomas as a great landmark in the historic struggle between the temporal and the spiritual powers. Leo X had shown no great concern for the celebration of the Jubilee of 1520 in England, and his successor seemed not to have held St Thomas in high esteem until his reputation was impugned by the king of England. In his breviate to Francis I of 26 July 1535, before news of More's death reached Rome, Paul III expressed his shock at the execution of Bishop Fisher: 'this most holy man laid down his life for God, for the Catholic religion, for justice, for truth, while he was defending not merely the particular rights of one only man [*sic*], as Thomas of Canterbury formerly did, but the truth of the universal church'.[24] But by

[22] In *The Practise: Expositions of Scripture and Practice of Prelates*, Parker Soc. (Cambridge, 1849), pp. 293, 309. Wolsey's pretensions were also contrasted to the virtues of Becket in a popular ballad, *c.* 1528: F. J. Furnivall (ed.), *Ballads from Manuscripts* 2 vols. (London 1868–72), vol. I, pp. 352–61.

[23] John Bale, *A brefe Chronycle concernynge the Examinacyon and death of the martyr... syr John Oldecastell...* (?Antwerp, 1544, reprinted London, ?1548), fol. A2v. I am grateful to Dr Lawrence Manley for this reference. Becket is also compared disparagingly with the Lollard knight. Cf. H. Christmas (ed.), *Select Works of John Bale, Bishop of Ossory*, Parker Soc. (Cambridge, 1849), pp. 55, 58.

[24] *LP*, vol. VIII, no. 1117; P. Janelle, (ed.), *Obedience in Church and State: Three Political Tracts by Stephen Gardiner* (Cambridge, 1930), pp. 12–13.

this stage, in England if not in Rome, Becket had come to represent the assertion of papal over regal rights, and after the most prominent victims of the royal supremacy had been cut down, the cult that commemorated a comparable defiance of royal authority came increasingly to be regarded as politically subversive.

For all his caution in moving against the potent symbols of papal authority in England, Henry did not distance himself from popular displays of anticlericalism. To mock the clergy's pretensions he was even prepared to put up with having himself portrayed on stage. The story is told by the imperial ambassador. In June 1535, within a week of the execution of Fisher and when More was still languishing in the Tower, the king went out of his way to attend an interlude that set forth, as Chapuys indignantly put it in a letter to Charles V, 'a gallant and notable interpretation of a chapter of the Apocalypse'. This was enacted on the eve of the Nativity of St John somewhere on the outskirts of London, and Henry concealed himself in a house where he could watch the show unobserved. He was so pleased at the depiction of himself cutting off the heads of the clergy that in order to laugh out loud and encourage the people, he made himself known to the rest of the audience.[25] Indeed the entertainment delighted him so much that he urged Queen Anne to see a repeat performance on St Peter's eve. Henry's indulgence of such antipapal and anticlerical demonstrations on red-letter days was extraordinary: in later reigns it was deemed tantamount to lese-majesty to represent a living sovereign on stage.

A number of former friars and monks played a crucial part in the discrediting of Becket. Both John Bale and William Barlow had left their orders in the early years of reform, and when images first came under concerted attack, Cromwell received useful intelligence from another turncoat. In 1535 the Observant friar, Robert Ward, was indicted for heresy at Chelmsford, and wrote to Cromwell to warn him about the obscurantist teaching of his fellow friars. The story of the martyrdom illustrated in the stained-glass windows of the church of St Thomas of Acre, depicting the humiliation of a naked Henry II kneeling at the shrine to be beaten by a monk, was misinterpreted by the pardoners, who told the unlearned that the martyr had been slain for resisting the king. Through such invidious words and pictures, according to Ward, simple folk were encouraged to resist the reform of pilgrimage and prayers to saints.[26]

---

[25] Chapuys to Granvelle, 30 June 1535: *LP*, vol. VIII, no. 949. White, *Theatre and Reformation*, p. 28.

[26] *LP*, vol. VIII, nos. 625–6 (n. d.).

Friar Arthur of the Greyfriars at Canterbury got into trouble in the same year for preaching an incendiary sermon at Herne on Easter Sunday. He was alleged to have denounced the reformers' attack on prayer, fasting and pilgrimages. 'I say, he that gives or offers one penny to St Thomas's shrine, it is more meritorious for the soul than he had given a noble to poor people, for one is spiritual and the other corporal.' On the face of it, this would appear to be one of the last recorded tributes paid to the efficacy of pilgrimage, but the friar claimed in his defence that he had been misreported. The friar's detractors cannot be taken on trust, and it looks as if Becket's memory had been invoked by partisans in a private quarrel in the ecclesiastical politics of the city when the campaign against images and shrines was gathering strength but before it had been sanctioned by the king.[27]

The miraculous properties of images were apparently first challenged in print in England by one of Cromwell's protégés in 1535. In a marginal note to his English translation of Martin Bucer's treatise on images, William Marshall recommended that the miracles associated with the images at Walsingham, Canterbury and other centres of pilgrimage should be 'well tried by Scripture, to see what article of our faith they have confirmed'.[28] Something of Cromwell's own beliefs is perhaps revealed in the changes that the civic humanist Thomas Starkey made at his instigation to the definition of 'policy' when invited to formulate his political philosophy in an exchange of letters in 1535. Starkey's revised position was that there were two 'policies', two manners of living, 'ii dyuerse fascuyons of passyng thys pylgrymage, the one cyuyle, polytyke & worldly, the other heuenly, spriritual & godly'.[29] If Cromwell and the politiques in his circle were already set upon a worldly pilgrimage in the king's service, they did not always follow the same path. In his *Exhortation to the people, instructynge theym to Unitie and Obedience*, published sometime before March 1536, with a preface addressed to the king, Starkey urged that religious reform be pursued with moderation. 'Things indifferent', *adiophoria*, should be left to be decided by secular policy, as indeed had

---

[27] PRO SP1/91, fol. 176 (*LP*, vol. VIII, no. 480). Elton comments that even if the sermon had been maliciously misreported 'it shows the friar's enemies displaying a vigorous imagination itself suggestive of the sort of things that were being said and causing unrest'. G. R. Elton, *Policy and Police: The Enforcement of The Reformation in the Age of Thomas Cromwell* (Cambridge, 1972), p. 16.

[28] Cited in M. Aston, *England's Iconoclasts, I: Laws against Images* (Oxford, 1988), p. 210.

[29] S. E. Lehmberg, 'Thomas Cromwell', pp. 143, 148. Lehmberg argues that Cromwell favoured the *via media* in religion, but his claim that, though opposed to the invocation of saints and the abuse of relics, images and pilgrimages, the minister was 'inclined to reform in these matters rather than total condemnation', does not seem to be borne out by the evidence.

happened in the case of the papal supremacy. Both faith and works were necessary for salvation, and pilgrimages, observances of holy days and the invocation of saints, once purged of their excesses, were acceptable as 'convenient means' to testify to inward faith. Likewise, the monasteries should be reformed but not abolished. In advocating the *via media*, Starkey seems to have been responding to Cromwell's earlier advice, but there was soon to be a parting of the ways as the minister decided on a more radical course of action.

The monastic visitors who reported late in 1535 drew attention to idolatry among the many abuses they found in the religious houses. The information contained in the *comperta* was used to justify the act for the dissolution of the smaller monasteries passed in the last session of the Reformation Parliament, but even before then it had been exploited in the preparation of a measure framed for the suppression of the monastic shrines. This abortive bill purported to give parliamentary sanction to injunctions to be issued by the vicar general, Thomas Cromwell, for prohibiting pilgrimages and the worship of relics. Though the draft survives in what appears to be a fairly finished state, without corrections, its status is problematic, so that no safe conclusions can be reached on whether it was seriously considered by the makers of policy. It reflects some of Cranmer's known views and evidently derived from Cromwell's coterie of reformers, but whatever its provenance its significance lies in the fact that it outlines a reforming scenario in which the suppression of monastic sites of pilgrimage was envisaged prior to the dissolution of the houses themselves. The preamble makes a distinct connection between the iniquities of the monks and the abuses of pilgrimages, though the remedy proposed was to purge the crime, not to abolish the monastic orders or houses. The abolition of pilgrimage is represented as a necessary reform of the Christian commonwealth, and the main enacting clause prohibits any of the religious from seducing or alluring anyone

to runne abowte on pylgrymage to seek God in this place or that, and persuade the people to geve any peculiar office to any saynct, but playnly like Christen men to recognize all goodnes to come of God as the very fontayne and gever of all remedy bothe for the sowle and body, or that any suyche persons shall for lucre sett furth their images or reliques, whereby the glory and honor of God in any parte maye be lyke as in tymes past by suyche meanes not a litell hath ben debilitate and diminyshed.[30]

The penalties prescribed are the loss of their benefices and stipends, and expulsion from the place where the offence was committed. The argument against idleness and false religion was deployed to apply equally to monasticism and to pilgrimages, relics and saints. In the event no such

[30] PRO SP6/116/247–53; *LP*, vol. x, no. 246, item 16.

comprehensive denunciation of the monastic life, or of the unedifying and unprofitable religious observances it allegedly induced in the laity, was to be promulgated by the regime.[31] The king is commended for mercy and dedication to 'a charitable and quyet reformation' to the glory of God, the advancement of the true religion of Christ, the increase of honour and the discharging of his conscience. For all this blandishment, a drastic reform on the scale proposed evidently did not appeal to Henry at this stage; the bill was cast aside in favour of a piecemeal dissolution of the monasteries in which Cromwell proceeded 'little by little'.

Just as the decision to dissolve the lesser monasteries did not lead ineluctably to the abolition of all religious houses, so the campaign against the abbeys did not at first entail the systematic suppression of all the shrines. To begin with, the respective policies seem to have had a separate rationale and they continued to observe a different timetable. Not all the shrines that formed centres of pilgrimage were administered by the monks, and even as late as May 1538 Henry was engaged in re-founding monasteries, an indication of the haphazard and unsystematic character of the dissolution.[32] In some places monasteries and their relics were put down at the same time; in other cases, such as at Canterbury and Winchester, the suppression of the shrines preceded that of the religious houses.[33]

None of the provisions of the bill aborted in 1536 was salvaged for inclusion in the act for the dissolution of the greater monasteries, and at no stage was Parliament to have a voice in the suppression of the shrines or pilgrimages, or in sanctioning the injunctions issued by Cromwell in his capacity as either visitor general or vicegerent in spirituals. Henry may have balked at the implication in the draft bill that the prerogative powers of the supreme head required further parliamentary sanction. In formulating their Supplication against the Ordinaries in 1532, the Commons had protested about the excessive number of saints' days which, it was alleged, were observed with little devotion,[34] but they did not proceed to legislation and it was left to Convocation to institute a revision of the calendar of saints. An ordinance of 19 July 1536 restricted the number

---

[31] A faint echo of the complaint in the preamble about the diversion of alms for the poor is to be found in the injunctions of 1536. In the visitors' injunctions of 1535 the monks were enjoined to persuade pilgrims to donate their offerings to the poor rather than to the objects of veneration. BL Cotton MSS, Cleopatra Eiv, fols. 21–5, printed in J. Youings, *The Dissolution of the Monasteries* (London, 1971), pp. 149–52.

[32] J. J. Scarisbrick, *Henry VIII* (London, 1968), p. 512.

[33] G. W. O. Woodward, *The Dissolution of the Monasteries* (London, 1966), pp. 52–3.

[34] An undated draft address of the Commons to the king, proposing that there should be fewer holy days, especially at harvest time, because of the proliferation then of 'abominable and execrable vices, ydle and wanton sportes, and plaies of the staige', is cited without source reference in J. P. Collier, *The History of English Dramatic Poetry to the Time of Shakespeare*, 3 vols. (1831), vol. I, p. 126n.

of holy days, and the feasts of St Thomas were not explicitly included in the list of exceptions that could still be observed (Christmas Day and the feasts following it, Easter, Pentecost and Corpus Christi).[35] Another two years were to pass before this oblique omission became an overt condemnation, an interval that may be explained in part by the king's equivocation on the formularies of the faith in the late 1530s.[36]

The Ten Articles and Cromwell's first injunctions to the clergy of 1536 were categorical in defining as idolatrous the abuses of image-worship and of the honouring of saints. Pilgrimages were discouraged but not forbidden: the clergy were not to extol any images, relics or miracles 'for superstition or lucre', but to exhort the people that offerings to images and relics would be better bestowed upon the poor. This latter point had been the burden of Erasmus's satire on pilgrimage to Walsingham and Canterbury, composed in Latin around 1511. It was printed in an anonymous English translation, *Ye pylgremage of pure deuotyon*, some time in 1536–7. Nothing is known of the circumstances of publication but modern commentators have speculated that it was issued as part of Cromwell's propaganda campaign to discredit shrines and pilgrimages.[37]

The king's doctrinal views appear to be stated unequivocally in the Ten Articles, with their affirmation of the importance of penance as one of the three sacraments essential for salvation. Images are not to be venerated in themselves and saints are not to be revered with the worship due only to God. Pilgrimages as such are not mentioned, but it is declared that the saints in heaven should be prayed to only as intercessors for our sins, while Christ must be acknowledged as the only mediator for our salvation. The king's letters that accompanied copies of the ordinance of Convocation distributed to the bishops forbade the clergy from reading or speaking of the abrogated feasts, which included those that fell in harvest time: they were to 'pass them over with secret silence', so that they would be discontinued through neglect.[38] Henry was clearly not disposed to bring matters to a head by precipitate action against the shrines, and

---

[35] S. E. Lehmberg, *The Later Parliaments of Henry VIII* (Cambridge, 1977), pp. 39, 92, 293 n 147.

[36] For another reading of the evidence, see George Bernard's case for Henry's pursuit of a consistently moderate course in reforming the Church. Bernard, 'The Making of Religious Policy, 1533–1546: Henry VIII and the Search for the Middle Way', *HJ*, 41 (1998), 321–49.

[37] D. Erasmus, *A dialogue of communication of two persons, intitled ye pylgremage of pure deuotyon. Newly translated into Englishe*. London, *s.a.* V. Houliston, 'St Thomas Becket in the Propaganda of the English Counter-Reformation', *Renaissance Studies*, 7 (1993), 44; R. Marius, *Thomas More: a Biography* (London, 1984), pp. 332–3; H. de Vocht (ed.), *The Earliest English Translations of Erasmus' Colloquia* (Louvain, 1928), pp. lxv–lxviii.

[38] R. W. Dixon, *History of the Church of England from the Abolition of the Roman Jurisdiction*, 6 vols. (Oxford, 1878–1902), vol. I, pp. 424–5; vol. II, p. 69.

he continued to temporise on doctrinal reform. In his response to *The Institution of a Christian Man*, issued in September 1537, he expressed his reservation about the formula on prayers to the saints in heaven contained in section 33: he would have the saints acknowledged as mediators, and not merely intercessors, in prayers to God for salvation.[39] He was doubtless distracted by other concerns from insisting on such revision. When the second injunctions were devised twelve months later, he sanctioned a more radical reform from which there was to be no retreat.

The evidence suggests that in the intervening period the king was but gradually won over to approve the campaign against idolatry and the indiscriminate veneration of saints. In 1537 the 'reformed' enumeration of the Ten Commandments was adopted in which 'the prohibition of graven images is given special prominence by separation from the injunction to worship God alone'.[40] But as late as August of that year Cranmer despaired of persuading the people to desist from keeping the prohibited feasts and holy days when the court still observed them, 'ffor the kyngys own howse shal be an example unto al ye realme to breake his own ordinances'.[41] The clergy were also negligent in observing the order for abbreviating the calendar of saints, so that the archbishop had to reissue it on 16 September.[42] The more favourable conditions prevailing on the domestic and the international scene early in 1538, however, permitted Cromwell to advocate a more determined and consistent course of reform.

The official campaign of iconoclasm may be dated from the first of a series of sermons delivered at Paul's Cross by John Hilsey, bishop of Rochester. According to the chronicler Charles Wriothesley, Hilsey preached at Cromwell's instigation and with the king's permission. In February Hilsey exposed the deception of the Rood of Grace at Boxley Abbey, near Maidstone: It had been manipulated like a puppet by the monks, who used 'old wire' and 'rotten sticks' to cause its eyes and lips to move.[43] In a letter to Heinrich Bullinger, John Hoker used an extended dramatic metaphor to describe the successive scenes in its degradation.

---

[39] J. E. Cox (ed.), *Miscellaneous Writings and Letters of Thomas Cranmer*, Parker Soc. (Cambridge, 1846), p. 93; C. Haigh, *English Reformations: Religion, Politics and Society under the Tudors* (Oxford, 1993), pp. 132–3.

[40] Aston, *England's Iconoclasts*, pp. 371–92, 408–30.

[41] Cranmer to Cromwell, from his house at Ford, 28 Aug. [1537]: BL, Cotton MSS, Cleo. Ev, fol. 300. This section was added in the archbishop's own hand to the letter dictated to his clerk.

[42] *LP*, vol. XII (2), no. 703.

[43] Wriothesley states that Hilsey preached more frequently than any other bishop at Paul's Cross: 'when any abuse should be shewed to the people eyther of idolatrye or of the Bishop of Rome, he had the doeynge thereof by the Lord Vicegerentes commaundement from the Kinge'. *Wriothesley's Chronicle*, vol. I, p. 104. The conservative Bishop Stokesley of London challenged Hilsey's right to select the preachers: Millar Maclure, *The Paul's Cross Sermons, 1534–1642* (Toronto, 1958), p. 26.

The 'juggler' was revealed first from a platform to a jeering throng at Maidstone, and then to the king and the 'theatre' of the court, before the matter was referred to the Council. Within a few days the 'stroller' was made to perform its last miracle at Paul's Cross, where it was denounced from the pulpit by Hilsey before being hurled to the ground to be dismembered and burned by the indignant spectators. 'It is difficult to say whether the king was more pleased on account of the detection of the imposture, or more grieved at heart that the miserable people had been imposed on for so many ages.'[44] In 1510 Henry had made an offering of 6*s*. 8*d*. at the Rood of Grace. As Latimer later lamented, the king had been deceived too long by flattering preachers; he was at last convinced that the feigned relics and images should be destroyed.[45] If, in sanctioning the attack on idolatry, Henry was yielding to the persuasions of Cromwell and Cranmer, he was not thereby committing himself irretrievably to a reformist position. As Peter Marshall has demonstrated, the exposure of idolatrous duplicity, especially that perpetrated in the monasteries, was exploited to signal the supreme head's determination to cleanse the Church of the superstitions so long tolerated by the papacy. As such this form of iconoclasm could be 'of service both to evangelicals and conservatives within the Henrician establishment'. It enabled the king's envoys abroad to vindicate the royal supremacy as having a consistent goal in purifying the Church.[46]

In March 1538 Lord Lisle, the deputy of Calais, was informed by John Hussee, his factor in London, that 'Pilgrimage saints go down apace'.[47] The rumour spread in April that the figures of the Virgin of Walsingham and St Thomas of Canterbury, along with other images, would soon follow the Rood of Grace to perform miracles at Paul's Cross.[48] In May Friar Forest was condemned to death: the charge was denial of the royal supremacy but he had also affirmed that the Blessed Martyr, St Thomas of Canterbury, had died for the rights of the Church. The wooden image

---

[44] Trans. from the Latin in G. C. Gorham, *Gleanings of the Reformation in England, 1533–1588* (London, 1857), pp. 17–19.

[45] Maclure, *Sermons*, p. 30. For Latimer's comment, see note 60 below.

[46] P. Marshall, 'The Rood of Boxley, the Blood of Hailes and the Defence of the Henrician Church', *JEH*, 46, 1995, 689–96 (esp. 690), which also reviews the evidence for the claim that the articulated figures which were said to be manipulated by the monks to perform conjuring tricks were not necessarily fraudulent.

[47] M. St Clare Byrne (ed.), *The Lisle Letters*, ed. 6 vols. (Chicago, 1981), (ed.), vol. v, p. 1129.

[48] Nicholas Partridge (whose brother was reported to have been the first to expose the sham: *LP*, vol. XIII (1), no. 348) wrote to Bullinger on 12 April 1538 from the Frankfurt book fair, recounting news received from a member of the German merchant companies in London. *LP*, vol. XIII (1), no. 754.

of Derfel Gadarn ('the great god of Wales', as Latimer called it) was brought to London, broken up and used as tinder for burning the friar at the stake.[49] This public spectacle of execution and iconoclasm, accompanied by a three-hour sermon by Latimer, was stage-managed by Cromwell to enforce the royal supremacy. It can also be regarded as an opening gambit in his strategy to discredit Becket.

In Canterbury on 6 July the city pageant was mounted, as it turned out for the last time, and presumably on the following day the feast of the Translation of the Relics was celebrated, since there is no evidence that it was discontinued prior to the prohibitions of 19 July. On 9 August the archbishop was observed in his palace to be ostentatiously refraining from fasting on the vigil of St Lawrence.[50] It was Cranmer who instigated the proceedings against the shrine, 'by cause that I have in great suspect that St Thomas of Canterbury his blood, in Christ's church in Canterbury, is but a feigned thing and made of some red ochre or of such like matter'. Late in August the archbishop asked Cromwell to obtain a commission for one of his chaplains and Dr Legh, 'to try and examine that and other like things there'. The miraculous properties of the tincture of Becket's blood in the 'Canterbury water' which pilgrims took away with them, so that each phial was 'in effect a perambulatory shrine', were to be put to the test.[51] If as seems likely such an inspection did take place in Canterbury, independently of the attentions of the king's commissioners for the monasteries who actually dismantled the shrine, it would have questioned not only the therapeutic value of the 'miraculous blood' but perhaps the authenticity of the head reliquary as well ('other like things there'). The inquiry set in train by the archbishop may have been the basis for the subsequent rumour that surfaced in the final version of the papal bull excommunicating Henry, that the saint had been

---

[49] *LP*, vol. VIII, no. 626; P. Marshall, 'Papist as Heretic: The Burning of John Forest, 1536', *HJ*, 41 (1998), 351–74.

[50] Corpus Christi College, Cambridge MS 298, fol. 48r,: the Latin chronicle of a monk of St Augustine's Abbey, Canterbury, preserved by Cranmer. A near-contemporary English version of this document (BL Harleian MS 419, fols. 112–14) is printed in J. G. Nichols (ed.), *Narratives of the Days of the Reformation*, Camden Soc., o.s., vol. LXXVII, (1860), p. 285. This manuscript is a damaged fragment and, in the entry relating to Cranmer's non-observance of the fast, the name of the saint's day is lost. The missing words are conjectured ('Thomas Beckets I suppose') in a marginal note, possibly in Strype's own hand, on fol. 113v, and supplied in parenthesis in Nichols's edition of the text, with an acknowledgement to Strype. Cf. J. Strype, *Memorials of Archbishop Cranmer*, 3 vols. in 4 (1848–54), vol. I, p. 134 (61 in 1st edn). The inference has been repeated as fact by historians ever since.

[51] R. C. Finucane, *Miracles and Pilgrims in Medieval England* (London, 1977), p. 163. Cf. B. Spencer, *Pilgrim Souvenirs and Secular Badges: Medieval Finds from Excavations in London*, vol. VII (London, 1998), pp. 38–9.

summoned to a posthumous 'trial' for treason.[52] Another possible explanation for this report is that a scene depicting Thomas Becket called
to answer the charges laid against him, as it were at the bar of History,
may have featured in the dramatic performance that is known to have
been put on in the primatial see to coincide with the spoliation of the
shrine.[53] Henry and Cromwell were both in Canterbury at the time, but
Cranmer had remained at Lambeth, detained by the negotiations with
the German envoys, who did not leave the country until October. The
archbishop did not, it seems, contrive to remain detached from what was
about to unfold in his see, but his absence may well have saved him from
compromising the dignity of his office. Before Cromwell left London, he
authorised the removal of images from St Paul's Cathedral. On 23 August Sir Richard Gresham was informed of the minister's views by Robert
Barnes, and by the following day the dean had dismantled the offending
objects.[54]

The progress of the demonisation of Becket in official propaganda,
which followed rather than preceded the suppression of the cult, can
be traced in the series of orders issued by Henry and Cromwell between
September 1538 and early in the following year: the second injunctions to
the clergy, the royal proclamation of 16 November, and the king's letters
to the justices in December. In order fully to understand the way in which
the king's hostility to Becket was finally articulated, some account must
be taken of significant revisions that were made to these measures before
they were printed, as well as of the relevant section in a 'defence' of the
Henrician Reformation that was drafted in 1539 though not in the event
promulgated. The rewriting of the Becket story that they reveal may have
been coloured by what Henry witnessed in Canterbury.

We cannot be certain to what extent the king's activities during his
progress in Kent in the autumn of 1538 had been decided in advance –
except in one particular. Before Henry set out he altered his itinerary so
as to arrive in Dover two days earlier than had been planned. This was
to enable him to reach the port in time to meet Anne Gouffier de Boisy,
the wife of Raoul Vernon, Sieur de Montreuil-Bonin, who was about to
depart for France after a visit to Madelaine of France, the short-lived
Queen of Scotland. Mme de Montreuil visited Canterbury on the last
day of August to pay her respects to the shrine, the last dignitary to do

[52] Cox, *Cranmer Letters*, p. 378.; Elton, *Policy and Police*, p. 257, n. 1. For an exposé of
the forged documents which purported to confirm the canard, see J. H. Pollen, S. J.,
'Henry VIII and St Thomas Becket', *The Month*, 137 (1921), 119–28, 324–33.

[53] I am indebted to Dr Richard Rex for the suggestion that this was a possible scenario for
the performance at St Stephens.

[54] Wriothesley's *Chronicle*, I, p. 84. For the discussions with the envoys, see D. MacCulloch,
Cranmer A Life (New Haven, CT and London, 1996), pp. 215–23.

so, and was shown around the cathedral by her escort on the journey, William Penison, who reported her impressions to Cromwell. She duly marvelled at the splendour of the shrine, though (like Dean Colet on his pilgrimage in the company of Erasmus) she refused to kiss the saint's skull when offered it by the prior. It is conceivable that, dazzled as she was by the worldly rather than the spiritual riches of the shrine, her subsequent recounting of the experience to the king at Dover (as Diarmaid MacCulloch has suggested) 'clinched a plan of action already in Henry's mind'.[55] She may even have acted as an unwitting advocate of Cromwell's designs.

That much is speculation, but there is firmer evidence to indicate that the final decision of policy on shrines and pilgrimages was taken only after the arrival of the court at Canterbury. An early version of Cromwell's second injunctions to the clergy, which *inter alia* authorised the dismantling of 'feigned images', is marked as 'exhibited', presumably to the king, on 5 September 1538. This was the day on which Henry reached Canterbury *en route* from Dover. The clergy were reminded that in instructing the laity, images served no other purpose than to put the unlearned in mind of 'the lives and conversacion' of the persons represented. These sentiments, conventional enough in themselves,[56] now appeared in a reformist context. The Word was to take precedence over images in worship, for it was the Bible in English that was to take pride of place in churches. No particular shrine or saint is named in the document; images *per se* were not forbidden but their abuse in the worship of saints and relics in superstitious pilgrimages and offerings is condemned. There is, besides, a hint at further action yet to come in the abolition of offensive images.[57] This promise was fulfilled in the section added to the document evidently after a consultation with the king at Canterbury. The last four items were incorporated before the injunctions were sent to Cranmer on 30 September and then, on 11 October, published under his mandate.

[55] De Vocht, *Erasmus' Colloquia*, pp. lxv–lxviii, *LP*, vol. XIII (2), nos. 257, 280, 288, 349, 1280; *SP*, *Henry VIII*, vol. I, p. 584; MacCulloch, *Cranmer*, pp. 226–8. In 1507 Mme de Montreuil had married Raoul Vernon, Sr de Montreuil-Bonin (d.1516), and in 1529 was appointed governess to Francis I's youngest son and daughters. I am indebted to Dr David Potter for this information.

[56] The Briggantine monk William Bonde drew a similar distinction between idols and images in *The Pylgrimage of Perfection* (1526, reprinted 1531), adding that images serve 'as books to the rude and unlearned people, and to move simple souls to devotion'. Cited in W. H. Frere and W. M. Kennedy (eds.), *Visitation Articles and Injunctions of the Reformation*, 3 vols. (London, 1910) vol. II, p. 38 n 3.

[57] The king 'hath in part already, and more will hereafter, travail for the abolishing of such images as might be an occasion of so great an offence to God, and so great danger to the souls of his loving subjects'. Frere and Kennedy (eds.), *Visitation Articles*, vol. II, pp. 34–43.

One of these additions forbade any further alteration in the order of divine service and fasting days without the king's further authority. The two feasts of St Thomas had already been silently removed from the calendar by Convocation, along with certain other holy days. It was now decreed that the eves of those abrogated feasts were no longer to be observed as fasting days, including the commemoration of Thomas Becket, 'sometyme archbishop of Canturburie, whiche shall be cleane omitted, and in the stede therof the feriall service used'.[58] The prohibition would extend to the civic aspect of the cult, the pageant that had been put on in Canterbury and elsewhere on 6 July. Becket was at last singled out for exceptional treatment in the calendar of saints, for nothing was to be permitted that would serve to keep alive the memory of *his* life and conversation. The last item in the additions endorsed an important liturgical reform: in church processions intercessory prayers to saints were to be omitted in favour of those addressed to God and to Christ. This signified that Henry had at last overcome his scruple on the vexing matter of the role of the saints, relinquishing the conservative position that he had taken in response to the 'Bishops' Book'. It may safely be assumed that he authorised these revisions to the injunctions before the demolition of the shrine began during his visit.

The Cistercian Abbey of Hailes in Gloucestershire, where the reliquary was supposed to contain the very blood of Christ shed upon the Cross, was suppressed later in the year. In another sermon at Paul's Cross on 24 November, Bishop Hilsey denounced 'the Blood of Hailes' as fraudulent.[59] By this time Becket had been decanonised, and his bones and those of the other saints at Canterbury disposed of. There is no direct record of Henry's personal view of Becket, expressed on this or any other occasion, but his disillusionment with relics at this time may be gauged from his reaction to the revelation that the Blood of Hailes was an imposture. This was related by Latimer in one of his digressions in the sermon preached before Edward VI on 19 April 1549: 'What a do was it to brynge thys out of the kynges head, this abominacyon of the bloud of Hales could not be taken a great whyle out of his mynd!'[60] Bishop Hilsey had preached against the relic at Paul's Cross and exposed it as a forgery before the

---

[58] *LP*, vol. XIII (2), no. 281; D. Wilkins, *Consilia Magnae Britanniae et Hiberniae*, 4 vols. (London, 1737), vol. III, 817. R. B. Merriman, *The Life and Letters of Thomas Cromwell*, 2 vols. (Oxford, 1902), vol. II, no. 273. C. C. Butterworth, *The English Primers, 1529–1545: A Chapter in the History of the English Bible and the English Reformation* (Philadelphia, 1953), p. 169 (where the desecration of the shrine is misdated to October). Cf. D. MacCulloch, *Cranmer*, pp. 226–7, where it is surmised that the first version of the injunctions was presented to Henry during his progress somewhere in Kent.

[59] Maclure, *Sermons*, pp. 187–8.

[60] Latimer may have recalled this episode with rueful irony, since he had been forced to recant his views on images, purgatory and pilgrimage when accused of heresy in

king and council. It appears that Henry was particularly incensed by the iniquity of a dissembling 'miracle' that profaned the sacrament of the altar. His initial objection to the shrine at Canterbury was of a different order, but any lingering scruples he might have had about disturbing the relics there could well have been dispelled on receiving, presumably on his arrival in the city, a report from Cranmer's agents to confirm the archbishop's suspicion that the 'miraculous blood' of the 'martyr-saint' was spurious.[61]

If the final decision to proceed against the cult of Becket was not taken until a late stage in the progress in Kent, there is at least some evidence to suggest that Cromwell had arranged matters beforehand so that Henry could witness for himself the suppression of the most important centre of pilgrimage in the kingdom. The visit may indeed have been considered necessary to forestall a violent popular reaction such as was provoked by the suppression of the priory at Walsingham in 1537.[62] Henry's presence in Canterbury accompanied by his armed guard of honour gave a seal of legitimacy to the act of desecration, which might otherwise have been challenged or resisted. The arrangements made at Canterbury for the entertainment of the court certainly indicate that at least the minister's plans had been laid some time in advance. The king's itinerary in Kent in the autumn of 1538 can be established from the surviving state papers, which include the 'Lisle Letters' and Cromwell's financial accounts.[63] The preparations made at Canterbury for the arrival of the king and court can be traced in the chamberlain's accounts, though the entries are less full than those for some previous royal visits.[64] Henry usually stayed

Convocation in 1531–2. Henry had not responded to Latimer's appeal on that occasion, and in his court sermon of 1549 the bishop proceeds to urge courtiers and royal chaplains to refrain from giving sycophantic advice to rulers, and adds: 'Unpreacheynge Prelates haue been the cause, that the bloud of Hales did so long blynd the kynge'. *The seconde [to seventh] sermon[s] of Master Hughe Latemer . . . preached before the Kynges maiestie* (London, 1549), leaf Dd iii r–v

61 That the 'abuses' at Canterbury were treated by the king's commissioners as comparable to those of Boxley appears from the letter of T.Wriothesley *et al.* from Brussels, 20 Nov. 1538, explaining how they had defended the king's actions to Antony Barough, the Margrave of Berghen op Zoom. *SP, Henry VIII*, vol. VIII, no. 97.

62 *LP*, vol. XIII (1), no. 194; C. E. Moreton, 'The Walsingham Conspiracy of 1537', *Historical Research*, 63 (1990), 29–43.

63 Cf. the itinerary of Henry VIII, compiled from entries in *LP*: PRO OBS1/1419, fol. 61v. For Cromwell's itinerary, see Merriman, *Letters*, vol. II, app.

64 A payment authorised by the mayor and aldermen to Master Alen, one of the king's servants, is immediately followed in the chamberlain's accounts by one of 13s. 4d. to the four serjeants of the city 'towards their cootes [coats] on bysshop beckettes nyght'. This was not a reference to the entertainment put on for the king, but rather a delayed disbursement for the last performance of the pageant mounted on 6 July 1538 (the accounts for previous years contain similar entries of payments made in arrears) CCA, FA12, fol. 374.

in a *tentorium*, 'the hall in the Blean', erected for each visit, and one of the king's guard came ahead of the court to find out if the city was free of infection. On 5 September, payments were made to Kyrke, the clerk of the market who accompanied the royal entourage to arrange purveyance, as well as rewards to the king's trumpeters and footmen.[65]

Lord Lisle, deputy of Calais, was present at Canterbury to receive the king and to solicit his favour. The letters written on 8 and 10 September by John Hussee from Dover to Lady Lisle at Calais provide us with one of the two extant contemporary accounts of what transpired in the cathedral during the king's sojourn in the city. In the first letter Hussee gives an ironic account of the spoliation of the shrine by the king's commissioners. Richard Pollard was 'too busy night and day in prayer with offering unto S. T. shrine and head, with other dead relics, that [he] could have no idle worldly time' to consider any other business. He was still engaged on the task when Hussee wrote again two days later: Lisle had stayed every night in Cromwell's lodging and had not been out of his company except when he went to the king.[66] From the Lisle correspondence it may be deduced that the 'disgarnishing' of the shrine had begun by 7 September at the latest and had continued for at least another two days, aided by the monks and officers of the priory.[67] After a significant delay, the shrine of the most important English saint was at last destroyed: the relics were desecrated and the precious donations appropriated by the Crown. The rumour circulated that twenty carts were required to convey the treasure to the Tower of London,[68] an inflated estimate of its quantity that has been uncritically repeated by modern historians. Another contemporary assessment, equally unreliable, is preserved in the chronicle of Elis Gruffydd who, after relating the diversity of opinion on the martyr-saint, records a fellow Welshman's sardonic appraisal of the king's motives:

Look, I cannot contradict anything that is done by God and the king, but it is fairly certain that he [Becket] did nothing against King Henry the Eighth, unless it is held against him for being so diligent in preserving so much treasure – gold,

---

[65] Among the next entries in the accounts are payments for swans, a dish fit for a king, and for the cleaning of the door of the Guildhall 'ayenst the kynges comyng to Canterbury'. *HMC, IXth Report, Apx*, pp. 144–5, 148–53.

[66] *LP*, vol. XIII (2), nos. 302, 317.

[67] At the end of September payments of £23 16*s* 'in sundry parcels' were doled out by Thomas Wriothesley 'by way of his Majesty's rewards' to several monks and chief officers of Christ Church and to servants and labourers. BL Arundel MS 97, fol. 34b; *LP*, vol. XIII (2), no. 1280.

[68] The estimate is based on the unreliable testimony of a Frenchman captured at Dover who had also put it about that the king intended to pull down all the parish churches as well as the abbeys. *LP*, vol. XIV (1), no. 1073.

silver, and precious stones worth 20,000 marks. And so if he was a traitor to other kings, it is certain that he is a loyal treasurer to today's king.[69]

According to John Stow, whose description of the decoration of the shrine and its treasure is probably based on more accurate documentation, the gold and precious stones filled two large chests, which were so heavy that it required six or eight strong men to carry them one at a time out of the church.[70]

Henry had hesitated before authorising the spoliation; he would soon tergiversate on other matters of doctrine but this act was irreversible. According to an entry in the Latin chronicle written by a monk of St Augustine's Abbey until its dissolution in 1540, both the desecration and the prohibition of the cult of Becket took place on one day, the feast of the Nativity of the Virgin, 8 September. This is almost certainly a simplification of the record by a scandalised observer of the sacrilege.[71] The king left Canterbury for Sittingbourne on this day, which is also the date on which Cromwell's accountant, Thomas Avery, made a payment of 40 shillings to 'Balle and his ffelowes . . . given to them by my lordes commaundment at Saynt Stephens besydes Caunterbury for playing before my lorde'.[72] Historians of drama are generally agreed that this must refer to John Bale and the company of players now sponsored by Cromwell. It is also assumed by most of these modern writers that the play was of Bale's own composition, though there is no consensus as to which one it was, or indeed on the exact place of performance.[73]

Paul Whitfield White has explored the possibility that the play was Bale's *God's Promises*, which is generally accepted to have been particularly

---

[69] NLW Mostyn MS 158, fol. 527. Writing as he did in a secret tongue, and with no intention of publicising in his own lifetime his extensive commentary on contemporary events, Elis did not go in for the self-censorship observed by the English chroniclers. I am grateful to Professor Patrick Ford, the leading authority on the text as a literary source, for valuable help in deciphering the chronicler's tortuous syntax.

[70] John Stow, *The Annales of England to 1605* (London, 1605), p. 970.

[71] Corpus Christi College, Cambridge, MS 298, fol. 28, an entry that is missing from the fragmentary Tudor transcript of the English translation printed in *Narratives of . . . the Reformation*. The entry conveys the impression that the two feasts were declared to be discontinued simultaneously with the demolition of the shrine, though the writer notes elsewhere that the Feast of the Translation was prohibited earlier in the same year: *Narratives*, p. 185.

[72] *LP*, vol. XIV (2), no. 337. In a Latin 'autobiography' of 1557, Bale acknowledged Cromwell's support for his 'comedies'. Peter Happé (ed.), *The Complete Plays of John Bale*, 2 vols. (Woodbridge, 1985), vol. I, p. 147.

[73] P. W. White, *Theatre and Reformation*; G. Walker, *Plays of Persuasion: Drama and Politics at the Court of Henry VIII* (Cambridge, 1991); S. B. House, 'Literature, Drama and Politics', in D. MacCulloch (ed.), *The Reign of Henry VIII: Politics, Policy and Piety* (London, 1995), pp. 181–201.

suited to church performance.[74] However, the reference to St Stephens in Avery's accounts need not be to the church; in May 1535 Cromwell had acquired a share in the rectory of the parish of Hackington, and it is more likely that it was there, in the dwelling-house next to the church, that Bale and his company enacted their play.[75] Hackington rectory had been the property of the archdeacon of Canterbury since 1227. As a favour to Archdeacon William Warham, his nephew and namesake, Archbishop Warham had considerably extended and refurbished the rectory, so that it would have resembled a mansion house with a hall large enough to stage an entertainment for Cromwell's household and guests.[76] Under the same date in Avery's accounts, ten shillings apiece were dispensed to the trumpeters and the 'kings lowed pypes' at St Stephens, which suggest that Henry himself was Cromwell's guest at this entertainment.[77] Those who paid the piper acted the host on such occasions: the city had also rewarded the king's trumpeters on his arrival. On the feast of the Nativity of the Virgin, Henry would have attended mass, presumably in St Stephen's Church rather than the cathedral, before the play was put on, and afterwards taken his leave of Canterbury while it was still daylight.

Bale wrote twenty-four plays, the texts of only five of which have survived, the most important being *Kynge Johan*. We know that an 'enterlude concernyng King John' was enacted before Cranmer over the Christmas season, 1538–9, not in Canterbury apparently but in his house at Ford. It seems safe to assume that this was Bale's play in the repertoire of the players on tour in Kent. Judging by the testimony of two of those present, the audience was swayed by its propaganda, though an altercation ensued when they later related its antipapal message to a third party. On the following day, John Alforde, aged eighteen, gave a report of what he had seen to a company gathered at the house of another spectator, Thomas Browne

[74] White, *Theatre and Reformation*, pp. 149–58.
[75] The grant was to Cromwell, John Palmer and John Johnson alias Antony, who were to be seised in fee of the rectory of St Stephens, the messuages and appurtenances, with 20 acres of adjacent land. This outright grant of 12 May 1535 predated the measures to dissolve the monasteries and was confirmed by Archbishop Cranmer and Prior Goldwell of Christ Church. CCA, DCC/T2 (Priory Register, 1533–40); P. Clark, *English Provincial Society from the Reformation to the Revolution: Religion, Politics and Society in Kent 1500–1640* (Hassocks, 1977), 51 and n 54.
[76] CCA U3/39/28/6, pp. 17–20, 318; Matthew Parker, *De Antiquitate Britanniae Ecclesiae* (1572), p. 380 (*sub* 1532); William Lambarde, *Perambulation of Kent* (London, 1576), pp. 251–3. J. Strype, *Life and Acts of John Whitgift*, 3 vols. (London, 1718), vol. III, p. 286. The archbishop died at the house in 1532, and his nephew was succeeded as archdeacon by Edmund Cranmer on 9 March 1534. J. Le Neve, *Fasti Ecclesiae Anglicanae, 1300–1541*, vol. IV (London, 1963), p. 15.
[77] The same company played again before Cromwell in the New Year, presumably at his house in Stepney, for which a payment of 30s. (less generous than the 40s. reward on 8 Sept.) was made on 31 Jan. 1539: *LP*, IV (2), no. 782, pp. 337, 339.

of Shorncliffe, Kent. It was clear that the parallel intended to be drawn between King John and Henry VIII had been appreciated by Alforde and Browne, both of whom were convinced that the authority of 'the bishop of Rome' had been rightfully curtailed. Henry Totehill, another guest at Browne's house, dissented from this view, and (as recounted in Browne's deposition) objected vehemently: 'That it was petie and nawghtely don, to put down the Pope and Saincte Thomas: for the pope was a good man, and Saincte Thomas savid many suche as this deponent was from hangyng.' Cranmer relayed this 'naughty communication... concerning the bishop of Rome and Thomas Becket' to Cromwell.[78] From these descriptions it has been assumed by students of English Reformation drama that the play had treated of both these subjects.

In his reconstruction of the text, Greg Walker argues convincingly against the supposition that the play on King John enacted in 1538–9 contained an onslaught on Becket.[79] One of the surviving texts of Bale's Kynge Johan does indeed include a scene in which Becket is berated, but this is most likely to have been a later recension. Walker construes Totehill's words as a denunciation of recent changes in policy rather than a direct comment on the play, which he himself had not seen. The rehabilitation of King John's historical reputation had long since been deployed in tracts written in defence of the king's great matter. A dramatisation of the contest between John and the pope would in itself have pleased Henry, but it does not follow that this was what was represented in the interlude sponsored by Cromwell in Canterbury on 8 September 1538. It would have been appropriate to the occasion for the players to have performed in the king's presence any one of the several plays written by Bale to denounce the pope and Roman pretensions to jurisdiction over the Church in England. There is, however, some evidence to suggest that the subject of the entertainment was highly topical.

Two of Bale's missing English plays were on an antipapal theme: one on the divorce of Henry and Catherine, the other an interlude called variously 'The Knaveries of Thomas Becket' and 'On the Treasons of Becket'. Since the Becket play is first noticed in a list of Bale's works compiled sometime between 1536 and 1539, it may already have been in the players' repertoire during their tour of Kent.[80] There is no definite

---

[78] Totehill was placed in the custody of Cranmer's servant Antony Marten, who testified at second hand to the reports of the words complained of, 'that it was petie that Saincte Thomas was put down, and that the olde was as good as the newe ... that the Bisshop of Rome was a good man'. Cox, Cranmer Letters, 387–8.

[79] Walker, Plays of Persuasion, pp. 172–5.

[80] In Anglorum Heliades (1536–9) this is entered as 'De Traditione Thome Becketi', and in Summarium of 1548 as 'De Thomae Becketi Imposturis'. Happé (ed.), The Plays of John Bale, vol. I, pp. 8–9.

record of specific performances, but it was evidently devised to counter the cult of Becket after the campaign against idolatry had been officially sanctioned and Cromwell had succeeded the earl of Oxford as Bale's patron. Given what is known of Bale's rewriting of the history of Henry II's reign, it would have fulfilled this purpose more effectively than the play *Kynge Johan* in its original form. Bale's views on the historical Becket and the role of the saints as intercessors for salvation can be traced in his sermons and works on English and British history, based as they were on copious research.[81] The library which was scattered when he fled in 1553 from the diocese of Ossory contained, as he lamented in a letter to Matthew Parker, 'the 554 epistles of Thomas Becket'.[82] In *The Englysh votaryes*, dedicated to Edward VI in 1551, his step-by-step deconstruction of the Becket mythos can be traced in the marginalia: 'The freshe and lustye begynnynges of Thomas Becket . . . Antichrist he preferreth to hys kynges obedyence . . . The trayterous code, and advauncement above Christ [in prayers of intercession] . . . The false miracles and canonifacyon of Becket.' And in the text: *'This Becket in all flourishing doings hearckened to the pope, defending his pompous kingdom, supporting his church's excess, and wretchedly died for the sinful liberties of the same.'*[83]

A play representing this revised version of the fate of Thomas Becket would have been the most apposite entertainment to present before the king in Canterbury.[84] The evidence is circumstantial but it may be suggested that the performance formed part of the ritual of decanonisation which passed through several distinct phases. Certain aspects of the cult were already vulnerable to the charge of idolatry: in the cathedral the saint's statue stood near the shrine and his image proliferated in stained glass. The feasts of St Thomas had been silently suppressed and his representation in effigy called in question; what remained to be discredited was the belief in the sanctity of the most precious relics, including the 'miraculous blood', a process set in train by Cranmer. Once that was accomplished, the iconoclasts proceeded to the spoliation of the shrine. Their action was then vindicated by the disparagement of Becket as a bogus saint and martyr.

---

[81] 'It is possible . . . to suggest the tendencies of the two lost plays' (on Becket and on the king's marriage): T. B. Blatt, *The Plays of John Bale: A Study of Ideas, Technique and Style* (Copenhagen, 1968), pp. 34–53.

[82] M. McKisack, *Medieval History in the Tudor Age* (Oxford, 1971), p. 21.

[83] John Bale, *The First Two Partes of the Actes or unchast examples of the Englysh votaryes*, fols. xci, xciii, xcvi–xcviiv. Bale also addressed those who compared 'their old canonized martyrs with our newly-condemned martyrs here', Anne Askew and her companions: *Select Works of John Bale*, ed. H. Christmas (Cambridge: Parker Soc., 1849), p. 190.

[84] S. B. House ('Literature, Drama and Politics', 189) assumes that the play was enacted in Cranmer's house, and this is accepted by MacCulloch, *Cranmer*, p. 227.

The injunctions of 1538 repeated the commonplace that images were little more than a visual aid to worship for the illiterate. The publicists of the break with Rome similarly recognised that the most immediate way to appeal to the unlettered masses lay through spectacle when they advocated the replacement of recreational folk drama with more sophisticated shows to convey a political and religious message. Cromwell's protégé, Richard Morison, believed that plays were even more effective than sermons, for 'into the commen people thynges sooner enter by the eies then by the eares'. Morison would have the interludes on Robin Hood supplanted by ones demonstrating the wickedness of the pope and the religious orders, and instructing the subjects in obedience to the king.[85] This was the argument that was to prevail in the reformers' opposition to traditional popular drama, though not with immediate effect. The pageant of St Thomas, performed to the accompaniment of the marching watch in the streets of Canterbury on the eve of the Translation of the Relics, was demoted to 'Bishop Becket's pageant' in 1536 but allowed to continue for another two years.[86] By 1538 Cromwell had taken heed of Morison's advice on the use of drama as propaganda to the extent of sponsoring his own troupe of players. In Canterbury in September he and Bale may have been concerned to convey a message to the king as much as to his subjects, to reassure him of the rightcousness of the action he had sanctioned. That Henry was receptive to interludes that humiliated the clergy emerges from the scene described by the imperial ambassador in 1535.

In the absence of a text we can only speculate on Bale's dramatic treatment of its subject. As has already been suggested, the device of a posthumous trial for treason may have been used to depict the protagonist of the traditional story as an anti-hero, in line with the debunking method followed in the dramatist's historical writings. His interludes are known to have shared some of the characteristics of the mystery plays. To discredit the martyr-saint, Bale would have re-staged the familiar scenes as represented in the city pageant to give them a hostile gloss consistent with the ongoing campaign against relics. The deceptions of the keepers of shrines in exploiting the credulity of the faithful with conjuring tricks had their correlatives in the theatrical devices used on the pageant wagon in the processions on St Thomas's eve. If as seems probable the play emulated the pageant by dramatising the scene of the murder in the cathedral, it would have done so to display the archbishop in the worst possible light. The greatest impact would have been conveyed by an enactment of the death scene which represented Becket's culpability, depicting the knight

[85] BL, Royal MS 18 A l; Cotton MS. Faustina C.ii, fols. 5–12. Sydney Anglo, *Spectacle, Pageantry and Early Tudor Policy* (Oxford, 1969), pp. 266–7.
[86] *HMC, IXth Report, App.*, pp. 152–3.

de Tracy as acting in self-defence when he delivered the fatal blow.[87] This retelling of the story was already in circulation; the first surviving evidence for its adoption as the authorised version to justify the degradation appears in the proclamation issued on 16 November 1538.

his dethe, whiche they vntruely called martyrdome, happened vpon a reskewe by him made, and that, as it is written, he gaue opprobrious wordes to the gentyll men, whiche then counsayled hym to leaue his stubbernesse, and to auoyde the commocion of the people, rysen up for that rescue. And he nat onely callyd the one of them bawde, but also toke Tracy by the bvsome, and violently shoke and plucked hym in suche maner, that he had almoste ouerthrowen hym to the pauement of the churche, So that vpon this fray one of their company perceiuinge the same, strake ym, and so in the thronge Becket was slayne.[88]

The climactic scene in the Becket story as described in the proclamation may well have been the denouement depicted in Bale's lost play. A dramatic re-enactment of these events in Canterbury, near the scene of the original crime, exculpating the violence of Henry II's knights as provoked by Becket's aggression and exposing his 'imposture', was doubtless intended to have a cathartic effect on its audience. The purpose of a local performance was conceivably not only to impress the king but to exorcise the 'superstition' induced by the pageant of St Thomas in its participants and spectators. One of the lessons to be taught to the credulous would have been that the 'miraculous blood' in the shrine was as much a sham as the pig's blood used by the actors in the pageant.[89] Bale's play would have called attention to the theatrical nature of the cult and, by confronting members of his audience with their own participation in the representation of Becket as a saint, sought to weaken belief in his holiness. If the murder in the cathedral was re-enacted as a psychodrama in this way to coincide with the dismantling of the shrine by the king's agents, then it may be accounted one of the most remarkable examples of the political uses of theatre in the Reformation. Along with the exposure of the more important relics as counterfeit, a spectacular parade of Becket's 'iniquities' may even have served finally to ease Henry's conscience on the troubling matter of the place of penance in pilgrimage.

In the proclamation the cult of Becket is singled out for execration more than two months after the destruction of the shrine. His images

---

[87] In a forthcoming publication Dr Margaret Aston will demonstrate the contribution of Cromwell's ally, Richard Tracy, the descendant of William de Tracy, to the rehabilitation of the family name that is reflected in this rewriting of history.

[88] Society of Antiquaries, proclamation no. 96; P. L. Hughes and J. F. Larkin, *Tudor Royal Proclamations, 1: The Early Tudors 1485–1553* (New Haven, CT and London, 1964), no. 186.

[89] J. B. Sheppard, 'The Canterbury Marching Watch with its Pageant of St Thomas', *Arch. Cant.*, 12 (1879), 27–46.

were now to be removed from churches and other places throughout the realm, his festivals were explicitly proscribed, and his name and that of the pope were to be erased from all liturgical books. The king's subjects should not be induced to commit idolatry, on pain of imprisonment at the king's pleasure. The last section of the proclamation was added after the other articles had been corrected in draft in the king's hand, and some historians have argued that it represented an effort by Cromwell and Cranmer to balance an otherwise conservative statement of religious views.[90] In the making of both the injunctions and the proclamation, it would appear, the attack on Becket was added at the last moment. While the former composition may indicate that the king had been persuaded to authorise the degradation only at a late stage in the proceedings, the peculiar diplomatic of the latter document should not be read as evidence that Henry had only reluctantly agreed to the contents.[91] He had after all been present in Canterbury when the shrine was destroyed and may well have witnessed, if not the act of desecration itself, then the drama that accompanied it. On his return from embassy in France at the end of September, the conservative bishop of Winchester, Stephen Gardiner, let it be known that he 'misliked not the doing at Canterbury, but rather semed to like it, sayeing, that if he had been at home, he would have given his counsail to the doing therof, and wisshed that the like were doon at Winchester'.[92] The proclamation contained an *ex post facto* justification of these events. On the day it was issued Henry presided over the trial of the heretic John Lambert, and when the tide of reform seemed to be turning, Cromwell in particular would have wished to underline the king's commitment to a *fait accompli*.

News of the desecration of the shrine had reached Rome by 25 October, when the pope in consistory commissioned a report on the matter by

[90] In the two surviving drafts of the proclamation, the king's own corrections can be seen in the second version, which is restricted to eight articles. The last two articles, which included the attack on Becket, were added before printing, and they have been interpreted by modern authorities as a triumph for the reformers in the council. Elton points out that the last item is the only one which specifies the advice of the council, and argues that it was the work of Cromwell, 'whose convictions and preoccupations it reflects'. Elton, *Policy and Police*, p. 257.

[91] *Pace* Greg Walker, who argues that Cromwell was using the injunctions and the proclamation to put pressure on a king who was reluctant to commit himself to further reform in the unsettled diplomatic situation: *Plays of Persuasion*, p. 207.

[92] As modern commentators have remarked, this was surely disingenuous, since by this time he would surely have heard of the desecration in the previous week of the shrine of St Swithun in his own see. T. Wriothesley to Cromwell, undated: *SP, Henry VIII*, vol. VIII, pp. 51–2; Glyn Redworth, *In Defence of the Church Catholic: The Life of Stephen Gardiner* (Oxford, 1990), p. 85. Wriothesley was informed by a correspondent on 31 March 1539 that the bishop had expressed his disapproval of the removal of the treasure of St Swithun: *LP*, vol. XIV(1), pp. 246–47.

Campeggio and three other cardinals.[93] This in turn may have been known in London within three weeks, calling for some kind of rejoinder, hence the proclamation of 16 November. The bull that excommunicated Henry VIII, reactivating the suspended instrument of 30 August 1535, was signed by the pope on 17 December, and was to be promulgated on the Kalends of January 1539.[94] It was probably at this time that Ralph Sadler, Cromwell's protégé and since 1536 a gentleman of the privy chamber, made a copy of the ten Constitutions issued by Henry II in Normandy, ordering the king's justices and bishops in England to swear to them so as to forestall the announcement of a papal interdict.[95] The king's excommunication had been long expected and the council no doubt considered steps to prevent the bull being smuggled into England. If this piece of historical research by Sadler denoted an intention by the king to emulate the action of Henry II, nothing was done in the event to revise or add to the oath of supremacy prescribed in the Act of 1534.

The proclamation had stated that offenders would be punished at the king's pleasure, but only statutes could create offences at common law. It was certainly not made a treasonable offence to defy the order, as some historians have claimed, and the penalities meted out in the event were not uniformly severe. We do not know the fate of Henry Totehill, but no proceedings were taken against Dr John Lusshe, vicar of Aylesbury, who early in 1539 was found to be in possession of sermons and papers praising Becket and the pope.[96] The abbot of Glastonbury was executed after being found in possession of a printed life of Becket in a collection that also contained a book against the king's great matter, papal pardons and bulls. Although in poor health, he was sent to the Tower, found on examination by Cromwell to have lent money to the rebels in the north in 1536, and executed.[97]

The order to remove the images of St Thomas and to delete his name, along with that of the pope, from liturgical books was but perfunctorily obeyed. The Kentish priest Henry Goderich preached against the common belief among the people that they could let the images stand as long as they 'transposed' them and set new tokens in their hands. The parishioners of Ashford had thus altered Becket's image in the church

---

[93] *LP*, vol. xiii(2), no. 684.

[94] H. Pollen, 'Henry VIII and St Thomas Becket', *The Month*, 137 (1921), 119–28.

[95] PRO, SP1/138/1–4; *LP*, vol. xiii (2), no. 685. These Constitutions were reproduced in the 'First' *Quadrilogus*, printed in Paris in 1495, and in most of the ms versions. Cf. BL Add. MS. 11506, fol. 11b (13th century); T. D. Hardy (ed.), *Descriptive Cat. of Materials Relating to the History of Great Britain and Ireland*, 3 vols. in 4 parts (London, 1862–71), vol. ii, pp. 384–5.

[96] Elton, *Policy and Police*, p. 23, n 2.   [97] Merriman, *Cromwell*, vol. i, p. 176.

into one of St Blaise.[98] A similar precaution was taken by a great man in a particularly sensitive position. Elis Gruffydd describes how the name of St Thomas inscribed on his effigy in the private chapel in Lord Lisle's residence at Calais was scratched out and 'St Nicholas' painted in its place.[99] The demotion of Thomas of Canterbury was evidently not interpreted as a disincentive to venerate other saints, as the humble and the exalted took advantage of a certain ambiguity in the injunctions and the proclamation.[100]

The widespread failure to obey the authority of the supreme head, and the circulation of rumours about his intentions, led to the issue of special letters to the justices of the peace in December 1538. Henry was particularly concerned to quash the false report that parish registers, which had been introduced in the proclamation, were devices for imposing new exactions on every subject at birth, marriage and death. It had been put about 'that therein we go about to take away the liberties of our realme, for conservacion wherof they fayne that Busshopp Beckett of Canterbury which they have tofore callyd seynt Thomas dyed for'. On the contrary, it was declared, he had resisted Henry II to prevent the clergy being called before the courts of the realm, though it was afterwards alleged to have been to advance such liberties of the church as he contended for in his lifetime with the archbishop of York to establish the precedence of Canterbury in officiating at the coronation of kings of England.[101] Even the king's letters failed to deter Thomas Tyrrell, the parson of Gislingham, Suffolk, from saying the 'service of Thomas Becott' on 29 December to an empty church. In a sermon on the following Sunday, Tyrrell urged his flock to go on pilgrimage; when later asked where they should go now that the shrines at Walsingham and Canterbury were put down, he told them to journey to Jerusalem.[102]

The revised account of the assassination of Becket given in the proclamation and the royal letters was further elaborated in the draft 'declaration of the faith' of 1539. This survives as an unfinished composition of four disparate pieces in the hand of Thomas Derby, clerk of the privy council. Its last section presents a justification of the dissolution

---

[98] *LP*, vol. XIV (1), no. 1053; PRO SP1/152/ 1–2; E. Duffy, *The Stripping of the Altars: Traditional Religion in England 1400–1580* (New Haven, CT and London, 1992), pp. 418–19.

[99] NLW MS. 158, fol. 527v.   [100] Aston, *England's Iconoclasts*, p. 228.

[101] This section was revised in a late draft of the letter to clarify the point that Becket had insisted on the prerogative of Canterbury. PRO SP1/ 140/ 211–7; *LP*, vol. XII (2), no. 1171 (two of the four drafts of this letter noticed in *LP* are no longer to be found in the PRO); two further versions are in the BL, Cotton Cleo.Evi, 222, 224; *LP*, vol. XII (2), no. 1171.

[102] PRO SP1/142, 62–5; *LP*, vol. XIV (1), no. 76.

and the reform of 'superstitious' practices such as supernumerary holy days, indulgences, and shrines. Images in churches ('bokes of the unlerned people') are not necessary and yet the king is pleased to tolerate them except when they lead to idolatry and pilgrims are tricked to worship counterfeit representations of the saints. In the case of the shrine at Canterbury, judgement had been pronounced not on a spurious image but on a bogus saint, for the archbishop of Canterbury 'whiche they called St Thomas, by good approbacions it appeareth clerely that his common legend is fals'. He had been reconciled to Henry II long before his death and had no quarrel directly with him but only with the archbishop of York 'which was for prowd prehemynence bitwen them, and by the strif thereof procured frowardly his own deth, which they untruely called martyrdome'. The scene of the murder in the cathedral is described as in the proclamation but the discourse goes further to represent the degraded Becket as a violent man, 'a grete warryer, brener of towns, [en]croacher of benefices, a hunter and a hawker, prowed and sedicious'.[103] Other charges were added or elaborated in emendations to the original draft of the 'declaration': Becket was also corrupt, having obtained the office of the king's chancellor as well as the archbishopric 'by money and . . . unlawful means'. As for the motive for the jurisdictional dispute with York, Becket had himself confessed this openly to Pope Alexander III. This much is found in the writings and chronicles of good record made by his chaplains and brethren, the bishops of England, 'and sundry of them above xl yeres prented in Parys and never reproved,' a reference to the black letter printing of the 'First' *Quadrilogus* in 1495.[104] These then were the 'good approbacions', the result of historical research conducted by Sadler and others which served to undermine the legend, and not of any forensic trial of the saint's claim to sainthood and martyrdom that was rumoured at the time.[105] When the tomb was opened the bones had been found to include the greater part of the skull, so that the contents of the head-reliquary were but 'a feigned fiction', and while there is a hint

---

[103] At the end the discourse turns to justifying the execution for treason of anointed priests and monks, and 'Thomas More, the gester, ffysher of Rochester, the [vain]glorious hypocrite, both the champions of superstycion and abuse'. PRO SP1/143/198–205v., esp. 204–5. J. Collier, *An Ecclesiastical History of Great Britain*, 2 vols. (London, 1708–14), vol. I, p. 39.

[104] Hardy, *Materials*, vol. IV (1879), pp. xix–xxi.

[105] The Greek Nicander Nucius Greek, who travelled in England *c*. 1545–6, reported the rumour that Henry VIII had appointed judges and commissioners to investigate Becket's status as a martyr-saint: they 'devoted two years to the inquiry . . . and they passed a note of censure against him as a rebel and revolutionist'. Nicander is also a source for the claim that Becket's relics were burned and the ashes fired from a cannon. J. A. Cramer (ed.), *The Second Book of the Travels of Nicander Nucius, of Corcyra* (Greek text and translation), Camden Soc., vol. XVII (1841), pp. 72–5.

that this might have been burned,[106] it is declared that the bones had been hidden so as not to give rise to further superstition. Neither this somewhat jejune corrective to contradictory rumours nor the embellishing of the demythologised version of the saintly tradition was publicised in the event, for no part of the 'declaration of the faith' was printed as an official circular or tract. The privy council may have concluded that to defend the king of England against specific charges of sacrilege, schism and tyranny was to give a hostage to fortune. If the claim advanced in the document that pilgrimages had not been completely banned was intended to placate an international audience, it surely struck an unconvincing note, while the denial of the rumour that the king had designs on all the monasteries was soon belied by events.

The revision of the saint's life advanced in all these documents as the authorised version was essentially the view refracted through the prism of the Lollard traditions and the writings of William Tyndale – and also, it would seem, those of John Bale.

When at the end of the decade the king called a halt to doctrinal reform, there was to be no change of mind or direction where images, saints and pilgrimages were concerned. The religious reaction that set in after Cromwell's downfall in 1540 did not involve a retreat from the iconoclasm or the ideological cleansing of the records that he and Cranmer had inaugurated. The removal from service books of all allusions to the pope and St Thomas was discussed with approval in parliament in 1540, although no formal measure was passed. During his progress in Yorkshire in the following year, Henry had cause to inform his archbishop that abused images and relics still remained in various places 'to allure our subjects to their former hypocrisy and superstition'. He ordered that all traces of such memorials and occasion of pilgrimage be eradicated.[107] When in 1542-3 Convocation was divided on proposals to advance religious reform, the bishops resolved, at Cranmer's initiative, that the clergy should take greater care in supervising the excisions from liturgical books.[108] While parishioners either obediently accepted the changes or conformed reluctantly and waited for a better day, John Bale suffered from the loss of

---

[106] 'If this hede was brent, was therefore St Thomas brent? Assuredly, it concludeth not.' Wriothesley notes in his Chronicle (p. 86) that the bones had been burned 'in the same church by my Lord Crumwell'.

[107] Cited in Aston, *England's Iconoclasts*, p. 238.

[108] The names of saints not authenticated in the Bible or by the venerable doctors of the Church were also to be erased. Lehmberg, *Parliaments*, pp. 39, 92, 293 n. 147. P. B. Roberts, 'Thomas Becket: The Construction and Deconstruction of a Saint, from the Middle Ages to the Reformation', B. M. Kienzle *et al.*, *Models of Holiness in Medieval Sermons* (Louvain-la-Meuve, 1996), pp. 16–17.

Cromwell's protection and went into exile in Germany in 1540. He had always been highly deferential to King Henry but his religious views had become too extreme to be tolerated. His printed books were included in a list of heretical works banned by proclamation in the last year of the reign.[109] In 1542 the lower house of Convocation registered a protest against interludes and comedies staged in London 'in contempt of God's word'.[110] Bale's plays may well have been included in this condemnation, but even if they were proscribed the impact on their audience of earlier performances could not be undone.

The last religious play to be enacted at Canterbury at the city's expense was in 1542–3, when payment was made to Bryce, a shoemaker, for four pairs of shoes 'for tormentors in the play'. This has been read by one modern commentator as evidence that a play of St Thomas had replaced the pageant, but the allusion is more likely to be to a Corpus Christi interlude, now sponsored by the city rather than the guild. In the same year 'the hole stage of the play' was sold for 11 shillings to Thomas Bathurst, one of the city's benefactors.[111] In the ideological cleansing in Canterbury, Cranmer had led the way by removing the scene of the martyrdom engraved in the archbishop's seal and replacing it with the image of Christ on the cross. The seal of Christ Church was similarly redesigned before the Priory was dissolved in 1539, and rather belatedly in 1541–2 the burghers of Canterbury paid for the removal of the depiction of the martyrdom from the city's common seal.[112] In London also, traces of tributes to Becket were effaced from the City arms and seal. The hospitals of St Thomas in both cities were dissolved and rededicated. The property of the foundation in London was acquired by the mayor and corporation, and in the next reign a royal charter was obtained by the City to enable the hospice to maintain its corporate identity and charitable status, its dedication now transposed to Thomas the Apostle. Many of the memorials of St Thomas of Canterbury in ornaments and liturgical books within churches and libraries up and down the country were defaced or removed by the more extreme Protestants of Edward VI's reign, while others escaped their attention. The likeness of the saint illuminated in stained glass in Canterbury Cathedral survived (possibly covered with whitewash) for another century, until

---

[109] His English printed books were included in the list of heretical works banned by proclamation in the last year of the reign. *Tudor Royal Proclamations*, vol. I, no. 272.

[110] Lehmberg, *Parliaments*, p. 165.

[111] CCA, FAC13, fol. 62v; G. E. Dawson (ed.), *Records of Plays and Players in Kent, 1450–1642*, Malone Collections, vol. VII (Oxford, 1965), pp. 188, 198. The Guild of Corpus Christi was finally abolished in the act against chantries in 1547.

[112] *HMC, IXth Report, App.*, p. 153.

most of the windows were put out by the more thorough-going puritan iconoclasts.[113]

The suppression of the cult associated with churches dedicated to St Thomas in other parts of the realm continued unabated after Cromwell's fall.[114] The most blatant disobedience of the prohibition of 1538 was reported in the first year of Edward's reign, when a Welsh gentleman was delated by the king's agents for erecting, on the altar in the parish church of New Radnor, an alabaster table of imagery depicting five scenes of Becket's life and death.[115] Nor was the ban on the traditional secular observances on the more popular of Becket's feast days always obeyed, even under Edward. One such defiance of the supreme head's authority resulted in an ironic conjunction of religious drama and political protest in 1549. There were disturbances in Kent, East Anglia, and the west country, but only the rebels in Devon and Cornwall expressed discontent at the passing of the old religious order. Kett's followers in Norfolk were not hostile to the Protestant regime of Protector Somerset; their grievances were economic ones and yet the rising broke out because the pageant, if not the feast, of St Thomas was still being observed at Wymondham, where there was a chapel in the high street dedicated to the saint. There had been stirrings beforehand but the country people were given an opportunity to discuss their grievances when they assembled in large numbers on 6 July, St Thomas's eve, 'att a certen night and daie playe', and the celebrations lasted for another two days.[116]

Thomas of Canterbury was duly restored to the calendar of saints with the restitution of the Roman obedience after Mary's accession.[117] Entries in the accounts for Canterbury Cathedral show how thorough was the campaign to reinstate the traditional saints' days, the Sarum service and sacred music of Roman Catholic worship. The rewards given by the Dean and Chapter to George Frevell in 1555 for 'writing of St Thomas

---

[113] John Watney, *Some Account of the Hospital of St Thomas of Acon* (London, 1892), p. 118; William Somner, *The Antiquities of Canterbury* (London, 1640), pp. 247–50; Richard Culmer, *Cathedrall Newes from Canterbury* (London, 1644), pp. 21–22.

[114] R. Whiting, *The Blind Devotion of the People: Popular Religion and the English Reformation* (Cambridge, 1989), pp. 116–17.

[115] K. Williams-Jones, 'Thomas Becket and Wales', *Welsh History Review*, 5 (1971), 364–5.

[116] 6 July was a Saturday, and the celebrations took the form of interludes and processions over three days: F. W. Russell, *Kett's Rebellion in Norfolk* (London, 1859), p. 25. The priory at Wymondham had been re-dedicated to St Mary and St Thomas after the martyrdom, and the chapel founded in honour of Becket in 1172. S. K. Land, *Kett's Rebellion: The Norfolk Rising of 1549* (Ipswich, 1977), p. 20.

[117] The old order of holy days, processions and ceremonies was restored by the proclamation announcing the injunctions for religion that had been authorised in the first parliament of the reign. *Tudor Royal Proclamations, II: The Later Tudors* (1969), p. 407.

Legends', and to John Marden in the following year 'for prickynge of St Thomas storrye', testify to the care with which the cult was revived in liturgy and music. The old pageant of St Thomas made its reappearance on 6 July 1554, when two 'chariots', equipped with a new 'scaffold' or stage, accompanied the marching watch through the city streets.[118]

The pageant was finally suppressed early in the reign of Elizabeth. In 1559 the mayor was discharged of the fine for not keeping the watch, though the new pageant wagon was not sold until 1564.[119] John Bale returned to Canterbury in 1560 as a prebendary of the cathedral, and in the following June he complained that the city authorities were tardy in dismantling the trappings of Catholic ritual and the pagan May-day rites. It was in these circumstances, in the face of the recidivism of the city fathers, that Bale finally revised the text of *Kynge Johan*. The lines relating to Becket are believed to have been added to the surviving B text after 1560,[120] and may perhaps have been taken by the dramatist from his other play. The character, 'Imperial Majesty', who figures in the later text of *Kynge Johan*, representing the spirit of rulership later to be embodied in Henry VIII, may conceivably have made an appearance in the lost part of the first version; the most significant new matter is the allusion to Queen Elizabeth, who is praised as a light to other princes. There is no record of any performance of the play before or after Bale's death in 1563. Thereafter the most influential counterblasts to the reputation of Becket appeared in the work of the Elizabethan Protestant antiquary, William Lambarde, *A Perambulation of Kent* (1576), and in the *Acts and Monuments* of John Foxe, Bale's successor as the chief polemicist of the English Reformation. Foxe points to the commendable service of the three agents of reformist propaganda: 'players, printers, preachers . . . be set up of God, as a triple bulwark against the triple crown of the pope, to bring him down'[121] – and (he could have added) against the cult of Becket. In successive editions of 'The Book of Martyrs', Foxe elaborates on the attacks of Tyndale and Bale by supplying evidence purporting to discredit Becket's sanctity. In the 1570 edition, he was concerned to answer

---

[118] CCA Lib. Mss MA 39, 40; J. B. Sheppard, *Arch. Cant.*, 11: 8–9.

[119] In 1563–4: 'Receyved of Mr Arden for a peyer of wheles and the bedd of an old pageant . . . iis. viid.' CCA AC2, fol. 124v; FA16, fol. 283v.

[120] These lines 'need not necessarily have occurred in the A text'; the paper on which the B text is written bears '1558' in its water mark: G. Walker, *Plays of Persuasion*, pp. 171 n 6, 175. For the view that the lines may have been present in the missing leaves of the A text, see B. B. Adams (ed.), *John Bale's King Johan* (San Marino, 1969), pp. 6–7, 144–7, 149.

[121] Cited in J. N. King, *English Reformation Literature: The Tudor Origins of the Protestant Tradition* (Princeton, 1982), p. 277.

Nicholas Harpsfield's criticism of the Protestant calendar of saints.[122] The printing, in the 1583 edition, of Henry VIII's proclamation of 1538 may have been intended as a reminder to Elizabeth, who had tried to rein in the iconoclasm of Protestant zealots, of the continuing need to purge the Church of 'idols'. By contrast, in his *Survey of London* the crypto-Catholic John Stow was altogether more ambivalent on the subject of Becket's contemporary and posthumous reputation.

There is a singular instance on record of the defiance of the Reformation ban on pilgrimages to Canterbury. Around 1580 the recusant Thomas Cowell of Northamptonshire, whose family came from Faversham, 'upon a vowe he had made went a-pilgrimage to Canterbury to visitt the holy places their', in what was perhaps the first post-dissolution quest for Becket's bones. He was moved to do so, it was said, by a troubled conscience for having purchased ex-monastic property. The family had continued to be true to the old faith, and Cowell had been arrested on suspicion of being a seminary priest. But he had not been in touch with the missionary 'underground' and it may well have been the lack of priestly counsel that precipitated his spiritual crisis.[123]

In Elizabeth's reign the cult of Becket was revived in both iconography and drama among the Catholic exiles on the Continent. The church dedicated to Becket at Padua and the English College at Rome contained paintings of the saint, the feasts of St Thomas were kept in the English seminaries, and the Society of Jesus commemorated his martyrdom in liturgy and drama. His memory was especially revered at St-Omer, where on his flight in 1164 Becket had taken refuge at the Abbey of St Bertin. St Thomas had become the patron saint of the Abbey, which was in confraternity with Christ Church Priory. An inventory drawn up in 1456 of the saints' relics kept at the abbey church included an ostrich eggshell containing part of a fabric stained with the brain and blood of the Blessed Thomas.[124] During the 'Counter-Reformation' the revivified cult served to fortify the resolve of the English priests, strangers and pilgrims in exile who as agents for the reconversion of England passed the time of their pilgrimage in fear. At the English school for the sons of English Catholics founded by the Jesuits at St-Omer in 1593, a Latin interlude on the

[122] John Foxe, *Actes and Monuments* . . . (London, 1570), pp. 691–5. Cf. D. Nussbaum, 'Reviling the Saints or Reforming the Calendar? John Foxe and his "Kalendar" of Martyrs', in S. Wabuda and C. Litzenberger (eds.), *Belief and Practice in Reformation England: A Tribute to Patrick Collinson* (Aldershot, 1998), pp. 113–36.
[123] *HMC, Rutland MSS*, vol. I, pp. 307–14, esp. 311; P. Clark, *English Provincial Society*, p. 179.
[124] *The Gentleman's Magazine*, n.s., 18 (Nov. 1842), 492–6 (a communication by J. G. Nichols).

theme of the martyrdom of Becket was performed by the pupils. The manuscript text of this religious drama, *Breuis Dialogismus*, dated 1599, survives in the Salisbury collection at Hatfield House: it is doubtless a copy procured by informers in the service of Sir Robert Cecil, the queen's Secretary.[125]

As the modern editor of the text has written, this 'allegorical playlet... is an intriguing witness to the martyrological fervour of the English Counter-Reformation'.[126] The dialogue is devotional rather than didactic; it would have been performed by the grammarians as part of the liturgical round rather than an academic exercise in a school that came to be distinguished for its teaching of Greek and Latin. It also had a distinctive moral purpose. The pupils and the audience were exhorted to emulate the sacrifice of Thomas the Martyr, and the audience would have included, among the guests of the school, the seminary priests on their way to the English mission.[127] Contemporary martyrs like Henry Walpole, who was executed in 1595 and had been among the founders of the school, were associated in the interlude with the martyrdom of 1170. In promoting Becket as an example to be followed in the schooling of recruits of the 'Enterprise of England', the Jesuits defied Henry VIII's iconoclasm but surely also the injunction that prohibited the missionary priests from courting martyrdom. The manuals of casuistry studied in the seminaries expounded the traditional teaching of the Church that martyrs were called by God, and Christians must not elect themselves to martyrdom.[128] St Thomas remained the inspiring patron saint of Saint-Omer until, shortly after its transfer to Stoneyhurst in 1794, he was superseded by St Aloysius.[129] By the early seventeenth century, in spite of the continued protection of the Most Catholic Kings, the students at the English colleges in Spain and in the Spanish Netherlands were reduced to taking out licences to collect funds for these foundations. One Welsh traveller reported that on every ship that sailed from Spanish ports to the West Indies a box for offerings was tied to the mast; adorned with a picture of Becket, it bore the superscription 'Sancte Thomas Cantuarensis, ora pro nobis'.[130]

---

[125] Cecil Papers, Hatfield, 139/116. V. Houliston, '*Breuis Dialogismus*', *English Literary Renaissance*, 23 (1993), 382–405.

[126] Houliston, '*Breuis Dialogismus*', 384.

[127] '[T]he reference in both the Prologue and the Epilogue to the performers as the English company (*Anglia cohors*) implies that it is addressed to a wider audience than the college itself'. *Ibid.*, 385.

[128] P. J. Holmes, *Elizabethan Casuistry*, Catholic Record Society, Records ser., no. 67 (1981), pp. 72–4.

[129] The school moved to Bruges in 1762, to Liège in 1773; St Aloysius may have replaced St Thomas as its patron between 1802 and 1818. Hubert Chadwick, SJ, *St Omers to Stonyhurst* (London, 1961), pp. 48, 374–5, 281, 384 *et seq.*

[130] Lewis Owen, *The Running Register* (London, 1626), cited in A. J. Loomie, SJ, *The Spanish Elizabethans: The English Exiles at the Court of Philip II* (New York, 1963), p. 202.

In his *Tres Thomae*, printed at Douai in 1588, Thomas Stapleton dwelt at length on the similarities between the three Thomases, More, the Apostle, and Becket. The Elizabethan author of a life of Thomas More that circulated in manuscript drew on the works of both Stapleton and Nicholas Harpsfield to compare More with Thomas of Canterbury and Thomas of Dover. He concludes that in him there was a deeper cause of martyrdom: 'St Thomas of Canterbury died because he would not consent to any abridgement of the Pope's authority; More died for the Pope's supremacy itself'.[131] Stapleton was the usual source for the Jesuit plays performed in the English seminaries on the continent. Thomas More was also the subject of dramatic performances at St-Omer in the early seventeenth century that, in Dr Houliston's judgement, were 'designed to associate Catholic loyalty and spirituality with English patriotism'.[132] Many of the pupils at St-Omer graduated to the English College at Rome, where *Thomas Morus, Captiva religio*, and *St Thomas Cantuarensis* are listed among the plays performed in 1612–13. In one of these communities at that time a silver medal was struck depicting the likeness of More 'martiris Angli' on the obverse, and on the reverse the figure of Becket, mitred and holding a cross and a book. Nothing is known of the medal's provenance, and it survives as a singular token of the merging cult of the two martyrs among the exiles.[133]

In this history most roads still lead to Canterbury. Even before the city had lost the bones of Becket, it had gained the skull of Thomas More – that is, if we are to believe the tradition which alleges that his severed head was recovered from Tower Bridge by his daughter Margaret Roper and buried in St Dunstan's Church. Since More's canonisation this relic has attained a certain cachet, though it can hardly be said to have become an object of pilgrimage.[134] The fate that befell the bones of St Thomas Becket in 1538, on the other hand, continues to fascinate the faithful and the curious.[135]

---

[131] Thomas Stapleton, *The Life and Illustrious Martyrdom of Sir Thomas More* [1588], ed. and trans. P. E. Hallett (London, 1928); E. V. Hitchcock and P. E. Hallett (eds.), *The Lyfe of Syr Thomas More, Sometime Lord Chancellor of England by Ro:Ba:* (London, 1950), pp. 266–71. The tract is attributed to Robert Bassett in app. 1. In the dedication to 'R. R.' the author explains that the work is largely a conflation of Stapleton and Harpsfield: Houghton Library, Harvard University, Eng. MS 765.

[132] Houliston, '*Breuis Dialogismus*', p. 384.

[133] '*The King's Good Servant': Sir Thomas More, 1477/8–1535*, catalogue of an exhibition at the National Portrait Gallery, London, compiled by J. B.Trapp and Hubertus Shulte Herbruggen (London, 1978), item 282, p. 138.

[134] Abbé Germain Marc'hadour in H. O. Albin (ed.), *Thomas More and Canterbury* (Bath, 1994), pp. 34–71.

[135] J. Butler, *The Quest for Becket's Bones: the Mystery of the Relics of St Thomas Becket of Canterbury* (New Haven, CT and London, 1995).

9 'To be a pilgrim': constructing the Protestant life in early modern England

N. H. Keeble

In 1510 a husband and wife, William and Alice Cowper, were summoned before Richard Fitzjames, bishop of London, to answer the charge that:

they had spoken against pilgrimages, and worshipping of images; but chiefly the woman who, having her child, on a time, hurt by falling into a pit or ditch, and being earnestly persuaded by some of her ignorant neighbours to go on a pilgrimage to St. Laurence for help of her child, said, That neither St. Laurence, nor any other saint could help her child, and therefore none ought to go on pilgrimage to any image made with man's hand, but only to Almighty God; for pilgrimages were nothing worth, saving to make priests rich.[1]

The resolute firmness of this testimony against pilgrimages is striking: not even the injury to her child can tempt Alice Cowper to accept the advice of her 'ignorant neighbours'. To readers of John Foxe's *Book of Martyrs*, however, this encounter between episcopal authority and unlettered commitment is also strikingly familiar. It takes its place in a long series of confrontations stretching back to the early Church, from which Foxe constructs a tradition of opposition between true believers and the forces of Antichrist. Repeatedly the latter are identified with the ecclesiastical powers of Rome, the former with 'poor and simple men and women'.[2] This opposition culminates in Foxe's record of the English experience of persecution under Mary, but that climax is foreshadowed by his account of Wycliffe and the Lollards. The case of William and Alice Cowper comes towards the end of a succession of fifteenth- and early sixteenth-century cases of persons brought before ecclesiastical tribunals for the Lollard emphases of their beliefs. 'Four principal points', says Foxe, 'they stood in against the Church of Rome: in pilgrimage, in adoration of saints, in reading Scripture-books in English, and in the carnal presence of Christ's body in the sacrament'.[3]

Hostility to pilgrimages comes first in this list, and it recurs time and again in Foxe's reports of examinations and trials and in his renderings

---

[1] John Foxe, *Acts and Monuments*, ed. Josiah Pratt, 8 vols. (London, 1877), vol. IV, p. 177.
[2] *Ibid.*, p. 179.   [3] *Ibid.*, p. 218.

of the professions of faith of the accused. These professions commonly adduce three arguments against the practice. First, pilgrimages are acts of idolatry, an infringement of the Second Commandment, bestowing upon objects and places the veneration that is due to God alone. In 1510 another suspected heretic, Joan Baker, admitted to Fitzjames that she regretted her pilgrimages 'to St. Saviour and other idols' since faith should be in 'God who is in heaven who only worketh all the miracles that be done, and not the dead images, which be but stocks and stones'. Secondly, pilgrimages divert funds from more practical charitable uses. James Brewster, a carpenter of Colchester burned at Smithfield in 1511, believed 'it was better bestowed money which was given to the poor, than that which was offered in pilgrimage'. And thirdly, as an expedient of the Roman Church to sustain (and increase) its material wealth, often through deceit and fraudulent contrivances, pilgrimages are but another example of its worldliness and covetousness. Such revelations in the 1530s as that the Holy Blood of Hales in Gloucestershire was in fact that of a duck, or that within the Rood of Grace at Boxley Abbey in Kent, 'a man should stand enclosed, with a hundred wires within the rood, to make the image goggle with the eyes, to nod with his head, to hang the lip, to move and shake the jaws, according as the value was of the gift which was offered', are adduced by Foxe as outrageous evidence of the cupidity of the Church of Rome and of its mendacious willingness to deceive 'simple people' for its own profit. In sum, as William Sweeting, Brewster's friend and fellow martyr, was reported to have said with patriarchal firmness to his wife when she purposed to go on a pilgrimage, 'it was to no purpose nor profit...it were better for her to keep at home, and to attend her business'.[4]

'And all this', Foxe pointedly observes of the Lollards' testimony, 'was before the name of Luther was heard of in these countries [i.e. counties] among the people'. A denial of the religious integrity or validity of pilgrimages is firmly established by the *Book of Martyrs* as a definitive mark of authentic Christian witness long before its narrative reaches the Reformation. Foxe thus prepares his readers to recognise in Protestantism's repudiation of pilgrimages one of its claims to religious legitimacy by setting that opposition within an historical tradition. Of those examined in 1507 at Amersham, Buckinghamshire by William Smith, bishop of Lincoln, Foxe reports that 'they were noted and termed among themselves by the name of 'known men', or 'just-fast-men': *as now they are called by the name of Protestants*'.[5] And as, for Foxe, hostility to pilgrimages is one of

---

[4] *Seriatim*: Foxe, vol. IV, pp. 175, 216; vol. V, pp. 179, 397; vol. VI, p. 215.
[5] *Ibid.*, vol. IV, pp. 217, 218 (my italics; cf. vol. IV, pp. 214, 241, 246).

the defining characteristics of reformed Christianity, so he underscores it as a feature of the newly established independent Church of England. He reports in full that in the Injunctions of 1536, issued without reference to Convocation in Henry VIII's first act as Supreme Head of the Church of England, the clergy were forbidden to 'set forth or extol any images, relics, or miracles, for any superstition or lucre, nor allure the people by any enactments to the pilgrimages of any saints', a prohibition reinforced by the Injunctions of 1538 (which further discouraged the practice by declaring Becket a rebel and no saint). The clergy of the Tudor Church were to

exhort as well their parishioners, as other pilgrims, that they do rather apply themselves to the keeping of God's commandments, and the fulfilling of his works of charity; persuading them that they shall please God more by the true exercise of their bodily labour, travail, or occupation, and providing for their families, than if they went about to the said pilgrimages; and it shall profit more their soul's health, if they do bestow that on the poor and needy, which they would have bestowed upon the said images or relics.[6]

This prohibition survived the conservative tendencies of Henry's later years. The reactionary Six Articles Act of 1539, which affirmed transubstantiation, communion in one kind, clerical celibacy, vows of chastity, private masses and auricular confession, said nothing to legitimise pilgrimages. In this regard, at least, there was to be no going back.[7] By then, the legislation of the Reformation Parliament, the dissolution of the monasteries and the activities of Cromwell had deprived the practice of pilgrimage of its administrative support. It dropped from the debates between reformers and Romanists who, in the changed political and theological situation of Henry's later years, confront each other over transubstantiation, the royal supremacy and the doctrine of justification by faith, not over the propriety of pilgrimages. And, in case there should be any lingering affection for the practice, parishioners of the Edwardian and Elizabethan Church of England heard the Homily 'Against the Peril of Idolatry' speak, with some asperity, of 'the madness of men' who

even in our time, in so great light of the Gospel . . . running on heaps by sea and land, to the great loss of their time, expense and waste of their goods, destitution of their wives, children, and families, and danger of their own bodies and lives, to Compostle, Rome, Jerusalem, and other far countries, to visit dumb and dead

---

[6] *Ibid.*, vol. v, pp. 166, 259. There are excerpts from the Injunctions (including the relevant passages) in H. Bettenson (ed.), *Documents of the Christian Church*, 2nd edn (London, 1967), pp. 230–3, and they are summarised in J. R. Tanner (ed.), *Tudor Constitutional Documents A.D. 1485–1603*, 2nd edn (Cambridge, 1930), pp. 93–4.

[7] Foxe, vol. v, pp. 262–3, 463. For the Six Articles, see Bettenson (ed.), *Documents*, pp. 233–4, and Tanner (ed.), *Tudor Documents*, pp. 95–8.

stocks and stones, doth sufficiently prove the proneness of man's corrupt nature to the seeking of idols once set up and the worshipping of them.[8]

There was, then, no doubt that pilgrimages and Protestantism did not mix; and yet, the most influential and enduring imaginative product of early English Protestantism is entitled *The Pilgrim's Progress*. Bunyan clearly anticipated that his fictional creativity might trouble his Protestant (and predominantly nonconformist) readers: he prefaced to Part I of his allegory apologetic verses explaining and justifying his figurative method. There is, however, no defence offered of his controlling metaphor of the pilgrimage; this is assumed to be uncontentious within his religious community. Indeed, the choice is presented as all but inevitable, coming apparently unbidden into the mind of this radical Protestant,[9] shaped by Independent and sectarian Puritanism, devotee though he was of Foxe's *Book of Martyrs*, which he had by him in Bedford gaol while writing *The Pilgrim's Progress*.[10] If, alerted by this case, we begin to look around, it is to find that, far from keeping home to attend their business, early English Protestants were forever on the road. They are an outdoor people, walking, journeying, wayfaring, sometimes running, clambering, often lost, but then seeking out signs and directions in order to return to the way, determined always to press onward. The emphasis is there from the earliest days, in the sermons of Latimer, for example, who, convinced that the foolishness of preaching (1 Cor. i.21) is the divinely ordained means of salvation, contrasts reformed and unreformed bishops in terms of action and inaction, the static and the dynamic, industry and idleness: 'Paul was no sitting bishop, but a walking and a preaching bishop'.[11] Thereafter, the spiritual and moral demands of the Christian life are repeatedly represented through the trials and obstacles of the road. The preface to the *Book of Homilies* itself adopts 'this our most dangerous pilgrimage' as its locution for human life.[12] For the John Milton who could not praise 'a

---

[8] *Certain Sermons or Homilies appointed to be read in churches in the time of Queen Elizabeth* (London, 1908), p. 262. The *Homilies* first appeared in 1547, and, after successive reprintings, were published in a revised text in 1559.

[9] John Bunyan, *The Pilgrim's Progress*, ed. J. B. Wharey, rev. R. Sharrock, 2nd edn (Oxford, 1960), p. I, lines 7–18 (hereafter cited as *PP*).

[10] John Brown, *John Bunyan (1628–1688): His Life, Times and Work*, tercentenary edn, ed. Frank M. Harrison (London, Glasgow and Birmingham, 1928), pp. 153–4; Christopher Hill, *A Turbulent, Factious and Seditious People: John Bunyan and His Church* (Oxford, 1988), p. 109. For a list of representative references to Foxe in Bunyan's work, see R. Sharrock (gen. ed.), *The Miscellaneous Works of John Bunyan*, 13 vols. (Oxford, 1976–94), vol. XII, p. xxxviii n 81 (hereafter cited as *MW*).

[11] G. E. Corrie (ed.), *Sermons by Hugh Latimer*, The Parker Society (Cambridge, 1844), p. 68.

[12] *Homilies*, p. vii.

fugitive and cloister'd vertue, unexercis'd & unbreath'd, that slinks ... out of the race, where that immortall garland is to be run for, not without dust and heat', the 'true Christian' is the 'wayfaring Christian'.[13]

And so the titles of Protestant sermons and works of practical divinity repeatedly configure the Christian life as a perambulation, a progress, a journey, even, in Edward Taylor's image of the saints 'Encoacht for Heaven', a stage-coach journey.[14] There are *pathways* to *praier* (Thomas Becon, 1542), to *perfect rest* (Edward Woolay, 1571), to *Canaan* (William Attersoll, 1609), to *please God* (Thomas Wallis, 1617), to *peace* (Thomas Gardener, 1643), and, of course, in that bestseller of the seventeenth century, a *Plaine Mans Path-way to Heauen* (Arthur Dent, 1601). *Counsel* is offered *to the Christian-Traveller* (William Shewen, 1683). Saints are given *Directions for a Comfortable Walking with God* (Robert Bolton, 1625) and *A Help to Holy Walking, or A Guide to Glory* (Edward Bury, 1675), while *Solemn Advice to Young Men* warns them *not to walk in the wayes of their heart* (Increase Mather, 1695). Believers are directed in *The Christians Daily Walke* (Henry Scudder, 1627) and described as *Children of Light Walking in Darkness* (Thomas Goodwin, 1636). *Christian Directions, Shewing how to Walk with God* gives *guidance in the way to heaven* (Thomas Gouge, 1661) while an account of *A Christians Walk and Work on Earth until he attain heaven* gives the believer *plain direction in his pilgrimage thither* (Christopher Ness, 1678).

Whence came all this talk of walking and of pilgrimages? Curiously, it was encouraged by that very antipathy to pilgrimages that was so marked a feature of early Protestantism. This hostility did not expel *pilgrimage* from the religious lexicon; rather, it appropriated it to new purpose. Once again, Lollardy provided the cue. As part of his press campaign to discredit the old order, that committed but intemperate reformer John Bale published in 1544 *A Brefe Chronycle* of the trial in 1413 of the Lollard Sir John Oldcastle. The articles put to Oldcastle for subscription by Thomas Arundell, archbishop of Canterbury, and his 'unlearned clergy' (dismissed by Bale as a 'foolish and blasphemous writing') included the affirmation that 'it is meritorious to a christian man to go on pilgrimage to holy places; and there specially to worship holy relics and images of saints, apostles, martyrs, confessors, and all other saints besides

---

[13] John Milton, *Areopagitica* (1644), in C. A. Patrides (ed.), *John Milton: Select Prose* (Harmondsworth, 1974), p. 213. (Patrides notes that in some copies of the 1644 edn *wayfaring* has been changed by hand to *warfaring*.)

[14] Edward Taylor, 'The Joy of Church Fellowship Rightly Attended', line 4, *Gods Determinations Touching his Elect*, in D. E. Stanford (ed.), *The Poems of Edward Taylor*, 2nd abridged edn (New Haven, CT, 1963), p. 334.

approved by the church of Rome'. Oldcastle, however, entertained quite
a different notion of pilgrimage:

in this I am fully persuaded, that every man dwelling on this earth is a pilgrim,
either towards bliss or else towards pain; and that he which knoweth not, nor will
not know, nor yet keep the holy commandments of God in his living here, (albeit
that he goeth on pilgrimage into all quarters of the world,) if he departeth so,
he shall surely be damned. Again, he that knoweth the holy commandments of
God, and so performeth them to the end of his life to his power, shall without
fail be saved in Christ, though he never in his life go on pilgrimage, as men use
now-a-days to Canterbury, Walsingham, Compostella, and Rome, or to any other
such place else.[15]

Just this view had been published a few years earlier, perhaps by William
Tyndale, in the edition put out in 1530 of William Thorpe's record of his
examination by Arundell in 1407 on suspicion of Lollardy. Thorpe, accused of preaching 'that pilgrimage is not leful; and . . . that those men and
women that go on pilgrimages to Canterbury, to Beverley, to Karlington,
to Walsingham, and to any such other places, are accursed and made
foolish, spending their goods in waste', developed an extended distinction between 'two manner of pilgrimages'. On the one hand, 'I call them
true pilgrims travelling toward the bliss of heaven, which, in the state,
degree, or order that God calleth them to, do busy them faithfully for
to occupy all their wits bodily and ghostly, to know truly and to keep
faithfully the biddings of God'. Through experience, however, Thorpe
has learned that 'the most part of men and women, that go now on pilgrimages' can rarely repeat the Pater Noster, Ave Maria or Creed 'in any
manner of language', nor call to mind a single Commandment. They
undertake pilgrimages 'more for the health of their bodies than of their
souls; more for to have riches and prosperity of this world, than for to
be enriched with virtues in their souls; more to have here worldly and
fleshly friendship, than for to have friendship of God and of his saints in
heaven'. As he develops this theme, Chaucer's Miller can be heard piping
the pilgrims from the Tabard Inn at Southwark:

I know well that when divers men and women will go thus after their own wills, and
finding out one pilgrimage, they will ordain with them before to have with them
both men and women that can well sing wanton songs, and some other pilgrims
will have with them bag-pipes; so that every town that they come through, what
with the noise of their singing, and with the sound of their piping, and with the
jangling of their Canterbury bells, and with the barking out of dogs after them,

[15] John Bale, *A Brefe Chronycle Concernynge the Examinacion and Death of the Blessed Martyr
Syr John Oldecastell* (1544), in Henry Christmas (ed.), *Select Works of John Bale*, The
Parker Society (Cambridge, 1849), pp. 15, 25, 27.

that they make more noise than if the king came there away, with all his clarions, and many other minstrels.[16]

Such 'pilgrimage-going is neither praiseable nor thankful to God'; indeed, it is no pilgrimage properly so-called, for its business has nothing to do with keeping the biddings of God.

In early English Protestant writing this distinction between true and false pilgrimages became a distinction between the figurative and the literal, with the literal unexpectedly associated with the false. When Latimer speaks of the 'very godly and ghostly pilgrimage ... which all saints whilst they were in this world walked',[17] this spiritual pilgrimage is implicitly opposed as true and devout (*very godly*) to the actual, but false, pilgrimages of Rome. The 'godly and ghostly pilgrimage' of Protestantism is constructed precisely as an alternative to the Roman practice: the Christian's true pilgrim way is not literally from place to place but metaphorically from this world to the next. When, in the allegorical *The Parable of the Pilgrim* (1665), the central figure Theophilus encounters a 'cluster of *Pilgrims* (as they called themselves)' making for 'Loretto, the Holy Land, or such like places', it is to have their credulity and susceptibility to 'lying legends' and the silly 'relations of the dronish Monks' mocked by his guide's story of 'the Holy Cock and Hen' of Compostela to which they give full credence. Speaking through the voice of this guide, the author Symon Patrick, afterwards successively bishop of Chichester and of Ely, denies that sanctity can be acquired through any journey, or that 'there is any holiness in that Land [of Palestine] more then in any other'. He allows spiritual progress as the only genuine pilgrimage: 'These are the Holy Places which we desire to behold. A man dying unto sin, presents us with the fairest sight of Christs Sepulchre. It sets us upon Mount *Olivet* when we meet with a Soul of a Coelestial conversation.'[18]

For this pilgrimage, unlike those of Rome, there was good scriptural warrant. It lay in the presentation of the Old Testament Patriarchs as models of faith in chapter xi of the epistle to the Hebrews. In Tyndale's rendering (substantially retained by the Geneva and King James Bibles):

And they all dyed in fayth, and receaved not the promyses: but sawe them a farre of, and beleved them, and saluted them: and confessed that they were straungers and pilgrems on the erthe. They that say soche thinges, declare that they seke a countre. Also if they had bene myndfull of that countre, from whence they came oute, they had leasure to have returned agayne. But now they desyre a better,

---

[16] *The Examinacion of Master William Thorpe Preste* (1530), in Bale, *Select Works*, pp. 99, 100, 101. Whether Bale, Tyndale or George Constantine was responsible for this publication is undecided.

[17] Latimer, *Sermons*, p. 490.

[18] Symon Patrick, *The Parable of the Pilgrim* (1665), pp. 428, 437, 438, 445.

that is to saye a hevenlye. Wherfor God is not a shamed of them even to be called their God: for he hath prepared for them a citie.[19]

Tyndale's gloss on Hebrews xi was that 'Fayth and trust inchrist only, is the lyfe and quyetnes of the conscience, and not trust in workes, how holye soeuer they appere.'[20] The similar emphasis in the annotations of the Geneva Bible encouraged early Protestant writers to turn to this chapter almost as often as to Romans when seeking to press home the primacy of faith.[21] Useful though it was in promoting solifidianism, however, its so-teriological work was as nothing compared to its imaginative contribution to the establishment of Protestant identity. Hebrews xi is an exercise in Biblical hermeneutics, turning Old Testament story to Christian purpose through what might be called 'experiential typology'. The Old Testament recounts the history of the election of Israel and the course of its covenant relationship with Jehovah in narratives in which religious dedication and desert journeys are so interconnected that the landscapes of nomadic wanderings become emblems of moral conditions and the journey the means by which spiritual destinies are fulfilled. In the two traditions of Israel's origins, in the Abraham legends and the Exodus saga, is repeated the same pattern of decision to leave, journey under divine guidance, testing in the wilderness and covenant. This pattern came to control the narrative shape of the Protestant – still more, Puritan – imagination, for here was a Biblically authorised model for the representation of experi-ence. It is an anomaly of the cultural history of Protestantism that, despite its stress upon plainness in artistic as well as in liturgical and devotional practice, allegorical and symbolic hermeneutical methods and literary modes survived the Reformation.[22] Traditional typological readings of the Old Testament were developed in such works as *Christ Revealed: or the Types and Shadows of Our Saviour in the Old Testament* (1635) by the early seventeenth-century English Puritan divine Thomas Taylor, in the massive *Tropologia: a Key to Open Scripture Metaphors* (1681) by Bunyan's contemporary, the English Baptist Benjamin Keach, and in *The Figures or Types of the Old Testament* (1683) by the ejected Congregational minis-ter Samuel Mather, brother of the New England divine Increase Mather.

[19] Hebrews xi.13–16, as rendered in N. Hardy Wallis (ed.), *The New Testament Translated by William Tyndale 1534* (Cambridge, 1938), p. 516.

[20] Wallis (ed.), *New Testament*, p. 515.

[21] Geneva's page headlines to this chapter were 'Of faith', 'The force of faith' and 'How faith worketh', and its chapter headnote identified three foci: '*1. What faith is, and a com[m]endacion of the same. 9. Without faith we can not please God. 16. The stedfast belefe of the fathers in olde time*' (L. E. Berry (ed.), *The Geneva Bible: a facsimile of the 1560 edition* [Madison, Milwaukee and London, 1969]).

[22] On this anomaly see Thomas H. Luxon, *Literal Figures: Puritan Allegory and the Refor-mation Crisis in Representation* (Chicago, 1995).

They engaged the imagination of the New England minister and poet Edward Taylor in a collection of thirty-six (then unpublished) sermons *Upon the Types of the Old Testament*.[23] In such works, the details of Old Testament narratives became something more than 'some outward or sensible thing ordained of God under the Old Testament to represent and hold forth something of Christ in the New'.[24] They were read as symbolic anticipations not only of New Testament events, but also of an individual's personal experience, and as allegorical representations of the general experiences of saints, sinners and nations: for Taylor, the Bible was 'a notable guide through this pilgrimage of our life' in whose narratives the reader could 'see his owne case'.[25]

The key to such typological reading of the individual's case lay in Hebrews. Its presentation of Noah, Abraham, Moses and other Old Testament figures as Christian exemplars seizes on migrancy as the condition of their faith (they 'seek a country'). This figuring of the life of the faithful as nomadic, and particularly the phrase 'strangers and pilgrims on the earth', came to inform representations of the Protestant life as a journey or pilgrimage from unregeneracy, represented as a rural wasteland or an urban slum; through conversion, represented in the decision to leave; temptation, moral growth and spiritual enlightenment, presented as incidents and locations on the way; to eternal bliss located in the far country, holy mountain or eternal city of the journey's end. This, of course, is the pattern of *The Pilgrim's Progress*,[26] as it is of Patrick's *Parable of the Pilgrim* in which Theophilus, 'being weary of the Country where he dwelt' and hearing of the attractiveness of 'a place called *Jerusalem*' resolves to set out for it, though 'the weather was cold, the wayes dirty and dangerous, and the journey . . . long'.[27] Though in a different genre, George Herbert's thirty-five-line lyric 'The Pilgrimage' is similarly structured: the poem's

[23] Edited by C. W. Mignon, 2 vols. (Lincoln, NA and London, 1989).

[24] Samuel Mather, *The Figures or Types of the Old Testament* (1705), p. 52. For discussion of the literary consequences of typology in the early modern period, see: Sacvan Bercovitch (ed.), *Typology and Early American Literature* (Amherst, MA, 1972); Joseph A. Galdon, *Typology and Seventeenth-Century Literature* (The Hague, 1975); Paul J. Korshin, *Typologies in England, 1650–1820* (Princeton, 1982); Mason I. Lowance, *The Language of Canaan* (Cambridge, MA, 1980); Earl Miner (ed.), *Literary Uses of Typology* (Princeton, 1977). For Bunyan in particular, see R. Greaves, G. Midgley and W. R. Owens in *MW*, vol. VIII, pp. xliii–l, vol. VII, pp. xv–xxvi and vol. XII, pp. xxxviii–xlvii.

[25] Thomas Taylor, *David's Learning, or The Way to True Happiness* (1617), pp. 183, 190–1 (quoted by W. R. Owens in *MW*, vol. XII, p. xxxix). This paragraph, and some passages which follow, derive from the discussion of Puritan fiction in ch. 9 of N. H. Keeble, *The Literary Culture of Nonconformity in Later Seventeenth-century England* (Leicester, 1987), pp. 263–82.

[26] On Hebrews as a source for *PP* see Brainerd P. Stranahan, 'Bunyan and the Epistle to the Hebrews', *Studies in Philology*, 79 (1982), 279–96.

[27] Patrick, *Parable of the Pilgrim*, pp. 2, 3, 5.

first-person narrator travels between 'The gloomy cave of Desperation' and 'The rock of Pride', through 'Fancies medow', 'Cares cops' and 'the wilde of Passion' and he is, at the poem's close, making his way to death.[28] It was to Hebrews xi.13 ('And they confessed, that they were strangers, and pilgrims on the earth') that Herbert's younger contemporary, and admirer, Henry Vaughan turned for the epigraph to his poem of longing for release from mortality entitled 'The Pilgrimage'.[29] Exceptionally, the journey of Sir Walter's Ralegh's pilgrim, though metaphorical, is not through life to death but along bejewelled 'holy paths' leading from death to 'the land of heauen'. Exceptional, too, is the fact that, with his 'Scallop shell of quiet' and his 'staffe of faith', he continues to bear the insignia, and with his 'Gowne of Glory' to wear the attire, of the medieval Roman Catholic pilgrim; while in his 'bottle of salvation' he carries such a prize as the phials of holy water and blood that once pilgrims carried from Becket's shrine at Canterbury.[30]

It is not, ordinarily, what he carries that distinguishes the Protestant pilgrim. Geneva's gloss on Hebrews xi.13 was 'And therefore put not their confidence in thi[n]gs of this worlde'. This unworldliness and otherworldliness are the true distinguishing marks, as in the following characterisation of the late seventeenth-century nonconformist saint John Janeway:

For the latter part of his life, he lived like a man that was quite weary of the world, and that looked upon himself as a stranger here, and that lived in the constant sight of a better world. He plainly declared himself but a Pilgrim that looked for a better Country, a City that had foundations, whose builder and maker was God. His habit, his language, his deportment, all spoke him one of another world.[31]

It was to this image that the Quaker William Penn turned when, rejecting the hedonistic culture of the Restoration, he urged mortification and self-denial:

The true self-denying man is a pilgrim; but the selfish man is an inhabitant of the world: the one uses it, as men do ships, to transport themselves or tackle in a journey, that is, to get home; the other looks no further, whatever he prates, than to be fixed in fulness and ease here, and likes it so well, that if he could, he would not exchange.[32]

[28] George Herbert, *The Works*, ed. F. E. Hutchinson (Oxford, 1941), pp. 141–2.
[29] Henry Vaughan, *The Complete Poems*, ed. A. Rudrum (Harmondsworth, 1976), pp. 224–5.
[30] Sir Walter Ralegh, 'The Passionate Mans Pilgrimage', in *The Poems*, ed. A. Latham, 2nd edn (London, 1962), pp. 49–51. Such details raise questions about the attribution to Ralegh of this poem, as of the ballad beginning 'As you came from the holy land/ Of Walsinghame ...' (pp. 22–3).
[31] James Janeway, *Invisible Realities, Demonstrated in the Holy Life and Triumphant Death of Mr. John Janeway* (1671), p. 91.
[32] William Penn, *No Cross, No Crown*, ed. N. Penney (York, 1981), p. 40.

True faith reduces the believer to the status of an exile, an outcast. As the Tudor homily 'The Fear of Death' had it, 'life in this world is resembled and likened to a pilgrimage in a strange country far from God; and ... death, delivering us from our bodies, doth send us straight home unto our country'. Christian and Faithful are derided at Vanity Fair as 'Outlandish-men', that is, as foreigners. 'Bear yourselves as inhabitants of another country' said the Presbyterian nonconformist John Howe. 'As birds robbed of their native wood/ ... with the thought of home do pine', so Vaughan's pilgrim longs for release from mortality. 'I am', says the Christian Professor in Keach's allegorical dialogue *War with the Devil* (1673), 'a Stranger, and I am going Home'.[33]

Abraham was taken as the exemplar of such a 'self-denying man': '*Abraham* ... was the founder of your Order' his guide tells Theophilus.[34] In biographical fact, his calling 'to get thee out of thy country' Haran and to journey 'unto a land that I will show thee', and his exodus, in obedient response, from a centre of civilisation and from his family, who remained in Mesopotamia, to live as a nomadic tent-dweller in 'the foreign and hostile land of Canaan' (Gen. xii.1–10, xiv.4, 10) anticipated the demands their religious commitment placed upon many sixteenth-century Protestant exiles. Many later Puritans felt compelled by their 'differences about Religious Matters' with the Royalists to take up what Richard Baxter called 'this moving Life' in the New Model Army.[35] George Fox is only the most notable example of many seekers after truth who, during the Interregnum, travelled 'up and down as a stranger on the earth' 'to look for comfort' from despair.[36] The heroic evangelistic journeys undertaken by Fox after his convincement are legendary, but Restoration persecution compelled nonconformists of many persuasions to follow demanding, if less dramatic, itinerant ministries. The Yorkshire Presbyterian Oliver Heywood, for example, regularly travelled 1,000 miles a year 'in my Lords work'.[37] Even those nonconformists who did not travel had nevertheless effectively chosen exile. Many knew the social ostracism which, in his Biblical commentary (1708–10) the Presbyterian Matthew Henry conjectured was Abraham's lot since the Canaanites 'were likely to be but

[33] *Certain Sermons*, p. 99; *PP*, p. 90; John Howe, *The Works*, ed. Henry Rogers, 6 vols. (London, 1862–3), vol. II, p. 217; Vaughan, 'The Pilgrimage', lines 17–20, in *Complete Poems*, pp. 224–5; Benjamin Keach, *War with the Devil*, 22nd edn (1776), p. 105.

[34] Patrick, *Parable of the Pilgrim*, p. 148.

[35] Richard Baxter, *Reliquiae Baxterianae* (1696), I.31, §49 and I.58, §85.

[36] J. L. Nickalls (ed.), *The Journal of George Fox*, corrected reprint (London, 1975), pp. 3–4, 5, 6, 10.

[37] Oliver Heywood, *His Autobiography, Diaries, Anecdote and Event Books*, ed. J. Horsfall Turner, 4 vols. (Brighouse and Bingley: printed for the editor, 1882–5), vol. II, pp. 225, 227–8.

bad neighbours, and worse landlords'.[38] Some, however, literally chose exile in the Great Migration of the 1630s. The earliest such group was John Robinson's separatist church at Scrooby in Nottinghamshire which, in 1608, decided to emigrate to Amsterdam, 'to go into a country they knew not ... for their desires were set on the ways of God'. In 1620 that same resolution took them, as the colonists known to history as the Pilgrim Fathers, to New England: they were, Cotton Mather later wrote, '*satisfy'd*, they had as plain a command of Heaven to attempt a Removal, as ever their Father *Abraham* had for his leaving the *Caldean* Territories'. William Bradford, Plymouth colony's historian and governor for most of its first thirty-five years, could with justice claim that, like Paul (2 Cor. xi.26–7), the Pilgrims had been 'in journeyings often ... in perils in the wilderness', and he could reflect, in a poem published in *New England's Memorial* (1669), Nathaniel Morton's history of Plymouth based upon Bradford's own journal:

> [God] call'd me from my native place
> For to enjoy the means of grace.
> In wilderness he did me guide,
> And in strange lands for me provide.
> In fears and wants, through weal and woe
> A pilgrim passed I to and fro.[39]

For New Englanders like Bradford, Exodus was as sigificant a precedent as Abraham's emigration. That Jehovah had led his people home through the wilderness from their Egyptian captivity inspired Puritan emigrants seeking in New England relief from persecution by undertaking what Samuel Darnforth called their *Errand into the Wilderness* (1670). Given their Eurocentric assumptions, we could understand Puritan emigrants to America believing that they were embarked for a wilderness, but when, in her untitled poem 'As weary pilgrim', the New England poet Anne Bradstreet creates a wilderness as the context of her mortal life, beset by 'dangers', 'travails', 'burning sun', 'briars and thorns', 'hungry wolves', 'erring paths' and 'parching thirst', it is not Massachusetts she is describing. Bunyan, after all, found precisely the same topography in Bedfordshire, England: the narrator of *The Pilgrim's Progress* walks 'through the wilderness of this world' and it was 'from the *Lions Dens*', from the prison where 'I stick between the Teeth of the Lions in the

---

[38] Matthew Henry, *An Exposition of All the Books of the Old and New Testament*, 3 vols. (London, Glasgow and Edinburgh, 1867), vol. I, p. 42.

[39] William Bradford, *Of Plymouth Plantation*, ed. S. E. Morrison (New York, 1952), vol. II, p. 329; Cotton Mather, *Magnalia Christi Americana: or the Ecclesiastical History of New England* (1702), I.6, §3; Nathaniel Morton, *New England's Memorial*, in *Chronicles of the Pilgrim Fathers*, [ed. A. Young], Everyman's Library (London, 1910), p. 173.

Wilderness' that Bunyan addressed the reader of his autobiographical *Grace Abounding*.[40] In early modern Protestant texts, England no less than New England appears an uncultivated wasteland of scrub and brambles, scorched by a relentless sun, prowled by wild beasts; signposting is poor and travellers are prone to lose themselves in featureless deserts. Clearly, these details do not derive from observation; the descriptive authority of such passages is not experiential but intertextual. They are recalling a far distant land and time in order to trace in their authors' and readers' experience the patterns of significance that Hebrews taught them to read in Old Testament story.

In the Pentateuch narratives the Israelites, of course, are seeking a homeland. However, in the passage in Hebrews that inspired Richard Baxter's *The Saints Everlasting Rest* (1650), the 'rest' denied to the erring Israelites is identified as eternal bliss (iii.7–4, 16). Abraham's preference for exile over return to Mesopotamia is similarly rendered as the hope 'for a better country, that is an heavenly' (xi.8–16). With eternal salvation replacing Canaan as the journey's destination, allegorical and narrative logic demands that the wilderness topography of the desert wanderings signifies the mortal experience that leads to that destiny. As journeys not for temporal possession but for an eternal kingdom, the Israelites' forty years of desert wandering thus provide a narrative and figurative model for Christian experience. The Geneva Bible supplied Numbers xxxiii with a map showing 'the way, which the Israelites went for the space of fourtie yeres from Egypt through the wilderness of Arabia, vntil they entred into the land of Canaan'. Clearly marked is the wilderness of Sin (Exod. xvii.1). When, in 1655, Faithful Teate published *A Scripture-Map of the Wildernesse of Sin, and the Way to Canaan. Or the Sinners Way to the Saints Rest* (1655) he explained that the wilderness he described was '*the WILDERNESSE OF SIN spiritually so called*'. He did not '*deny in the least the Historicall respect some Scriptures have*', but, reading them '*mystically*', he understands '*by the Antitype, by the Wildernesse*' the state of unregeneracy: 'my work is Topographical to draw out the Map of the wilderness . . . of unconversion'.[41] What Bradstreet and Bunyan describe, then, is not a particular, geographical location. It is rather an imaginative terrain, the landscape of an idea, the image of a spiritual conviction. To walk by faith is to perceive oneself a pilgrim providentially led like the Israelites through the desert. As George Fox put it, 'it is the great love of God to make a wilderness of that which is pleasant to the outward

---

[40] Anne Bradstreet, *The Works*, ed. J. Hensley (Cambridge, MA, 1967), p. 283; *PP*, p. 9; John Bunyan, *Grace Abounding to the Chief of Sinners*, ed. R. Sharrock (Oxford, 1962), p. 1.

[41] Faithful Teate, *A Scripture-Map of the Wildernesse of Sin, and the Way to Canaan* (1655), pref. ep., sigs. A4v, aa1, 2.

eye and fleshly mind'.[42]Consequently, one could as readily discern the wilderness in Elizabethan or Restoration London as in New England. The work in which the Presbyterian nonconformist Thomas Gouge, addressing London apprentices, wrote that we are to live 'as a citizen of heaven, and a pilgrim on the earth' is entitled *The Young Man's Guide through the Wilderness of this World to the Heavenly Canaan* (1670).

The pilgrim way through this wilderness begins in an initial act of commitment. The observation in Hebrews that 'by faith' Abraham 'went out not knowing whither he went' (Heb. xi.8) was picked up in the gloss in the Genevan version of the Bible on Genesis xii.1: 'In appointing him no certeine place, he [God] proueth so muche more his faith and obedience'. The point was to be a standard one in Protestant commentaries: for Matthew Henry, for example, Abraham's removal 'was designed to try his faith and obedience, and also to separate him, and set him apart, for God'. Abraham was 'tried whether he loved God better than he loved his native soil and dearest friends', and, as he was told nothing about the promised land, he 'had no particular securities given him that he should be no loser by leaving his country to follow God. Note, those that deal with God must deal on trust.'[43] Protestant story takes its rise from such an act of trust, which is represented time and again in the decision to relinquish security and stability and to venture into the unknown against, as it seems, common sense. In *The Pilgrim's Progress*, departures repeatedly affront the advocates of worldly caution: Faithful's prudent neighbours, for example, stigmatise his pilgrimage as a 'desperate journey', while, in Part II, Mrs. Timorous leaves Mercy 'to go a fooling' with the tart comment that 'while we are out of danger we are out; but when we are in, we are in'.[44] Just such attempts are made to dissuade the hero of Keach's *War with the Devil* from setting out:

> Who would for Things which so uncertain are,
> Such losses suffer, and such Labour bear?
> A Bird i' th' Hand's worth two i' th' Bush, you know,
> This Zeal, poor Lad, will work thy Overthrow.[45]

So to argue from worldly security – 'I have married a Wife, I have a Farm, I shall offend my Landlord, I shall offend my Master, I shall lose my Trading...therefore, *I dare not come*' – is to betray the moral turpitude of the unregenerate. Lot's wife, after all, paid a heavy price for looking longingly back at what she had to leave; by contrast, Lot did not even turn to see what had become of her.[46] Equally admonitory is the

[42] Fox, *Journal*, p. 13.   [43] Henry, *Exposition*, vol. I, pp. 40–1.   [44] *PP*, pp. 67, 183–4.
[45] Keach, *War with the Devil*, p. 107.   [46] *MW*, vol. V, pp. 165, 176–7.

reminder of Theophilus' guide who, alluding to Numbers xi.5, recalls
that 'no less than six hundred thousand Travellers to *Jerusalem* in ancient
times . . . left all their carkasses buried in the Desarts' because, although
they 'left *Egypt*, as you are now going to forsake the world', it was 'in their
Bodies only, and not in their hearts and affection . . . They loved the Country from whence they were departed'. By contrast, 'the name of *Pilgrim*'
requires its bearer to 'forsake his home, his wife, his children, and all
he hath'.[47] Bunyan's uncompromising dramatisation of the injunction of
Luke xiv.26 in Christian's determination to abandon his family, creates
what must surely be one of the most disconcerting opening scenes of any
fiction, affronting not only, as it seems, common sense, but also common
decency.[48]

To make such a reckless decision and to insist on undertaking so foolhardy a journey argues an audacious and intrepid character. 'Hee that
at euery steppe, lookes at euery stoppe, and numbers his perils with his
paces, either turnes aside faintly, or turns back cowardly' admonished the
early seventeenth-century Puritan divine Thomas Adams; 'The boldness
of Christians is the honour of Christ' wrote Henry.[49] 'Play the man'
echoes like a refrain through *The Pilgrim's Progress*. Christian is not to be
deterred from his pilgrimage by its hazards and dangers. In his Pauline ar-
mour of faith engaging Apollyon he has a good deal of the martial chivalric
hero about him; so has that 'man of his Hands' Valiant-for-Truth who
'fought with most Courage' when his 'Sword did cleave to my Hand' with
blood. Bunyan's most famous contribution to hymnody after all invites
us to discern '*true Valour*' in the Christian pilgrim undismayed by lion,
giant, hobgoblin or foul fiend.[50] Cowardice is not the least of the failings
of the Philistine champion Harapha as he faces the prowess of Milton's
Samson, and it is Samson who informs Penn's encomium of Fox, whom
he never knew 'out of his place, or not a match for every service and
occasion', 'For in all things he acquitted himself like a man, yea, a strong
man'.[51]

To recount the Protestant pilgrimage is hence to tell an adventure story.
'Faith is an adventuring upon the truth of God, an adventuring our lives,
and adventuring our souls' wrote Gouge in his *Young Mans Guide*. 'I
must venture' resolves Christian confronted by the lions of persecution

[47] Patrick, *Parable of the Pilgrim*, pp. 34, 51.

[48] For an argument countering this view, see N. H. Keeble, 'Christiana's Key: The Unity
of *The Pilgrim's Progress*', in Vincent Newey (ed.), *The Pilgrim's Progress: Critical and
Historical Views* (Liverpool, 1980), pp. 1–20.

[49] Thomas Adams, *The Workes* (1630), p. 652; Henry, *Exposition*, vol. III, p. 863.

[50] *PP*, pp. 59–60, 291, 295.

[51] John Milton, *Samson Agonistes* (1671), lines 1061–244, in *Complete Shorter Poems*, ed.
J. Carey, 2nd edn (Harlow, 1997), pp. 392–8; Fox, *Journal*, p. xlvii.

before the House Beautiful.[52] By daring to venture, to take the risk, the Protestant hero assumes to himself something of the quality of the old heroes of chivalric romance, and it is the unexpectedness of the next *aventure* that in his story, as in medieval romance, provides the suspense of his narrative. Despite Protestantism's predominantly predestinarian theological bias, journey's end is not a foregone conclusion. Though they might well hold a Calvinist view of election and reprobation, divines commonly taught that assurance was a gift, which might be withheld, and that uncritical reliance upon the doctrine of the necessary perseverance of the saints fostered complacency and hypocrisy. Sermons and guides to godliness repeatedly urge watchfulness and caution upon their readers since one can never be sure what awaits around the next bend. Christian learns this lesson the hard way: it is after turning aside into the lands of Giant Despair that he meets the shepherds Watchful and Experience. 'Way-fairing men' are 'seldom at a Certainty': 'sometimes our way is clean, sometimes foul; sometimes up-hill, sometimes down-hill.' When, in *The Pilgrim's Progress*, Honest, 'an old man' who has 'bin a Traveller in this Rode many a day', has seen pilgrims 'set out as if they would drive all the World afore them. Who yet have in a few days, dyed as they in the Wilderness, and so never gat sight of the promised Land', it would be a foolhardy wayfarer who supposed that beginning on the way guaranteed successful completion of the journey. Bunyan's Honest there alludes, as did Theophilus' guide in Patrick's *Parable of the Pilgrim*, to Israel's wanderings in Sinai: 'Almost all the many Thousands of the Children of Israel in their Generation, fell short of *Perseverance*, when they walk'd from *Egypt* towards the Land of *Canaan*. Indeed, they went to the work at first pretty willingly, but they were very short-winded, they were quickly out of Breath, and *in their Hearts they turned back again into* Egypt.'[53]

This need for determination and resolution was articulated through an-other Biblical image of the road. Glossing Matthew vii.13–14 ('Enter ye in at the strait gate'), Henry writes: 'Conversion and regeneration are *the gate* by which we enter into this way'; 'This is a *strait gate*, hard to find, and hard to get through, like a passage between two rocks' (I Samuel xiv.4).[54] What obscures the gate is the difficulty of distinguishing outward religious observance from inner spiritual renewal. Bunyan's Christian, who 'could not tell which way to go', has a flirtation with formalism and moralism before being directed by Evangelist to the Wicket-Gate of true conver-sion. Formalist and Hypocrisy, of course, never do enter by the gate but

---

[52] Thomas Gouge, *The Works* (1798), pp. 383–4; *PP*, p. 43.
[53] *PP*, pp. 120, 257, 275; *MW*, vol. v, pp. 160–1.   [54] Henry, *Exposition*, vol. III, p. 44.

come 'tumbling over the Wall, on the left hand of the narrow way'.[55] That narrow way, 'as straight as a Rule can make it',[56] derives from the contrasting Old Testament images, invoked by Jesus' injunction in Matthew, of the straight way of the righteous, 'in the pathway there of there is no death' (Prov. v.8, xii.28), and the crooked way of the wicked leading to destruction (Prov. ii.15, iv.19; Isa. lix.7–10). It is a way undeviating and uncompromising (*straight*), demanding and difficult (*strait*). Save for a very few antinomian and enthusiastic voices, Protestant divines of all persuasions were univocal in their insistence that only continuing moral and spiritual effort could keep one in the way to its end. For Richard Baxter it was axiomatic that '*Your Conversion is not sound if you are not heartily desirous to encrease*. Grace is not true, if there be not a desire after more':

I doubt it is the undoing of many to imagine, that if once they are sanctified, they are so sure in the hands of Christ, that they have no more care to take, nor no more danger to be afraid of, and at last think they have no more to do, as of necessity to Salvation; and thus prove that indeed they were never sanctified.[57]

Baxter's teaching on justification aroused the ire of such Calvinist divines as John Owen, but even a predestinarian like John Bunyan wrote *Christian Behaviour* (1663) to show 'the Beauty & Excellency' of good works. The fate of Ignorance in *The Pilgrim's Progress* should not blind us to Christian's declaration, in dismissing Talkative, that 'The Soul of Religion is the practick part'.[58] In Talkative was represented a moral failing that Protestant divines had long sought to discountenance: 'The *Apostle [Paul]* chargeth vs', wrote Adams, 'to walke, not to talke of loue: One steppe of our feet, is worth ten words of our tongues.'[59] 'True faith', Bishop John Jewel had written in his foundational *Apologie of the Church of England* (1562), 'is lively, and can in no wise be idle . . . therefore we teach the people, that God called us . . . as Paul saith, "unto good works, to walk in them" [1 Thess. iv.7; Eph. ii.10]'; and this, for the next century and a half, sermons were tirelessly to reiterate: 'there is nothing of Christianity got by idleness' admonishes Bunyan; 'no hinderance . . . lyes in our way but only our own laziness' agrees Patrick.[60]

---

[55] *PP*, pp. 9, 39, 48. In fact, Bunyan's 'Wicket-Gate' seems not to derive from this Matthean passage or its Lucan equivalent (Luke xiii.24) which, in *The Strait Gate* (1676), Bunyan interprets as referring to the gate of heaven rather than to the '*door of faith*' (John x.9; Acts xiv.27) which leads to a committed Christian life (*MW*, vol. v, pp. 74–5). In Bunyan's *The Heavenly Foot-man* (1698) it is this latter, not Matthew's strait gate, that sets the believer in the right way of Christ (John xiv.6) (*MW*, vol. v, p. 152).

[56] *PP*, p. 27.

[57] Richard Baxter, *Directions for Weak Christians* (1669), part I, 17–18 (sigs. G8-G8v).

[58] *MW*, vol. III, p. 9; *PP*, p. 79.   [59] Adams, *Workes*, p. 802.

[60] T. L. Parker (ed.), *English Reformers* (London, 1966), pp. 32–3; *MW*, vol. v, p. 84; Patrick, *Parable of the Pilgrim*, p. 192.

This gives to Protestant story an insistent onward pressure. The word 'progress' impels the saint forward, preventing any antinomian rest just within the gate: 'You have hit of the right way, but you have your Journey yet to go'.[61] And it is a long journey. 'Departing from iniquity', wrote Bunyan, 'is not a work of an hour, or a day, or a week, or a month, or a year: But it's a work will last thee thy life-time'. 'It is a work of continuance . . . of time, of all thy time'.[62] Like Abraham, like the Israelites, Christians must expect to be tried and to have to endure: '*that which heads it against the greatest Opposition*', opines Bunyan's Honest, '*gives best demonstration that it is the strongest*'. 'You must', Evangelist warns Faithful and Christian, 'through many tribulations enter into the Kingdom of Heaven . . . in every City, bonds and afflictions abide in you: and therefore you cannot expect that you should go long in your Pilgrimage without them.'[63] Just so, Herbert's pilgrim is allowed no relief: 'A long it was and weary way', a 'foul journey' of relentless effort and disappointment, seemingly thankless and without reward. When the poem opens, he is already on the road, 'travelling on', struggling through adverse terrain 'With much ado'. When, midway through the poem, he attains the 'gladsome hill,/ Where lay my hope' it is to be bitterly disappointed to discover that 'My hill was further'; and so he ends the poem as he began, 'flinging away' and journeying on.[64]

This point was often made by associating with the figures of the journey and the pilgrimage the Pauline image of the race for the prize or crown of salvation (1 Cor. ix.24; Gal. v.7; Phil. ii.16; Heb. xii.1). Noting that '*Olympus* in the Heathen *Poets* is commonly used for heaven, so the *Olympick* exercises may well be used to resemble those for heaven, and the heavenly Crown likened to the *Olympick* Garland', the Restoration episcopalian Mark Frank derives from the analogy the necessity of strenuous effort: 'Running is a violent exercise'; 'The word run is no idle word, there is pains and labour in it.' Auditors of the Presbyterian Thomas Manton's 1662 farewell sermon heard that 'a Christian's life is like a race from earth to heaven . . . Running is a motion, and a speedy motion; there is no lying, sitting or standing, but still there must be running'. It is with the verse from 1 Corinthians ix that Evangelist encourages Christian and Faithful to bear the suffering that lies in store for them at Vanity Fair.[65] But this is a long-distance race: 'It is an easy matter for a Man to *Run hard for a spurt*, for a Furlong, for a Mile or two: O but to hold out for a Hundred, for a Thousand, for *Ten Thousand Miles*; that a Man that doth this, he must look to meet with Cross, Pain, and Wearisomness to the Flesh.' Those

---

[61] Gouge, *Works*, pp. 296–7.   [62] *MW*, vol. ix, pp. 276, 277.   [63] *PP*, pp. 87, 265.
[64] Herbert, *Works*, pp. 141–2.
[65] Mark Frank, *LI Sermons* (1672), pp. 288, 289, 296; Thomas Manton, *The Works*, 5 vols. (London, 1870–2), vol. ii, pp. 59–60; *PP*, p. 86.

words are from Bunyan's *The Heavenly Foot-man* (1698), a sermon treatise on 1 Corinthians ix.24 ('So run that ye may obtain') in which the race (a 'running with all might and main', 'thorow all difficulties', 'to the end of ... Life') becomes a prolonged Biblical migration:

the *way is long*, (I speak Metaphorically) and there is many a dirty step, many a high Hill, much Work to do, a wicked Heart, World and Devil to overcome. I say, there are many steps to be taken by those that intend to be Saved, by running or walking in the steps of that Faith of our Father *Abraham*. Out of *Egypt*, thou must go, thorow the *Red Sea*; thou must run a long and tedious Journey, thorow the wast howling Wilderness, before thou come to the Land of Promise.[66]

When Bunyan goes on to caution his readers to 'Beware of by-paths' and 'crooked Paths, Paths in which Men go astray, Paths that lead to Death and Damnation', and to resist the blandishments of those neighbours and others who 'do call after you', the race, the straight way, the journey and the migration combine to create the allegorical world of *The Pilgrim's Progress*.[67] No wonder: for by the late seventeenth century Protestants had long been accustomed to imagining theirs to be the way of the 'very godly and ghostly pilgrimage'.[68]

[66] *MW*, vol. v, pp. 148, 149, 150, 161.   [67] *MW*, vol. v, pp. 155, 157.
[68] In *PP*, p. 1, Bunyan says that, when writing of '*the Way/ And Race of Saints*', he fell '*suddenly into an Allegory/ About their Journey, and the Way to glory*'. It is generally supposed that *The Heavenly Footman* is the book to which Bunyan here refers: see Roger Sharrock's note in *PP*, p. 312, and Graham Midgley's remarks in *MW*, vol. v, pp. xlix–li, with the several anticipations of *The Pilgrim's Progress* observed in his notes.

Index

(Page numbers in italics refer to illustrations)

abbeys, 211; *see also* religious houses, dissolution of
Abraham, 2, 245, 246, 248, 251, 255, 256
abuses, 210
accidents, 129, 131
Act of Succession, 193, 194, 197
Adorno, Anselm, 141, 151, 152
adventure stories, 252–3
Agaune, 34
Agnes de Courtenay, 41
agrarian reform, 189, 190, 191
Alan of Tewkesbury, 64, 68
Alban, St *see* St Albans Abbey
Albert of Aachen, 2
Alexander III, pope, 71, 84
allegory, 241, 244, 245, 246, 250, 256
almsgiving, 33, 192
Alphege, St, 75, 78, 83, 91, 105
altars, 53, 55, 59, 91, 100, 163
    Canterbury, 101, 103, 104
ambulatories, 95, 96, 98, 100, 104, 106
Amesbury, 23
Amphibalus, St, 20
ampullae, 48, 50, 112, 136
Anagni Cathedral, 51
Angers, 13, 28
Angevins, 12, 13, 51, 52;
    see also Plantagenets
Anglo-Saxons, 13–14, 22, 31, 40, 44, 91, 97, 167
Anne, St, 137
Annunciation, 136, 137, 138
Anselm, St, 78, 105, 106
anthropology, 12, 14, 17, 28
anticlericalism, 208, 223
apse, 90, 91; *see also* east ends
Aquitaine, 26, 27
Arbroath Abbey, 85
architecture, 1, 90

Decorated style, 106
Early Gothic, 96–7
east ends, 96, 97–8
pavements, 91, 93–4, 96, 106
Perpendicular, 102, 104
raised shrines, 95, 96
Romanesque, 90, 91, 98
screens, 100–1, 102, 104, 105, 107, 171
shrine-bases, 99
Trinity Chapel, 95, 96
art, 3, 10, 46–8, 85, 87, 91, 154, 171, 173;
    see also images
Asia, 146, 147, 148, 161
Aske, Robert, 178, 179, 180, 182, 186, 188–9, 192
Augustine, St, 35, 78, 135
    shrine of, 90, 91

badges, 1, 6, 48, 136, *137*, 170, 183, 195
Bainham, James, 202
Baldwin, abbot, 96, 114, 115
Bale, John, 171, 207, 208, 221ff, 226, 231–2, 2324, 242
Bale, Norfolk, 138
baptisms, 191
Barlow, William, 201–2, 208
Barnes, Robert, 205
Barnham Broom, Norfolk, 171
Barton, Elizabeth, 200, 205
Battle Abbey, 13–14
battles, 24–6
Bawburgh church, Norfolk, 109, 111, 117, 125, 127–8, 166–71
    chapel, 170–1
    guild, 170
    miracles, 169
Baxter, Richard, 248, 250, 254
Becket, Thomas *see* Thomas, St; *see also* Canterbury, cult of Thomas Becket
Benedict of Canterbury, 46, 55, 59, 80

Benedictines, 90, 125
benefactions *see* gifts
Bergen, 50
Bernard, George, 203
Bernard of Clairvaux, St, 31, 34, 46–7,
    89, 159
Bethlehem, 159
Bible, 6, 78, 217, 244–56; *see also* New
    Testament; Old Testament
Birgitta, St, 150, 155
bishops, 135–6, 212, 230
Black Prince, 104, 106
Blaise, St, 80
blindness, 115–16, 131, 133
blood, 168, 239, 247
    Christ, 34, 36–7, 218
    Thomas Becket, 48, 49, 58, 112, 121,
        215, 219, 224, 226
Blythburgh church, 172
Bocking, Dr Edward, 205
Bologna, 163
Book of Hours, 173
Book of Martyrs, 234, 238, 239, 241
books, 52, 64, 87, 143, 146–8, 175, 228,
    231, 232
Bouchier, archbishop, 105
Bowen, John Atherton, 92
Boxley Abbey, Kent, 172, 213–14
    Rood of Grace, 214, 239
Bradstreet, Anne, 249, 250
Bramfield church, 172
Brasca, Santo, 146, 148
Bretons, 24, 25, 28
Brewster, James, 239
Bristol, 28
Bromholm Priory, Norfolk, 27, 123, 136,
    167, 173
Browne, Thomas, 222–3
Bruges, Jerusalem Church, 151–3
Bunyan, John, 10–11, 111, 160, 164, 250,
    254, 255, 256
    Pilgrim's Progress, 10, 241, 246, 249,
        251, 252, 253, 254, 256
burials, 59, 164
Burlingham St Andrews, 171
Bury St Edmunds, 18, 23, 25, 28, 38,
    90, 91, *118*, 172, 173
    healing, 112, 113, 114, 117, 119,
        120, 121

Caister, Richard, 128
Calvary, 35, 153, 154, 155, 159
Calvinism, 253, 254
Campin, 154
canon law, 1, 17
Canaan *see* Israelites

canonisation, 28, 33, 42, 97, 98–9, 132,
    166, 169
Canterbury, cult of Thomas Becket, 3, 8,
    31, 129, 169
    burial, 59, 62–3, 72, 94, 104
    destruction of shrine, 199, 201, 211,
        217, 220–1, 224, 227
    discrediting of, 202, 215, 216, 224, 230,
        232–3, 234
    feast days, 26, 212, 215, 218, 224, 233
    Henry II and, 16, 17, 23, 26, 28
    Henry VIII and, 200–1, 203, 205ff,
        211–12, 216ff, 227
    images, distribution of, 48–52, 83–4,
        85, 87
    martyrdom, 49, 53–5, 59, 64, 67, 71,
        72, 80, 83, 89, 225–6, 230, 236
    miracles, 75, 78, 116, 119
    pageant, 225, 226, 233, 234
    popularity, 85
    prohibition, 218, 227, 230
    relics, 34, 48, 49, 50, 51, 58, 93, 96,
        112, 121, 215, 219, 224, 226
    restoration, 233–4, 235–7
    Trinity Chapel, 47, 52, 72, 75, *76*, *77*,
        81–3, 85, *86*, 87, *88*, 90, 93, 95, 96,
        105, 106–7
    wealth of, 47
    windows, 72, 75, *76*, *77*, *82*, *86*, *88*
    see also Canterbury Cathedral;
        Thomas, St
Canterbury Cathedral, 90, 98, 101–7,
    233, 234
    ambulatories, 96, 106, 104, 106
    'Bell Harry', 101
    Corona, 96, 106, 107
    crypt, 94, 96, 103, 104
    Martyrdom Altar, 101, 103, 104
    Meopham's Tomb, 105–6
    Morton's monument, 104
    nave, 102
    new choir, 91
    new east end, 95–6
    north choir aisle, 102–3
    pavements, 91, 93, 96, 106
    rebuilding, 101, 103, 104
    reredos, 100, 105
    Rood, 102
    screens, 100, 102, 104, 105, 107
    shrines, 105–7
    south transept, 103, 104–5
    vaults, 96
    wax chamber, 103
    see also Canterbury, cult of Thomas
        Becket
Canterbury Tales see Chaucer, Geoffrey

Capetians, 30, 39, 41, 71
'Captain Poverty' movement, 180, 181,
    192, 195; see also Pilgrimage of Grace
Capua Cathedral, 51, 52
Carpenter, David, 26
Catalonia, 51
Catherine, St, 8, 81, 146, 151
Catholicism, 6, 10, 11, 162, 163, 195,
    207, 233, 234, 235–6, 237, 238, 239
Cavenham, Suffolk, 171
Cawston, 173
ceremonial, 1, 29, 33–4, 43, 159
chancel, 90, 97, 128
chantry chapels, 100, 101, 102, 104, 128,
    170–1
chapels, royal, 34
Chapuys, Eustace, 179, 180, 203, 208
charity, 33, 142, 167, 192, 239, 240
Charlemagne, 14, 42, 43, 81
Charles V, Emperor, 179, 203
Chartres Cathedral, 19, 49, 67–71, 69, 70,
    72, 75, 81, 87
châsses, 46, 49, 50–1, 53n, 56, 59, 62–3,
    64, 87; see also reliquary boxes
Chaucer, Geoffrey, 1, 2, 8, 17, 112, 120,
    141, 160, 243
Chester, 99
childbirth, 134–8
children, 121, 129, 131, 133, 135, 136
Christ, 55, 64, 67, 71, 72, 78, 80, 83, 136,
    155, 160, 180, 181, 185, 195, 212
    blood, 34, 36, 57, 59
    healing, 110, 113, 119
    sufferings, 123, 149, 151
Christ Church Priory, Canterbury, 64, 84,
    205, 206, 232, 235
Christianity, 7, 33, 34, 242, 243, 244
Church, English, 83, 85, 186, 189, 193,
    206, 218, 231–3, 240
    and Becket, 201
    ceremonial, 33–4
    Convocation, 211, 212, 218, 231, 232
    and healing, 108, 110
    and miracles, 111
    see also religious reformers
churches, 1, 7, 9, 13, 34, 90, 191–2
    Becket images, 232, 233
    order of service, 218
    sanctuaries, 90, 97
    sepulchres, 156
    see also east ends
Cicero, 1
clergy, 9, 143, 163, 186, 187, 189, 193,
    194, 196, 201, 212, 213, 229, 240
Cluniacs, 123, 125
coins, 30

Coldstream, Dr Nicola, 99
Colet, Dean, 101, 103
Cologne, 42, 63, 64, 75, 136, 176
combs, 56, 63n
'commons', 180, 181, 182, 183, 186, 187,
    193, 194, 196, 198
commonwealth, 178, 179, 184, 188,
    189–92, 194
communitas, 14, 15, 17, 121, 165,
    174, 177
Compostela, 7, 18, 19, 20, 30, 141, 145,
    244
Constantine, 1, 15
continuity, 4, 161
conversion, 246, 253, 254
Corinthians, epistle to, 255, 256
Cosmati pavements, 93
Counter-Reformation, 235–6
courage, 252, 253
Cowell, Thomas, 235
Cowper, William and Alice, 238
Cranmer, Thomas, 199, 203, 204, 210,
    213ff, 222, 223, 224, 227, 231, 232
Cromwell, Thomas, 189, 190, 193, 197,
    199–200, 203, 206, 208, 209, 216,
    219, 222, 224
    injunctions, 210, 211, 212, 225, 227,
    229
Crook, Dr John, 90, 91
Crophill, John, 113, 139
crosses, 13, 35, 154, 182, 194, 195
Crown, 193, 203; see also Act of
    Succession; royal supremacy
Crown of Thorns, 34, 35
crusades, 1–2, 7, 13, 17, 18, 29, 179, 183,
    187
Cumberland, 181, 182, 188, 189, 197
cures see healing
Cuthbert, St, 90, 91, 98, 182, 183, 186,
    187, 194; see also Durham Cathedral
Cyprus, 145

Dakyn, John, 181, 185
Darcy, Lord, 183, 189
David, St, 24
de Bec, Lady Mabel, 121, 131
de Chauliac, Guy, 138–9
de Deguileville, Gillaume, 2, 110, 159
de Lusignan family, 41
de Mézières, Philippe, 143
de Tracy, 226
death, 129, 164, 247, 256
dementia, 133, 134
demonic possession, 129, 134
Denis, St, 78
des Roches, Peter, 27, 37

devotion, 9, 146, 149, 156, 171
  royal, 21, 22–9
diaries, 144–5, 150–1
diet, 133
discontinuity, 4
disease, understanding of, 132–3
distances, 174
Doncaster, 182, 183, 187, 196, 197
Dover, 216, 217, 220, 237
drama, 110, 156, 199, 216, 221–6, 232,
    233, 235–6, 237
  anti-Becket, 223–4, 225
  anti-Catholic, 208
  Kynge Johan, 222, 223, 224, 234
  popular, 225
  propaganda, 225, 226
Dunstan, St, 75, 78, 83, 91, 105
Dupront, Alphonse, 31
Durham, county of, 181, 183, 188, 197
Durham Cathedral, 91, 95, 98, 100, 195

East, 1, 13, 29, 144, 146–7, 148, 161
East Anglia, 166, 168
  healing, 110–17ff
  shrines, 108–9, 125, 127–9
  Virgin Mary cult, 125, 136 *see also*
    Norfolk; Suffolk; Walsingham
East Barsham, Norfolk, 137
east ends, 90–1, 95, 96, 97–8, 99, 101, 102
East Riding, 185, 197
Easter sepulchres, 156–9
Edington, 159
Edmund, St, 23, 25, 112, 116, 117, 119, 132,
    133, 171; *see also* Bury St Edmunds
Edmund of Canterbury, 19
Edward I, 18, 19, 22, 38, 42
Edward IV, 170
Edward VI, 218, 224, 232, 233
Edward the Confessor, 36, 40, 42, 114,
    171
  canonisation, 28, 33
  relics, 25, 26
  shrine, 93, 99
Egypt, 9, 146, 252, 253, 256
Eleanor of Aquitaine, 27, 40
Eleanor of Provence, 23
Elizabeth I, 173, 234–5
Elizabeth of York, 176
Ely Cathedral, 28, 98, 114, 131, 171
emigrants, 246, 249
endurance, 252, 255
England, 250
  and Jerusalem pilgrimage, 142–3, 146–9
  legends, 166–71
  see also English kings

English Catholic exiles, 235–7
English kings, 7, 8
  chapels, 34
  devotions, 21, 22–9
  protection of pilgrims, 29–30
  sacrality, 12, 28, 29, 31, 36–44
  and saints, 31–5, 40–3
  see also Plantagenets
Entombment of Christ, 155, 159
epilepsy, 138
Erasmus, 101, 103, 123, 212
ergotism, 133
Erkenwald, St, 94, 99
Essex, 29, 171, 208
Ethelreda, St, 171; *see also* Ely Cathedral
eucharist, 121, 155
Eustace, St, 80–1
ex votos, 125–6
exile, 2, 248, 249, 250
Exodus, 245, 248, 249, 250

fairy-tales, 170
faith, 2, 210, 240, 245, 250, 251, 254
family, abandonment of, 252
fasting days, 23, 218
feast days, 25, 26, 33, 172, 184, 185, 212,
    213, 215, 218, 233; *see also* saints' days
fertility, 136–8, 169
Feyerabend, 161
Finchams of Norfolk, 128
Finucane, R.C., 134
fiscal reforms, 190–1
Fisher, Bishop John, 206, 207
FitzUrse, 85, 87
Fleury, 46
Fontevraud, 23, 27
Foster, Thomas, 194
Fox, George, 248, 250, 252
Foxe, John, 234, 238–40, 241
Foxearth, Essex, 171
France, 7, 13, 14, 18, 19, 24, 26–7, 30, 39,
    81, 97, 163
  Becket images, 49–50, 67–71
Francis of Assisi, St, 84–5
Franciscans, 9, 142, 144, 149, 154, 163
Freiburg, 156
Frevell, George, 233
friars, 208–9
Frideswide, St *see* Oxford
Fulk Nerra, Count, 13

Gardiner, Stephen, 227
Garnier, 49
Gascony, 27, 30
Gatele, Thomas, 129

'gate', 253, 255
Geary, Patrick, 165
gender, 135, 187
Genesis, 248, 251
Geneva Bible, 247, 250, 251
gentry, 128, 178, 186, 187, 189
George, St, 183, 196
Germany, 31, 52, 142, 154
Gervase, 95, 96, 105
gifts, 87, 126–7, 128, 170, 173
    royal, 16, 20, 27, 29, 30–1, 33, 34–6
Gilbert of Sempringham, St, 31, 32, 33
Gilbertus Anglicus, 126
Glastonbury Abbey, 94, 167, 168
Godmersham, Kent, 53n
Godric of Finchale, St, 32
Godstow, 41–2
Gomez-Géraud, Marie-Christine, 4
good works, 210, 254
Görlitz, 153
gospel books, 52, 78
Gouge, Thomas, 242, 251, 252
Gouffier de Boisy, Anne, 216–17
grace, 176, 178, 179, 184, 185, 188, 196,
    197; see also Pilgrimage of Grace
Great Ashfield, Suffolk, 173, 174
Gregory, St, 2, 80, 83, 105
Grim, Edward, 53, 67
Gruffydd, Elis, 199, 220, 229
guidebooks, 143–4
guilds, 156, 162, 165, 170

Hackington, Lincolnshire, 156, 158
hagiography, 31, 63, 83, 111–12, 116–17,
    129
Hailes Abbey, Gloucestershire, 168, 218,
    239
Hakluyt, 10, 161
halo, 63, 64, 67
Hamo of Savigny, 25
Harpsfield, Nicholas, 235, 237
Harrison, William, 93–4
Hatfield House, 236
Hautbois, 109
healing, 8, 41, 49, 75, 87
    cost of medicines, 113
    cults, 108
    expectations, 131, 132
    folk, 138–9
    and gender, 134–5
    and liminality, 117, 119–21
    medical treatment, 116, 132, 133
    miracles, 110, 111, 113, 119, 120,
        123, 125, 126, 129, 131, 139, 143,
        169, 170

royal, 38–9
    surgery, 114, 116, 131
Hebrews, Epistle to, 2, 245–6, 247, 250,
    251
Helena, St, 15, 161, 173
Henry, Matthew, 251, 252, 253
Henry I, 32
Henry II, 12, 21, 27, 30, 52, 85, 201, 228
    and Canterbury, 16, 17, 23, 26, 28
    charters, 20, 44
    devotions, 22, 23, 24, 25, 37
    family tradition, 13, 14
    gifts, 16, 29, 34–7, 44
    images, 67, 71
    prophecies about, 31, 32–3
    sacrality of, 38, 42
Henry III, 12, 15, 18–19, 33, 99
    devotions, 23, 24, 25–6, 27, 37
    gifts, 20, 34–7
    sacrality of, 37, 38, 40, 43
Henry IV, 106, 107
Henry VI, 128, 171
Henry VIII, 179, 180, 181, 188, 190, 196,
    222, 223
    and Canterbury, 216, 217, 219–21
    excommunication of, 228
    and pilgrimage, 200–1, 210–11
    and saints, 200–1, 211–13, 218–19, 231
    see also Proclamation (1538)
Henry of Blois, Bishop, 40
Henry of Fordwich, 75
Henry the Lion, 52, 78
Henry the Young King, 18, 19, 24–5, 40
herbalism, 110, 113, 133, 138
Herbert, George, 246–7, 255
Hereford Cathedral, 174
heresy, 185, 186, 197, 206, 227, 232, 239
Higgins, Iain, 147
Hilsey, John, bishop of Rochester, 213,
    214, 218
Hilton, Walter, 2, 159–60
historiography, 3, 4, 5–6, 12, 230
Hitton, Thomas, 206
Hoker, John, 213
Holy Blood of Hailes see Hailes Abbey,
    Gloucestershire
Holy Land, 13, 18–19, 30, 142–4
    see also Holy Sepulchre Church,
        Jerusalem; Jerusalem pilgrimage
holy people, visits to, 8–9, 128, 150
Holy Rood see Bromholm Priory, Norfolk
Holy Sepulchre Church, Jerusalem, 1, 2, 6,
    35, 94–5, 144
    images, 151–4, 156, 162
    miracles, 143

Holy Sepulchre Church, Jerusalem (*cont*.)
    tomb-shrine, 93, 94
    see also Jerusalem pilgrimage
Holy Trinity Church, Long Melford, *124*,
    125, 135
holy water, 48, 121, 122, 131, 136, 247
Horstead, Norfolk, 172
hospices, 116, 232
hospitality, 192
Hospitallers, 35
hospitals, 29, 108, *115*, 116, 138, 232
Houghton, Norfolk, 138
Howard, Lord John, 172–3
Hugh, Bishop of Lincoln, 21, 31, 33, 41,
    98, 99
human remains, ingestion of, 122
humility, 16, 167
Huntingfield Psalter, 71, 78, 80
Hussee, John, 220

iconoclasm, 6, 200, 203, 214, 216, 217,
    230, 231, 232–3
idolatry, 205, 209, 210, 212, 213, 214,
    224, 227, 230, 239
illuminated books, 53, *66*, *118*
images, 5, 8, 9, 23, 101, 120, 209, 212,
    217, 225, 232, 233
    distribution, 48–52, 83–4, 85, 87, 171,
        172
    East Anglia, 171, 172–3
    elevation of saints, 63
    Jerusalem, 151–9
    origins of, 154–6
    quantity of, 85, 87
    role of, 48
    see also iconoclasm; idolatry
incantations, 138, 139
indulgences, 19, 143, 163, 175, 176
injunctions
    1536, 212, 240
    1538, 217, 225, 229, 240
inscriptions, 52–3
insignia, 1, 17, 20
Ipswich, 113, 131, 134
Ireland, 24
Isabella, Queen, 19, 27
Islam, 7, 95
Islip, Abbott, 100, 102
Israelites, 2, 245, 248, 250, 251, 253
Italy, 7, 10, 18, 31, 50–1, 142, 153, 155

James, M.R., 168
James, St, 71
    hand of, 19, 24, 25, 29
    see also Reading Abbey

Janeway, St John, 247
Jerome, St, 35
Jerusalem pilgrimage, 3, 4, 6–7, 8, 9, 29
    Angevins and, 13
    England and, 142–3, 150, 156–9
    images, 151–9
    inner experience of, 148–50, 159–60
    literary accounts, 143–51, 161–2
    special quality, 141
    tradition of, 15
    see also Holy Sepulchre Church,
        Jerusalem
Jesuits, 236, 237
Jewel, Bishop John, 254
jewels, 39, 47, 48, 127, 172
John, King, 18, 19, 21, 22, 27, 33, 34, 42,
    72, 223
    burial, 98
    penance, 23
    see also drama
John de Montmirail, 41
John of Bridlington, 166
John of Salisbury, 37, 49, 55, 58–9, 64
journals *see* diaries
journeys, 1, 2, 10, 15, 23–4, 166, 174,
    184, 244, 246ff, 250
    destination, 253
    hazards, 252, 254, 255, 256
    as metaphor, 241–2, 245
    see also travellers

Keach, Benjamin, 245, 248, 251
Kempe, Margery, 9, 128, 134, 136,
    149–50, 160, 175, 177
Kent, 216, 217, 219–21, 222, 223, 228,
    233, 234
Kett's rebellion (1549), 233
Kings Lynn, 6
king's touch, the, 38
Knaresborough, 31
Koziol, Geoffrey, 39–40

labour, 174
Lacy, Edmund, Bishop of Hereford, 175
Lady Chapel, 97, 98, 104, 125
laity, 9, 156, 165, 173, 193
Lambarde, William, 234
Lancashire, 181, 188
Lancaster Herald, 182, 191
Langland, William, 180–1, 182, 195
Langton, Stephen, Archbishop of
    Canterbury, 53, 71–2, 89
language, 1–2, 9, 11, 132, 164, 179
Latimer, Bishop, 10, 202, 214, 215, 218,
    241, 244

Latin, 7, 145, 161, 167, 212, 221
law courts, 30
Lawrence, St, 80, 83
Le Huen, Nicolas, 151
Le Vigean, 63, 64
legends, 9, 166–7, 168, 169, 170
leprosy, 119, *122*
Lesnes Missal, 55, 85, 87
Leyser, Karl, 39
Limoges, 27, 50, 53n, 56, 57, 59, 62–3
Lincoln Cathedral, 21, 98–9, 156, *157*
Lincolnshire rebellion (1536), 178, 190,
    194, 195, 198; *see also* Pilgrimage of
    Grace
Lisle, Lord, 214, 219, 220
Litcham All Saints, 171
literature, 10, 11, 143–51, 161–2, 175,
    180, 245, 246–7, 252
liturgy, 2, 4, 6, 9, 218
Lollards, 150, 174, 199, 201, 231, 238,
    239, 242–3
London, 181, 182, 187, 196, 232
Long Melford, Suffolk, 125, 135
Lords, 186, 187, 192, 193, 196; *see also*
    nobility
Louis VII of France, 71, 72, 75, 84
Louis IX of France, 16–17, 19, 27, 36, 41
Lovell, Sir Gregory, 169
Loyola, Ignatius, 162
Lucca, 51
Ludham, 171
Luke, St, 185
Lumley, Lord George, 182, 183, 184
Lusshe, Dr John, 228
Lutherans, 201, 205
Lydgate, John, 135, 159, 168
Lyngsjö, 50, 67, *68*, 78

magic, 39, 43, 111, 127, 138–9, 173
Maidstone, 206, 214
malaria, 131
Mandeville, Sir John, 147–8, 161
manuscripts, 50, 53, 64, *66*, 147, 148
Map, Walter, 15, 37
marble
    Belgian, 96, 106
    Purbeck, 93, 94, 105
    Roman, 93
    Tournai, 105–6
    Wealden, 106
Marden, John, 234
Margaret, St, 138
Margaret of Anjou, 127, 136
Margaret of Scotland, 40
Mariano da Siena, 150–1

Mark, St, 5
Marshall, William, 209
Martial, St, 25, 63
Martin, St, 13, 17, 80, 81, 83
martyrdom, 53–5, 71, 78, 80, 89, 236
Mary, Queen, 197, 200, 233, 238
Mary Magdalene, 18, 80, 136
Mason, Emma, 26
Mather, Cotton, 249
Mather, Increase, 242, 245
Mather, Samuel, 245
Matilda, 52, 75
Maurice, St, 34
medicine *see* healing; herbalism
memorials, 1, 4, 5, 151
Mercers' Hall, London, 159
Michael, St, 24, 25
migration, 246, 249, 256
military pilgrimage, 179, 181, 187–8, 197;
    see also Pilgrimage of Grace
Milton, John, 241–2, 252
miracles, 9, 40, 41, 42, 75, 94, 108
    critics of, 209
    healing, 110, 111, 113, 119, 120, 123,
        125, 126, 129, 131, 139
    Jerusalem, 143
    legends, 168, 169, 170
mitre, 49, 51, 52, 57, *58*, 80
monasteries, 211; *see also* religious houses,
    dissolution of
monks, 9, 16, 20, 25, 102, 103, 104, 135,
    186, 192, 208, 210
Monreale Cathedral, 51, 52, 80
Montfort, John de, 41
Montfort, Simon de, 41
Montjoux, hospital of, 29
morality, 8, 170, 236, 241, 245, 246, 251,
    252–4
More, Sir Thomas, 134, 201, 206–7, 237
Morison, Richard, 225
Morton, Cardinal, 101, 104
Morton, Nathaniel, 249
mysticism, 141, 149

narrative, 67, 75, 84, 143–51, 160–1, 163,
    170, 250, 251, 252–3, 255
Nativity, 155
Netherlands, 162, 249
New England, 249, 251
New Radnor, 233
New Testament, 78, 155, 156, 246, 252,
    253, 255, 256; *see also* Hebrews,
    Epistle to
New York, 52, 53, *56*, *60*, 78, *79*
Niccolò of Poggibonsi, 146, 148

Nicholas, St, 13, 80, 81, 108
nobility, 7, 34, 136, 167, 169, 170,
        193, 194
nomads, 245, 246
nonconformists, 241, 248
Norfolk, 6, 27, 114, 138, 167, 171,
        172, 233
    healing shrines, 109, 111, 117, 123,
        128, 131, 136, 169, 170
Normans, 13, 25, 27, 31, 38
North Riding, 197
northern risings see Pilgrimage of Grace
Norton, Dr Christopher, 91
Norway, 50
Norwich, 111, 125, 128, 135, 136, 138
    Cathedral, 112, 113
Numbers, Book of, 250, 252
nuns, 23, 41
nutrition, 133, 134

oath of supremacy, 220
Odoric of Pordenone, 147
Old St Paul's Cathedral, 93–4, 99, 172, 216
Old Sarum, 94
Old Testament, 2, 78, 164, 244–52, 253,
        254, 255, 256
Oldcastle, Sir John, 242, 243
Osmund, St, 94, 96, 97, 167
Oswald, St, 98
Osyth, St, 35
Ottomans, 146, 162, 163
outcasts, 247, 248
Oxford, 25, 95, 99

paganism, 111, 138, 234; see also magic
pageants, 225, 226, 233, 234
Parable of the Pilgrim, The (1665), 244,
        246, 252, 253, 254
Paris, 72, 78, 230
Paris, Matthew, 40, 41
parish registers, 229
Parliament, 186, 193, 210, 211, 231
Pascha, Jan, 163
Passionate Man's Pilgrimage, 11
pathways, 242, 254, 256
Patricelli, Francesco, 163
Patrick, Symon see Parable of the Pilgrim,
        The (1665)
Patrington, Yorkshire, 156
patronage, 7, 10, 127–8
Paul, St, 255
payments, 174–5, 176; see also gifts
peasants, 189, 191
Pembroke, 24
penance, 13, 16, 17–18, 19, 22, 24, 38,
        173–4, 176, 200, 212

Penn, William, 247, 252
Percy family, 183, 193
Peter of Alexandria, 80
Peter of Blois, 15, 38, 44
Peter of Tarantaise, 39
Peterborough Abbey, 98
Petroc, St, 34
phials, 49
Philip, St, 34
Pickering, Friar, 184, 194
Piers Plowman see Langland, William
piety, 6, 7, 8, 170, 173; see also devotion
Pilate, 154, 155
Pilgrim Fathers, 249
pilgrimage, 44, 229
    banning of, 198, 231, 235
    critics of, 44, 179, 209, 210–11, 212,
        238–41, 242
    definition, 1–2, 10–11, 14–15, 17
    international, 3, 6–7, 8, 13, 14, 141–5
    Latin character, 7 and liminality, 6, 7, 8,
        14, 28, 117, 119–21, 165–6, 177
    local, 6, 19, 127–8, 165, 166, 172–3,
        175, 177
    as metaphor, 2, 9–11, 159–60, 164,
        241ff
    motivation, 8, 87, 120, 146, 149,
        175, 176
    popularity, 9, 94
    promotion of, 168
    role of art, 47, 87
    royal protection, 29–30
    secular, 31, 42
    and social status, 1, 7, 8, 14, 17, 127,
        134–5
    surrogates, 173, 174–5, 176
    true and false, 243–4
    see also royal pilgrimages
Pilgrimage of Grace:
    aims of, 178–9, 181, 183, 184–5,
        188–90, 197
    badges, 183
    banners, 182, 183–4, 186, 194–5
    and Commonwealth, 189–94
    concept of revolt, 178
    cross-bearers, 182, 195
    as crusade, 179, 183, 187, 197
    economic grievances, 189–92
    1537 revolts, 186, 196
    oaths, 178, 181, 182, 189, 194
    pardons, 196, 197
    petitions, 189, 190, 195, 196
    pilgrimage aspects, 194–8
    political factors, 186–7, 189, 190, 193–4
    religious factors, 184–6, 188, 192, 195
    social factors, 193–4

songs, 184, 188, 194
  terminology of, 178–80
Pilgrimage of the Lyfe of the Manhood, 165
Pilgrimage to Parnassus, The, 10
pilgrims:
  Affagart, Greffin, 162
  Arundel, earl of, 10
  Aymer de Lusignan, 41
  Baylis, Mistress, 166
  Bernard of Breydenvach, 153
  Berners, Sir James, 131
  Brygg, Thomas, 155
  Burghesh, Bartholomew, 142
  East, Margaret, 176
  Fabri, Felix, 142–3, 144, 148, 162
  FitzEisulf, Jordan, 87
  Godia, 121
  Gurwain, 135
  Guylforde, Sir Richard, 144, 145
  Henry Bolingbroke, 142
  Herfast, Bishop, 114, 116
  Lanier, Nicholas, 10
  Marshal, William, 18
  Matthew, Tobie, 10
  Mowbray, Thomas, 142
  Neville, Hugh, 142
  Ormesby, Sir Arthur, 142
  Paston, John, 127
  Scorel, Jan van, 162
  Sieldeware of Belaugh, 134
  Wey, William, 145–6, 159
  William of Perth, 97
Pilgrim's Progress see Bunyan, John
plague, 123, 135
Plantagenets
  court, 33–5
  desacralisation, 39–40
  family tombs, 27, 99
  and international shrines, 18–20
  itinerary, 14–15, 21, 22, 31
  and prophecies, 32–3
  and Saxon kings, 40
  spirituality, 28, 29
Plymouth colony, 249
poetry, 2, 11, 111, 145–6, 159, 160,
    246–7, 249
  legends, 168–71
Poitiers, 30, 46
politics, 7–8, 19, 26–9, 39, 190, 193, 200,
    205, 209
Pollard, Richard, 220
Pontefract, 179, 182, 184, 186, 189, 192
Poore, Bishop Richard, 98
pope, 33, 71, 176, 180, 195, 203, 207–8,
    227–8, 237
porphyry, 93, 94

Pottergate, Norwich, 136, *137*
poverty, 33, 128, 133, 142, 180, 181, 190,
    191, 192, 195, 197
prayer, 120, 139, 145, 184, 186, 195, 206,
    212, 213, 218
Prayer Book (1549), 6
Presbyterians, 248, 251
Prestwich, Michael, 12
privileges, 20, 30, 175
proclamation (1538), 226–7, 228, 229,
    235
progress, 242, 255
prophecies, 32–3
Protestantism, 4, 10–11, 160, 162–3, 195
  early tradition, 245
  hostility to pilgrimage, 239–41, 242, 243
  pilgrimage elements in, 241–56
  see also religious reformers
Proverbs, 254
psalters, 50, 59, 63, 64, 68, 71
psychosomatic disorders, 132
Purchas his Pilgrims, 10
Puritanism, 241, 245, 248–54
Pynson, Richard, 168

'race', 255–6
Radegund, Ste, 46
Ralegh, Sir Walter, 11, 247
Ramsbury, rector of, 173
Ranieri of Pisa, St, 8
Reading Abbey, 19, 29, 34; *see also*
    James, St
Reformation, 4, 6, 156, 160, 184–5, 199,
    200–1, 234, 245
relics, 1, 5, 13, 14, 21, 25, 26, 43, 46, 49ff,
    94, 103, 186, 220, 226, 230, 231, 237
  cults, 90
  as gifts, 34–7, 159
  and healing, 108, 121, 123, 125
  royal chapel, 34
  theft of, 34
  translation of, 91, 96
  see also reliquaries
religious houses, dissolution of, 178, 184,
    185–6, 191, 192, 210, 211
religious reformers, 10, 184–6, 201–3,
    205–6, 208–9ff, 218, 231–3
reliquaries, 36, 37, 46, 83, 218
reliquary boxes, 46, 49, 50–1, 53, 53n, 55,
    57, 59, *60*, *61*, 62–3, 64, 78, 87
Renaissance, 146
reredoses, 100
Reuwich, Erhard, 153
rewards, 47, 87
Richard I, 7, 8, 17–18, 23, 25, 27, 30,
    42, 43

Richard of Chichester, St, 33
Richmond, Yorkshire, 181, 185, 188, 189,
    195, 196
ritual, 27–8, 43, 119, 120, 121, 128,
    139, 181
'roads', 255
Robert of Normandy, 13
Robert the Bruce, 127
Rocamadour, 22, 26, 28, 49, 172
Rochester Cathedral, 97, 98, 167
Roger of Wendover, 123
Romanesque style, 63, 90, 91, 98
Rome, 7, 14, 15, 18, 20, 29, 51, 93, 141,
    163, 174–5, 235, 237
Rood of Grace see Boxley Abbey, Kent
roods, 27, 172, 214, 239
royal pilgrimages, 127
    and battles, 24, 25, 26
    ceremonial, 33–5
    exceptionality, 15–17, 21
    gifts, 16, 20, 27, 29, 30–1, 33
    influence of, 31
    and life events, 23–4
    mishap and illness, 22, 27
    penance, 13, 16, 17–18, 22, 24
    political events, 26–9
    thanksgivings, 24, 26
royal supremacy, 201, 205, 206, 214, 215,
    228, 240
Russell, Josiah Cox, 42

Saidnaiya, 35
St Albans Abbey, 18, 20, 23, 24, 90, 91,
    95, 99, 100
St Amand, 63
St Augustine's Abbey, Canterbury, 93
St Bartholomew's Priory, Yarmouth, 108,
    123
St Benet Hulme Abbey, 115
Saint-Denis, 7, 19, 30
Ste Foi, 46
St Frideswides, Oxford, 95, 99
'Saint-Fuscien' Psalter, Amiens, 50, 64,
    65, 78
St Leonard's, Norfolk, 128
St Mary's, Bury St Edmunds, 171
Saint-Michel, 24
Saint-Omer, 63, 72, 235–6, 237
St Stephen's, nr Canterbury, 221, 222
St Thomas of Acre, 208
saints, 9, 22, 212, 213
    Becket and, 78, 80, 81, 83
    images, 63, 80–1, 83, 171
    intercession, 23, 24, 32, 121, 140, 185,
        186, 218

and kings, 24–5, 31–5, 36, 37, 40–3
    legends, 166–7
    prohibition of, 217–19, 221, 228–9,
        231, 232
saints' days, 184, 185, 195, 211–12, 233;
    see also feast days
Saladin, 95
Salimbene, 16
Salisbury Cathedral, 94, 96–7, 100, 174;
    see also Osmund, St
salvation, 187, 188, 210, 241
San Vivaldo, Tuscany, 153
sanctuaries, 90, 97, 195
Sardenay, 146
Sassia, 29
satire, 8, 110, 212
Sawley ballad, 188
Scandinavia, 50, 67, 68, 78
science, 110, 138, 139
screens see architecture
scrip, 1, 17, 20
sculptures, 48, 49, 50, 87, 101, 156
sea journeys, 23–4, 142, 145, 162, 163
seals, 52, 53, 89, 232
self-denial, 247, 248
self-expression, 148–50
Seligenthal Abbey, 52, 56–7
Sens, 16, 49, 53n, 71, 72, 73, 74, 80–1, 87
sermons, 21, 188, 209, 213, 218, 224,
    241, 242, 246, 253, 255, 256
Seville, 154
sexual depravity, 119
Shaxton, Nicholas, 138
shrine-keepers, 8, 116, 121, 129, 132,
    186, 225
shrines, 1, 3, 4, 14, 21, 94, 105–7
    access to, 90, 100, 101, 102
    bases, 99, 106
    raised, 95, 96
    remodelling, 99–100
    reputation, 48
    suppression of, 198, 211, 227, 228
    tombs, 94, 106
Sicily, 51
Simon of Meopham, 105–6
sin, 19, 22, 23, 24, 119, 132, 139, 250,
    251, 254
Sinai, 8–9, 146
Sion, Mount, 142, 143, 144
Six Articles Act (1539), 240
social class, 1, 7, 8, 14, 17, 127, 134–5,
    136, 165, 187, 193–4
souvenirs, 34, 87, 173
Spain, 51, 154, 236
Sparham, 171

spiritual benefits, 174–6
Spiritual Pilgrimage (1563), 163
spirituality, 2, 87, 119, 123, 149, 150, 154,
    159–60, 163, 244
staff, 1, 17, 18
Stapleton, Thomas, 237
Stapulton, William, 178, 185
Starkey, Thomas, 209–10
'stations', 145, 154
Statute of Uses, 190, 197
Stephen, St, 32, 80, 83
stones, 39, 47, 221
strangers, 1, 2
Stow, John, 221, 235
suffering, 119, 120, 123, 132, 151, 255
Suffield, Walter, 128
Suffolk, 112, 113, 125, 131, 135, 172, 173
Sweden, 50, 67, 68
Sweeting, William, 239
Swithun, St, 40, 90, 91, 97; *see also*
    Winchester Cathedral
symbolism, 2, 4, 9–10, 159, 160, 164, 174,
    241, 242, 243, 244, 245, 246ff

Tafur, Pero, 146
Tarragona, 51
Tarrasa, 51, 53, 54, 64
taxes, 190, 191, 193, 197
Taylor, Edward, 246
Taylor, Thomas, 245
Ten Articles, 212
Ten Commandments, 213
tenants' rights, 192–3
Thetford, Norfolk, 125, 129, 136
Thomas, St, 26, 29, 171, 237
    canonisation, 49
    decanonisation, 201, 218, 224
    letters, 64, 224
    life, 84, 231
    murder, 59, 85, 91, 101, 225–6, 230
    posthumous treason trial, 216, 225
    saintly lineage, 78, 80, 81, 83
    see also Canterbury, cult of Thomas
        Becket
Thomas of Florence, 153
Thomas of Monmouth, 113, 117, 120,
    121n, 129
Thomas the Apostle, 232, 237
Thorneton, William, 182
three kings of Cologne, 42, 176
time, awareness of, 132
tomb-shrines, 94, 106
Torkyngton, Richard, 144, 145, 176
Totehill, Henry, 223, 228
Tours, 13, 17

'transcience', 14, 15
transept, 97, 98, 103, 104–5
transubstantiation, 240
travel literature, 10, 144–51
travellers, 1, 3, 8–9, 10, 144–51, 161–2,
    176, 248; *see also* journeys
treason, 193, 196, 216, 225, 228
True Cross, 13, 123, 173
truth, 160, 243–4, 254
Tucher, Hans, 144
Turner, Victor and Edith, 5–6, 14, 15,
    117, 119, 121, 164–5
Tyndale, William, 202, 206, 207, 231,
    243, 244–5
Tyrrell, Thomas, 229

Umpton, William, 202

Vaughan, Henry, 247, 248
Venice, 4–5, 6–7, 142, 143, 144,
    162, 163
Victoria and Albert Museum, 62, 63
Virgin Mary, 9, 19, 22, 34, 54, 63, 64, 80,
    123, 125, 126, 127, 129, 135, 138, 155
    image shrines, 172–3
voluntary act, 17
votive offerings, 27, 125–7, 173
vows, 2, 17, 18, 20, 176, 181, 194, 240

Wade, Laurence, 204
Walker, Greg, 223
walking, 242, 254
Walpole, Henry, 236
Walsingham, 6, 7, 9, 109, 111, 123, 125,
    126–7, 136, 166, 172
    legends, 168
    suppression, 219
Walstan, St, 132–3, 166–71
    cures, 169, 170
    images, 171
    wider cult, 171
    see also Bawburgh church, Norfolk
Walter, Hugh, Archbishop of Canterbury,
    95
Ward, Benedicta, 111
Warham, Archbishop, 103, 201, 222
watchfulness, 253
wax, 30, 103, 131, 173
wealth, 17, 20, 30, 47, 87, 128, 189, 190,
    192, 239
West Riding, 181, 185
Western Europe, 1, 3, 4, 141, 144, 151,
    153, 155–6, 235–6
Westminster Abbey, 7, 25, 36, 37, 93, 95,
    99, 100, 101

Westmorland, 181, 185, 188, 189, 195
wilderness, 2, 245, 249–51, 253
Wilfred, St, 185
William, Archbishop of Champagne, 49
William of Boldensele, 146, 147
William of Canterbury, 50
William of Malmesbury, 91
William of Norwich, St, 112, 113, 117, 119, 120, 121, 125, 129, 133, 135, 138, 140, 171
William of Rochester, 167
William of Sicily, 51
William of York *see* York Minster
William the Conqueror, 13, 25, 114
Willis, Professor Robert, 95
Winchelsey, Archbishop, 105

Winchester Cathedral, 22, 40, 41, 91, 95, 97–8, 100, 211
windows, 47, 49, 67, 72, 75, *76*, *77*, 80, 81, *82*, 83, 85, *86*, 87, *88*, 91, 94, 96, 103, 106, 208, 232–3
Withburge, St, 171
Wolsey, Thomas, 207
women, 110, 11, 112, 113, 114, 119, 120, 121, 126, 133, 134–8
Woolpit, Suffolk, 109, 125, 172–3
Worcester Cathedral, 27, 98, 164
Wulfric of Haselbury, 32
Wulstan, St, 98
Wymondham, Norfolk, 233

York Minster, *122*
Yorkshire, 126, 188, 193, 195
Yrieix, St, 27